HARCOURT · TROPHIES ·

A HARCOURT READING/LANGUAGE ARTS PROGRAM

ON YOUR MARK

TEACHER'S EDITION

SENIOR AUTHORS
Isabel L. Beck ◆ Roger C. Farr ◆ Dorothy S. Strickland

AUTHORS
Alma Flor Ada ◆ Marcia Brechtel ◆ Margaret McKeown
Nancy Roser ◆ Hallie Kay Yopp

SENIOR CONSULTANT
Asa G. Hilliard III

CONSULTANTS
F. Isabel Campoy ◆ David A. Monti

⧉Harcourt

Orlando   Boston   Dallas   Chicago   San Diego

Visit *The Learning Site!*

www.harcourtschool.com

ISBN 0-15-3397543

2 3 4 5 6 7 8 9 10   073   10 09 08 07 06 05 04

Program Authors

SENIOR AUTHORS

Isabel L. Beck
Professor of Education and Senior Scientist at the Learning Research and Development Center, University of Pittsburgh

Research Contributions: Reading Comprehension, Beginning Reading, Phonics, Vocabulary

Roger C. Farr
Chancellor's Professor of Education and Director of the Center for Innovation in Assessment, Indiana University, Bloomington

Research Contributions: Instructional Assessment, Reading Strategies, Staff Development

Dorothy S. Strickland
Samuel DeWitt Proctor Professor of Education, Rutgers University

Research Contributions: Early Literacy, Elementary Reading/Language Arts, Writing, Intervention

AUTHORS

Alma Flor Ada
Director of Doctoral Studies in the International Multicultural Program, University of San Francisco

Research Contributions: English as a Second Language, Bilingual Education, Family Involvement

Marcia Brechtel
Director of Training, Project GLAD, Fountain Valley School District, Fountain Valley, California

Research Contributions: English as a Second Language, Bilingual Education

Margaret McKeown
Research Scientist at the Learning Research and Development Center, University of Pittsburgh

Research Contributions: Reading Comprehension, Vocabulary

Nancy Roser
Professor, Language and Literacy Studies, University of Texas, Austin

Research Contributions: Early Literacy, Phonics, Comprehension, Fluency

Hallie Kay Yopp
Professor, Department of Elementary Bilingual and Reading Education, California State University, Fullerton

Research Contributions: Phonemic Awareness, Early Childhood

SENIOR CONSULTANT

Asa G. Hilliard III
Fuller E. Callaway Professor of Urban Education, Department of
Educational Foundations, Georgia State University, Atlanta

Research Contributions: Multicultural Literature and Education

CONSULTANTS

F. Isabel Campoy
Former President, Association of Spanish Professionals in
the USA

Research Contributions: English as a Second Language,
Family Involvement

David A. Monti
Professor, Reading/Language Arts Department, Central Connecticut
State University

Research Contributions: Classroom Management, Technology,
Family Involvement

PROFESSIONAL DEVELOPMENT FOR READING
Supports Research-Based Instruction

Professional Development for Reading *guides teachers through the process of delivering research-based instruction in phonemic awareness, phonics, fluency, vocabulary, and text comprehension.*

COURSES

■ **Teaching Phonemic Awareness, Grades K–1** The role of phonemic awareness in learning to read and strategies for teaching

■ **Teaching Phonics, Kindergarten** Systematic, explicit phonics instruction including special attention to letter-sound relationships

■ **Teaching Phonics, Grade 1** Teaching letter-sound relationships, word blending and word building, and reading decodable texts

■ **Teaching Phonics, Grade 2, and Strategies for Intervention, Grades 3–6** Principles of decoding and research-based intervention strategies for older students

■ **Teaching Fluency, Grades 1–6** The progression from efficient decoding to text comprehension

■ **Teaching Vocabulary, Grades K–2** The progression of vocabulary through primary grades, including its role as a bridge between phonics and comprehension

■ **Teaching Vocabulary, Grades 3–6** The role of vocabulary learning strategies in improving reading in older students

■ **Teaching Text Comprehension, Grades K–1** The role of listening comprehension in learning to read and the transition from listening to reading comprehension

■ **Teaching Text Comprehension, Grades 2–6** Techniques for teaching reading strategies for students to use

■ **Assessment to Inform Instruction, Grades K–6** Entry-level, monitoring, and summative assessments

■ **An Overview of Reading Instruction for Teachers, Administrators, and Parents, Grades K–6** The building blocks of research-based reading instruction: phonemic awareness, phonics, fluency, vocabulary, and text comprehension

Q **How is Word Blending taught in *Trophies*?**

A The purpose of Word Blending instruction is to provide students with practice in combining the sounds represented by letter sequences to decode words. *Trophies* employs the cumulative blending method, which has students blend sounds successively as they are pronounced.

Q **How does *Trophies* use Word Building to help students with decoding (reading) and encoding (spelling)?**

A In the decoding portion of Word Building, teachers first tell students what letters to put in what place. For example, students are told to put *c* at the beginning, *a* after *c*, and *t* at the end. They are asked to read the word *cat* and then are asked to change *c* to *m* and read the new word, *mat*. In Word Building activities that help encoding, students are asked which letter in the word *cat* needs to change to make the word *mat*. This encoding approach is used to build spelling words throughout the first grade program.

Q **How are students taught to decode multisyllabic words?**

A Students are taught to see words as patterns of letters, to identify long words by breaking them down into syllable units, and to blend the syllables to form and read long words. Decoding lessons throughout grades 2–6 directly and explicitly provide students with various strategies, including understanding syllable types and patterns and recognizing such word structures as prefixes, suffixes, and root words, to decode multisyllabic words.

Look for

✓ Phonics and spelling lessons
✓ Word Blending
✓ Word Building
✓ Decoding/Phonics lessons in Grades 2–6
✓ Additional Support Activities to reteach and extend

READING ALOUD

Reading aloud to students contributes to their motivation, comprehension, vocabulary, fluency, knowledge base, literary understanding, familiarity with academic and literary terms, sense of community, enjoyment, and perhaps to a lifetime love of literature.

Sharing and responding to books during read-aloud time helps develop communication and oral language skills and improves comprehension. Literature that is read aloud to students serves as the vehicle for developing literary insights, including sensitivity to the sounds and structure of language. Students learn how powerful written language can be when fluent readers read aloud, interpreting a text through appropriate intonation, pacing, and phrasing. Comprehension skills are developed as students ask and answer questions and share their personal understandings. More advanced students who are read to and who get to talk with others about the best of written language learn both to discuss texts knowingly and to interpret their meanings expressively.

Reading aloud exposes students to more challenging texts than they may be able to read independently. Vocabulary development is fostered by listening to both familiar and challenging selections read aloud. Texts read aloud that are conceptually challenging for students can effectively improve language and comprehension abilities. Listening to challenging texts also exposes students to text structures and content knowledge that are more sophisticated than they may encounter in their own reading.

Listening skills and strategies are greatly improved during read-aloud activities. When students are encouraged to respond to stories read aloud, they tend to listen intently in order to recall relevant content. When students listen responsively and frequently to literature and expository texts, they hone critical-thinking skills that will serve them in many other contexts. In sum, reading aloud

- models fluent reading behavior
- builds students' vocabularies and concepts
- creates an interest in narrative structures
- builds background knowledge by introducing children to new ideas and concepts and by expanding on what is familiar to them
- exposes students to different text structures and genres, such as stories, alphabet books, poetry, and informational books

" Sharing literature with children increases their vocabulary and their understanding of how language works. Sharing stories, informational books, and poetry with children has become increasingly valued for its cognitive contribution to children's literary development. "

— **Dorothy S. Strickland**
Samuel DeWitt Proctor
Professor of Education,
Rutgers University

Q **How does *Trophies* provide opportunities for teachers to read aloud to their students?**

A *Trophies* provides a comprehensive collection of read-aloud selections for all levels of instruction. In kindergarten through grade 2, the program includes read-aloud options for students every day. In grades 3–6, a read-aloud selection accompanies every lesson in the *Teacher's Edition*. Read-aloud selections are available in *Read-Aloud Anthologies* for kindergarten through grade 2, the *Library Books Collections* for kindergarten through grade 6, and several other formats.

Q **What genres can students meet through read-alouds?**

A Students encounter a wide variety of literary genres and expository texts through read-aloud selections in all grades. Expository nonfiction becomes more prevalent as students move up the grades. Other genres include poetry, finger plays, folktales, myths, and narrative nonfiction. In lessons in grades 3–6 with Focus Skills, such as narrative elements or text structure, the genre of the read-aloud selection matches the genre of the reading selection.

Q **What kind of instruction accompanies read-aloud selections in *Trophies*?**

A In kindergarten and grade 1, the instruction that accompanies Sharing Literature includes three options:
- Build Concept Vocabulary
- Develop Listening Comprehension
- Listen and Respond

In grade 2, options include Develop Listening Comprehension, Set a Purpose, and Recognize Genre. The instructional focus in kindergarten centers on concepts about print and beginning narrative analysis (characters, setting, important events). As students move up the grades, they are taught more complex literary skills, such as following the structure of stories, recognizing their beginnings, middles, and endings, and even occasionally generating alternative endings. In grades 3–6, read-alouds also serve as a vehicle for exploring expository text structures.

Look for

✔ Daily "Sharing Literature" activities in Kindergarten through Grade 2
✔ Read-aloud selections and instruction with every lesson in Grades 2–6
✔ *Library Books Collections* at all grades
✔ *Read-Aloud Anthologies* in Kindergarten through Grade 2

COMPREHENSION

Reading comprehension is the complex process of constructing meaning from texts. Recent comprehension research has been guided by the idea that the process is strategic and interactive.

Comprehension is the construction of meaning through an interactive exchange of ideas between the text and the reader. Comprehension strategies are interactive processes that allow readers to monitor and self-assess how well they understand what they are reading. These processes include determining the purpose or purposes for reading, such as to obtain information or to be entertained. After the purpose is determined, readers activate prior knowledge about the content of the text and its structure. Research has shown that the more readers know about the content of a particular text, the more likely they will understand, integrate, and remember the new information. Familiarity with the genre or text structure also fosters comprehension.

Most students need explicit instruction in comprehension skills and strategies. Research shows that comprehension skills and strategies are necessary for student success and that they do not develop automatically in most students. Without explicit instruction and guidance, many readers fail to acquire automatic use of these skills and strategies and show little flexibility in applying them to understand a variety of texts. Research shows that poor readers who are directly taught a particular strategy do as well as good readers who have used the strategy spontaneously. Typically, direct instruction consists of

- an explanation of what the skill or strategy is and how it aids comprehension
- modeling how to use the skill or strategy
- working directly with students as they apply the skill or strategy, offering assistance as needed
- having students apply the skill or strategy independently and repeatedly

Students need extensive direct instruction, guidance, and cumulative practice until they can independently determine the method of constructing meaning that works for them.

Students need to learn strategies for comprehending a wide variety of texts, including both fiction and nonfiction. In kindergarten, students should be taught to understand narrative structure. They should learn to identify the beginning, middle, and ending of a story and other literary elements, such as characters and setting. Then they can use their knowledge of these elements to retell stories they have listened to. In first through third grade, readers deepen their knowledge of these narrative elements and interact with others as book discussants and literary meaning makers. They learn to use the specific language of literature study, such as *point of view* and *character trait*. By grades 4–6, students must have the skills, strategies, and knowledge of text structures to comprehend complex nonfiction texts, including those in the classroom content areas. Students need to be explicitly and systematically taught the organizational structure of expository text, e.g., compare/contrast, cause/effect, and main idea and details. These organizational structures should be taught systematically and reviewed cumulatively.

> " One of the fundamental understandings about the nature of reading is that it is a constructive act. Specifically, a reader does not extract meaning from a page, but constructs meaning from information on the page and information already in his/her mind. "
>
> — **Isabel L. Beck**
> **Professor of Education and Senior Scientist at the Learning Research and Development Center, University of Pittsburgh**

Q **How does *Trophies* provide explicit instruction in comprehension?**

A *Trophies* features systematic and explicit comprehension instruction grounded in current and confirmed research. Comprehension instruction in kindergarten focuses on helping students construct meaning from stories read to them. From the earliest grades, teachers guide students before, during, and after reading in the use of strategies to monitor comprehension. Guided comprehension questions ask students to apply a variety of comprehension skills and strategies appropriate to particular selections. Each tested skill is introduced, reinforced, assessed informally, retaught as needed, reviewed at least twice, and maintained throughout each grade level.

Q **How does comprehension instruction in *Trophies* build through the grades?**

A Comprehension instruction in *Trophies* is rigorous, developmental, and spiraled. Students gain increasingly sophisticated skills and strategies to help them understand texts successfully. In the instructional components of the earliest grades, emergent and beginning readers develop use of strategies as they respond to texts read by the teacher, and more advanced students begin to apply skills and strategies to texts they read themselves. Students demonstrate their comprehension through asking and answering questions, retelling stories, discussing characters, comparing stories, and making and confirming predictions. As students progress through the grades, they build upon their existing skills and read a more extensive variety of texts.

Q **How is instruction in genres and text structures developed in the program?**

A The foundation of *Trophies* is a wide variety of fiction and nonfiction selections, including many paired selections to promote reading across texts. Instruction in both the *Pupil Edition* and *Teacher's Edition* helps students develop a thorough understanding of genre characteristics and text structures. In kindergarten, students explore story elements, such as characters, setting, and important events. As students move up the grades, they analyze both literary elements and devices and expository organizational patterns, such as cause/effect and compare/contrast, to understand increasingly difficult texts.

Look for

✔ Focus Strategies and Focus Skills
✔ Diagnostic Checks
✔ Additional Support Activities
✔ Guided Comprehension
✔ Strategies Good Readers Use
✔ Ongoing Assessment
✔ Comprehension Cards

VOCABULARY

A large and flexible vocabulary is the hallmark of an educated person. The more words students acquire, the better chance they will have for success in reading, writing, and spelling.

Students acquire vocabulary knowledge through extensive reading in a variety of texts. The amount of reading students do in and out of school is a strong indicator of students' vocabulary acquisition. Research supports exposing students to rich language environments through listening to literature and reading a variety of genres independently. Their vocabulary knowledge grows when they hear stories containing unfamiliar words. As students progress through the grades, their reading of books and other materials contributes more significantly to vocabulary knowledge than viewing television, participating in conversations, or other typical oral language activities. In other words, increasing students' volume of reading is the best way to promote vocabulary growth.

Students need multiple encounters with key vocabulary words in order to improve comprehension. Current and confirmed research has shown that students need to encounter a word several times before it is known well enough to facilitate comprehension. Direct instruction in vocabulary has an important role here because learning words from context is far from automatic. After being introduced to new words, students need opportunities to see those words again in their reading and to develop their own uses for the words in a variety of different contexts, in relationship to other words, and both inside and outside of the classroom. For instruction to enhance comprehension, new words need to become a permanent part of students' repertoires, which means instruction must go well beyond providing information on word meanings.

Students can benefit from direct instruction in vocabulary strategies. Although estimates of vocabulary size and growth vary, children likely learn between 1,000 and 5,000 words per year—and the average child learns about 3,000 words. Since wide reading provides a significant source for increasing word knowledge, it is imperative that students learn key strategies to help them learn new words as they are encountered. Vocabulary strategies students should know by third grade include

- using a dictionary and other reference sources to understand the meanings of unknown words
- using context to determine the meanings of unfamiliar words
- learning about the relationships between words (synonyms, antonyms, and multiple-meaning words)
- exploring shades of meaning of words that are synonyms or near-synonyms
- using morphemic analysis—breaking words into meaning-bearing components, such as prefixes and roots

At grades 3 and above, morphemic analysis becomes an even more valuable dimension of vocabulary instruction. For example, learning just one root, *astro,* can help students unlock the meanings of such words as *astronaut, astronomy, astrology,* and *astrological.*

> " Research on vocabulary shows that for learners to come to know words in a meaningful way, they need to engage with word meanings and build habits of attending to words and exploring their uses in thoughtful and lively ways. "
>
> — Margaret C. McKeown
> **Research Scientist**
> **Learning Research and Development Center,**
> **University of Pittsburgh**

Q **How does *Trophies* provide exposure to a wide variety of texts?**

A *Trophies* provides students with a wealth of opportunities to read a rich variety of texts. The *Pupil Editions,* the nucleus of the program in grades 1–6, feature a variety of high-quality literature selections that help students build vocabulary. *Trophies* also provides students with extensive reading opportunities through such components as these:

- *Big Books* (kindergarten and grade 1)
- *Read-Aloud Anthologies* (kindergarten through grade 2)
- *Library Books Collections* (kindergarten through grade 6)
- *Books for All Learners* (grades 1–6)
- *Intervention Readers* (grades 2–6)
- *Teacher's Edition* Read-Aloud Selections (grades 2–6)

Q **How does the program provide multiple exposures to key vocabulary?**

A Students are given many rich exposures to key vocabulary through the following program features:

- Vocabulary in context on *Teaching Transparencies*
- *Pupil Edition* and *Teacher's Edition* Vocabulary Power pages
- *Pupil Edition* main selections
- Word Study pages of the *Teacher's Edition* (grades 3–6)
- Additional Support Activities in the *Teacher's Edition*
- *Practice Books*
- *Books for All Learners*
- *Intervention Readers*

Q **How does *Trophies* facilitate the teaching of vocabulary-learning strategies?**

A Lessons include explicit teaching and modeling of vocabulary strategies. Specific lessons in both the *Pupil Edition* and *Teacher's Edition* provide direct instruction that helps enable students to increase their vocabulary every time they read. Strategies include using a dictionary, using context to determine word meaning, and understanding word structures and word relationships.

Look for

✓ Building Background and Vocabulary
✓ *Big Book* lessons
✓ Listening Comprehension
✓ Word Study (grades 3–6)
✓ Lessons on word relationships and word structure (grades 3–6)
✓ Additional Support Activities

FLUENCY

Research recognizes fluency as a strong indicator of efficient and proficient reading. A fluent reader reads with accuracy at an appropriate rate, attending to phrasing. When the reading is oral, it reflects a speech-like pace.

Oral fluency is reading with speed, accuracy, and prosody—meaning that the reader uses stress, pitch, and juncture of spoken language. Researchers have repeatedly demonstrated the relationship between fluency and reading comprehension. If a reader must devote most of his or her cognitive attention to pronouncing words, comprehension suffers. It follows then that students who read fluently can devote more attention to meaning and thus increase their comprehension. This is why oral reading fluency is an important goal of reading instruction, especially in the elementary grades. Word recognition must be automatic—freeing cognitive resources for comprehending text. If word recognition is labored, cognitive resources are consumed by decoding, leaving little or no resources for interpretation. In kindergarten and at the beginning of grade 1, oral reading may sound less like speech because students are still learning to decode and to identify words. Nevertheless, with appropriate support, text that "fits," and time to practice, students soon begin to read simple texts in a natural, more fluent, manner. By the beginning of grade 2, many students have come to enjoy the sounds of their own voices reading. They choose to read and reread with the natural sounds of spoken language and have few interruptions due to inadequate word attack or word recognition problems.

Fluent readers can
- recognize words automatically
- group individual words into meaningful phrases
- apply strategies rapidly to identify unknown words
- determine where to place emphasis or pause to make sense of a text

Fluency can be developed through directed reading practice, opportunities for repeated reading, and other instructional strategies. The primary method to improve fluency is directed reading practice in accessible texts. Practice does not replace instruction; it provides the reader opportunity to gain speed and accuracy within manageable text. One form of directed reading practice is repeated reading, which gives a developing reader more time and chances with the same text.

Repeated reading
- provides practice reading words in context
- produces gains in reading rate, accuracy, and comprehension
- helps lower-achieving readers

" Children gain reading fluency when they can read at a steady rate, recognizing words accurately and achieving correctness in phrasing and intonation. **"**

— Nancy Roser
Professor, Language and Literacy Studies
The University of Texas at Austin

Q How does *Trophies* teach and assess oral reading fluency?

A Toward developing fluent readers, *Trophies* provides explicit, systematic phonics instruction to build word recognition skills that enable students to become efficient decoders. (See the Phonics section of these pages for more information.) *Trophies* also provides the following tools that enable teachers to assess student progress on an ongoing basis:

- Oral reading passages in the back of each *Teacher's Edition* (grades 2-6)
- Guidelines to help teachers use these passages (grades 2-6)
- *Oral Reading Fluency Assessment*

Q How does *Trophies* provide intervention for students who are not developing oral reading fluency at an appropriate pace?

A In the grades 2-6 *Intervention Resource Kit*, every day of instruction includes a fluency builder activity. Students are assigned repeated readings with cumulative texts. These readings begin with word lists, expand to include multiple sentences, and eventually become extended self-selected passages. Fluency performance-assessment activities are also provided in the *Intervention Teacher's Guides*.

Q How does *Trophies* provide opportunities for repeated readings?

A In grades 1–6, the Rereading for Fluency features offer a wide variety of engaging activities that have students reread with a focus on expression, pacing, and intonation. These activities include

- **Echo Reading**—Students repeat (echo) what the teacher reads aloud.
- **Choral Reading**—Groups of students read aloud with the teacher simultaneously.
- **Repeated Reading**—The teacher models, and students reread several times until fluency is gained.
- **Readers Theatre**—Students assume roles and read them aloud from the text.
- **Partner Reading**—Students take turns reading aloud with a partner.
- **Tape-Assisted Reading**—Students listen to an audiotext and read along with the recording.
- **Phrase-Cued Text**—Students read texts that have been "chunked" into syntactic phrases.
- **Shared Reading**—Students join in as the teacher reads to the whole group.

Look for

- ✔ Rereading for Fluency
- ✔ Oral reading passages in the *Teacher's Edition*
- ✔ *Oral Reading Fluency Assessment*
- ✔ *Fluency Routine Cards*
- ✔ *Intervention Teacher's Guides*

ASSESSMENT

Assessment is integral to instruction. By choosing the appropriate assessment tools and methods, you can find out where your students are instructionally and plan accordingly.

Assessment is the process of collecting information in order to make instructional decisions about students. Good decisions require good information and to provide this information, assessment of students and their learning must be continuous. Because the reading process is composed of many complex skills, such as comprehension, word attack, and synthesis of information, no one assessment tool can evaluate completely all aspects of reading. Teachers need to gather information about their students in many ways, both formally and informally. Assessment helps them plan instruction, and ongoing assessments throughout the instructional process should guide their decisions and actions.

Assessment must systematically inform instruction and help teachers differentiate instruction. The first tool the classroom teacher requires is an entry-level assessment instrument to identify students' instructional level and potential for participating in grade-level instruction. This diagnostic instrument should be sensitive to gaps and strengths in student learning. After placement, teachers need differentiation strategies that are flexible and that can be easily adapted according to continual monitoring of student progress.

Assessments for monitoring progress should be used to determine ongoing priorities for instruction. The use of both formal and informal tools and strategies, including formative and summative assessments, provides a comprehensive picture of students' achievement as they progress through an instructional program. Informal assessments encourage teachers to observe students as they read, write, and discuss. These assessments provide immediate feedback and allow teachers to quickly determine which students are having difficulty and need additional instruction and practice. Formal assessments provide opportunities for teachers to take a more focused look at how students are progressing. Whether formal or informal, monitoring instruments and activities should be

- frequent
- ongoing
- easy to score and interpret

Teachers should be provided with clear options for monitoring and clear pathways for providing intervention and enrichment as needed. Less frequent summative assessments may be used to gauge long-term growth.

Student progress needs to be communicated to parents and guardians on a regular basis. As students become more accountable for their learning through standards-based testing, teachers are becoming more accountable not only to administrators but also to families. A complete instructional program should offer means for teachers to communicate with families about how their students are progressing and how families can contribute to students' growth.

> **Knowing how well a student can use literacy skills such as reading, writing, listening, and speaking is vital to effective instruction.**
>
> — **Roger Farr**
> Chancellor's Professor and Director of the
> Center for Innovation in Assessment,
> Indiana University, Bloomington

Q **How does *Trophies* integrate entry-level group and individual assessments with instruction?**

A The *Placement and Diagnostic Assessment* provides an overview of specific diagnostic information about prerequisite skills for each grade level. In addition, *Reading and Language Skills Assessment* pretests can be used to determine whether students need additional instruction and practice in phonics, comprehension skills, vocabulary, writing, and writing conventions.

Q **What monitoring instruments are included with *Trophies*?**

A Formative assessments that facilitate monitoring student progress include

- Diagnostic Checks at point of use for immediate assessment of understanding, with follow-up Additional Support Activities in the *Teacher's Edition*
- Ongoing Assessment to assess and model the use of reading strategies, in the *Teacher's Edition*
- *Intervention Assessment Book*
- Performance Assessment activities in the *Teacher's Edition*
- *End-of-Selection Tests* to monitor students' comprehension of each selection

In each theme's *Teacher's Edition,* the Theme Assessment to Plan Instruction section provides a clear road map for using assessment to adapt instruction to student needs.

Q **What other assessment instruments are used in *Trophies*?**

A The *Reading and Language Skills Assessment,* which includes posttests for end-of-theme assessment and Mid-Year and End-of-Year Tests, provides information about students' mastery of reading skills. Other assessment instruments in *Trophies* include

- *Holistic Assessment,* which uses authentic, theme-related passages and provides a more global, holistic evaluation of students' reading and writing ability
- *Oral Reading Fluency Assessment,* which monitors accuracy and rate
- *Assessment Handbook* (Kindergarten)

Look for

In the *Teacher's Edition*
✓ **Diagnostic Checks**
✓ **Ongoing Assessment**
✓ **Performance Assessment**
✓ **Theme Assessment to Plan Instruction**

Other Components
✓ ***Placement* and *Diagnostic Assessments***
✓ ***Reading and Language Skills Assessment* (Pretests and Posttests)**
✓ ***Holistic Assessment***
✓ ***Oral Reading Fluency Assessment***
✓ ***Assessment Handbook* (Kindergarten)**

WRITING

Good writing skills are critical both to students'
academic achievement and to their future success
in society.

Writing instruction should incorporate explicit modeling and practice in the conventions of written English. All students can benefit from systematic instruction and practice in spelling, grammar, usage, mechanics, and presentation skills, such as handwriting and document preparation. Mastering these conventions enables students to communicate their ideas and information clearly and effectively.

- In kindergarten, children should use their growing knowledge of language structure and the conventions of print to begin expressing their ideas through words and pictures and putting these ideas into writing, with words spelled phonetically.

- In grades 1–3, students should continue to transfer their developing reading skills to writing conventions by using their knowledge of word structure and phonics to spell new words. They should learn and apply the fundamentals of grammar, mechanics, and sentence structure.

- In grades 4–6, instruction should build advanced spelling, grammar, and mechanics skills and should apply them in student writing of narratives, descriptions, and other extended compositions. Students should be systematically taught to apply writing conventions in purposeful writing activities.

Students should learn about and practice the process skills that good writers use. Many students do not realize, until they are told, that most stories and articles are not written in one sitting. Good writers plan, revise, rewrite, and rethink during the process of writing. Instruction in writing processes can spring from author features and interviews with the writers whose works students are reading. The teacher's modeling of effective prewriting, drafting, revising, proofreading, and publishing techniques should build upon this understanding. Particular attention should systematically be paid to revision strategies such as adding, deleting, clarifying, and rearranging text. Students should apply these strategies to their own work repeatedly and should learn new techniques gradually and cumulatively.

Systematic instruction in writer's craft skills should be applied to the process. Students should be taught that, whatever the form of their writing, they must determine a clear focus, organize their ideas, use effective word choice and sentence structures, and express their own viewpoint. These writer's craft skills should be taught through focused exercises and writing tasks and should be reinforced cumulatively in lessons that teach the elements of longer writing forms.

> ❝ Effective writing is both an art and a science. The ability to generate interesting ideas and a pleasing style characterizes the art side; mastering the craft and its conventions characterizes the science side. Good instruction judiciously attends to both. ❞
>
> — **Dorothy S. Strickland**
> Samuel DeWitt Proctor
> Professor of Education,
> Rutgers University

Q **How does *Trophies* provide instruction and practice in the conventions of written English?**

A *Trophies* provides systematic, explicit instruction and abundant practice in spelling, grammar, usage, and mechanics in daily, easy-to-use lessons. Transparencies, activities, and practice sheets are provided for modeling and practice. Presentation skills are also formally taught, with an emphasis on handwriting at the lower grades. Spelling instruction, especially at the primary grades, is closely linked to phonics instruction. All skills of conventions are applied in purposeful writing activities.

Q **How does *Trophies* teach the process of writing?**

A From the earliest grades, students using *Trophies* learn that good writers plan and revise their writing. Students are guided through the prewriting, drafting, revising, and proofreading stages with models, practice activities, graphic organizers, and checklists. Instruction in presentation skills, such as handwriting and speaking, guides the publishing stage. Teacher rubrics for evaluation are provided at point of use, and reproducible student rubrics are provided in the back of the *Teacher's Edition*.

Q **How does *Trophies* apply writer's craft instruction to the writing process?**

A In kindergarten, students begin to write sentences and brief narratives about familiar experiences. Students also engage in shared and interactive writing in kindergarten through grade 2. In grades 1 and 2, instruction in story grammar and sentence types becomes more sophisticated, with students learning about and applying one component, such as capitalization, at a time. In grades 2–6, explicit writer's craft lessons are built into the writing strand and follow this format:

- Weeks 1 and 2 of the unit present writer's craft skills, such as organizing, choosing words, and writing effective sentences. Students complete targeted exercises and apply the craft in relatively brief writing forms.
- Weeks 3 and 4 present longer writing forms, emphasizing the steps of the writing process. The writer's craft skills learned in Weeks 1 and 2 are applied in longer compositions.
- In grades 3–6, Week 5 presents a timed writing test in which students apply what they have learned.

Look for

✔ Writer's Craft lessons
✔ Writing Process lessons
✔ Timed or Tested Writing lessons
✔ 5-day grammar and spelling lessons
✔ Traits of good writing

LISTENING AND SPEAKING

Increasingly, young people must comprehend, and are expected to create, messages that are oral and visual rather than strictly written. Listening and speaking skills are essential to achievement in both reading and writing.

Listening to narratives, poetry, and nonfiction texts builds thinking and language skills that students need for success in reading and writing. The domains of the language arts (listening, speaking, reading, and writing) are closely connected. Listening instruction and speaking instruction are critical scaffolds that support reading comprehension, vocabulary knowledge, and oral communication skills. Classroom instruction must be focused on these skills and must also strategically address the needs of students with limited levels of language experience or whose language experiences are primarily in languages other than English.

Listening instruction and speaking instruction should progress developmentally through the grades. In the primary grades, instruction should focus on

- listening to and retelling stories, with an emphasis on story grammar (setting, characters, and important events)
- explicit modeling of standard English structures, with frequent opportunities to repeat sentences and recite rhymes and songs
- brief oral presentations about familiar topics and experiences
- developing familiarity with academic and literary terms

As students move up the grades, they should develop increasingly sophisticated listening and speaking skills, including the more complex production skills. By grades 4–6, students should be increasingly capable of

- delivering both narrative and expository presentations using a range of narrative and rhetorical devices
- modeling their own presentations on effective text structures they have analyzed in their reading
- orally responding to literature in ways that demonstrate advanced understanding and insight
- supporting their interpretations with facts and specific examples
- interpreting and using verbal and nonverbal messages
- analyzing oral and visual messages, purposes, and persuasive techniques

❝ Oral response activities encourage critical thinking and allow students to bring their individuality to the process of responding to literature. ❞

— Hallie Kay Yopp
Professor
Department of Elementary Bilingual
and Reading Education,
California State University, Fullerton

Q **How does *Trophies* provide rich listening experiences that build understanding of language structures and texts?**

A From the very first day of kindergarten through the end of grade 6, *Trophies* provides abundant and varied texts, support, and modeling for listening instruction. With resources such as *Big Books, Read-Aloud Anthologies,* and Audiotext of the reading selections, the teacher has every type of narrative and expository text available. *Trophies* also provides direct instruction and engaging response activities so that teachers can use each listening selection to its full advantage. The *English-Language Learners Resource Kit* provides additional opportunities for students with special needs to develop an understanding of English language structure, concept vocabulary and background, and listening comprehension skills.

Q **How does *Trophies* develop listening through the grades?**

A Listening is developed through the Sharing Literature features in kindergarten through grade 2 with such options as Build Concept Vocabulary, Develop Listening Comprehension, and Listen and Respond and through the *Read-Aloud Anthologies.* In grades 3–6, read-alouds serve as a vehicle for setting a purpose for listening and develop listening comprehension and listening strategies.

Q **How does *Trophies* provide instruction in speaking and in making presentations?**

A *Trophies* provides instruction to guide students in making both narrative and expository presentations. In kindergarten, each lesson offers formal and informal speaking opportunities through the Share Time feature. In grades 1 and 2, speaking activities are included in the Rereading for Fluency and in the Wrap-Up sections of the lesson. The Morning Message feature in kindergarten through grade 2 provides additional informal speaking opportunities. In grades 3–6, presentation skills become more sophisticated. Students are asked to make such presentations as extended oral reports, multimedia presentations, debates, and persuasive speeches.

Look for

✔ **Develop Listening Comprehension**
✔ **Daily "Sharing Literature" activities (Kindergarten through Grade 2)**
✔ **Read-Aloud selections and instruction with every lesson (Grades 2–6)**
✔ **Morning Message (Kindergarten–Grade 2)**
✔ **Author's Chair presentations (Kindergarten–Grade 2)**
✔ **Rereading for Fluency**
✔ **Listening and Speaking Lessons (Grades 3–6)**
✔ **Presentation Rubrics (Grades 2–6)**
✔ ***Read-Aloud Anthologies* (Kindergarten–Grade 2)**

REACHING ALL LEARNERS

Students come to school with diverse experiences and language backgrounds. Teachers, who are charged with providing universal access to high-quality instruction, require specially designed plans and materials to help all students meet or exceed grade-level standards.

Curriculum and instruction must be carefully planned to provide for students who need varying levels of intervention and challenge. Students require additional instruction, practice, and extension at different times and in different degrees. Some students need occasional reteaching and slight modifications in pacing, while others are at greater risk and require more intensive intervention. Research shows that students with learning difficulties need more review and practice to perform a new task automatically. Instruction should cumulatively integrate simpler or previously learned tasks with newer, more complex activities. In addition, research shows the following:

- Reading difficulties can stem from inaccuracy in identifying words.
- Intervention should be geared toward a student's level of reading development.
- Diagnostic testing results should show what students know and what they need to know; frequent assessment is critical.
- Instruction should be direct and explicit.

Curriculum and instruction must be structured to meet the needs of English-language learners. The 2000 U.S. Census confirmed what many educators already knew: more and more students do not speak English as their first language. Widely ranging levels of English proficiency in mainstream classrooms present special challenges and opportunities for teachers. Depending on their level of English acquisition and their grade placement, English-language learners need varying degrees of additional support in areas such as oral language, English phonology, vocabulary, background information, and the academic language of school.

Students who already meet or exceed grade-level expectations need opportunities for enrichment or acceleration. They need to be challenged by vocabulary extension study and exposure to sophisticated literature in a variety of genres. Students may also be encouraged to carry out investigations that extend their learning. Such activities should promote sustained investigative skills: raising questions, researching answers, and organizing information. Several research studies have shown the importance of setting high standards for advanced learners. An instructional program that clearly provides for differentiation at a variety of levels can be the tool teachers need to provide universal access to high-level standards.

> **❝** In the process of helping students learn, we want to support them in discovering that each person is unique and has a unique contribution to make towards creating a better world for all. **❞**
>
> — **Alma Flor Ada**
> Director of Doctoral Studies in the
> International Multicultural Program
> University of San Francisco
>
> — **F. Isabel Campoy**
> Former President, Association of
> Spanish Professionals in the USA

Q **How does *Trophies* provide differentiated instruction at a variety of levels?**

A *Trophies* was designed to accommodate a diverse student population, with tiers of differentiation for different needs. Diagnostic Checks, with brief activities, are positioned at point of use within each lesson in the *Teacher's Edition* so that specific needs of students can be identified and addressed. Additional Support Activities, tied closely to the lessons, are provided for further differentiation. The three types of activities address below-level readers, advanced students, and English-language learners. In addition, Alternative Teaching Strategies are provided for students who perform below level on the *Reading and Language Skills Assessments*. The *Library Books Collections* and the *Books for All Learners* also provide students at all levels with a wealth of reading opportunities in a variety of genres.

Q **What additional support does *Trophies* provide?**

A An *Intervention Resource Kit* and an *English-Language Learners Resource Kit* are available for students with greater needs.

Both kits

- align closely with the core program
- provide rigorous daily lessons
- provide abundant cumulative, spiraled practice

For below-level readers, the *Intervention Resource Kit* preteaches and reteaches the same skills and concepts that are taught in the core program. The *English-Language Learners Resource Kit* builds background, vocabulary and concepts, academic language, comprehension, and language arts. Finally, to guide teachers in making instructional decisions, *Trophies* provides a complete assessment program, with instruments for entry-level assessment, monitoring of progress, and summative assessment. (See the Assessment section of these pages for more information.)

Look for

- ✓ **Reaching All Learners**
- ✓ **Diagnostic Checks**
- ✓ **Additional Support Activities**
- ✓ **Practice pages for all levels**
- ✓ *Books for All Learners*
- ✓ *Intervention Resource Kit*
- ✓ *English-Language Learners Resource Kit*
- ✓ *Library Books Collections*
- ✓ *Placement and Diagnostic Assessments*

WHAT RESEARCH SAYS ABOUT
CLASSROOM MANAGEMENT

The task of managing the classroom is becoming increasingly complex. Teachers are seeking to maximize instructional effectiveness for students with a diverse range of skills and backgrounds.

Classroom management is a critical variable related to student achievement. Research shows that the more time teachers spend dealing with student behavior and interruptions in instruction, the more student achievement suffers. A classroom environment that promotes student growth and learning results from making effective decisions about the organization and scheduling of instruction and the physical arrangement of the classroom.

Effective organization includes differentiating instruction to engage all students in instructional-level activities. Grouping strategies are important for addressing diverse needs, but grouping must never be treated as an aim in itself. Flexible grouping can help ensure that all students meet instructional goals, and it can be effective in helping students participate and contribute in a learning environment. Grouping should be fluid and temporary, varying according to individual students' progress and interests and should allow time for students to function independently and be responsible for their own work. The types of instruction that are most successful in the major grouping patterns include

Whole Group

- Sharing literature
- Developing concepts
- Providing modeling
- Presenting new knowledge

Small Group

- Developing skills
- Practicing processes
- Collaborating on projects
- Providing challenge activities

After flexible work groups are established, effective classroom organization should focus on scheduling classroom activities and creating a classroom arrangement that facilitates learning. Initially, teachers might establish one or two learning centers based on tasks that are familiar to students. Then teachers can develop other centers and routines as needed. Before beginning a routine, teachers should introduce students to the procedures for using each area, ensuring that students understand what they are to do and how much time they should spend in each area. A rotation schedule should be established so that students can easily move from one area to another as tasks are completed. Helping students become familiar with schedules and routines enables the teacher to devote more time to individual and small-group instruction.

> **" The organization of the classroom should provide students with many opportunities to share with teachers and other students the things they are reading and writing. "**
>
> **— Roger Farr**
> Chancellor's Professor and Director of the Center for Innovation in Assessment, Indiana University, Bloomington

Q How can teachers keep other students engaged in meaningful experiences while providing instruction to students with special needs?

A *Trophies* provides an abundance of productive materials and ideas for independent and small-group work

- Managing the Classroom sections in the back of the *Teacher's Editions* that provide clear instructions in arranging the classroom with centers or stations, using a Work Board with center icons to help organize routines and schedules, and tracking student progress.

- Classroom Management and Reading and Writing Routines sections in the *Teacher's Editions* (grades 1–2) that provide suggestions for individual, whole-group, and small-group activities.

- Cross-Curricular Centers and Stations with pacing suggestions to regulate student participation

- Lesson-specific Workboards to help teachers manage groups and individuals simultaneously

- Integration of content from social studies, science, and other content areas

- *Books for All Learners* to allow students to read independently at their own level

- Practice pages for students with diverse skills and language backgrounds

- Theme Projects for extended group work

- Comprehension Cards, *Library Books Collections,* and other resources to facilitate group and independent reading

Q How does *Trophies* help teachers manage its instructional pathways for classrooms with diverse learners?

A *Trophies* provides a clear, manageable system of diagnostic assessment checkpoints, ongoing formal assessment and performance-based opportunities, and instructional pathways for teachers to follow based on results. In addition to easy-to-use lesson planners that include suggested pacing, the system provides

- Diagnostic Checks and customized activities at point of use

- Additional Support Activities to reinforce, reteach, and extend key concepts in every lesson

- *Intervention Resource Kits* and *English-Language Learners Resource Kits* for more intensive instruction

- Alternative Teaching Strategies for additional options to modify instruction

For more information, see Theme Assessment to Plan Instruction in each *Teacher's Edition.*

Look for

- ✓ Diagnostic Checks
- ✓ Cross-Curricular Centers or Stations
- ✓ Work Boards
- ✓ *Books for All Learners*
- ✓ *Library Books Collections*
- ✓ Practice pages
- ✓ Theme Projects
- ✓ Comprehension Cards
- ✓ Managing the Classroom

Contents

Reference Materials

School-Home Connections

Additional Reading / T101

Additional Resources

Introducing the Book

Discuss the Title and Cover Illustration

Invite students to discuss the title and the cover illustration. Ask what the title, *On Your Mark*, might mean. Discuss what the tortoise and the hare in the picture might be doing and what feeling the picture gives students.

Discuss the Book's Organization

Discuss the letter to the reader. Have students read the letter on page 3 of the *Pupil Edition*. Discuss how reading can take people on different and exciting paths.

Examine other parts of the book. Have students turn to each feature. Briefly discuss how each part helps readers use the book and understand the literature.

- Table of Contents—shows titles, authors, and page numbers
- Using Reading Strategies—describes tools readers can use
- Theme Table of Contents—lists literature in that theme
- Vocabulary Power—introduces selection vocabulary words
- Genre Notes and Labels—describe the different types of literature
- Making Connections—provides questions and activities relating to the literature
- Focus Skill—provides instruction in skills relating to the literature
- Test Preparation—reinforces the Focus Skill with sample test questions
- Writer's Handbook—explains the writing process and how to use reference sources
- Glossary—contains all vocabulary words and their definitions
- Index—provides page numbers of alphabetized literature titles and authors

HARCOURT
· T R O P H I E S ·

HARCOURT
· T R O P H I E S ·

A HARCOURT READING/LANGUAGE ARTS PROGRAM

ON YOUR MARK

SENIOR AUTHORS
Isabel L. Beck ◆ Roger C. Farr ◆ Dorothy S. Strickland

AUTHORS
Alma Flor Ada ◆ Marcia Brechtel ◆ Margaret McKeown
Nancy Roser ◆ Hallie Kay Yopp

CONSULTANTS
F. Isabel Campoy ◆ Asa G. Hilliard III ◆ David A. Monti

Harcourt

Orlando   Boston   Dallas   Chicago   San Diego

Visit *The Learning Site!*

www.harcourtschool.com

HARCOURT
· T R O P H I E S ·

A HARCOURT READING/LANGUAGE ARTS PROGRAM

ON YOUR MARK

Dear Reader,

Are you ready? You are about to travel on an exciting path. You may be surprised at how much you learn on the way.

In **On Your Mark,** the stories, poems, and articles will take you to many exciting places. Some places are in the past, some are in outer space, and some are at the center of the earth! You will meet many unusual characters and read about interesting facts. Some stories might even make you laugh out loud.

As you read this book, you will learn to be a better reader. You will learn about many new and interesting topics. Take the time to enjoy everything you learn along this reading journey.

On your mark, get set, read!

Sincerely,

The Authors

The Authors

4

5

6

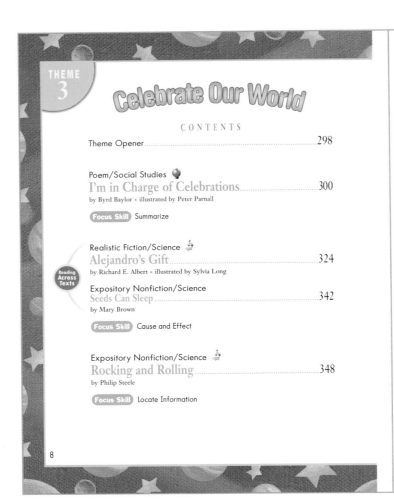
8

9

xxxviii   On Your Mark

Using Reading Strategies

Introduce the Concept

Discuss with students what they do when they read. They may mention things that they do before, during, or after reading. Ask questions such as these: **What do you do to get yourself ready to read? What do you do when you don't understand something you are reading? What do you do when you come to a word you don't know?** Make a list on the board of students' answers. Tell students that they have named some good reading *strategies*. Explain that a strategy is a plan for doing something well.

Explain Strategies Good Readers Use

Have students read pages 10–11. Explain that these are the strategies they will be focusing on as they read the selections in this book. Discuss with students a brief explanation of each strategy:

- **Use Decoding/Phonics**   Look for familiar spelling patterns and word parts to help you decode longer words as you read.

- **Make and Confirm Predictions**   Think about what might happen next in a story. Read to find out whether you are right. Make new predictions as you read.

- **Create Mental Images**   Sometimes, picturing in your mind what you are reading can help you understand and enjoy a selection. Pay attention to descriptive details.

- **Self-Question**   Have you ever found that you have questions as you are reading? Learn to ask yourself good questions as you read. This will help you check your understanding and focus on important ideas in the selection.

- **Summarize**   Tell or list the main points of the selection or the main things that happened. This will help you understand and remember what you read.

- **Read Ahead**   If you are having trouble understanding something in a selection, such as who a certain character is, don't give up. Keep on reading. The meaning may become clearer when you have more information.

- **Reread to Clarify**   If something doesn't make sense, you may have missed an important point. Try reading the passage again or going back to an earlier part of the selection.

- **Use Context to Confirm Meaning**   After you read an unfamiliar or difficult word, ask yourself whether what you read makes sense in the sentence and whether it fits what is happening in the selection. By paying attention to the words around unfamiliar words, you can learn many new words and become a stronger reader.

- **Use Text Structure and Format**   Find clues to meaning by looking at how the author organized the information. Is it arranged in time order? By main idea and details? Look at headings and captions.

- **Adjust Reading Rate**   Think about the type of selection you are reading. A selection that has a lot of facts and details, such as a selection about volcanoes, may have to be read more slowly than a story about a character your age.

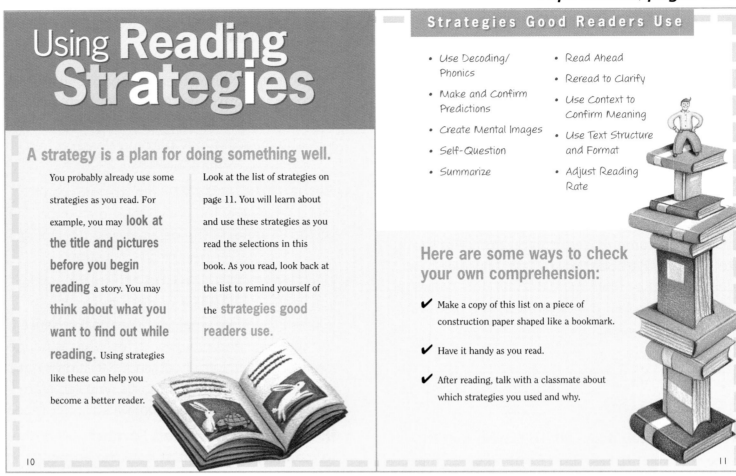

Using Reading Strategies

Monitor Comprehension   Distribute copies of Thinking About My Reading and My Reading Log, pages R42–R43. Have each student begin a personal reading portfolio. Students can use the forms to record how they choose self-selected books, the strategies they use during reading, how long they read outside of class each day, and other reading behaviors.

Strategy Bookmark   Have students make a bookmark from a sheet of heavy paper and write the strategies on the bookmark. Invite students to decorate their bookmarks. As they read, they should refer to the bookmark to help remind them of the strategies they can use.

Response Journal   Explain to students that they should keep a journal to record their responses to selections and to monitor their progress as readers. They may use a spiral-bound notebook or sheets of paper stapled together. In the notebook, they should create sections to write about which strategies work best for them and to develop their own plans for reading different kinds of selections. You may want to have them record here rather than on the My Reading Log copying master how long they read each day. They should also set aside a section of the notebook for a Word Bank, where they will list new or interesting words they come across in their reading.

Celebrate Our World

In this theme, students explore our Earth and our Universe. As they read and listen to selections about people and animal characters appreciating the world around them, they will come to view their own world through fresh eyes.

Theme Resources

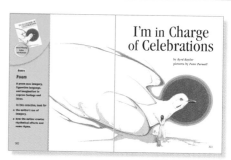

▲ **"I'm in Charge of Celebrations,"**
pages 302–317
POEM

▲ **"Alejandro's Gift,"**
pages 326–340
REALISTIC FICTION

READING ACROSS TEXTS
"Seeds Can Sleep,"
pages 342–343
EXPOSITORY NONFICTION

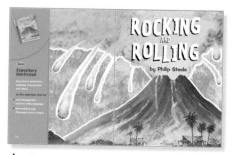

▲ **"Rocking and Rolling,"**
pages 350–364
EXPOSITORY NONFICTION

▲ **"The Armadillo from Amarillo,"**
pages 372–391
INFORMATIONAL NARRATIVE

READING ACROSS TEXTS
"Mapping the World,"
pages 394–395
EXPOSITORY NONFICTION

▲ **"Visitors from Space,"**
pages 402–411
EXPOSITORY NONFICTION

SEE ALSO INTERVENTION READER:
Bright Surprises
- "Book of Days"
- "The Hummingbird Garden"
- "A Mountain Blows Its Top"
- "The Place in Space"
- "A Meteor Stopped Here"

 Selections are available on *Audiotext 6.*

INDEPENDENT/SELF-SELECTED READING

These books are available through Harcourt.

Library Books Collection

Teaching plans for the Library Books Collection can be found on pages **417Q–417T**.

▲ **Earth: Our Planet in Space**
by Seymour Simon

▲ **Jordi's Star**
by Alma Flor Ada

Books for All Learners

BELOW-LEVEL

ON-LEVEL

ADVANCED

ELL

Teaching suggestions for the **Books for All Learners** can be found on pages **323K–323N, 347K–347N, 369M–369P, 399M–399P,** and **417K–417N.**

Reading Outside of Class Additional trade book titles can be found on page T101. Have students complete the "My Reading Log" form on page R42 for each book they read.

TECHNOLOGY RESOURCES

Available at *The Learning Site:* www.harcourtschool.com

- *Writing Express*™ CD-ROM
- *Grammar Jingles*™ CD
- *Media Literacy and Communication Skills Package* (Video)
- *Reading and Language Skills Assessment* CD-ROM

Resources for Teachers
- Graphic Organizers
- Language Support
- Classroom Management
- Lesson Planner

Student Activities
- Author/Illustrator Information
- Skill Activities
- Test Tutor
- Writing Activities
- Grammar Activities

Resources for Parents
- Helping Your Child Learn to Read
- Helping Your Child Learn to Write
- Helping Your Child Take Tests
- Internet Safety
- Homework Helper

PROFESSIONAL DEVELOPMENT

Professional Development for Reading courses combine current, scientifically-based research with practical classroom strategies. Topics include

- Phonemic Awareness
- Phonics
- Vocabulary
- Fluency
- Text Comprehension
- Assessment

	I'm in Charge of Celebrations pp. 300A–323N	Alejandro's Gift pp. 324A–347N
• **Reading** • **Vocabulary** • **Comprehension**	**Read** Free-Verse Poem **Guided Comprehension** **Summarize T** **Fact and Opinion T** **Selection Vocabulary T** *signal, celebrations, choosy* *average, tracks, admiring*	**Read** Realistic Fiction **Guided Comprehension** **Read Across Texts** "Seeds Can Sleep" EXPOSITORY NONFICTION **Cause and Effect T** **Paraphrase** **Selection Vocabulary T** *windmill, cherished, furrows* *ample, shunned, growth*
• **Independent Reading**	**Books for All Learners** **Below-Level:** *Music Makes Joy* **On-Level:** *City Celebrations* **Advanced:** *What Is a Desert?* **English-Language Learners:** *My School Year*	**Books for All Learners** **Below-Level:** *The Burro's Land* **On-Level:** *A Circle Story* **Advanced:** *Liberty* **English-Language Learners:** *In the Garden*
• **Writing** • **Grammar** • **Spelling**	**WRITER'S CRAFT: Word Choice T** **Writing Form: Poem** **More Irregular Verbs T** **Words with Suffixes -er, -ful, -ly, -able T**	**WRITER'S CRAFT: Word Choice T** **Writing Form: Thank-you Letter** **The Verb** *Be* **T** **Changing** *y* **to** *i* **T**

• **Cross-Curricular Stations**	**Science**
	 Make a Desert Diorama
	
	  Social Studies
	 Research Local Geography
		Science
		 Report on Desert Animal Adaptations
		
		  Social Studies
		 Compare Desert Environments

T = tested skill

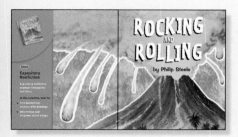

Rocking and Rolling
pp. 348A–369P

Read Expository Nonfiction

Guided Comprehension

Locate Information T

Graphic Aids T

Cause and Effect

Selection Vocabulary T

magma, edges, range

epicenter, coast, peak

 Books for All Learners

Below-Level: *Ring of Fire*

On-Level: *The Perfect Ending*

Advanced: *Rock Hounds*

English-Language Learners:
This Land

WRITING PROCESS: Play T

Apply Writer's Craft: Word Choice

Contractions T

Contractions T

 Science
Wave Action

 Science
Earth in the Making

The Armadillo from Amarillo
pp. 370A–399P

Read Informational Narrative

Guided Comprehension

Read Across Texts
"Mapping the World" EXPOSITORY NONFICTION

Cause and Effect T

Locate Information

Graphic Aids

Make Inferences

Selection Vocabulary T

eventually, converse, continent

sphere, universe, homeward

 Books for All Learners

Below-Level: *From Here to There*

On-Level: *Amazing Armadillos*

Advanced: *The Bald Eagle*

English-Language Learners:
Finding Your Way

WRITING PROCESS: Invitation T

Apply Writer's Craft: Word Choice

Adverbs T

Words That End Like *ever* T

 Science
Map Vegetation Areas

 Social Studies
Draw State Symbols

Visitors From Space
pp. 400A–417N

Read Expository Nonfiction

Guided Comprehension

Locate Information T

Graphic Aids T

Selection Vocabulary T

force, nucleus

loops, solar wind

particles, fluorescent

 Books for All Learners

Below-Level: *Hale and Bopp: Two Guys Make History*

On-Level: *Our Moon*

Advanced: *Sky Tales*

English-Language Learners:
What Shape Is That?

WRITING PROCESS: Story T

Apply Writer's Craft: Word Choice

Comparing with Adverbs T

Words Ending with *-le* or *-al* T

 Science
Research Constellations of Stars

 Science
Create a Solar System Map

Theme Assessment
to Plan Instruction

Entry-Level Assessment *Assesses essential prior knowledge and skills*

PLACEMENT AND DIAGNOSTIC ASSESSMENT
Use to diagnose individual students and to make placement decisions.

• **Reading and Language Skills Assessment: Pretest**

Administer the Pretest	
Diagnosis	**Prescription**
IF performance is	**THEN** use these available resources:
BELOW-LEVEL	• Core Instruction in the Teacher's Edition • Below-Level Reaching All Learners notes (at point of use in the Teacher's Edition) • Extra Support Copying Masters • Intervention Resource Kit
ON-LEVEL	• Core Instruction in the Teacher's Edition • Cross-Curricular Stations • Practice Book
ADVANCED	• Core Instruction in the Teacher's Edition • Advanced Reaching All Learners notes (at point of use in the Teacher's Edition) • Challenge Copying Masters

Monitoring of Progress *Lesson resources and assessment instruments*

• **End-of-Selection Test (in Practice Book)**

• **Oral Reading Fluency Assessment**

Assess progress and customize instruction	
Diagnosis	**Prescription**
IF students do not perform well on the • Performance Assessments • Diagnostic Checks (at point of use in the Teacher's Edition) • Oral Reading Fluency Assessment • End-of-Selection Tests (in Practice Book) • Diagnostic checks (point of use)	**THEN** choose from these available resources: • Additional Support Activities, pp. S66–S95 • Books for All Learners • Intervention Resource Kit • Extra Support Copying Masters
IF students do perform well on the • Performance Assessments • Diagnostic Checks (at point of use in the Teacher's Edition) • Oral Reading Fluency Assessment • End-of-Selection Tests (in Practice Book) • Diagnostic checks (point of use)	**THEN** choose from these available resources: • Additional Support Activities, pp. S66–S95 • Challenge Copying Masters • Books for All Learners

Summative Assessment *Assesses mastery of theme objectives*

- **Reading and Language Skills Assessment: Posttest**
- **End-of-Year Reading and Language Skills Assessment**
- **Holistic Assessment**

Administer Theme Posttests

Diagnosis	Prescription
IF performance is	**THEN** use these available resources:
BELOW-LEVEL	• Alternative Teaching Strategies, T70–T77 • Intervention Resource Kit • Chart their progress. See pages R39–R41.
ON-LEVEL	• Chart their progress. See pages R39–R41.
ADVANCED	• Provide accelerated instruction in higher-grade-level materials. • Chart their progress. See pages R39–R41.

Technology

Reading and Language Skills CD-ROM

Use this CD-ROM to

- administer assessments electronically
- customize assessments to focus on specific standards
- track students' progress

Reaching All Learners

■ BELOW-LEVEL

Levels of Support

Point-of-use notes

in Teacher's Edition, pp. 300K, 322, 323E, 324K, 346, 347E, 348K, 368, 369G, 370K, 398, 399G, 400K, 416, 417E

Extra Support Copying Masters

pp. 49–50, 53–55, 58–61, 64–65, 68–69

Additional Support Activities

- Vocabulary, pp. S66, S72, S78, S84, S90

- Comprehension and Skills, pp. S68, S74, S80, S86, S92

- Grammar and Writing, pp. S70, S76, S82, S88, S94

Intervention Resource Kit

■ ENGLISH-LANGUAGE LEARNERS

Levels of Support

Point-of-use notes

in Teacher's Edition, pp. 300K, 322, 323E, 324K, 346, 347E, 348K, 368, 369G, 370K, 398, 399G, 400K, 416, 417E

English-Language Learners Copying Masters

pp. 49–50, 53–55, 58–61, 64–65, 68–69

Additional Support Activities

- Vocabulary, pp. S67, S73, S79, S85, S91

- Comprehension and Skills, pp. S69, S75, S81, S87, S93

- Grammar and Writing, pp. S71, S77, S83, S89, S95

English-Language Learners Resource Kit

■ ADVANCED

Levels of Support

Point-of-use notes

in Teacher's Edition, pp. 300K, 322, 323E, 324K, 346, 347E, 348K, 368, 369G, 370K, 398, 399G, 400K, 416, 417E

Challenge Copying Masters

pp. 49–50, 53–54, 58–61, 64–65, 68–69

Additional Support Activities

- Vocabulary, pp. S67, S73, S79, S85, S91

- Comprehension and Skills, pp. S69, S75, S81, S87, S93

- Grammar and Writing, pp. S71, S77, S83, S89, S95

Accelerated Instruction

- Use higher-grade-level materials for accelerated instruction.

- Theme Project, p. 298J

Combination Classrooms
Literature Circles

Form groups of five or six students. Make sure that groups reflect a range of ages and reading levels; check that books selected are ones that below-level readers can handle. Have each group set a reading schedule. Then assign group members these jobs:

- **discussion leader**— develops questions and leads discussion.
- **summarizer**— summarizes the selection.
- **literacy reporter**— finds and reads aloud passages that stand out because they are especially sad or happy, are key moments in the plot, or are especially well written.
- **illustrator**— creates a drawing or graphic that captures some aspect of the selection.
- **word chief**— notes difficult words and confusing passages.
- **connector**— finds links between the book and others the class has read.

Have two literature circles meet each day so you can oversee their discussions. Gradually, allow them more independence.

Students with Special Needs
Building Confidence for Below-Level Readers

Students who associate reading with failure or frustration require extra help and encouragement in order to become successful readers.

- **Teach students to be strategic readers.** Help students focus on what they can do instead of what they cannot do. Call attention to students' successes. Ask questions to elicit strategies students used while reading. Give plenty of positive feedback on what they did well. Avoid correcting miscues as students are reading aloud; give them time to self-correct.

- **Prepare students for success.** Before asking a student to read a passage aloud, read it aloud yourself as students follow along silently, or give students an opportunity to read aloud chorally to build their confidence. Before you call on students, give them advance notice that you will be asking them to read or respond to a question.

- **Help develop reading fluency** by having students reread familiar text silently and aloud.

Make an Observation Poster

OBJECTIVE

To use a tool to observe and study minute details of objects.

45-90 Minutes per Week

Materials

- hand lenses
- pencils
- colored markers
- paper
- paste
- poster board

Project Question

How can taking a very close look at something change the way you see it?

1 **CHOOSE AN OBJECT** Ask each student to choose a small object from the school environment to research, such as a rock, a leaf, a feather, the surface of a hand, a piece of wood, and so on.

2 **EXAMINE** Have students use hand lenses to examine and study the surface of their object. Have pairs of students describe the up-close views and tell how the object looks different when viewed through the lens.

3 **DRAW** Each student should create detailed drawings of both the life-sized object and its magnified image.

4 **DESCRIBE** Have students write a brief description of the differences between the two views.

5 **POST** Each student can make a poster featuring the drawings and written descriptions. Display the posters on a bulletin board, and invite students to describe them. You may wish to use the Rubric for Presentations on page T92.

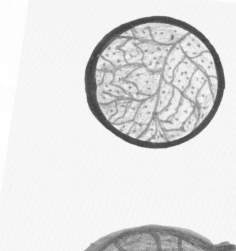

Additional Homework Ideas

Visit *The Learning Site*: www.harcourtschool.com. See Resources for Parents and Teachers: Homework Helper.

	Vocabulary	Comprehension	Literature Response	Grammar/Writing	Spelling
WEEK 1	Write four pairs of **rhyming sentences.** Use at least one vocabulary word from "I'm in Charge of Celebrations" in each pair of sentences.	Choose one of the stories from the previous theme and write a **summary** of it.	If you were to create your own celebration, what day would it be? What would you celebrate? **Explain the celebration** in a paragraph.	Write a poem about your favorite holiday or celebration. Use **figurative language** and **strong imagery.**	Make a four-column chart with headings *-er, -ful, -ly,* and *-able.* Write at least four new words in each column.
WEEK 2	**Write a paragraph** describing a farm. Use at least four of the vocabulary words from "Alejandro's Gift" in your paragraph.	Create a **cause-and-effect chart** to show how and why animals adapt to the desert environment.	Draw "before" and "after" pictures of a desert showing **how a water hole would change the environment.**	Write a thank-you letter to someone who has done something nice for you recently. Circle any **forms of the verb *be*** in your letter.	Write five pairs of sentences. Use the **singular and plural forms** of a spelling word in each sentence pair.
WEEK 3	**Write a short story** about an island volcano. Use all of the vocabulary words from "Rocking and Rolling" in your story.	Think of a book that you would like to read. List the **book parts** for this imaginary book and write a sentence describing the information contained in each part.	"Rocking and Rolling" contains a lot of information about geology, the study of the earth. **Write a paragraph describing the geological information** you find most interesting.	Write a scene from a play you might write about an exciting event at school. Use **contractions** in the **dialogue.**	Write a paragraph that warns local residents about an oncoming tsunami. Use three of the spelling words and the six words that make them up in your paragraph. Circle the **contractions.**
WEEK 4	**Write an imaginary first-person account** of a trip into space and back. Use several vocabulary words from "The Armadillo from Amarillo" in your note.	Think about how Armadillo has changed by the end of the story. Write a paragraph describing some of the **effects** of his travels and their **causes.**	**Draw a picture** of what your house and town might look like to an eagle flying overhead. Label streets and add signs for stores and businesses.	Invite a friend to set out on Armadillo's journey with you. Use at least four **adverbs** in your invitation.	**Write a paragraph** about your town that includes at least five of the spelling words.
WEEK 5	**Draw and label** pictures that show the meanings of at least three of the vocabulary words from "Visitors from Space."	Find a nonfiction book about the Solar System. Use self-stick notes to mark the **different parts of the book.** On each note, write the information that can be found in that part.	Write a letter to the author of "Visitors from Space." Tell her **your favorite part of the selection** and explain why you like it. Then **ask questions** you have about the Solar System.	Write a short story about the life of an astronaut. Use **adverbs to compare** the astronaut's life to your own.	Make a two-column chart. Label one column *-le* and one column *-al.* Then add at least five new words to each column.

Build Background

Discuss the meaning of *celebrate.*

Write the theme title *Celebrate Our World* on the board. Ask a volunteer to tell what it means to *celebrate* something. Ask:

- *What kinds of events do you celebrate?*
- *What do you think it means to "celebrate your world"?*

Preview the Theme. Ask students to read the table of contents. Discuss familiar authors or titles. Have students write three questions about the theme that they would like answered by the time they finish reading.

Develop Concepts

Make an ABC list. Have students create an alphabetical list of things worth celebrating. List the letters of the alphabet down the left side of the list, and ask students to name some things in the world worth celebrating that begin with each letter. Record their suggestions on the list.

ABC List

A- acing a test, animals, achievements
B - birthdays, beginnings, babies
C - circus, camp, cats
D - daybreak, dumplings, dogs etc...

THEME 3

Celebrate Our World

298

CONTENTS

299

Build Theme Connections

Begin an ongoing graphic organizer.
Invite students to create a graphic organizer that will help them record information about the things that people do to celebrate the natural world. You may want to keep the organizer on a computer, a chart, or a bulletin board. Students can return to it as they read the theme selections to add new ideas or information. Ask:

How do people celebrate the world?			
WHO	WHAT	WHEN	WHERE
my class and I	planted trees	on Arbor Day	in Liberty Park
the teacher and students	recycle paper	every day	in our classroom

 QUICKWRITE

Have students make a chart with these headings in their journals: *place, time of year, what I see*. In the chart, have them write details about a variety of favorite places.

 Apply to Writing

Tell students to check carefully the pattern of letters in final syllables as they proofread their writing. Have them look for words ending in unstressed syllables.

Teacher Notes

300BB

THEME CONNECTION:
Celebrate Our World

GENRE:
Poem

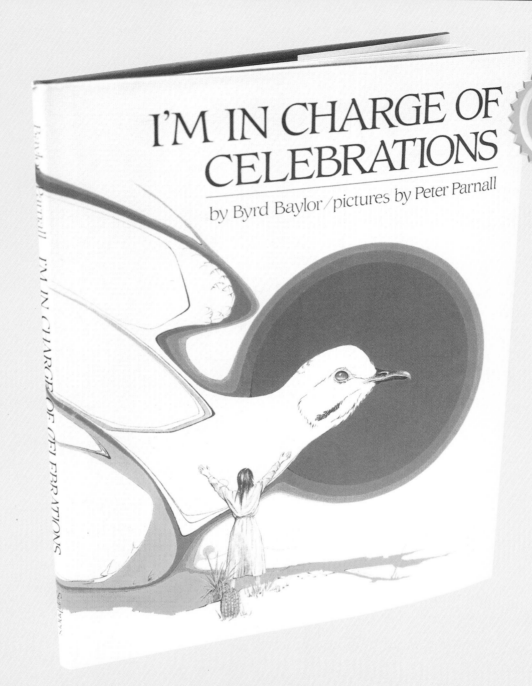

I'M IN CHARGE OF CELEBRATIONS

by Byrd Baylor / pictures by Peter Parnall

Award-Winning Author and Illustrator

SUMMARY:

A young girl explores an American Southwest desert. When she witnesses a natural wonder, she records the date in her notebook and creates a way to celebrate the event. Every year, she celebrates each of her special days.

 All selections available on *Audiotext 6*

Books for
All Learners

Lesson Plans on pages 323K–323N

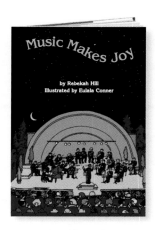

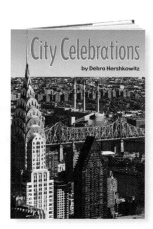

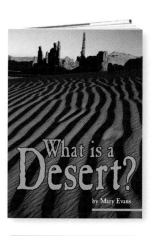

BELOW-LEVEL	ON-LEVEL	ADVANCED	ELL
• Lesson Vocabulary	• Lesson Vocabulary	• Challenge Vocabulary	• Concept Vocabulary
• Focus Skill: Summarize	• Focus Skill: Summarize	• Focus Skill: Summarize	• Focus Skill: Summarize

MULTI-LEVEL PRACTICE

Extra Support, pp. 49–50

Practice Book, pp. 49–52

Challenge, pp. 49–50

English-Language Learners, pp. 49–50

ADDITIONAL RESOURCES

Spelling Practice Book, pp. 95–97

Language Handbook, pp. 151–153

Audiotext 6

Intervention Resource Kit, Lesson 26
  • Intervention Reader, *Included in Intervention Resource Kit*

English-Language Learners Resource Kit, Lesson 26

Technology

• *Writing Express™* **CD-ROM**

• *Grammar Jingles™* **CD**

• *Media Literacy and Communication Skills Package* (Video)

• *Reading and Language Skills Assessment* **CD-ROM**

• *The Learning Site:* **www.harcourtschool.com**

ORAL LANGUAGE

- **Question of the Day**
- **Sharing Literature**

SKILLS & STRATEGIES

- **Comprehension**

- **Vocabulary**

READING

- **Guided Comprehension**

- **Independent Reading**

- **Cross-Curricular Connections**

LANGUAGE ARTS

- **Writing**

  Daily Writing Prompt

- **Grammar**

  Daily Language Practice

- **Spelling**

Daily Routines
- Question of the Day
- Daily Language Practice
- Daily Writing Prompt

Day 1

Question of the Day, p. 300H
What is your favorite celebration? Why is it your favorite? When and how is it celebrated?

Literature Read-Aloud, pp. 300G–H

Comprehension:
 Summarize, p. 300I **T**
 Create Mental Images, p. 300J

Vocabulary, p. 300L

Read: Vocabulary Power, pp. 300–301
Vocabulary Power Words:
admiring, choosy, average, signal, tracks, celebrations

 Independent Reading
~~Books for All Learners~~

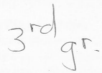 Zach.

 3rd gr.

DLP ↓

1. Have you ever see a desert. (seen; desert?)
2. A desert is home to many plant and animal. (plants; animals)

Spelling:
Words with Suffixes *-er, -ful, -ly, -able*, p. 323G **T**

Day 2

Question of the Day, p. 300H
What is a natural wonder that you think is worthy of a celebration? How would you celebrate it?

Think and Respond, p. 316

Comprehension:
 Summarize, pp. 302–319 **T**

Decoding/Phonics:
Word Structure: Prefix + Root Word + Suffix, p. 323A

Reading the Selection, pp. 302–319
Vocabulary Power Words

 Independent Reading
Books for All Learners

SOCIAL STUDIES Research Local Geography
SOCIAL STUDIES Population Density

Writing: Writer's Craft, p. 323C

Writing Prompt:
You are a scientist who discovered how to control the weather. Every day you can make the weather just the way you want it. Write a story about a day you controlled the weather.

Grammar:
Extend the Concept, p. 323E **T**

Daily Language Practice

1. Pay atention to nature? (attention; nature.)
2. Have you ever taken a walks and seen an animal up close! (walk; close?)

Spelling:
Word Sort, p. 323G **T**

T = tested skill

Focus Skill

Summarize

Objectives of the Week:

- To summarize important information in text
- To read and understand a free-verse poem
- To recognize and understand the various tenses of irregular verbs
- To use figurative language and imagery to write a poem

Day 3

Question of the Day, p. 300H
If you spotted a coyote or another animal in the wild, what would you do? How do you think you would feel?

Oral Grammar, p. 323F

Comprehension:
 Summarize, pp. 322–323 **T**
Test Prep

Word Study:
Suffixes, p. 323I

Rereading for Fluency, p. 315

[handwritten notes: 9:10 – 9:40, ela / reading + written, 1:40 – 2:10, Math, Mitchell]

Daily Language Practice

1. you will not seen these thing unless you are quiet.
   (You; see; things)
2. Sometimes you has to be still for a long time
   (have; time.)

Spelling:
Word Parts, p. 323H **T**

Day 4

Question of the Day, p. 300H
Would you like to live in a desert? Why or why not? Use reasons or facts to support your opinion.

Fact and Opinion, p. 323B **T**

Self-Selected Reading, p. 300F

 Independent Reading
Books for All Learners

SOCIAL STUDIES Native American Folklore and Customs

Writing: Writer's Craft, p. 323D

 Writing Prompt:
Imagine that you can climb a rainbow. Think about what it would be like to climb up a rainbow and then slide down it. Now write a paragraph titled "How to Climb a Rainbow."

Grammar:
Using Irregular Verbs, p. 323F **T**

Daily Language Practice

1. The author say she once come upon a rabbit.
   (says; came)
2. Her and the rabbit seen the same triple rainbow.
   (She; saw)

Spelling:
Concentration, p. 323H **T**

Day 5

Question of the Day, p. 300H
What special celebrations are there in your community? If you can't think of any, what celebrations do you think there should be?

Listening and Speaking
Poem, p. 323J

Comprehension:
 Summarize, pp. 323K–M **T**

Word Study:
Homographs, p. 323I

Self-Selected Reading, pp. 319, T101

Independent Reading
Books for All Learners

SCIENCE Experiment with Mirrors
SOCIAL STUDIES Draw a Map

Writing: Writer's Craft, p. 323D

Writing Prompt:
The natural world is full of beautiful and surprising things. Think about something beautiful or surprising you have seen in the natural world. Now write about what you saw.

Grammar:
Verb Tenses, p. 323F **T**

Daily Language Practice

1. is it lonely in the desert. (Is; desert?)
2. will we see the desert on our vaccation.
   (Will; vacation?)

Spelling:
Posttest, p. 323H **T**

Cross-Curricular Stations

SOCIAL STUDIES

Research Local Geography

OBJECTIVE: To locate various geographical features in the local region

"I'm in Charge of Celebrations" tells about many of the natural wonders that can be found in the desert. Use a map to find the desert nearest to your home. Then look for the nearest mountains, valleys, lakes, and rivers. Make a list of these places. Find out what you can about each one. Then use that information to create a travel brochure to convince people to visit your region for its natural wonders!

Materials

- U.S. map
- travel guidebooks for your region
- paper
- markers

SCIENCE

Make a Desert Diorama

OBJECTIVE: To examine the diverse life forms found in the desert

The narrator of "I'm in Charge of Celebrations" mentions different plants and animals that live in a Southwestern desert. Work with a partner to create a diorama of a desert. Follow these steps.

- Use an encyclopedia to find out about the desert ecosystem. Look for answers to questions such as these:
  - What is the terrain like in a desert?
  - What kinds of plants and animals live there?

Materials

- encyclopedia or computer with Internet access
- empty shoe box
- diorama materials, such as sand, glue, clay, cardboard, cotton, toothpicks, paints, markers
- slips of paper
- pens or pencils

The lizard and snake stay in the shade during the hottest part of the day. The barrel cactus has a thick stem to store water.

barrel cactus   snake   lizard

- Use what you learn to create a three-dimensional model of a desert that includes some plants and animals.
- Label the plants and animals. Include captions that tell how each one survives in the desert environment.

 Use the Internet to look for information about and photographs of the desert ecosystem.

LIBRARY CENTER

Self-Selected Reading

OBJECTIVE: To independently select and read books

Look for these books about communities and desert life:

- *Cactus Hotel* by Brenda Z. Guiberson. Henry Holt, 1991. NONFICTION
- *Archibald Frisby* by Michael Chesworth. Farrar, Straus & Giroux, 1994. FICTION
- *Water Dance* by Thomas Locker. Harcourt Brace, 1997. POETRY

Remember to

- select a book that interests you.
- keep track of what you read each day in your Reading Log.

Materials

- self-selected book
- *My Reading Log* copying master, p. R42

INQUIRY PROJECT

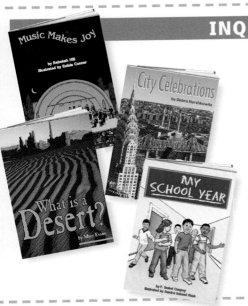

Extending the Selection

OBJECTIVE: To select a focus for an inquiry project

"I'm in Charge of Celebrations" may spark your interest in various topics. Share your ideas with a group of your classmates. You might use one of these books to get ideas for a project.

- *Music Makes Joy*
- *What Is a Desert?*
- *City Celebrations*
- *My School Year*

Materials

- research materials
- paper
- pencils, pens

TECHNOLOGY

Author Search

OBJECTIVE: To use technology to find out about and write to a favorite author

Many authors of children's books have websites that give biographical information. With a partner, choose an author to whom you would like to write. Search the Internet for that author's website. Then use the e-mail address to write to the author.

- Have one or two additional authors in mind.
- Show the author respect when you write your e-mail message.
- Use the rules for Internet safety.

Materials

- computer with Internet access
- paper
- pencils

Read Aloud

SET A PURPOSE
Listen to Understand and Enjoy

Read aloud the introduction slowly, asking students to listen for information about the role of dance in Native American communities. Then guide students to understand that poetry is often read to be enjoyed. Read the poem aloud with expression, emphasizing the rhythm.

LISTENING STRATEGY
Create Mental Images

Explain that one way to better understand a poem is to try to create a mental picture of what is being described. Have students listen with their eyes closed and try to picture the time of day and the events described in this poem.

DISCUSS GENRE

Point out that this selection is poetry. Students will also read poetry in this lesson.

Celebration
by Alonzo Lopez

Dance is one of the most common ways that people express themselves. In fact, in many cultures, dance is one of the most important forms of communication. Native Americans sometimes dance for healing or to tell a story. Sometimes they dance just for the fun of it.

For Native Americans, dance has always been a means for showing tribal unity. Because of that, for a long time the U.S. government actually outlawed Native American dancing! However, special ceremonies such as the Sun Dance, performed by the Sioux tribe in North Dakota, are still performed.

Dances that welcome the harvest, social dances, and powwows continue to be an important part of celebrating the Native American culture.

Celebration

I shall dance tonight.
When the dusk comes crawling,
There will be dancing
   and feasting.
I shall dance with the others
   in circles,
      in leaps,
         in stomps.
Laughter and talk
   will weave into the night,
Among the fires
   of my people.
Games will be played
And I shall be
   a part of it.

LISTENING COMPREHENSION

- **What are some reasons why Native Americans dance?**
  (Possible responses: to show tribal unity; to heal the sick, to tell a story, for fun, to welcome the harvest)
  CAUSE-EFFECT/IMPORTANT DETAILS

- **How would you sum up the events described in this poem?**
  (Possible responses: People gather together around several fires to celebrate by dancing, feasting, and playing games.)
  SUMMARIZE

- **What does the dance look like?** (Possible response: The dancers circle, leap, and stomp.) VISUALIZE

Question of the Day

DEVELOP ORAL LANGUAGE

- Display the first question on Teaching Transparency 235 or write it on the board. Ask a volunteer to read it aloud.

- **Response Journal**   Explain to students that they should think about the question throughout the day and write their responses in their journals. Tell students to be prepared to discuss the answer or answers to it by the end of the day or at another time that you choose.

- You may want to repeat this process daily for each of the five discussion questions.

OBJECTIVE

To summarize important information in text

▼ **Teaching Transparency 236**

FOCUS SKILL
SUMMARIZE

- **Summarizing** is telling the main ideas in a text in your own words. A summary is much shorter than the original text.
- A good summary gives only the most important ideas in a text.
- A good summary does not give details or your ideas or opinions.
- Summarizing helps readers share what they have read with others.

EXAMPLE:

Summary of Page 198 of "Boom Town"

> After a twenty-one day trip to California, this family discovers that they can't live near the gold fields. The town they have to live in isn't much of a town.

"I'm in Charge of Celebrations" Focus Skill: Summarize
Celebrate Our World, Theme 3 **236** Harcourt

BELOW-LEVEL

Additional Support
- *Intervention Teacher's Guide,* p. 260

ENGLISH-LANGUAGE LEARNERS

Additional Support
- *English-Language Learners Teacher's Guide,* p. 153

⭐ Focus Skill Summarize

REVIEW THE SKILL

Discuss summarizing.   Have students describe how to summarize a selection. (Possible response: Retell the important events or ideas in your own words.) Then discuss what makes a good summary. (Possible responses: It should be shorter than the original selection; it should include only the most important ideas or events; it should not include the opinions of the person who is summarizing.)

TEACH/MODEL

Display Transparency 236.

- **Have a volunteer read aloud the bulleted items.**
- **Then read aloud *Pupil Edition* page 198.**
- **Have a volunteer read aloud the example summary and lead a discussion about the merits of the summary.**

Text Structure.   Explain that "I'm in Charge of Celebrations" is a poem that tells a story and that stopping often to summarize the important ideas will help them to understand and enjoy the text.

PRACTICE/APPLY

Students can use a flow chart like the one below to help them keep track of the date and focus of each celebration described in the poem.

Date: Celebration:	→	Date: Celebration:

For opportunities to apply and reinforce the skill, see the following pages:

During reading: pages 306, 308, 310, and 312

After reading: *Pupil Edition* pages 322–323

 **Focus Strategy**

Create Mental Images

REVIEW THE STRATEGY

Explain to students that "I'm in Charge of Celebrations" is a free form poem. Discuss why imagination is important when reading poetry. (Imagination helps the reader create the images that the poet describes.)

TEACH/MODEL

Remind students that good readers often create pictures in their minds of what is being described in a poem or story. Point out that creating mental pictures helps readers better understand the ideas an author is trying to communicate.

Reread page 198 and then use this to model the strategy.

> **MODEL** As I read this page, I create a mental image in my mind of the long, bumpy stagecoach ride to California. Then I imagine what a tent city would look like. Finally the author helps me picture the "town" that Ma refers to by saying that the area was wide and lonesome and had very few buildings.

SKILL ⟷ STRATEGY CONNECTION

Point out to students that creating mental images of the things an author or poet describes can help them get a clearer understanding of the main ideas that should be included in a summary.

PRACTICE/APPLY

Remind students to use the Create Mental Images strategy to help them understand what the poet is describing. For opportunities to apply and reinforce the strategy **during reading**, see pages 307, 309, and 313.

Strategies Good Readers Use

- Use Decoding/Phonics
- Make and Confirm Predictions
- **Create Mental Images** **Focus Strategy**
- Self-Question
- Summarize
- Read Ahead
- Reread to Clarify
- Use Context to Confirm Meaning
- Use Text Structure and Format
- Adjust Reading Rate

Building Background

ACCESS PRIOR KNOWLEDGE

Ask students to name a special day that they like to celebrate. Ask: **Why is this day special to you? In what ways do you celebrate? Who celebrates with you?** Help students to develop this idea using a chart like this one.

Celebration	Why People Celebrate	How It Is Celebrated
birthday	to remember the day someone was born	by giving a party with a birthday cake, music, games
Mother's Day	to thank mothers	by giving cards and gifts; by making breakfast

technology

Visit *The Learning Site:*
www.harcourtschool.com
See Building Background.

DEVELOP CONCEPTS

Help students develop the concepts further by asking questions such as these:

- **What do you like to do at a celebration?**
  (eat, talk, sing, dance)

- **Who helps you celebrate?**
  (friends, family members)

- **Would you celebrate events that happen in nature? Why or why not?**
  (Responses will vary.)

- **What event in nature would you want to celebrate? What would you do to celebrate it?**
  (Responses will vary.)

Tell students they will be reading a poem about a woman who celebrates events in nature.

REACHING ALL LEARNERS

Diagnostic Check: Vocabulary

If . . . students have not mastered at least five of the six vocabulary words . . .

Then . . . have pairs of students take turns giving definition clues and holding up corresponding word cards.

ADDITIONAL SUPPORT ACTIVITIES

BELOW-LEVEL	Reteach, p. S66
ADVANCED	Extend, p. S67
ENGLISH-LANGUAGE LEARNERS	Reteach, p. S67

Vocabulary

Vocabulary

admiring looking at with wonder or respect

choosy picky, hard to please

average ordinary, not special

signal to make known, to announce

tracks prints left in the ground by an animal or person

celebrations joyous events that honor holidays, achievements, or happy occasions

TEACH VOCABULARY STRATEGIES

Decode multisyllabic words. Display Transparency 237, and have students read the first two lines of the poem. Remind them that when they come to a new word, they can look for syllable patterns they know to help them figure out the word. Model using syllable patterns to decode the word *admiring*.

MODEL I see the VCCV pattern in this word. I know that I have to divide between the two consonants. When I do, I see that the word begins with the short *a* sound. I then see the CVC pattern, so I know that the next syllable has the long *i* sound. The last syllable is -*ing*. When I blend the parts, I get /ad•mīr′ ing/. That means "looking at with wonder." It makes sense in the sentence.

Have students read the rest of the poem. Call on volunteers to decode the vocabulary using the strategy. Tell students they can confirm their pronunciations by using the glossary. Then discuss the meaning of each word.

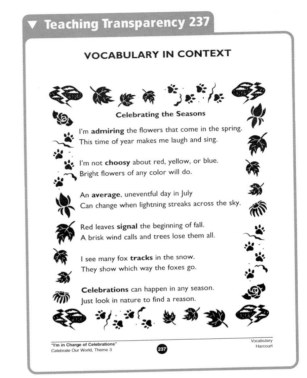

▼ **Teaching Transparency 237**

VOCABULARY IN CONTEXT

Celebrating the Seasons

I'm **admiring** the flowers that come in the spring.
This time of year makes me laugh and sing.

I'm not **choosy** about red, yellow, or blue.
Bright flowers of any color will do.

An **average**, uneventful day in July
Can change when lightning streaks across the sky.

Red leaves **signal** the beginning of fall.
A brisk wind calls and trees lose them all.

I see many fox **tracks** in the snow.
They show which way the foxes go.

Celebrations can happen in any season.
Just look in nature to find a reason.

"I'm in Charge of Celebrations"
Celebrate Our World, Theme 3   237   Vocabulary Harcourt

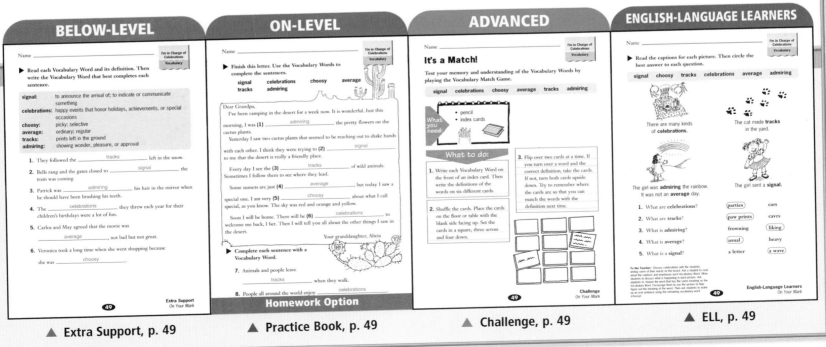

| **BELOW-LEVEL** | **ON-LEVEL** | **ADVANCED** | **ENGLISH-LANGUAGE LEARNERS** |

▲ Extra Support, p. 49   ▲ Practice Book, p. 49   ▲ Challenge, p. 49   ▲ ELL, p. 49

Vocabulary Power

Have a volunteer read aloud the first paragraph on page 300. Then ask students to read the remaining text silently. Remind them to apply the strategy of using syllable patterns to decode words.

Practice other vocabulary strategies. Have students answer questions with sentences that show what the vocabulary words mean. MEANINGFUL SENTENCES

- Is a person's birthday an *average* day or a special day? Explain why. **EXPLANATION**

- What are you *choosy* about? Tell how you are choosy. **DESCRIPTION**

- What are some good places to find animal *tracks*? **PRIOR KNOWLEDGE**

- How would you *signal* to ask someone to be quiet? to stand up? to sit down? **EXAMPLE**

- How can you tell if someone is *admiring* something? **DESCRIPTION**

- How would you complete this analogy: <u>celebrities</u> is to <u>special people</u> as *celebrations* is to _____? **RELATED WORDS**

▲ I'm in Charge of Celebrations

average

celebrations

choosy

tracks

signal

admiring

Vocabulary Power

o you enjoy the outdoors? The author of "I'm in Charge of Celebrations" loves nature and her home in the desert. People who live in other places also love their homes and the plants and creatures that live near them.

These pinecones may look **average**, but when they are painted and trimmed with ribbons, they will not be ordinary pinecones! They will brighten the house for holiday **celebrations**. We often include things from nature in our joyous events.

300

Winters in the north are cold and snowy. In the wild, animals can't be too **choosy** about their food. They must eat whatever they can find. We leave birdseed outside for the birds. Look at the **tracks** in the snow. It looks as if a squirrel has found the birdseed, too!

We enjoy this little plant that blooms to **signal** the end of winter. Its cheerful flowers announce the arrival of spring. Here is my mother **admiring** them. They are her favorite flowers, and she loves to look at them.

**Vocabulary-Writing
CONNECTION**

What clues might tell you whether the season has changed? Write a paragraph that describes one or two things that **signal** the beginning of each new season.

301

 QUICKWRITE

VOCABULARY–WRITING CONNECTION

Encourage students to use vivid descriptive words in their paragraphs. They may wish to add these descriptive words and the Vocabulary Power words to their Word Banks to use in future writing assignments.

Prereading Strategies

PREVIEW AND PREDICT

Have students read the **genre** information on page 302. Then, have students preview the selection by looking at the illustrations. Ask them what they think this selection is about, based on their preview and the characteristics of poetry. Then ask them to make predictions about what kinds of things the narrator celebrates. They can use a Flow Chart to record the celebrations. See *Transparency E*.

Date: (March 11) Celebration: (Dust Devil Day)	→	Date: Celebration:

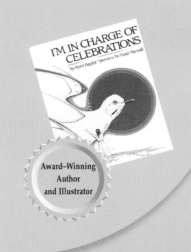

Award–Winning Author and Illustrator

Genre

Poem

A poem uses imagery, figurative language, and imagination to express feelings and ideas.

In this selection, look for

- **the author's use of imagery.**

- **how the author creates rhythmical effects and some rhyme.**

302

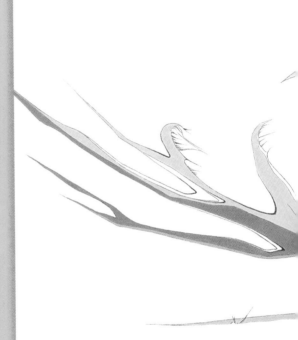

BELOW-LEVEL	ON-LEVEL	ADVANCED	ENGLISH-LANGUAGE LEARNERS
Guide students as they preview the selection. Discuss the meaning of these words and phrases: *date, lonely, in charge of, myself, rainbow, remember*. Help students set a purpose for reading through page 309. SMALL GROUP	Students can read the selection with a partner. Use the Guided Comprehension questions and Ongoing Assessments to gauge students' understanding. PARTNER	Students can write down interesting words and phrases in their journals as they read the selection independently. INDEPENDENT	Read aloud the selection or have students listen to it on *Audiotext 6*. Then have students read aloud selected pages as a group to develop oral fluency. SMALL GROUP

BELOW-LEVEL ADDITIONAL SUPPORT

ADDITIONAL SUPPORT
Intervention Reader: Bright Surprises Intervention Teacher's Guide, pp. 260–263

ENGLISH-LANGUAGE LEARNERS ADDITIONAL SUPPORT
See *English-Language Learners Resource Kit*, Lesson 26. *English-Language Learners Teacher's Guide*, pp. 153–154

I'm in Charge of Celebrations

by *Byrd Baylor*

pictures by *Peter Parnall*

303

SET PURPOSE

Read to be informed and entertained.
Remind students that one purpose for reading is to learn about something, and another is for enjoyment. Then ask students to set their own purposes. Offer this suggestion:

MODEL The text mentions different desert plants and animals. I would like to find out if these are part of any celebrations the narrator makes. I'll read to find out.

Focus Strategy **Create Mental Images** Have students use this strategy to help them understand the places, creatures, and events the narrator describes.

 "I'm in Charge of Celebrations" is available on *Audiotext 6.*

COMPREHENSION CARD 26

Think-Along Use the Think-Along strategy to help students understand the key points of the text.

Comprehension Card 26,
Page T81 ▶

▶ **Think Along** COMPREHENSION CARD **26**

I'm in Charge of Celebrations
You may wish to have students respond to the Think-Along questions in writing in their Response Journals.

1. How do you think the narrator will answer the question about being lonely? Why? (Possible answer: She will say she is not lonely, because she knows the desert.)

2. Why does the narrator laugh? (Possible answer: She can't understand why other people would think the desert was a lonely place.)

3. How do you think the narrator feels about celebrations? Explain. (Possible answer: She feels that they are important, but you have to be very excited for it to be a celebration.)

4. What do you think is going to happen next? (Possible answer: She is going to want to dance with the dust devil.)

5. What are you thinking about? (Possible answer: Seeing a dust devil would be very exciting.)

6. Is there anything in your life that once you start you can't stop? What is it? (Possible answer: Sometimes when I laugh I can't stop, and when I try to it makes me laugh even more.)

7. What do you think the rabbit would do if it saw the narrator? (Possible answer: It would probably run away.)

8. What celebration would you like to invent? Why? (Possible answer: Responses will vary.)

9. Why did the narrator want to celebrate seeing the green cloud? (Possible answer: It was very rare and beautiful.)

10. How do you think the narrator might have met the coyote? (Possible answer: They were walking on the same path.)

11. What are you thinking about now? (Possible answer: I am thinking that I would be afraid that the coyote might not be friendly.)

12. How might meeting the coyote have changed the narrator's life? (Possible answer: She felt really close to nature that day and wanted to keep feeling that way.)

13. Why might the narrator think that eating in that place would make the celebration even better? (Possible answer: Maybe she hopes the coyote will come back and eat with her.)

14, 15. What words might describe how the narrator felt after she saw the fireball? (Possible answer: happy, thankful, peaceful)

Guided Comprehension

1 **IMPORTANT DETAILS** **What details in the text tell you what the desert is like?** (Possible response: names of plants—beargrass, yuccas, cactuses; names of landforms—deep ravines, cliffs; mentions of signs of animal life—hawk nests, coyote trails that wind across the hills)

2 **CHARACTERS' EMOTIONS** **Does the narrator feel lonely in the desert? How do you know?** (Possible response: No, she names many things that are in the desert; she laughs and is surprised when people ask her if she is lonely.)

3 **MAKE PREDICTIONS** **Based on what the narrator has said about the desert so far, what do you think she will say is "worth a celebration"?** (Responses will vary.)

Sometimes
   people ask me,
    "Aren't you lonely
   out there
   with just
   desert
   around you?"

I guess they mean
   the beargrass
   and the yuccas
   and the cactus
   and the rocks.

I guess they mean
   the deep ravines
   and the hawk nests
   in the cliffs
   and the coyote trails
   that wind
   across the hills. **1**

"Lonely?"

I can't help
   laughing
   when they ask me
   that.

I always look at them . . .
   surprised. **2**

And I say,
   "How could I be lonely?
   I'm the one
   in charge of
   celebrations."

Sometimes
   they don't believe me,
   but it's true.
   I am.

I put
   myself
   in charge.
   I choose
   my own.

Last year
   I gave myself
   one hundred and eight
   celebrations—
   besides the ones
   that they close school for.

I cannot get by
   with only
   a few.

Friend, I'll tell you
   how it works.

304

BELOW-LEVEL

To help students understand and follow the structure of this narrative poem, display page 304 and read it aloud, running your finger below the text as you do so. If necessary, explain that you first read the left-hand column from top to bottom before moving on to read the right-hand column from top to bottom.

I keep a notebook
and I write the date
and then I write about
the celebration.

I'm very choosy
over
what goes in
that book.

It has to be something
I plan to remember
the rest of my life.

You can tell
what's worth
a celebration
because
your heart will
POUND
and
you'll feel
like you're standing
on top of a mountain
and you'll
catch your breath
like you were
breathing
some new kind of air.

Otherwise,
I count it just
an average day.
(I told you
I was
choosy.) ❸

305

ONGOING ASSESSMENT

Monitor Progress

Use Text Structure and Format

Ask students to explain how to read this poem. (Possible response: Read the first column from top to bottom. Then read the right-hand column.)

If students are unable to answer, use this model:

MODEL I can use the way the text is organized to help me figure out how to read it. The poem is divided into two columns. I will start with the column on the left and read it from top to bottom, before reading the column on the right.

SOCIAL STUDIES

Population Density Ask students to tell why the people who talk to the narrator might think of the desert as a lonely place. (Possible response: Deserts are hot, dry places with lots of sand and not many plants, animals, or people.) Use students' responses to discuss why certain regions of the world are more populated than others. Guide students to look at maps to help them understand how geography (physical features of the land), climate (temperature and the amount of rainfall), and natural resources (water and fertile land) are important in determining population density.

Guided Comprehension

4 **AUTHOR'S CRAFT/IMAGERY** **What does the narrator say the whirlwinds do that only people can really do?** (call to friends; dance to music)

5 (Focus Skill) **SUMMARIZE** **What happens on Dust Devil Day?** (The narrator sees seven giant whirlwinds and then dances near them.)

6 **IMPORTANT DETAILS** **How does the narrator feel when she sees the whirlwinds? What words help you know that?** (Possible responses: excited, joyful; *we turned around and around; something goes kind of crazy in you; yelling; you have to whirl around*)

Friend, I wish you'd been here
for Dust Devil Day.

But since you weren't,
I'll tell you how
it got to be
my first
real
celebration.

You can call them
whirlwinds
if you want to.
Me, I think
dust devils
has a better sound.

Well, anyway,
I always stop
to watch them.
Here, everyone does.

You know how
they come
from far away,
moving
up from the flats,
swirling
and swaying
and falling

and turning,
picking up sticks
and sand
and feathers
and dry tumbleweeds.

Well, last March eleventh
we were all going somewhere.
I was in the back
of a pickup truck
when the dust devils
started
to gather.

You could see
they were
giants.

You'd swear
they were
calling
their friends
to come too.

And they came—
dancing
in time to
their own
4 windy music.

306

ENGLISH-LANGUAGE LEARNERS

To assist students in understanding some of the longer stanzas in this poem, you may want to restate a complex sentence as several simpler ones. For example, you might read the stanza that begins at the bottom of the first column on page 306 as follows: *You know how the whirlwinds come from far way. They are moving up from the flats.*

They are swirling and swaying and falling and turning. They are picking up sticks and sand and feathers and tumbleweeds.

You may also want to explain the meanings of the following expressions in the poem: *cannot get by with* (page 304) and *catch your breath* (page 305).

We all started counting.
We all started looking
for more.

They stopped that truck
and we turned
around
and around
watching them all.
There were seven.

At a time like that,
something
goes kind of crazy
in you.
You have to run
to meet them,
yelling
all the way.

You have to
whirl around
like you were
one of them, **5**
and you can't stop
until
you're falling down. **6**

And then all day
you think
how
lucky
you were
to be there.

Some of my best
celebrations
are sudden surprises
like that.

If you weren't outside
at that
exact
moment,
you'd miss them.

I spend a lot of time
outside
myself,
looking around.

307

ONGOING ASSESSMENT

Monitor Progress

(Focus Strategy) **Create Mental Images**

What do the whirlwinds look like? (Possible response: swirling clouds of dust, sticks, sand, feathers, and tumbleweeds that seem to dance across the desert)

If students are unable to answer the question, model the strategy:

MODEL To get a better picture of the whirlwinds, I'll reread the text and then close my eyes and imagine what they look like. The words *swirling, swaying, falling,* and *turning* help me picture whirling clouds of dust that spin across the desert.

SCIENCE

Objects in Motion Have students brainstorm a list of words to describe the motion of the objects picked up by the whirlwinds. (Possible responses: whirling, spinning, twirling, turning, swirling, revolving, rotating) Record these on the board. Then provide students with some objects, such as a basketball or a top. Ask students to experiment with how to make these objects move in a way similar to that of the objects in the whirlwind. After they have practiced for a while, ask volunteers to show their objects in motion and describe them using the words on the board.

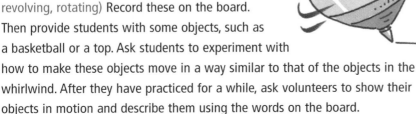

I'm in Charge of Celebrations **307**

Guided Comprehension

7 **SYNTHESIZE** Does the narrator think seeing the triple rainbow and the rabbit is special? How do you know? (Yes. She says she may be the only person to see that; she says it is worth a celebration.)

8 **CHARACTERS' TRAITS** What do the narrator's reactions to the whirl-winds and the rainbow tell you about her? (Possible response: She enjoys being out in nature and seeking out its wonders.)

9 (Focus Skill) **SUMMARIZE** What happens after Dust Devil Day? (Possible response: On August ninth, the narrator sees a triple rainbow and then comes across a jackrabbit looking at the same thing. On February sixth, she sees a green cloud that looks like a parrot flying in the sky.)

Once
I saw a triple rainbow
that ended in a canyon
where I'd been
the day before.

I was halfway up a hill
standing
in a drizzle of rain.

It was almost dark
but I wouldn't go in
(because of the rainbows,
of course),
and there
at the top of the hill
a jackrabbit
was standing
up on his hind legs,
perfectly still,
looking straight
at that same
triple
rainbow.

I may be
the only person in the world
who's seen
a rabbit
standing in the mist
quietly watching
three rainbows.

That's worth
a celebration
any time. **7**

I wrote it down
and drew the hill
and the rabbit
and the rainbow
and me.

Now
August ninth
is Rainbow Celebration Day. **8**

308

REACHING ALL LEARNERS

Diagnostic Check: Summarize

If . . . students are unable to identify the most important information in a text . . .

Then . . . work with them to break the text down into smaller chunks. In small groups have them create a poster showing the important events. Ask groups to write captions (summary statements) for each event.

ADDITIONAL SUPPORT ACTIVITIES

BELOW-LEVEL Reteach, p. S68

ADVANCED Extend, p. S69

ENGLISH-LANGUAGE LEARNERS Reteach, p. S69

I have
Green Cloud Day
too.

Ask anybody
and they'll tell you
clouds
aren't
green.

But
late one winter afternoon
I saw
this huge
green cloud.

It was not
bluish-green
or grayish-green
or something else.
This cloud
was
green . . .

green as a jungle parrot.

And the strange thing was
that it began
to take a parrot's shape,
first
the wings,
and then the head
and beak.

High in the winter sky
that green bird
flew.

It didn't last
more than a minute.
You know how fast
a cloud
can change,
but I still
remember
how it looked.

So I celebrate
green clouds
on February sixth. **9**

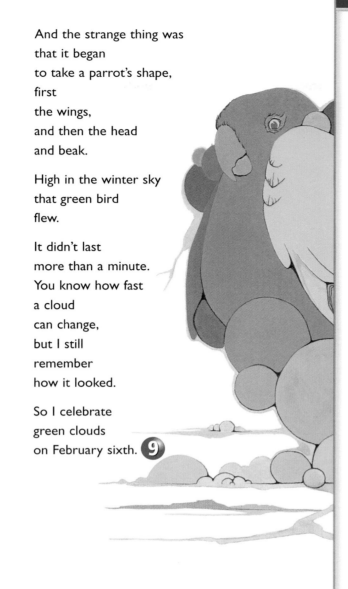

309

Monitor Progress

★
(Focus Strategy) **Create Mental Images**

What do you think the narrator means when she writes *High in the winter sky that green bird flew*? (Possible response: The green cloud that looked like a parrot was moving, so it looked as if the parrot was flying.) **Ask students how the Create Mental Images strategy could help them answer the question.**

If students have difficulty, provide this model:

MODEL **As I read about the green parrot cloud, I imagine what it looks like in my mind. I picture a green cloud that has the shape of a parrot with a head, beak, and wings. As the wind blows, the cloud moves across the sky as if the parrot were flying.**

SCIENCE

Refracted and Reflected Light Ask students who have seen a rainbow to tell when they saw it and what it looked like. If necessary, explain that rainbows usually occur when sunlight hits rain or mist. The sunlight enters the drops of water and is *refracted*, or bent, at different angles. The different angles of light are *reflected* out of the drops as different colors. Have students find and interpret a diagram in an encyclopedia or a book about color or weather that explains this effect.

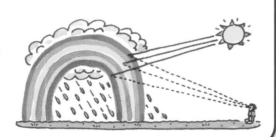

I'm in Charge of Celebrations **309**

Guided Comprehension

10 **(Focus Skill)** **SUMMARIZE** **Why does the narrator think she is lucky?** (Possible response: She was in the right place at the right time to see the coyote. They shared an experience that changed her life.)

11 **CHARACTERS' EMOTIONS** **How do you think the narrator feels after she and the coyote look at each other?** (Possible response: surprised and excited)

12 **IDENTIFY WITH CHARACTERS** **How do you think you would feel if you saw a coyote? Why?** (Responses will vary. Example: I'd feel excited but also a little scared because I wouldn't be sure what the coyote would do.)

At times like that,
I always think,
"What if I'd missed it?
What if I'd been
in the house?
Or what if I hadn't
looked up
when I did?"

You can see I'm
very lucky
about things
like that.

And
I was lucky
on Coyote Day,
because
out of all time
it had to be
one moment
only
that
a certain coyote
and I
could meet—
and we did. **10**

Friend, you should have
been here too.

I was following
deer tracks,
taking my time,
bending down
as I walked,
kind of humming.
(I hum a lot
when I'm alone.)

310

Draw students' attention to the last three stanzas on page 311, beginning with *I saw her eyes*. Have a volunteer read them aloud. Point out that characters in literature and real people often have experiences that change them in some important way. Challenge students to suggest some important events in young people's lives that might change them in some way. (Possible responses: getting a baby brother or sister; learning to read and write; going to school) Volunteers may like to share positive experiences that have changed their lives.

I looked up
in time to see
a young coyote
trotting
through the brush.

She crossed
in front of me.
It was a windy day
and she was going east.

In that easy
silent way
coyotes move,
she pushed
into the wind.

I stood there
hardly breathing,
wishing I
could move
that way.

I was surprised
to see her
stop
and turn
and look
at me.

She seemed to think
that I was
just
another
creature
following another
rocky trail.

(That's true, of course.
I am.)

She didn't hurry.
She wasn't afraid.

I saw her eyes
and she saw
mine. **11**

That look
held us
together.

Because of that,
I never will
feel
quite the same
again. **12**

311

Monitor Progress

Reread to Clarify

What does the narrator mean when she says that the look between her and the coyote "held us together"? (Possible response: She and the coyote both understood that they are creatures living together in the desert.)

If students are unable to answer the question, model the strategy:

MODEL Looking back, I see that the narrator says the coyote thinks of her as just another creature in the desert. She agrees. The look holds the two together because the girl feels she is a part of the desert world, just as the coyote is.

SOCIAL STUDIES

Native American Folklore and Customs

Remind students that the coyote is often a clever trickster in Native American tales. Invite students to share any coyote tales or other Native American stories they know. Then ask them what they know about the folklore and customs of Native American groups in the local area or region. Interested students might research Native American tribes to identify the groups in your area and find out more about their folklore, customs, traditions, and beliefs. Have them share what they discover with the class.

Guided Comprehension

13 (Focus Skill) **SUMMARIZE** **How does the narrator celebrate Coyote Day?** (Possible response: She walks the trail that she walked the day she saw the coyote; she brings food for the coyote.)

14 **CAUSE/EFFECT** **How do the meteor showers affect the narrator?** (Possible response: They amaze her.)

15 **MAKE AND CONFIRM PREDICTIONS** **Which of your predictions about the poem have been correct?** (Responses will vary.) **What else do you think will happen?** (Possible response: I think the girl will see other special things in the desert.)

So
on September twenty-eighth
I celebrate
Coyote Day.

Here's what I do:
I walk
the trail
I walked that day,
and I hum
softly
as I go.

Finally,
I unwrap
the feast
I've brought for her.

Last time
it was three apples
and some pumpkin seeds
and an ear of corn
and some big soft homemade
ginger cookies.

The next day,
I happened to pass
that way again.
Coyote tracks
went all around
the rock
where the food had been,
and the food
was gone.

Next year
I'll make it even better.
I'll bring
an extra feast
and eat there too. **13**

312

REACHING ALL LEARNERS

Diagnostic Check: Summarize

If . . . the students are unable to summarize text using the main ideas and details . . .

Then . . . have them list details about the main characters, the setting, and several events. Have students use their list to write a summary.

ADDITIONAL SUPPORT ACTIVITIES

BELOW-LEVEL Reteach, p. S68

ADVANCED Extend, p. S69

ENGLISH-LANGUAGE LEARNERS Reteach, p. S69

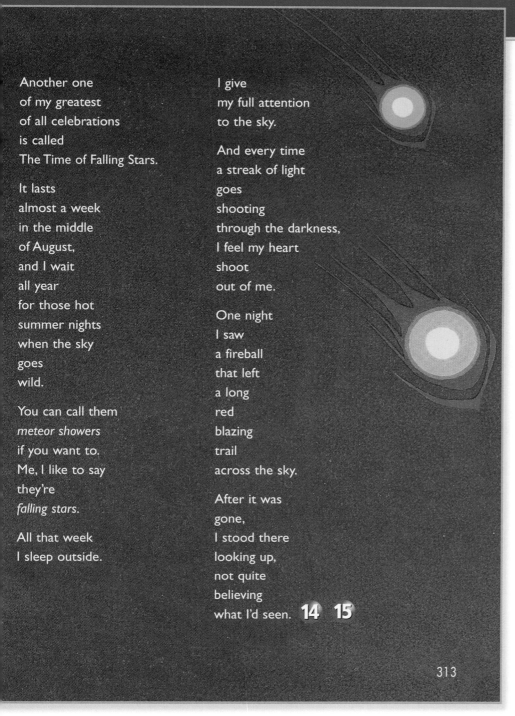

Another one
of my greatest
of all celebrations
is called
The Time of Falling Stars.

It lasts
almost a week
in the middle
of August,
and I wait
all year
for those hot
summer nights
when the sky
goes
wild.

You can call them
meteor showers
if you want to.
Me, I like to say
they're
falling stars.

All that week
I sleep outside.

I give
my full attention
to the sky.

And every time
a streak of light
goes
shooting
through the darkness,
I feel my heart
shoot
out of me.

One night
I saw
a fireball
that left
a long
red
blazing
trail
across the sky.

After it was
gone,
I stood there
looking up,
not quite
believing
what I'd seen. **14** **15**

313

ONGOING ASSESSMENT

Monitor Progress

Create Mental Images

What does the meteor shower look like?
(Possible response: many streaks of light shooting across the night sky)

Have students model how the strategy of creating mental images can help them understand the narrator's reaction to the meteor shower.

MODEL The narrator says that streaks of light go shooting through the darkness. I can picture many bright streaks of light against a dark sky. Picturing the falling stars helps me understand why the girl is so amazed by them.

LITERARY ANALYSIS

Free-Verse Poem Ask students to look back through the poem and tell how it is alike and different from other poems they have read. (Possible response: Alike—It is broken into stanzas or small parts; it uses lots of images; Different—The words at the end of the lines don't rhyme; there is no regular beat or rhythm.) Explain that poems without regular rhythm or rhyming patterns are called *free verse.* Then provide students with a poetry anthology and have them identify other free-verse poems.

Guided
Comprehension

16 **DRAW CONCLUSIONS** What do you think the girl and the man talk about? (Possible response: the meteor shower)

17 **IMPORTANT DETAILS** Why doesn't January first feel like New Year's Day to the narrator? (It seems just like any other winter day to her.)

18 **MAKE JUDGMENTS** When does the narrator celebrate the new year? (when spring arrives) **Do you think this is a good idea? Why or why not?** (Possible response: Yes, because it's a time of new beginnings; it's a time of year when new things start to grow.)

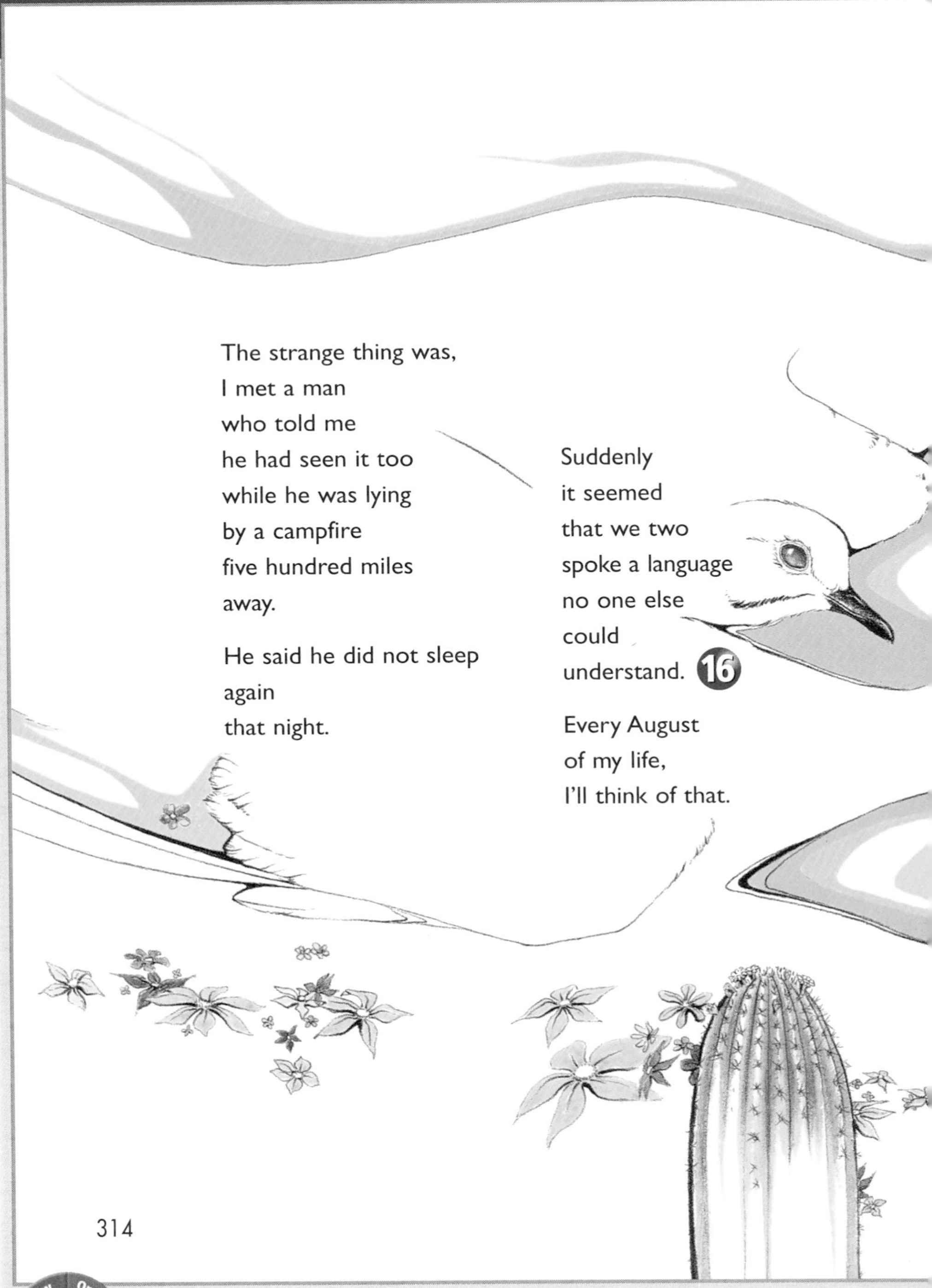

The strange thing was,
I met a man
who told me
he had seen it too
while he was lying
by a campfire
five hundred miles
away.

He said he did not sleep
again
that night.

Suddenly
it seemed
that we two
spoke a language
no one else
could
understand. **16**

Every August
of my life,
I'll think of that.

314

BELOW-LEVEL

Draw students' attention to the sentence *Suddenly it seemed that we two spoke a language no one else could understand* on page 314. Ask students who the word *we* refers to and what they talked about. (the girl and the man; the meteor shower) Point out that when two people talk about a special event that they have both experienced, they might feel like only they know what happened and how it felt to experience the event.

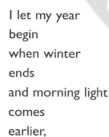

Friend,
I've saved
my New Year Celebration
until last.

Mine
is a little
different
from the one
most people have.

It comes in
spring.

To tell the truth,
I never did
feel like
my new year
started
January first.

To me,
that's just
another
winter day.

I let my year
begin
when winter
ends
and morning light
comes
earlier,
the way it *should*.

That's when
I feel like
starting
new.

I wait
until
the white-winged doves
are back from Mexico,
and wildflowers
cover the hills,
and my favorite
cactus
blooms. **18**

315

Monitor Progress

Use Decoding/ Phonics

Point to the word *wildflowers* in the last stanza on page 315. Ask: **What two smaller words can help you figure out this word? What does the word mean?** (*wild* and *flowers*; flowers that grow in the wild)

If students have difficulty responding, model the strategy:

MODEL I recognize two smaller words in this word, *wild* and *flower*. When I blend those two words together, I get *wildflower*. If I put together the meanings of the smaller words, I can figure out that wild-flowers are flowers that grow in the wild.

REREADING FOR FLUENCY

Echo Reading Read aloud a page of "I'm in Charge of Celebrations." Then read a chosen section one sentence or phrase at a time, pausing to have students read the sentence or phrase back to you. Point out to students that although the text is broken into many very short lines, they should still pay attention to punctuation to know when to pause or stop. Model fluent reading and use an appropriate tone of voice. For support, see Fluency Routine Cards in Theme Resources, pp. T80a–T80b.

Note: For assessment of oral reading accuracy and fluency, see pages T78–T80.

Guided Comprehension

RETURN TO THE PREDICTIONS/PURPOSE

Were your predictions about the poem correct? Did you change any of them? When? Discuss with students whether their purposes for reading were met.

Think and Respond

Answers:

1 Possible response: School holidays are not enough, and she thinks a celebration should be about something she will always remember; she writes about them in her book. **SUMMARIZE**

2 Possible response: because she can't imagine being lonely with all the plants, animals, and special things around her in the desert. **MAIN IDEA**

3 Possible response: She likes to wait until spring begins, when everything feels new. To her, this is the start of a new year. **IMPORTANT DETAILS**

4 Response will vary. **PERSONAL RESPONSE**

5 Accept reasonable responses. **READING STRATEGIES**

OPEN-ENDED RESPONSE

Write a paragraph explaining what you think the author of this poem is trying to teach readers.

It always
makes me think
I ought to bloom
myself.

And
that's when
I start to plan
my New Year
Celebration.

I finally choose
a day
that is
exactly
right.

Even the air
has to be
perfect,
and the dirt
has to feel
good and warm
on bare feet.

(Usually,
it's a Saturday
around the end
of April.)

I have a drum
that I beat
to signal
The Day.

Then I go
wandering off,
following all
of my favorite
trails
to all of the
places
I like.

I check how
everything
is doing.

316

COMPREHENSION

End-of-Selection Test

To evaluate comprehension, see *Practice Book* pages A41–A44.

I spend the day
admiring
things.

If the old desert tortoise
I know from last year
is out
strolling around,
I'll go his direction
awhile.

I celebrate
with horned toads
and ravens
and lizards
and quail. . . .

And, Friend,
it's not
a bad
party.

Walking back home
(kind of humming),
sometimes
I think about
those people
who ask me if
I'm *lonely* here.

I have to
laugh
out
loud.

Think and Respond

1 Why does the narrator choose her own **celebrations**? How will she remember them all?

2 Why does the narrator laugh out loud when people ask if she is lonely?

3 Why does the narrator have her New Year Celebration in April instead of January?

4 Which of the celebrations in the poem is your favorite? Why do you like it?

5 Describe a reading strategy that helped you understand or enjoy the poem.

317

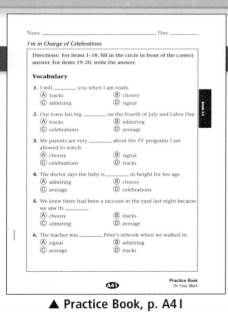

▲ Practice Book, p. A41

▲ Practice Book, p. A44

Meet the Author
Byrd Baylor

Dear Friends,

I'm in Charge of Celebrations is about my life and my home. I was born in Texas, and I spent many summers on a West Texas ranch. I love living where I can see cactus and red cliffs. I love hearing coyotes on cold, clear nights. These are the things I celebrate.

You can celebrate nature, too. Listen to the birds, and look at the flowers and the stones. Feel the wind and the sun and the rain. There are so many reasons to celebrate!

Yours truly,

Byrd Baylor

318

ABOUT THE AUTHOR

Byrd Baylor has written about such diverse topics as petroglyphs, the ancient pottery traditions of the Anasazi, rock collecting, and the creatures of the desert.

Have students discuss how "I'm in Charge of Celebrations" might have been different if the author had grown up in a different place, such as an island in the Caribbean. (Possible response: She might have written about the natural wonders that can be found at the seaside.)

Additional information about the author and illustrator can be found at *The Learning Site* at **www.harcourtschool.com**

Meet the Illustrator
Peter Parnall

Dear Readers,

I love to study nature, especially animals. I almost became a veterinarian, but I decided I liked drawing animals more than doctoring them. I have been very happy drawing pictures for other authors' books. I have also written and illustrated some of my own books.

I now live and work on a farm in Maine. I enjoy taking long walks in the woods near the farm and sharing my art with children. I hope you enjoyed my pictures in *I'm in Charge of Celebrations*.

Yours truly,

Peter Parnall

Visit *The Learning Site!*
www.harcourtschool.com

319

related books

You may want to recommend these titles to students interested in books about the natural world.

LIBRARY BOOKS COLLECTION

Earth: Our Planet in Space
by Seymour Simon

ADDITIONAL READING

- *By a Blazing Blue Sea*
  by S. T. Garne. Harcourt, 1999. **EASY**

- *The Desert Is Theirs*
  by Byrd Baylor. Aladdin, 1987. **AVERAGE**

- *One Day in the Desert*
  by Jean Craighead George. HarperCollins, 1996. **CHALLENGING**

ABOUT THE ILLUSTRATOR

The long walks **Peter Parnall** takes in parks and wooded areas have helped inspire many of his works. His detailed drawings reflect how carefully he observes the natural world around him. He says, "I found I wanted to share some of my love of nature and ecology with children and chose to do it by writing about 'stuff' . . . that is hanging around here and there, like a woodpile, or maybe a stone wall."

Have students talk about how the jobs of a veterinarian and an illustrator of wildlife are different. Then challenge them to discuss what a veterinarian and an illustrator of wildlife might have in common. (Possible response: They both love animals.)

Making Connections

COMPARE TEXTS

Answers:

1 Possible response: by writing down and celebrating events such as seeing a green cloud or a coyote **AUTHOR'S VIEWPOINT**

2 Possible response: because they both saw the same thing and felt the same way about it, even though they did not know each other and were many miles apart **CHARACTERS' EMOTIONS**

3 Possible response: Her New Year celebration does not fall on the same day every year. The other celebrations are on certain dates. **COMPARE AND CONTRAST**

4 Responses will vary. **COMPARE AND CONTRAST**

5 Responses will vary. **SYNTHESIZE**

▲ I'm in Charge of Celebrations

Making Connections

Compare Texts

1 How does the author of "I'm in Charge of Celebrations" show her feelings about nature?

2 Why does the girl feel a close connection to the man who was five hundred miles away from her when he saw the fireball?

3 How is the girl's New Year celebration different from the other celebrations in the poem?

4 Think of another poem you have read. How is that poem like and unlike "I'm in Charge of Celebrations"?

5 What questions do you have about the desert as a result of reading "I'm in Charge of Celebrations"?

Write a Conversation

The girl in "I'm in Charge of Celebrations" tells about meeting a man who had also seen the fireball in the sky. Think about what these two people might have said to each other about the fireball. Write a conversation to express their thoughts and feelings. Use a graphic organizer like this one to plan your written conversation.

Writing CONNECTION

GIRL: _____
MAN: _____
GIRL: _____
MAN: _____
GIRL: _____

320

Experiment with Mirrors

The girl in the poem celebrates the day she saw a triple rainbow. Rainbows can occur when sunlight hits rain or mist. The light is bent at different angles by the drops of water and then is reflected out of the drops. Try to make a rainbow with mirrors or other shiny objects. Then look in a science book to find out why you did or did not succeed.

Science CONNECTION

Draw a Map

"I'm in Charge of Celebrations" tells about life in a desert. Do research to learn about the desert that is closest to you, whether it is nearby or far away. Draw a map that shows where the desert is and also shows where your town or city is. Label the desert, your state, your town or city, and other states that may also be shown on your map. Identify and label other important features in your local region, such as lakes, rivers, oceans, mountains, or valleys.

Social Studies CONNECTION

321

Making Connections

HOMEWORK FOR THE WEEK

Students and family members can work together to complete the activities on page T96. You may want to assign some or all of the activities as homework for each day of the week.

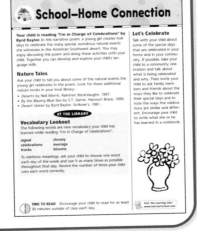

technology
Visit *The Learning Site:*
www.harcourtschool.com
See Resources for Parents and Teachers: Homework Helper.

Teacher's Edition, p. T96 ▶

Write a Conversation   Point out that the graphic organizer on *Pupil Edition* page 320 is set up like lines in a play. Write a sample conversation on the board. Model how to turn these lines into quotations using quotation marks, punctuation and capitalization, and such phrases as *the girl said*.

📁 **PORTFOLIO OPPORTUNITY**
Students may add their written conversations to their portfolios.

Experiment with Mirrors   Provide small mirrors and other shiny surfaces, as well as prisms if possible, and discuss safe handling with students. You may want to allow students to experiment outside using sunlight for best results.

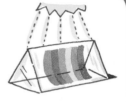

Draw a Map
Provide local maps for students to consult. To extend the activity, encourage students to add captions that give facts about the desert and other regions shown, such as elevation, amount of annual rainfall, animals and plants living there, and so on.

Summarize

SKILL TRACE

SUMMARIZE	
Introduce	p. 14I
Reteach	pp. S4, S16, T2
Review	pp. 34, 59B, 60I, 92
Test	Theme I Vol. 2
Maintain	**pp. 300I, 322**

RETURN TO THE SKILL

Have students read page 322 in the *Pupil Edition*. You may wish to use this model:

MODEL The statements about the girl's hair and her experience with the rabbit and the triple rainbow are details. The statement about where she lives is a main idea. I'd include that one in a summary of the selection.

Have students explain how summarizing helped them remember the main ideas in "I'm in Charge of Celebrations."

PRACTICE/APPLY

Ask students to give a brief oral summary of a story or nonfiction selection they have read recently on their own. Tell them to recall the main ideas in the selection in order to organize their summaries. **PERFORMANCE ASSESSMENT**

Visit *The Learning Site:*
www.harcourtschool.com
See Skill Activities and Test
Tutors: Summarize.

▲ I'm in Charge of Celebrations

Summarize

You know that to make a good summary, you tell the most important ideas or events from a story in your own words. There is also another way to think about a summary. Only main ideas are included. Supporting details are not included.

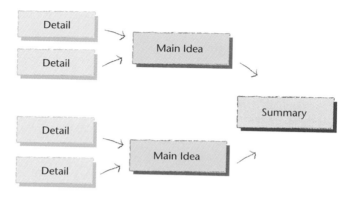

Think about the main ideas you would include in a summary of "I'm in Charge of Celebrations." Which of these statements belongs in a summary? Which are supporting details?

- A girl lives in the desert.
- She has long, dark hair.
- The girl once saw a rabbit watching a triple rainbow.

Visit *The Learning Site!*
www.harcourtschool.com
See *Skills* and *Activities*

322

REACHING ALL LEARNERS

Diagnostic Check: Comprehension and Skills

If . . . students are having difficulty summarizing . . .

Then . . . help them list the key events. Ask small groups to act out those events. Other students can provide an oral summary of the scene.

ADDITIONAL SUPPORT ACTIVITIES

BELOW-LEVEL Reteach, p. S68
ADVANCED Extend, p. S69
ENGLISH-LANGUAGE LEARNERS Reteach, p. S69

Focus Skill

Test Prep
Summarize

▶ **Read the paragraph.**

The Cactus

Most types of cactus plants are well suited to the hot, dry climate of the desert. Their stems are large and can hold a lot of water. Many stems have special shapes that cause rain to run directly to the roots. The roots are near the surface and spread out over a wide area so they can take in any rain that falls. The plants usually grow far apart from each other so that each one has a large area of soil from which to soak up water.

Now answer Numbers 1 and 2. Base your answers on "The Cactus."

1. **Which of the following ideas belongs in a summary of the paragraph?**

    A how much water a cactus can hold

    B which parts of a cactus help it survive in the desert

    C what cactus stems look like

    D whether you have ever seen a cactus

Tip Rule out the choices that give supporting details.

2. **Write a sentence that summarizes the paragraph.**

Tip Remember that a good summary tells about the main ideas from the paragraph.

323

Test Prep

Summarize Have students read the paragraph carefully and think about what the details tell about. Use the Tips to reinforce good test-taking strategies. (I.B,

2. Possible response: The desert cactus has special features that allow it to live well in that hot, dry climate.)

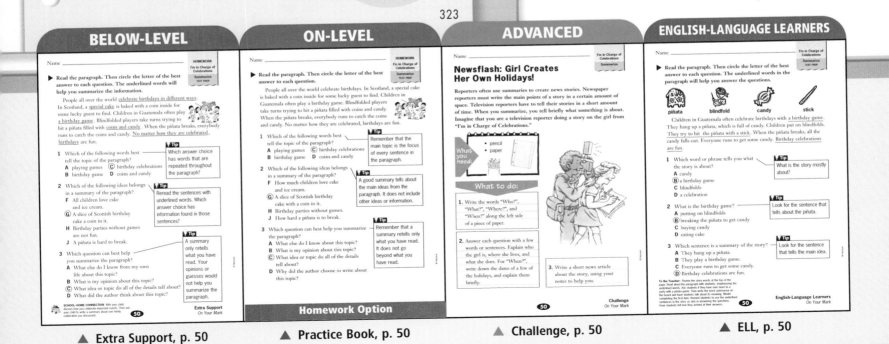

BELOW-LEVEL ▲ Extra Support, p. 50

ON-LEVEL ▲ Practice Book, p. 50

Homework Option

ADVANCED ▲ Challenge, p. 50

ENGLISH-LANGUAGE LEARNERS ▲ ELL, p. 50

Phonics

Decoding/Phonics

Word Structure: Prefix + Root Word + Suffix

OBJECTIVE

To decode and understand words with prefixes and suffixes

SKILL TRACE

WORD STRUCTURE: PREFIX + ROOT WORD + SUFFIX

Introduce	Grade 2
Maintain	**p. 323A**

ONGOING ASSESSMENT

If students are not able to fluently read approximately 114 words per minute, **then** they require phonics instruction and will also benefit from fluency practice.

NOTE: For assessment of oral reading accuracy and fluency, see pages T78–T80.

Phonics Practice Book, *Intermediate*, pp. 265–277.

REVIEW THE SKILL

Discuss prefixes and suffixes. Write this sentence on the board and read it aloud:

I have seen some unbelievable sights in the desert.

Point to the word *unbelievable*. Ask students to identify the prefix (un-), the root word (believe), and the suffix (-able) in this word. Then have students blend the parts to read the word aloud. Explain that often a root word may have both a prefix and a suffix added to it. Remind students that a prefix and suffix will change a word's meaning. Review prefixes and suffixes using a chart similar to the one below:

Prefix	Suffix	Meaning
bi-		"two"
dis, in-, non-, un-		"not"
	-ful	"full of"
	-ly	"in a way that is"
	-able, -ible	"can be"

PRACTICE/APPLY

Decode words with prefixes and suffixes. Write these words on the board. Have students identify the prefix, root word, and suffix for each word. Then have students read the words aloud. PERFORMANCE ASSESSMENT

disagreeable	reviewer	uneventful
biweekly	disapproving	nonreturnable
unhelpful	indescribable	dishonestly

Fact and Opinion

Comprehension

REVIEW THE SKILL

Discuss facts and opinions. Review with students that facts are statements that can be proven, and opinions are statements that tell what a person thinks or believes. An opinion cannot be proven. Have students suggest words that often signal opinions. (Possible responses: good, bad, best, worst, I think, I believe)

Next, read aloud the first three stanzas on *Pupil Edition* page 306. Model how to identify facts and opinions.

> **MODEL** The narrator says readers weren't around on the first Dust Devil Day. This is a fact since you can prove it. In the next stanza, the words *I think* and *better* help me know the narrator is expressing her opinion about the whirlwinds and dust devils.

PRACTICE/APPLY

Distinguishing between facts and opinions. Write on the board the following excerpts from the poem. Call on students to tell whether the sentence states a fact or an opinion, and to explain how they know.

- **Page 304: I gave myself one hundred and eight celebrations.**
  (fact; can be proven)

- **Page 307: You have to whirl around like you were one of them.**
  (opinion; tells what the narrator believes)

- **Page 308: I wrote it down and drew the hill and the rabbit and the rainbow and me.** (fact; can be proven)

- **Page 310: You can see I'm very lucky about things like that.**
  (opinion; expresses how the narrator feels)

Assign pairs of students these parts of the poem: pages 311–312, pages 314–315. Have them identify at least one fact and one opinion in their assigned section. **PERFORMANCE ASSESSMENT**

Summarize. Ask a volunteer to describe the differences between facts and opinions. (Possible response: A fact is a statement that can be proven or checked, while an opinion cannot be. Opinions tell what a person thinks or feels.)

OBJECTIVE
To distinguish between fact and opinion

SKILL TRACE
FACT AND OPINION

Introduce	p. 146I
Reteach	pp. S36, S48, T38
Review	pp. 166, 193D, 194I, 220
Test	Theme 2 Vol. 2
Maintain	**p. 323B**

ENGLISH-LANGUAGE LEARNERS
Below On-Level Advanced ELL

Have students work with English-proficient partners, who can point out words that signal opinions, such as *think*, *feel*, and *seems*.

Writer's Craft

Poem

Writer's Craft: Word Choice

TRAITS OF GOOD WRITING

	INTRODUCE AND PRACTICE	APPLY TO LONGER WRITING FORMS
Focus/Ideas	329E-F (3-1)	355E-F, 387E-F (3-1)
Organization	167C-D, 193E-F (3-2)	221E-F, 261E-F (3-2)
Voice	41C-D, 67E-F (3-1)	99E-F, 129C-D (3-1)
Word Choice	**323C-D, 347C-D (3-2)**	**369E-F, 399E-F (3-2)**
Development	303E-F, 329E-F (3-1)	355E-F, 387E-F (3-1)
Effective Sentences	35E-F, 59E-F (3-2)	93E-F, 117C-D (3-2)
Effective Paragraphs	181E-F, 205E-F (3-1)	223E-F, 255C-D (3-1)
Conventions	(See Grammar and Spelling Lessons.)	(Applied to all writing lessons.)

technology

Writing Express™ CD-ROM
Visit *The Learning Site:*
www.harcourtschool.com
See Writing Detective,
Proofreading Makes Perfect.

TRAITS OF GOOD WRITING

- **Focus/Ideas:** The poet clearly states the topic in the title and the beginning of the poem.

- **Organization:** The poet separates the ideas into two stanzas. The poet breaks lines in order to help readers understand and enjoy the poem.

- **Voice:** The poet's voice is personal and natural.

- **Word Choice:** The poet uses vivid language to create images and figurative language to describe something by comparing it to something else.

- **Development:** The poet uses details to create an image for the reader.

- **Effective Sentences:** The poet crafts sentences to be either long or short, depending on the rhythm wanted.

DAY 1 — TEACH/MODEL

CONNECT READING TO WRITING
Tell students that "I'm in Charge of Celebrations" is an unrhymed poem expressing the poet's thoughts and feelings about the wonders of nature.

WORD CHOICE Display Transparency 238A and read the introduction and the poem aloud. Ask students what the poet compares the snow on the ground to. (white paint)

Explain that a poem creates a picture, or image, in the reader's mind. Point out that poets use colorful, vivid language to show readers how things look, sound, taste, feel, and smell.

▼ Teaching Transparency 238A

STUDENT MODEL: POEM

A poem is one form a writer uses to describe something or to express feelings about a subject. Poets use vivid words and phrases to help readers picture what they are describing. A **rhyming** poem is a poem in which some or all of the lines end with rhyming words. An **unrhymed** poem does not have a regular pattern of rhyme and rhythm. Here is a short, unrhymed poem a student wrote for a school poetry contest.

Title	First Snow
First image	The first big snow, the one that covers everything, makes me think that
Comparison/ colorful words	someone painted the whole world white.
Second image Comparison/ colorful words	I wonder how many cans of paint that would take.

"I'm in Charge of Celebrations"
Celebrate Our World, Theme 3
238A
Student Model: Poem
Harcourt

DAY 2 — WRITER'S CRAFT

USE DESCRIPTIVE LANGUAGE
Display Transparency 238B. Read the introduction to Part A aloud. Then have students complete the activity.

Explain that good writers often describe things by comparing them to something else. Display Part B of the transparency and have students complete the activity.

APPLY TO WRITING Have students choose their favorite season. Then ask them to write several sentences in which they use colorful language to "paint a picture" of what that season looks like.

▼ Teaching Transparency 238B

WORD CHOICE: IMAGERY AND FIGURATIVE LANGUAGE

PART A Poets often use **imagery** to help readers create mental pictures of their subjects or what the poets are writing about. Poets often use colorful words to create these images.

Directions: Choose words from the box to write a sentence about each of the things below. Try to create a clear image of what you are describing.

lake _____
sun _____
trees _____

blue-green	blazing	tall
hot	still	shady

PART B When poets use **figurative language**, they describe one thing by comparing it to something else.

Directions: Read each sentence. Then draw a line under the thing that the word in dark type is being compared to.

The **sun** rose like an <u>orange balloon</u>.
The **diver** shot through the air like an <u>arrow</u>.
She swam as smoothly as a <u>fish</u>.

"I'm in Charge of Celebrations"
Celebrate Our World, Theme 3
238B
Writing
Harcourt

5 Day Plan

APPLY TO LITERATURE Have students read the last four stanzas on page 306. Ask them what the poet is comparing dust devils to. (giants) Have students make a list of the things that the dust devils are doing. (calling their friends, dancing)

Then ask students to read the last stanza on *Pupil Edition* page 315. Have them make a list of all the phrases the poet uses to create images of spring. (white-winged doves, wildflowers cover the hills, cactus blooms)

WRITING PROMPT: *Suppose that your class is having a poetry contest. Write an unrhymed poem about something you enjoy doing outdoors, such as planting seeds, playing in leaves, or building a snowman. Use words that express your thoughts and feelings.*

PREWRITE Tell students to decide on a topic. As a prewriting activity, students might draw a picture and then brainstorm images and descriptive words.

DRAFT Have students use the steps below to draft their poems:

1. **Introduce** the topic and write down the first image.

2. **Add** descriptive words and figurative language to describe the image.

3. **Write** about another image and repeat step two.

4. **Check** that the lines break in places that will help the reader understand and enjoy the poem.

5. **Write** a title for the poem.

Have students refer to their Word Banks for adjectives they might use in their poems.

REVISION FOCUS: CLARIFYING WORDS Explain to students that as they revise their poems, they will want to make sure they have used words that clearly express their ideas. Offer this example: *The cloud was big and fluffy.* Ask: **How could you create a clearer image of what the cloud looked like?** Work with students to rewrite the sentence to create a strong image. (Possible example: The cloud looked like a mountain of marshmallows.)

PEER CONFERENCE CHECKLIST Have partners use this checklist to discuss and revise their poems.

✓ Do the title and opening lines state the topic of the poem?

✓ Does the poem have images that show how the writer feels about the topic?

✓ Are colorful words used to describe the images?

✓ Does the poem make any interesting comparisons?

Language Handbook, pp. 18–21

Grammar

More Irregular Verbs

REACHING ALL LEARNERS

Diagnostic Check: Grammar and Writing

If . . . students are having difficulty forming the tenses of irregular verbs . . .

Then . . . write irregular verb forms on slips of paper and put them in a container. Students should choose a word and use it in a sentence.

ADDITIONAL SUPPORT ACTIVITIES

BELOW-LEVEL	Reteach, p. S70
ADVANCED	Extend, p. S71
ENGLISH-LANGUAGE LEARNERS	Reteach, p. S71

technology

Grammar Jingles™ CD,
   Intermediate: Track 11
Visit *The Learning Site:*
www.harcourtschool.com
See Grammar Practice Park,
Multimedia Grammar Glossary.

DAY 1 — TEACH/MODEL

DAILY LANGUAGE PRACTICE
1. Have you ever see a desert.
   (seen; desert?)
2. A desert is home to many plant and animal.
   (plants; animals)

INTRODUCE THE CONCEPT Remind students that an **irregular verb** is one that does not end with *-ed* in the past tense.

Display Transparency 239. Ask students to read sentences 1–4 and tell which verb is irregular and how they know. Discuss the forms of irregular verbs shown in the chart. Then have students rewrite sentences 5–8, using the form of *give* in parentheses.

▼ Teaching Transparency 239

MORE IRREGULAR VERBS

1. The coyote tastes the apples.   2. The coyote tasted the apples.
3. The coyote eats the apples.   4. The coyote ate the apples.
The verb *eat* is irregular. It does not end with *-ed* in the past tense.

Some Irregular Verbs

Verb	Present	Past	Past with Helping Verb
eat	eat, eats	ate	(have, has, had) eaten
give	give, gives	gave	(have, has, had) given
go	go, goes	went	(have, has, had) gone
ride	ride, rides	rode	(have, has, had) ridden
take	take, takes	took	(have, has, had) taken

5. I _____ the coyote a snack. (past) gave

6. I _____ the coyote a snack. (present) give

7. She _____ the coyote a snack. (present) gives

8. She had _____ the coyote a snack. (past with helping verb) given

"I'm in Charge of Celebrations"
Celebrate Our World, Theme 3   239   Grammar
                                                    Harcourt

DAY 2 — EXTEND THE CONCEPT

DAILY LANGUAGE PRACTICE
1. Pay atention to nature? (attention; nature.)
2. Have you ever taken a walks and seen an animal up close! (walk; close?)

BUILD ORAL LANGUAGE Have students take turns using present, past, and past-with-helping-verb forms of *eat*, *give*, *ride*, and *take* to complete this oral sentence:

She _____ it.

(*She eats it, She ate it, She has/had eaten it,* and so on.)

PERFORMANCE ASSESSMENT

Practice Book, p. 51

Name _____

Skill Reminder • *An irregular verb is a verb that does not end with –ed to show past tense.*

▶ Rewrite each sentence. Change present-tense verbs to past-tense. Change past-tense verbs to present tense.

1. I give each day a name.
   I gave each day a name.
2. Today I rode in a pick up truck.
   Today I ride in a pick up truck.
3. Seven dust devils went by.
   Seven dust devils go by.
4. I take pictures of the dust devils.
   I took pictures of the dust devils.
5. I write about special days in my journal.
   I wrote about special days in my journal.

▶ Complete each sentence with the correct past-tense form of the verb in parentheses ( ).

6. Later, I ___went___ down to the canyon. (go)
7. I always ___took___ a sketchpad with me. (take)
8. Once, I had ___taken___ a picture of a hawk. (take)
9. The hawk had ___ridden___ on the wind. (rode)
10. Then it ___ate___ something in the field. (eat)

TRY THIS! Use past-tense forms of the verbs *go, ride,* and *take*. Write three sentences about a place you like to visit.

Homework Option

▲ Practice Book, p. 51

5 Day Plan

DAILY LANGUAGE PRACTICE

1. **you will not seen these thing unless you are quiet.** (You; see; things)
2. **Sometimes you has to be still for a long time** (have; time.)

MORE IRREGULAR VERBS Have students work in groups. Display the chart on Transparency 239. Ask students to take turns choosing one verb form and using it in a sentence. The other students in the group should identify the tense being used.

Test Prep Tip

"When you take language tests, watch for sentences with the helping verb *have, has,* or *had.* Be sure to use the correct helping-verb form for the tense of the main verb."

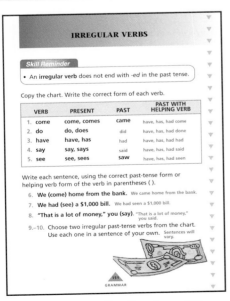

▲ Language Handbook, p. 151

DAILY LANGUAGE PRACTICE

1. **The author say she once come upon a rabbit.** (says; came)
2. **Her and the rabbit seen the same triple rainbow.** (She; saw)

USING IRREGULAR VERBS Have students look for irregular verbs in a piece of their own writing. Ask them to list the ones they find, identify the tense, and check the spelling.

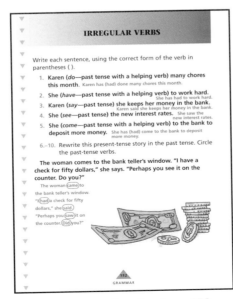

▲ Language Handbook, p. 152

DAILY LANGUAGE PRACTICE

1. **is it lonely in the desert.** (Is; desert?)
2. **will we see the desert on our vaccation.** (Will; vacation?)

LABEL VERB TENSES Have students copy each sentence below, underline the verb, and label it *past* or *present.*

1. I <u>gave</u> her an apple. (past)
2. She <u>took</u> it from me. (past)
3. Here she <u>comes</u> now. (present)
4. She <u>carries</u> the food to the hill. (present)
5. Sally <u>ate</u> the apple last. (past)
6. I <u>haven't ridden</u> a horse in years. (past)
7. Why can't you <u>go</u> with us? (present)
8. My mother <u>gives</u> advice to my father. (present)

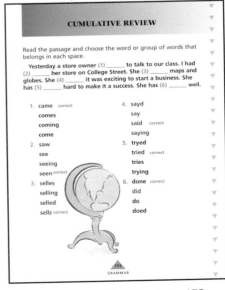

▲ Language Handbook, p. 153

I'm in Charge of Celebrations **323F**

Spelling Words

1. **farmer**
2. **useful**
3. **softly***
4. **suitable**
5. **lonely***
6. **quietly***
7. **teacher**
8. **thankful**
9. **exactly***
10. **readable**
11. **nicer**
12. **safer**
13. **harmful**
14. **playful**
15. **suddenly**

Challenge Words
16. **breathing***
17. **pleasant**
18. **beautiful**
19. **float**
20. **gentle**

* Selection Words

Spelling

Words with Suffixes -er, -ful, -ly, -able

DAY 1 — PRETEST/SELF-CHECK

ADMINISTER THE PRETEST Use the Dictation Sentences under Day 5. Help students self-check their pretests using Transparency 240.

ADVANCED

Use the Challenge Words in these Dictation Sentences:

16. We practiced **breathing** underwater.
17. It's **pleasant** out in the garden.
18. Everyone admired her **beautiful** dress.
19. We watched the feather **float** to the ground.
20. You must be **gentle** when you pick up a bunny.

DAY 2 — TEACH/MODEL

WORD SORT Display Transparency 240. Make sure students know the meanings of the words. Then ask students to copy the chart and to write each Spelling Word where it belongs.

Point to and read the word *farmer*. Ask students what suffix they see at the end of the word. *(-er)* Have a volunteer circle the suffix. Repeat the procedure with the words *useful*, *softly*, and *suitable*. Have students read the generalization to confirm their conclusion.

HANDWRITING Form the lower loop of an *f* correctly, so it doesn't look like a *b*.

▼ Teaching Transparency 240

WORDS WITH SUFFIXES
-er, -ful, -ly, -able

Spelling Words

1. farmer	6. quietly	11. nicer
2. useful	7. teacher	12. safer
3. softly	8. thankful	13. harmful
4. suitable	9. exactly	14. playful
5. lonely	10. readable	15. suddenly

• Some words end with the suffix -er, -ful, -ly, or -able.

Words that end with -er	Words that end with -ful	Words that end with -ly	Words that end with -able
farmer	useful	softly	suitable
teacher	thankful	lonely	readable
nicer	harmful	quietly	
safer	playful	exactly	
		suddenly	

"I'm in Charge of Celebrations"
Celebrate Our World, Theme 3 — 240 — Spelling Harcourt

▲ Practice Book, page 52

▲ Spelling Practice Book, page 95

DAY 3
SPELLING STRATEGIES

WORD PARTS Write the base words *teach*, *thank*, *quiet*, and *read* in a column on the board. In another column write the endings *-er*, *-ful*, *-ly*, and *-able*. Ask volunteers to read the base words and draw a line connecting each base word to the word ending that is across from it. Then have them read the word that is created. (teacher, thankful, quietly, readable) Ask students what the suffix *-able* means. (can be, is able to be)

✏️ Apply to Writing

Have students use the word parts strategy as they proofread. Have them look for words that end with *-er*, *-ful*, *-ly*, and *-able* to be sure they have spelled them correctly.

DAY 4
SPELLING ACTIVITIES

CONCENTRATION Have students write the Spelling Words on small cards, with the base word on one card and the ending on another. Have them play with a partner. One student shuffles the cards and places them face down in six rows of five cards. Partners take turns turning up two cards at a time. If the two cards form a Spelling Word, the student spells the word, keeps the pair, and continues. If a Spelling Word is not formed, the cards are turned face down again. The game ends when all the cards are gone. The player with the most cards wins.

DAY 5
POSTTEST

DICTATION SENTENCES

1. The **farmer** milked the cows.
2. A screwdriver is a very **useful** tool.
3. The father spoke **softly** to the baby.
4. Those shoes are not **suitable** for the hike.
5. She is **lonely** without her dog.
6. We walked **quietly** during the fire drill.
7. Who is your math **teacher**?
8. Be **thankful** that it is not raining.
9. I have **exactly** twenty-five cents.
10. These tongue twisters are not **readable**.
11. Do you think this park is **nicer** than the one by the market?
12. It is **safer** to walk across the street than to run.
13. The sun's rays can be **harmful**.
14. My puppy is very **playful**.
15. The cat ran off **suddenly**.

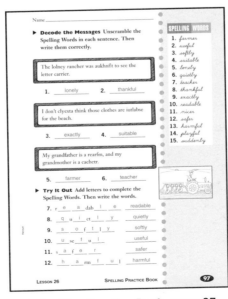

▲ Spelling Practice Book, page 96

▲ Spelling Practice Book, page 97

Word Study

WORD PARTS

Suffixes

OBJECTIVE

To use knowledge of the suffix -ion to determine word meaning

Write the word *celebration* on the board. Ask students to name the root word in this word. (celebrate) Cover the root so that only the suffix *-ion* is visible. Explain that many words contain this suffix, which is pronounced /shən/, means "action or process of," and is sometimes spelled *-tion* or *-ation*.

Ask students to generate a list of words that contain a form of this suffix. Write them on the board. Then have students take turns using each word in a sentence to demonstrate its meaning.

sense   fascinate   -ion/-tion/-ation

imagine   explore   converse

ADVANCED

Ask students to brainstorm pairs of sentences containing homographs and draw pictures to go with each pair. Have volunteers take turns displaying their pictures and sentences, reading the sentences aloud and then giving the meanings of the homographs.

MULTIPLE-MEANING WORDS

Homographs

OBJECTIVE

To use knowledge of homographs in order to determine word meaning

Remind students that two words can be spelled the same way but have different pronunciations and meanings. Point to the word *wind* in the third stanza of the first column on *Pupil Edition* page 304. Read the word aloud and explain that it means "to twist or turn." Then ask a volunteer to pronounce another word that is spelled the same way, and to tell its meaning. (*wind*; moving air) Call on another student to use this word in a sentence to demonstrate its meaning.

Next, provide pairs of students with these words: *bow, close, content, present, tear.* Ask partners to use a dictionary to find the pronunciations of each homograph and to list the definitions of each word. Then have them read the words aloud, explaining their meanings.

bow   bow

Speaking and Listening

Reciting a Poem

OBJECTIVE

To recite a poem from memory

Students may wish to publish their poems by reciting them before the class.

Organization Share these **organizational tips** with students.

- Read your poem once carefully, highlighting those words and phrases that you would like to emphasize.

- Think about the rhythm or beat of your poem.

Delivery Share the following **practice tips** with students.

- Reread your poem several times until you know it by heart.

- As you recite your poem, look around the room to establish eye contact with the audience.

Students can recite their poems in a "Poetry Slam," in which audience members listen to evaluate each poem based on pre-established criteria.
PERFORMANCE ASSESSMENT

Listening to a Poem

OBJECTIVE

To listen for pace and rhythm in poetry to identify important ideas

Listening Tips

- Listen to poetry for enjoyment and understanding.

- Close your eyes.

- Focus on changes in pace or rhythm that might signal important ideas.

- Identify the musical elements of the poem as you listen.

Have students listen for the message in each poem, as well as the imagery used to convey it. Share the Listening Tips with students.

POETRY SLAM Have students organize a poetry slam to evaluate and award prizes to the poems. To begin, have students work together to create a list of criteria for judging the poems. Tell them to list several categories; for example, *good imagery, use of vivid words, clear message, interesting delivery, strong rhythm*, and so on. Then have them evaluate each poem, based on their criteria, and vote on which prize to award it.

technology
Media Literacy and Communication Skills Package
(Video)

Books for All Learners

Reinforcing Skills and Strategies

■ BELOW-LEVEL

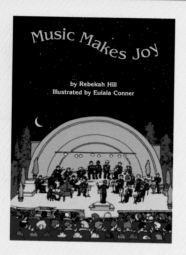

Music Makes Joy

by Rebekah Hill
Illustrated by Eulala Conner

 Focus Skill: Summarize

 Focus Strategy: Create Mental Images

✓ **Vocabulary:** *admiring, choosy, average, signal, tracks, celebrations*

Genre: Poem
Social Studies Connection: Countries and Traditions

SUMMARY This unrhymed poem describes the musical traditions of several countries from around the world and explores the theme that people everywhere celebrate life through music and dance.

 Visit *The Learning Site:*
www.harcourtschool.com
See Resources for Parents and Teachers: Books for All Learners.

BEFORE READING

Preview/Set Purpose Ask students to preview the poem. Guide students to set a purpose for reading.

Reinforce Summarize Help students make an outline they can fill in as they read to help them summarize what they learn about the music and dance of each country. SUMMARIZE/GRAPHIC AIDS

Music Makes Joy

I. China _____

   A. string instrument—qin _____

   B. music to dream by _____

Reinforce Vocabulary Ask questions such as: "What *celebrations* do you know of?" "What do you do in an *average* day?"

READING THE BOOK

Page 10 What picture do you create in your mind about the music of Tibet? (Monks are standing on mountaintops blowing horns; the music echoes from peak to peak.) What other mental images do you get from this poem? (Answers will vary.) CREATE MENTAL IMAGES

Pages 2–16 What is the poet saying in the first stanza on page 2 and the last one on page 16? (Possible response: that music and dance are part of every country and culture) INTERPRET THEME

Reread for Fluency Have students prepare, practice, and perform a choral reading of the poem. Model reading slowly and rhythmically.

RESPONDING

Outline Students can use their completed outlines to retell the important points the poet makes.

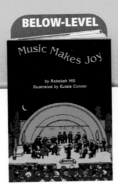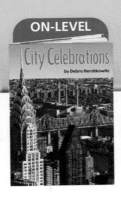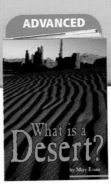
Oral Reading Fluency

Use Books for All Learners to promote oral reading fluency.

See Fluency Routine Cards, pp. T80a–T80b.

▲ page 323M   ▲ page 323N

■ ON-LEVEL

 Focus Skill: Summarize

 Focus Strategy: Create Mental Images

 Vocabulary: *admiring, choosy, average, signal, tracks, celebrations*

Genre: Realistic Fiction
Social Studies Connection: Cities of the United States and Their Celebrations

SUMMARY This story, written in the form of a young boy's travel journal, describes visits to six big cities throughout the United States and highlights their special celebrations and traditions. It ends by describing an event celebrated by Americans everywhere.

 Visit *The Learning Site:* www.harcourtschool.com
See Resources for Parents and Teachers: Books for All Learners.

BEFORE READING

Preview/Set Purpose Ask students to preview the book by reading the dates and city names and viewing the illustrations. Ask them what they think the book will be about, and why they would like to read it.

Reinforce Summarize Have students create a chart to help them record the important ideas about each city.

READING THE BOOK

Pages 8–9 What picture did you create in your mind of the mall in Washington, D.C.? (It is a long, wide strip of green grass with big, beautiful buildings lining each side.) What does the mall probably look like in April? (It probably has blooming cherry trees along it, full of pink blossoms.) CREATE MENTAL IMAGES

Pages 2–16 How is this book organized? Why do you think the author chose this way of organizing it? (It is organized according to the months and seasons. The author probably wanted to describe events that take place throughout the year, from winter through summer.) TEXT STRUCTURE AND FORMAT

Why do you think the author ends by describing the Fourth of July? (probably to show that there are some holidays everyone in the United States celebrates) DRAW CONCLUSIONS/AUTHOR'S CRAFT

Rereading for Fluency Have each student select the event or celebration that seemed most interesting and read aloud the two pages that describe it.

RESPONDING

Summary Chart Ask students to use their completed chart to summarize what the author has said about the events and traditions different cities celebrate.

Books for
All Learners
Reinforcing Skills and Strategies

■ ADVANCED

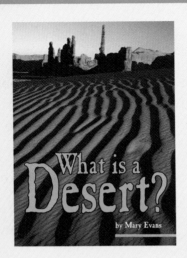

What is a Desert?
by Mary Evans

 Focus Skill: Summarize

 Focus Strategy: Create Mental Images

 Vocabulary: *admiring, choosy, average, signal, tracks, celebrations, survive, formation*

Genre: Nonfiction
Science Connection: Living Things in an Ecosystem

SUMMARY This selection describes what makes a desert a desert and explains how plants and animals in different deserts around the world survive in the hot, dry climate.

 Visit *The Learning Site:*
www.harcourtschool.com
See Resources for Parents and Teachers: Books for All Learners.

BEFORE READING

Preview/Set Purpose Have students preview the book. Ask students to predict what the book is about and select a purpose for reading it.

Reinforce Summarize Begin a fact web about the desert. Invite students to fill it in as they read to help them summarize the important ideas. SUMMARIZE/GRAPHIC AIDS

characteristics of deserts — deserts — desert plants

Expand Vocabulary Write *survive* and *formation* on the board. Ask students if they know what these words mean, and have them confirm these meanings in a dictionary. Then ask students to describe some different rock formations they have seen or seen pictures of.

READING THE BOOK

Pages 2–7 How are all deserts alike? (They all receive very little rain.) How are deserts different? (Some deserts are high and others are low; some are cold and rocky and others are hot and sandy; some have rivers flowing through them and others don't.) SUMMARIZE

Pages 8–16 Describe some plants and animals of the desert. (plants—barrel cactus, saguaro cactus; animals—Gila monster, different kinds of lizards, lake shrimp, Gila woodpecker, kangaroo rat) NOTE DETAILS

Rereading for Fluency Have students reread a portion of the selection aloud. Suggest that they read information about types of deserts, desert plants, or desert animals.

RESPONDING

Desert Tour Have students summarize the selection by conducting a "desert tour" or by presenting an oral summary.

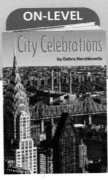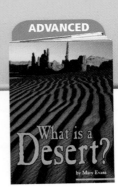

Managing Small Groups

While you work with small groups have other children do the following:
- Self-selected Reading
- Practice Pages
- Cross-Curricular Centers
- Journal Writing

▲ page 323K   ▲ page 323L

■ ENGLISH-LANGUAGE LEARNERS

 Focus Skill: Summarize

 Focus Strategy: Create Mental Images

 Concept Vocabulary: *nervous, museum, excited, speech*

Genre: Realistic Fiction
Social Studies Connections: Immigration; Customs and Traditions

SUMMARY Eight-year-old Juan has recently moved to the United States from Mexico. He is nervous about fitting in, but during his first year he learns a new language, makes new friends, and joins the soccer team.

 Visit *The Learning Site:*
www.harcourtschool.com
See Resources for Parents and Teachers: Books for All Learners.

BEFORE READING

Tap Prior Knowledge   Write *moving* on the board and read it aloud. Ask students who have moved to the United States to describe these experiences: going to a new *school*; *learning* a new *language*; making new *friends*.

Total Physical Response   Write the words *friends* and *moved* on the board. Then give a clue for each word and have students point to the word that fits the clue. (Examples: People you like a lot are your friends . If you went to a new place to live, you   moved .)

Display Vocabulary/Concept Words   Write the vocabulary words on the board. Read each word aloud and use it in an oral sentence about the challenges of moving to a new country and making new friends.

Preview the Book   Point out the main character, Juan, and read aloud the first paragraph on page 2. Have students preview the pictures and predict what happens to Juan during his first six months in the United States.

READING THE BOOK

Pages 4–7   Who are Juan's new friends? (Tomás and Gan) How do they help Juan? (Tomás helps Juan learn English; Gan helps Juan fit in.) SUMMARIZE

Page 16   How does Juan feel at the end of the story? Why? (He feels at home in the United States; he has learned English and made some new friends.) UNDERSTAND CHARACTERS' EMOTIONS

Rereading   Reread the book aloud with students. Ask volunteers to retell sections of their choice.

RESPONDING

Sequence Chart   Use a flow chart to help students summarize Juan's first six months in the United States.

Teacher Notes

Teacher Notes

THEME CONNECTION:
Celebrate Our World

GENRE:
Realistic Fiction

Award-Winning Illustrator

Comparing Realistic Fiction and Expository Nonfiction

▲ **READING ACROSS TEXTS:** "Seeds Can Sleep," by Mary Brown
GENRE: Expository Nonfiction

SUMMARY:

Alejandro's lonely desert life changes forever when he digs a secluded water hole for his animal neighbors. His gift is also a gift to himself, for as the animals visit, Alejandro's loneliness disappears.

 Selections available on *Audiotext 6*

Books for
All Learners

Lesson Plans on pages 347K–347N

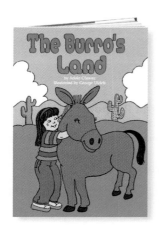

BELOW-LEVEL	ON-LEVEL	ADVANCED	ELL
• Lesson Vocabulary • Focus Skill: Cause and Effect	• Lesson Vocabulary • Focus Skill: Cause and Effect	• Challenge Vocabulary • Focus Skill: Cause and Effect	• Concept Vocabulary • Focus Skill: Cause and Effect

MULTI-LEVEL PRACTICE

Extra Support, pp. 53–55

Practice Book, pp. 53–57

Challenge, pp. 53–54

English-Language Learners, pp. 53–54

ADDITIONAL RESOURCES

Spelling Practice Book, pp. 98–100

Language Handbook, pp. 74, 157–159

Audiotext 6

Intervention Resource Kit, Lesson 27
  • Intervention Reader, *Included in Intervention Resource Kit*

English-Language Learners Resource Kit, Lesson 27

Technology

• *Writing Express™* **CD-ROM**

• *Grammar Jingles™* **CD**

• *Media Literacy and Communication Skills Package* (Video)

• *Reading and Language Skills Assessment* **CD-ROM**

• *The Learning Site:* **www.harcourtschool.com**

5-15 Minutes

ORAL LANGUAGE

- **Question of the Day**

15-30 Minutes

- **Sharing Literature**

SKILLS & STRATEGIES

- **Comprehension**

- **Vocabulary**

30-45 Minutes

READING

- **Guided Comprehension**

- **Independent Reading**

- **Cross-Curricular Connections**

45-90 Minutes

LANGUAGE ARTS

- **Writing**

  Daily Writing Prompt

- **Grammar**

  Daily Language Practice

- **Spelling**

Daily Routines
- Question of the Day
- Daily Language Practice
- Daily Writing Prompt

Day 1

Question of the Day, p. 324H
Have you ever heard the term "a gift that keeps on giving"? What do you think it means?

Literature Read-Aloud, pp. 324G–H

Comprehension:
 (Skill) Cause and Effect, p. 324I **T**
 (Strategy) Read Ahead, p. 324J

Vocabulary, p. 324L

Read: Vocabulary Power, pp. 324–325
Vocabulary Power Words:
shunned, cherished, growth, windmill, ample, furrows

 Independent Reading
Books for All Learners

SCIENCE Report on Desert Animal Adaptations

Writing: Writer's Craft, p. 347C
Writing Prompt:
One day you find some animal tracks near your home, and you decide to follow them. Think about what animal made them and where they lead. Now write a story about the day you found some animal tracks.

Grammar:
The Verb *Be*, p. 347E **T**

Daily Language Practice
1. Alejandro and his burro. Lived alone in the desert (burro lived; desert.)
2. He planted a garden, and wateried it every day. (garden and; watered)

Spelling:
Changing *y* to *i*, p. 347G **T**

Day 2

Question of the Day, p. 324H
Where would you most like to live–in a desert, in a jungle, or on top of a mountain? Why? Where would you least like to live? Why?

Think and Respond, p. 340

Comprehension:
 (Skill) Cause and Effect, pp. 326–341 **T**

Decoding/Phonics:
Word Structure: Root Word + Inflection, p. 347A

Reading the Selection, pp. 326–341
Vocabulary Power Words

 Independent Reading
Books for All Learners

SOCIAL STUDIES Compare Desert Environments

Writing: Writer's Craft, p. 347C
 Writing Prompt:
What advice would you give to a friend who feels lonely? Think about what a lonely person could do to feel less lonely. Now write a paragraph that gives your suggestions.

Grammar:
Extend the Concept, p. 347E **T**

Daily Language Practice
1. all kinds of animals appeared near the garden? (All; garden.)
2. They was thirsty and wanted the water in the puddles (were; puddles.)

Spelling:
Word Sort, p. 347G **T**

Focus Skill

Cause and Effect

Objectives of the Week:
- To recognize cause and effect relationships
- To read and understand a realistic fiction selection; to read and understand a nonfiction article
- To use the verb *be* correctly
- To use vivid verbs and specific nouns to write a thank-you letter

Day 3

Question of the Day, p. 324H
If you found a 1,200-year-old seed like the one in "Seeds Can Sleep," where do you think would be the best place to plant it? Why?

Oral Grammar, p. 347F

Comprehension:
 Cause and Effect, pp. 346–347 **T**
Test Prep

Word Study:
Multiple-Meaning Words, p. 347I

Reading Across Texts
Genre: Expository Nonfiction
Rereading for Fluency, p. 339

 Independent Reading
Books for All Learners

SCIENCE Windmills
SOCIAL STUDIES What Desert Is It?

Writing: Writer's Craft, p. 347D

Writing Prompt:
Animals live everywhere, even in cities. Think about something people could do to help city animals survive. Now write about one thing people could do for animals that live in the city.

Grammar:
What Was He?, p. 347F **T**

Daily Language Practice
1. Alejandro made a watering hole for the animals but they didnt come (animals, but; didn't; come.)
2. It was to close to the house, and the animals was afraid. (too; were)

Spelling:
Spelling Rules, p. 347H **T**

Day 4

Question of the Day, p. 324H
Why would you want to paraphrase a story?

Paraphrase, p. 347B

Self-Selected Reading, p. 324F

 Independent Reading
Books for All Learners

SCIENCE The Saguaro Cactus and the Gila Woodpecker
SOCIAL STUDIES Map Making

Writing: Writer's Craft, p. 347D

Writing Prompt:
Water is necessary for survival. Think of two other things people cannot live without. Now write about three things we need to survive. (Water should be one of them.)

Grammar:
Changing Tense, p. 347F **T**

Daily Language Practice
1. Alejandro digged another holes and put plants around it. (dug; hole)
2. He waited soon the animals came again to drink. (waited. Soon OR waited, and)

Spelling:
Think and Spell, Writing Headlines, p. 347H **T**

Day 5

Question of the Day, p. 324H
To irrigate (or water) their land better, farmers often have to dig ditches that split it into smaller parts. How many ditches would you have to dig across a square area of farmland to make sixteen smaller squares of equal size?

Listening and Speaking
Oral Presentation, p. 347J

Comprehension:
 Cause and Effect, pp. 347K–M **T**

Word Study:
Analogies, p. 347I

Self-Selected Reading, pp. 343, T101

 Independent Reading
Books for All Learners

SOCIAL STUDIES Give an Oral Presentation

Writing: Writer's Craft, p. 347D

Writing Prompt:
You are lost in the desert, but you make it home safely with the help of a kind desert creature. Write a story about the day an animal helped you find your way home.

Grammar:
Irregular Verb Roundup, p. 347F **T**

Daily Language Practice
1. Alejandro gived the animals a usefull gift. (gave; useful)
2. He was'nt lonly anymore. (wasn't; lonely)

Spelling:
Posttest, p. 347H **T**

Cross-Curricular Stations

40 Minutes

Materials

- nature magazines, science textbook, or encyclopedia
- paper
- pencils
- poster board

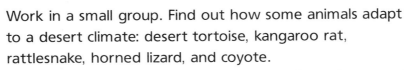
SCIENCE

Report on Desert Animal Adaptations

OBJECTIVE: To research and report on adaptations made by desert animals

Work in a small group. Find out how some animals adapt to a desert climate: desert tortoise, kangaroo rat, rattlesnake, horned lizard, and coyote.

- Look up each animal in a nature magazine, science textbook, or encyclopedia.
- Make a poster. Draw three desert animals, and write a caption which explains how the animal adapts to the desert.

 Use a computer to make captions for your poster.

30 Minutes

Materials

- encyclopedia or CD-ROM encyclopedia
- atlas
- paper
- pencils

SOCIAL STUDIES

Compare Desert Environments

OBJECTIVE: To compare and contrast the world's desert environments

Deserts exist in many countries, but no two deserts are the same. Each one has its own climate, terrain, and plant and animal life. The many deserts of the world include the Sahara, Gobi, Mojave, Australian, and Patagonian.

- Use an atlas to locate each desert and discover what countries it spans. Next, look up each desert in an encyclopedia. Find out its average rainfall, what animals and plants live there, and what the characteristics of the land are.
- Make a three-column chart. List the desert name in the left column, the desert location in the middle column, and all of the information you've gathered about the desert in the right column.

 Use a CD-ROM encyclopedia to learn about the world's deserts.

LIBRARY CENTER

Self-Selected Reading

OBJECTIVE: To independently select and read books

Look for these books about life in a desert:

- *Baby Rattlesnake* by Te Ata. Children's Press, 1989. FOLKTALE
- *Desert Voices* by Byrd Baylor. Scribner's, 1981. FICTION
- *Deserts* by Neil Morris. Raintree Steck-Vaughn, 1997. NONFICTION

Remember to

- keep track of what you read each day on your Reading Log.

20 Minutes a day

Materials

- self-selected book
- *My Reading Log* copying master, p. R42

INQUIRY PROJECT

Extending the Selection

OBJECTIVE: To select a focus for an inquiry project

Use "Alejandro's Gift" to think about related topics. Organize your ideas in a web. You can also look for ideas in these books:

- *The Burro's Land*
- *A Circle Story*
- *Liberty*
- *In the Garden*

30 Minutes

Materials

- research materials
- paper
- pencils

TECHNOLOGY

Information Search

OBJECTIVE: To use technology resources to research desert irrigation

Use the Internet or a CD-ROM encyclopedia to discover how water is brought and used in desert environments. Work with a partner.

Remember to

- explain the characteristics of desert climates.
- use the rules for Internet safety.

60 Minutes

Materials

- computer with Internet access or CD-ROM encyclopedia
- paper
- pencils

Read Aloud

Home Ranges
by Jim Arnosky

INTRODUCTION

Jim Arnosky likes to carry a small notebook with him as he wanders the woods and fields. He believes that everything we know about wildlife was discovered by watching. He wrote about his experience with wild animals in his book, *Secrets of a Wildlife Watcher: A Beginner's Field Guide.* In this excerpt, Arnosky describes the ranges that animals call home.

EXCERPT

Whenever you see a wild animal, the chances are that you are in its home range. Animals are creatures of habit. They travel the same paths again and again. They know all the feeding areas, water sources, sleeping spots, and hiding places.

Many animals live out their entire lives in a very small area. A woodchuck rarely ventures more than two hundred feet from its burrow. A cottontail's whole world need be only a few acres. White-tailed deer are born, live, and die in an area of one square mile.

Different animals can have overlapping ranges. On one short hike in a wrinkle of a mountain, I found fresh tracks of fox, coyote, weasel, bobcat, and bear. All are predators. They are natural enemies, competing for available food. I'm sure they avoided meeting one another, but their tracks crossed, paralleled, and often followed the same trails.

- **What is the main purpose of this passage?** (Possible response: to tell about the home ranges of wild animals) AUTHOR'S PURPOSE

- **How did Jim Arnosky learn about wild animals?** (Possible response: He went out and observed them in their natural environment.) CAUSE/EFFECT

- **In what ways are people similar to animals? In what ways are they different?** (Possible response: People have home ranges, too. Most sleep in the same bed night after night and travel the same roads to school or to work. But people can also travel farther in cars and planes than most animals.) COMPARE AND CONTRAST

- **Describe your "home range."** (Responses will vary.) EXPRESS PERSONAL OPINIONS

Question of the Day

DEVELOP ORAL LANGUAGE

- Display the first question on Transparency 243, or write it on the board. Ask a volunteer to read it aloud.

- **Response Journal** Explain to students that they should think about the question throughout the day and write their responses in their journals. Tell students to be prepared to discuss the answer or answers to it by the end of the day or at another time you choose.

- You may want to repeat this process daily for each of the five discussion questions.

▼ **Teaching Transparency 243**

QUESTION OF THE DAY

DAY 1: Have you ever heard the term "a gift that keeps on giving"? What do you think it means? Possible response: It means that some gifts can continue to make people happy long after they are given.

DAY 2: Where would you most like to live—in a desert, in a jungle, or on top of a mountain? Why? Where would you least like to live? Why? Responses will vary.

Day 3: If you found a 1,200-year-old seed like the one in "Seeds Can Sleep," where do you think would be the best place to plant it? Why? Possible response: A greenhouse; it provides a controlled amount of sunlight, and the seed can be watered regularly.

DAY 4: Why would you want to paraphrase a story? Possible responses: to show that you understand it; to tell someone else about it without giving away the best parts

DAY 5: To irrigate (or water) their land better, farmers often have to dig ditches that split it into smaller parts. How many ditches would you have to dig across a square area of farmland to make sixteen smaller squares of equal size? six

"Alejandro's Gift"
Celebrate Our World, Theme 3   **243**   Question of the Day
Harcourt

OBJECTIVE

To recognize cause and effect relationships

SKILL TRACE

CAUSE AND EFFECT	
Introduce	p. 324I
Reteach	pp. S74, S86, T71
Review	pp. 346, 369D, 370I, 398
Test	Theme 3 Vol. 2

▼ **Teaching Transparency 244**

CAUSE AND EFFECT

- A **cause** is something that makes something happen.
- An **effect** is what happens.
- Authors often use signal words, such as *because* or *as a result of*, to show a cause-effect relationship.
- Sometimes you need to figure out causes and effects on your own.

EXAMPLES:

CAUSE ⟶	EFFECT
The temperature dropped below freezing.	Ice formed on the pond.
Winter began.	Bears began to hibernate.
Our dog smelled a fox.	Our dog barked and barked.

Last week the wind blew so hard that it pushed over a tall tree in our yard. It was an old oak tree that had been in that spot for 150 years. Because it fell, some birds that had started a nest in the tree had to find a new place to build a home.

"Alejandro's Gift"
Celebrate Our World, Theme 3   **244**   Focus Skill
Harcourt

BELOW-LEVEL

Additional Support
- *Intervention Teacher's Guide*, p. 270

ENGLISH-LANGUAGE LEARNERS

Additional Support
- *English-Language Learners Teacher's Guide*, p. 159

⭐ Focus Skill · Cause and Effect

INTRODUCE THE SKILL

Access prior knowledge. Recall with students how the young girl in "I'm in Charge of Celebrations" was inspired by nature. Ask them to name some events that caused her to celebrate. (Possible responses: whirlwinds; a rainbow; a coyote; the arrival of spring)

TEACH/MODEL

Explain to students that a *cause* is an event that makes something happen, and an *effect* is what happens as a result of the cause. Tell them that understanding cause-effect relationships can help them know *why* and *how* things happen. Display Transparency 244.

- **Call on a volunteer to read aloud the first two bulleted items.**

- **Point out that several word phrases can signal a cause-effect relationship.**

- **Read the examples in the box. Emphasize how each cause leads to an effect.**

- **Read the paragraph aloud to students, and have them identify the *cause* and the *effect*. Also have them identify the signal word (*because*).**

PRACTICE/APPLY

Students can use a cause-effect chart like this to record the causes and effects of events in "Alejandro's Gift."

Cause-Effect Chart	
Cause	Effect

For opportunities to apply and reinforce the skill, see the following pages:

During reading: pages 328, 330, 336, and 342
After reading: *Pupil Edition* pages 346–347

Focus Strategy **Read Ahead**

INTRODUCE THE STRATEGY

Explain to students that the next selection is realistic fiction. Ask them what other realistic fiction stories they have read. Discuss what happens when a reader "gets stuck" while reading a story. Ask students how **reading ahead** may be helpful.

TEACH/MODEL

Remind students that good readers use strategies to solve problems as they read. If students become confused by something in a story, the Read Ahead strategy can sometimes help clear up the confusion.

Use the example paragraph on Transparency 244 to model the strategy.

> **MODEL** When I read the first sentence, I didn't understand the effects caused by the fallen tree. So, I decided to read ahead. Two sentences later, I saw the signal word *because*, and I understood—birds that had started a nest in the tree had to find a new place to live.

SKILL ⟷ STRATEGY CONNECTION

Tell students that **reading ahead** will help them understand **causes and effects** in the next story.

PRACTICE/APPLY

For opportunities to apply and reinforce the strategy **during reading**, see pages 333, 335, and 337.

Strategies Good Readers Use

- Use Decoding/Phonics
- Make and Confirm Predictions
- Create Mental Images
- Self-Question
- Summarize
- **Read Ahead** Focus Strategy
- Reread to Clarify
- Use Context to Confirm Meaning
- Use Text Structure and Format
- Adjust Reading Rate

Building Background

ACCESS PRIOR KNOWLEDGE

Ask students what they think it would be like to live in a desert. Ask: **What do people do in the desert for fun? What would your life be like?** Help students explore these ideas and develop a web like the one below.

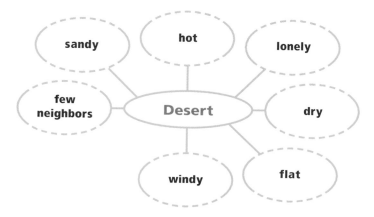

 technology

Visit *The Learning Site:*
www.harcourtschool.com
See Building Background.

DEVELOP CONCEPTS

Help students further develop the story concepts by asking questions such as these:

- **What might be good about life in the desert?** (few people, beautiful plants, warm to hot weather)

- **What might you dislike about living in the desert?** (hot, dry, dusty)

- **How might desert animals react to humans?** (fearful, curious)

- **What would you like to find out about living in a desert?** (Responses will vary.)

REACHING ALL LEARNERS

Diagnostic Check: Vocabulary

If . . . students have not mastered at least 5 of the 6 vocabulary words,

Then . . . have them use the glossary or a dictionary to find synonyms for the words to help reinforce the meanings.

ADDITIONAL SUPPORT ACTIVITIES

BELOW-LEVEL	Reteach, p. S72
ADVANCED	Extend, p. S73
ENGLISH-LANGUAGE LEARNERS	Reteach, p. S73

Vocabulary

Vocabulary

shunned stayed away from

cherished cared about deeply

growth plant life growing in a certain area

windmill a machine that uses the wind to generate power

ample more than enough

furrows long, deep grooves dug into soil

TEACH VOCABULARY STRATEGIES

Use sentence and word context. Display Transparency 245, and have volunteers read the paragraphs aloud. Remind students that they can often figure out the meaning of new words by using sentence and word context. Model using this strategy to determine the meaning of the word *shunned*.

MODEL At first I'm not sure what *shunned* means. In the next sentence I learn that Grandma didn't like crowds and noise. A city is a crowded, noisy place. *Shunned* must mean "to stay away from." When Grandma *shunned* the city, she stayed away from it.

Have students read the paragraphs silently. Discuss the meaning of each vocabulary word. Then ask volunteers to point out the words and phrases surrounding each word that give clues to its meaning.

Remind students to use context clues to help them figure out the meanings of unfamiliar words when they read. They can confirm meanings by checking the glossary.

▼ **Teaching Transparency 245**

VOCABULARY IN CONTEXT

Grandma's Desert Home

Grandma told me that even as a young woman she **shunned** the city. She never liked the crowds and always **cherished** quiet times. That's why she moved to the desert. The first time I visited her there, I was surprised. From the road, you could not see her house. It was hidden by tall grasses and other desert **growth**. I had not expected to see so many plants in the desert.

When Grandma and I walked behind her house, I saw a giant **windmill**. Its wooden arms were spinning slowly in the breeze. Grandma explained that as it spins, the windmill pumps water from her well. She has **ample** water for drinking and bathing. There's even enough for watering the vegetables that she has planted in **furrows** in the soil.

"Alejandro's Gift"
Celebrate Our World, Theme 3

245

Vocabulary
Harcourt

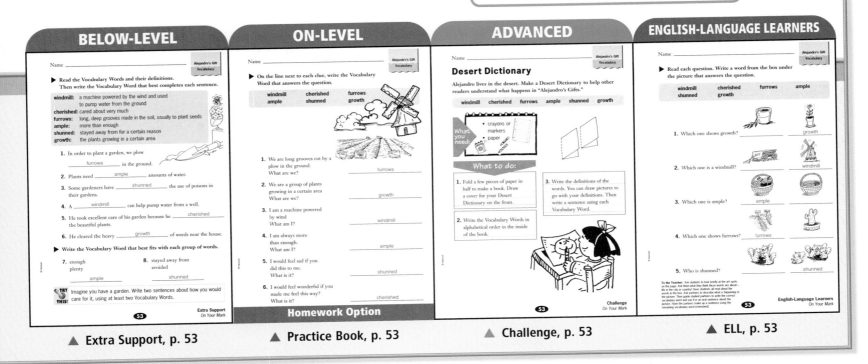

▲ Extra Support, p. 53   ▲ Practice Book, p. 53   ▲ Challenge, p. 53   ▲ ELL, p. 53

Vocabulary Power

APPLY STRATEGIES

Ask a volunteer to read aloud the first paragraph on page 324. Then have students silently read the remaining text. Remind them to apply the strategy of sentence and word context to figure out the meanings of unfamiliar words.

EXTEND WORD KNOWLEDGE

Practice other vocabulary strategies.

Have students answer the following questions with sentences that show the meanings of the Vocabulary Words. MEANINGFUL SENTENCES

- What kinds of *growth* might you find in a park? DESCRIPTION

- What objects might be *cherished* by the older members of your family? EXAMPLE

- Do farmers worry that their crops will dry up when there is *ample* rain? PRIOR KNOWLEDGE

- How could a *windmill* help a farmer? EXPLANATION

- What do *furrows* look like? DESCRIPTION

- What word means the opposite of "welcomed"? ANTONYM

▲ Alejandro's Gift

| growth |
| furrows |
| shunned |
| ample |
| windmill |
| cherished |

324

Vocabulary Power

In the next selection, you will read about Alejandro. He grows many kinds of vegetables in his garden. It takes hard work to grow crops, whether in a small garden or on a large farm.

FARMING

Before farmers can plant crops, they must prepare the soil. First, they clear away any weeds, bushes, and other plant **growth**. Then they plow the soil to loosen it. The farmer in this tractor is using a plow to make long, deep grooves called **furrows**. He will plant the seeds for his crop in the furrows.
Then he will cover the seeds with soil.

Farmers may spray or dust their crops with insect poisons. In recent years, some have **shunned** these sprays. They stay away from anything that may harm birds and other wildlife.

Crops can't grow without water. When there is **ample** rainfall, there is more than enough water to meet farmers' needs. When there is little rain, farmers need to get water in other ways. This **windmill** pumps water from the ground. It gets its power from the wind.

A farmer who has **cherished** his crop will usually have a good harvest. He will have worked hard because he cares deeply about the crop.

Vocabulary-Writing CONNECTION

What kinds of things have people **cherished** over the years? Write a paragraph that describes these things. Tell why you think people care about them.

325

QUICKWRITE

VOCABULARY-WRITING CONNECTION

Before they begin to write, encourage students to discuss the things they cherish most in their own lives and why they value them. Students should add the Vocabulary Power words to their Word Banks to use in future writing assignments.

Prereading Strategies

PREVIEW AND PREDICT

Have students read the **genre** information on page 326. Then have them preview the selection. Ask them what they think this selection is about, based on their preview and the characteristics of realistic fiction. Then have them record predictions about what might happen to Alejandro in the story. They can begin a chart to list the causes and effects of story events. See Transparency F on page T87.

Cause-Effect Chart	
Cause	Effect
Life in the desert was lonely.	Alejandro loved visits.

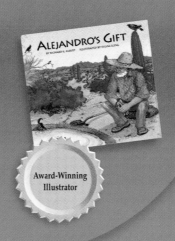

Award-Winning Illustrator

Genre

Realistic Fiction

Realistic fiction tells about characters and events that are like people and events in real life.

In this selection, look for

- **a main character who solves a problem.**
- **descriptive language that helps readers picture the setting.**

326

BY RICHARD E. ALBERT
ILLUSTRATED BY SYLVIA LONG

BELOW-LEVEL	**ON-LEVEL**	**ADVANCED**	**ENGLISH-LANGUAGE LEARNERS**
Preview the selection with students. Discuss the meanings of these words: *evening, garden, heat, thirsty, visitors,* and *water.* Help students set a purpose for reading through page 333. **SMALL GROUP**	Students can read the selection with a partner. Use the Guided Comprehension questions and Ongoing Assessments to help you assess students' understanding. **PARTNER**	Students reading on or above level can read the entire story silently. They can then discuss the Think and Respond questions on page 340 with another student who has also read independently. **INDEPENDENT/READER**	Read aloud the selection, or have students listen to it on *Audiotext* 6. Then have students read aloud selected pages as a group to develop oral fluency. **SMALL GROUP**

BELOW-LEVEL

ADDITIONAL SUPPORT

Intervention Reader: Bright Surprises Intervention Teacher's Guide, pp. 270–273

ENGLISH-LANGUAGE LEARNERS

ADDITIONAL SUPPORT

See *English-Language Learners Resource Kit,* Lesson 27. *English-Language Learners Teacher's Guide,* pp. 159–160

ALEJANDRO'S GIFT

327

SET PURPOSE

Read to understand. Tell students that one purpose for reading is to understand. Ask students to set their own purposes. Offer this suggestion:

MODEL I'll read to understand how Alejandro manages to live in a desert and what the "gift" is.

Focus Strategy **Read Ahead** Point out that using this strategy will help students understand this realistic story.

 "Alejandro's Gift" and "Seeds Can Sleep" are available on *Audiotext 6.*

COMPREHENSION CARD 27

Theme Have students use Comprehension Card 27 to discuss **Theme** in "Alejandro's Gift."

▶ Theme COMPREHENSION CARD 27

During Reading
1. From what you have read so far, what do you think the story is mostly about?
2. What point is the author trying to make? Why do you think that?
3. What do you remember most about the story so far?

Comprehension Card 27,
Page T82 ▶

Guided Comprehension

1 **NOTE LITERAL DETAILS** **What is Alejandro's home like?** (Possible response: He lives in a small adobe house in the desert by a road. It is hot and lonely. He has a garden where he grows vegetables. He has a windmill, a well, and a burro.)

2 (Focus Skill) **CAUSE-EFFECT** **Why does Alejandro plant a garden?** (Possible response: Working in the garden helped him feel less lonely.)

3 **MAKE PREDICTIONS** **Who do you think a visitor "from the desert itself" might be?** (Possible response: a wild animal)

Alejandro's small adobe house stood beside a lonely desert road.

Beside the house stood a well, and a windmill to pump water from the well. Water for Alejandro and for his only companion, a burro. **1**

It was a lonely place, and Alejandro welcomed any who stopped by to refresh themselves at the well. But visitors were few, and after they left, Alejandro felt lonelier than before.

ENGLISH-LANGUAGE LEARNERS

Point out and explain the words *companion* (p. 328), *refresh* (p. 328), and *endure* (p. 329). Use the following sentences:

- A *companion* is a friend.
- To *refresh* oneself is to pause for water, food, or rest. A thirsty person often feels refreshed after drinking water.
- If you *endure* something, you put up with it even if it is hard.

Visit *The Learning Site:*
www.harcourtschool.com
See Language Support.

To more easily endure the lonely hours, Alejandro planted a garden. A garden filled with carrots, beans, and large brown onions. **2**

Tomatoes and corn.

Melons, squash, and small red peppers.

Most mornings found Alejandro tending the garden, watching it grow. These were times he cherished, and he often stayed for hours, working until driven indoors by the desert heat.

The days went by, one after another with little change, until one morning when there was an unexpected visitor. This visitor came not from the desert road, but from the desert itself. **3**

329

ONGOING ASSESSMENT

Monitor Progress

Create Mental Images

How do you think Alejandro's face looked as he worked in his garden? (Possible responses: excited, happy, serious, content)

If students were unable to answer, use this model:

MODEL **I try to picture Alejandro's face as he works. The story tells me that the garden was very important to him and that he loved working there. Alejandro's face probably looked both serious and happy as he worked.**

SCIENCE

Windmills   Explain to students that windmills are tall structures that harness the wind as an energy source.

1. The wind turns arms or blades at the top of the windmill.

2. The arms turn a horizontal bar.

3. The spinning bar turns a vertical shaft.

4. The vertical shaft powers a water pump, a flour mill, or an electric generator at the windmill base.

Have students draw a windmill pumping water from a well. Label the following: *wind, arms, horizontal bar, vertical shaft, water pump.*

Guided Comprehension

4 (Focus Skill) **CAUSE-EFFECT** What causes the ground squirrel to visit Alejandro's garden? (It is thirsty.)

5 **IDENTIFY CHARACTERS' EMOTIONS** How does Alejandro feel after seeing the squirrel? (less lonely)

6 **SPECULATE** What small friends does the squirrel bring? What other animals might come? (Possible response: It brings other small animals such as wood rats, gophers, and rabbits; birds or larger animals might also visit.)

A ground squirrel crept from the underbrush. Moving warily over the sand, it hesitated and looked around. Alejandro paused, keeping very quiet as the squirrel approached the garden. It ran up to one of the furrows, drank its fill of water, and scampered away. After it left, Alejandro realized that for those few moments his loneliness had been all but forgotten.

330

REACHING ALL LEARNERS

Diagnostic Check: Comprehension and Skills

If . . . students are having difficulty understanding a character's motivation, . . .

Then . . . ask them to write a series of "why" questions about the character's actions. Have students put the questions and answers together into cause-effect statements.

ADDITIONAL SUPPORT ACTIVITIES

BELOW-LEVEL Reteach, p. S74

ADVANCED Extend, p. S75

ENGLISH-LANGUAGE LEARNERS Reteach, p. S75

And because he felt less lonely, Alejandro found himself hoping the squirrel would come again.

The squirrel did come again, from time to time bringing along small friends.

Wood rats and pocket gophers.

Jackrabbits, kangaroo rats, pocket mice.

331

ONGOING ASSESSMENT

Monitor Progress

Use Context to Confirm Meaning

What does the word *warily* mean in the second sentence on page 330? (carefully)

If students were unable to answer, use this model:

MODEL The beginning of the sentence tells me that the squirrel moved *warily*. The second part says that the squirrel *hesitated* and *looked around*. These clues tell me that *warily* must mean "carefully."

LITERARY ANALYSIS

MOOD   Explain to students that the **mood** of a story is what an author wants readers to feel. Point out the words *loneliness* and *lonely* on pages 330 and 331. Ask students what they think the mood of "Alejandro's Gift" is so far. (sad) Explain that the mood of a story can change. Ask students to think about the kinds of words the author might use to signal a change in mood. (pleased, hopeful) As they read, they should look for words that show that the mood of the story may be changing.

Alejandro's Gift   **331**

Guided Comprehension

7 **PROBLEM SOLVING**   **Why is time passing more quickly for Alejandro?** (Possible response: because he is spending time watching the desert animals that come to his garden)

8 **MAKE PREDICTIONS**   **Has the story described the kind of desert life you predicted?** (Responses will vary.) **What do you predict will happen next?** (Possible response: Alejandro might do something to keep his animal friends around.)

332

BELOW-LEVEL

Work with students to summarize what they have read so far.

- Alejandro lives a lonely life in the desert.
- He plants a garden.
- Desert animals begin to visit Alejandro's garden and drink water from the furrows.
- Alejandro becomes less lonely.

Have students set a purpose for reading through page 339.

Birds, too, became aware of Alejandro's garden. Roadrunners, gila woodpeckers, thrashers.

Cactus wrens, sage sparrows, mourning doves, and others came in the evening to perch on the branches of a mesquite bush, or to rest on the arms of a lone saguaro, before dropping down for a quick drink before nightfall.

Occasionally, even an old desert tortoise could be seen plodding toward the garden.

Suddenly, Alejandro found that time was passing more quickly. He was rarely lonely. He had only to look up from his hoe, or from wherever he might be at any moment, to find a small friend nearby. **7**

For a while this was all that mattered to Alejandro, but after a time he wasn't so sure. He began asking himself if there was something more important than just making himself less lonely. It took Alejandro little time to see there was. **8**

ONGOING ASSESSMENT

Monitor Progress

(Focus Strategy) **Read Ahead**

How could you find out what is more important to Alejandro than making himself less lonely? (I could try reading ahead to see if the story explains this.)

If students are unable to answer, provide this model:

MODEL I can't find the answer to this question unless I read ahead to the next page. Alejandro sees that animals visit his garden because they are thirsty, so he decides to give them water. Taking care of the animals is more important to Alejandro than being less lonely.

SOCIAL STUDIES

What Desert Is It? The plants and animals in "Alejandro's Gift" are found in a specific desert environment. Have students look up the following animals and plants in an encyclopedia, and list the place(s) where each is found.

Animals: coyote, jackrabbit, kangaroo rat, roadrunner, cactus wren, peccary, long-nosed coati

Plants: mesquite bush, saguaro cactus

Ask students to compare findings in a chart that lists animal and plant names and their habitats. Then ask students to name the desert environment in which the story is set. (the Sonoran Desert of southwestern North America)

Guided Comprehension

9 **SPECULATE** Why do you think the larger desert animals don't visit Alejandro's garden as the smaller animals do? (Possible response: They are more fearful of danger.)

10 **NOTE DETAILS** Why does Alejandro have plenty of water? (His windmill and well work together to provide water for his garden.)

He began to realize that his tiny desert friends came to his garden not for company, but for water. And he found himself thinking of the other animals in the desert.

Animals like the coyote and the desert gray fox.

The bobcats, the skunks, the badgers, the long-nosed coatis.

The peccaries, sometimes called *javelinas*, the short-tempered wild pigs of the desert.

The antlered mule deer, the does, and the fawns. **9**

Finding enough water was not a problem. With his windmill and well, Alejandro could supply ample water for any and all. **10** Getting it to those who needed it was something else.

334

ADVANCED

Use photographs from a nature magazine or encyclopedia to show that the illustrations of the bobcat, badgers, desert gray fox, and peccaries on pages 334–335 are accurate. Explain to students that long ago many nature illustrators were also scientists. Before the camera was invented, drawings were the only way some people could see many natural wonders. Sylvia Long's desert animal drawings in "Alejandro's Gift" are examples of this realistic style.

334 Celebrate Our World

335

ONGOING ASSESSMENT

Monitor Progress

Focus Strategy **Read Ahead**

How could you find out how Alejandro will get water to the animals who need it? (Try reading ahead; maybe the answer is on the next page.)

Ask volunteers to model how they would read ahead to discover Alejandro's solution.

If students have difficulty, provide this model:

MODEL I am not sure how Alejandro will get water to the animals. When I read ahead to the next page, I find out: Alejandro decides to dig a water hole for the animals.

SCIENCE

The Saguaro Cactus and the Gila Woodpecker The saguaro cactus and the gila woodpecker have a unique living arrangement— they rely on each other to survive. The large cacti provide food and shelter for the woodpeckers, and the birds do their part for the cactus by eating harmful insects, spreading cactus seeds, and helping pollinate flowers. Because of the gila wood-pecker's help, the giant saguaro cactus is the center of life for hundreds of desert animals. Students may want to research how other desert animals affect their environment.

Guided Comprehension

11 (Focus Skill) **CAUSE-EFFECT** Why does Alejandro go through the tiring work of digging a water hole? (Possible response: Helping his thirsty desert friends is all that matters to him.)

12 **TEXT STRUCTURE** Where on these pages can you find information to help you fill out your cause/effect chart? (Possible responses: The last word on page 336 is the signal word *so*, which identifies a cause-effect relationship; paragraphs 3 and 4 on page 337 tell me why the skunk avoided Alejandro's water hole.)

The something else, Alejandro decided, was a desert water hole.

Without delay, Alejandro started digging. It was tiring work, taking many days in the hot desert sun. But the thought of giving water to so many thirsty desert dwellers more than made up for the drudgery. And when it was filled, Alejandro was pleased with the gift he had made for his desert friends. **11**

There was good reason to suppose it would take time for the larger animals to discover their new source of water, so

336

REACHING ALL LEARNERS

Diagnostic Check: Comprehension and Skills

If . . . students are having difficulty understanding cause-effect relationships,

Then . . . have them work in pairs. Pairs should write simple cause-effect statements, such as "I overslept, so I missed the bus and was late for school."

ADDITIONAL SUPPORT ACTIVITIES

BELOW-LEVEL	Reteach, p. S74
ADVANCED	Extend, p. S75
ENGLISH-LANGUAGE LEARNERS	Reteach, p. S75

Alejandro was patient. He went about as usual, feeding his burro, tending the garden, and doing countless other chores.

Days passed and nothing happened. Still, Alejandro was confident. But the days turned to weeks, and it was still quiet at the water hole. Why, Alejandro wondered, weren't they coming? What could he have done wrong?

The absence of the desert folk might have remained a mystery had Alejandro not come out of the house one morning when a skunk was in the clearing beyond the water hole. Seeing Alejandro, the skunk darted to safety in the underbrush.

It suddenly became very clear why Alejandro's gift was being shunned.

Alejandro couldn't believe he had been so thoughtless, but what was important now was to put things right as quickly as possible.

ONGOING ASSESSMENT

Monitor Progress

(Focus Strategy) **Read Ahead**

What could you do to find out how Alejandro will "put things right"? (Read ahead. The next part of the story probably explains what he does.)

If students are unable to answer, ask: How could you find an answer to this question? If necessary, use this model:

MODEL **I am not sure how Alejandro will get animals to come to his water hole. I find out when I read ahead to the first sentence on the next page: Alejandro decides to dig a second water hole, one that is far from his house and hidden by desert growth.**

SOCIAL STUDIES

MAP MAKING   Ask students to work in pairs to draw a map of Alejandro's property, using clues from the illustrations on pages 328, 336, and 339 to help them. Explain that an aerial map shows what an area looks like from above. Remind students that the second water hole is far from the house—Alejandro can't even see it. After they have completed their maps, ask students to add the following labels: *road, house, stable, garden, windmill, water pump, water hole 1*, and *water hole 2.*

Guided Comprehension

13 INTERPRET STORY EVENTS Why do the animals come to the second water hole? (Possible response: It is far from Alejandro's house, and they feel safe.)

14 NOTE DETAILS   How does Alejandro know that the animals come to his second water hole? (Possible response: He hears singing birds, rustling bushes, and soft hoofbeats.)

15 IDENTIFY CHARACTERS' EMOTIONS   How do you think Alejandro feels when the larger animals finally come? Why? (Possible response: He is happy because he worked hard in the desert heat to dig the holes and give the animals water.)

Water hole number two was built far from the house and screened by heavy desert growth. When it was filled and ready, Alejandro waited with mixed emotions. He was hopeful, yet he couldn't forget what had happened the first time.

As it turned out, he was not disappointed.

The animals of the desert did come, each as it made its own discovery. Because the water hole was now sheltered from the small adobe house and the desert road, the animals were no longer fearful. And although Alejandro could not see through

338

 BELOW-LEVEL

Help students to understand the reasons why Alejandro digs the second water hole and some of the effects that resulted from its creation. Use the following sentences:

Causes:

Alejandro wanted to give water to the desert animals.

The first water hole was built too close to the house.

Alejandro built a second water hole.

Effects:

Desert animals could get as much water as they wanted.

Alejandro was happy and felt less lonely.

Invite students to predict how the story will end.

the desert growth surrounding the water hole, he had ways of knowing it was no longer being shunned.

By the twitter of birds gathering in the dusk.

By the rustling of mesquite in the quiet desert evening telling of the approach of a coyote, a badger, or maybe a desert fox.

By the soft hoofbeats of a mule deer, or the unmistakable sound of a herd of peccaries charging toward the water hole. **14** **15**

Monitor Progress

Use Decoding/ Phonics

Have students reading below level read aloud the last sentence on page 339. Listen for the pronunciation of the word *unmistakable*. If students do not pronounce it correctly, model the strategy:

MODEL This word is made up of the prefix *un-*, meaning "not," and the suffix *-able*, meaning "can be." I see that the root word is *mistake*, which means "get wrong." When I combine the prefix and suffix with the root word, I can sound out the whole word, *unmistakable*—"cannot be wrong." That makes sense.

REREADING FOR FLUENCY

Partner Reading Assign partners to read aloud passages from "Alejandro's Gift." While one partner reads, the other should listen critically so that he or she can provide feedback. Partners should then reverse roles. Remind students to pay attention to punctuation and to read with appropriate volume, rate, and expression.

For support, see Fluency Routine Cards in Theme Resources, pp. T80a–T80b.

Note: For assessment of oral reading accuracy and fluency, see pages T78–T80.

Guided Comprehension

RETURN TO THE PREDICTIONS/PURPOSE

Were you able to understand what life was like for Alejandro in the desert? Discuss with students whether their purposes for reading were met.

Think and Respond

Answers:

1 Possible response: Alejandro's gift to the animals is water. The animals make him feel less lonely. **SUMMARIZE**

2 Possible responses: kind, caring, patient; He cares about the animals. He figured out what was wrong and dug a second water hole. **CRITICAL THINKING**

3 Possible response: It was too close to Alejandro's house and to the road. The animals did not feel safe. **LITERARY ANALYSIS/TEXT STRUCTURE**

4 Possible response: Yes; I would enjoy watching the animals and learning more about the desert. **PERSONAL RESPONSE**

5 Accept reasonable responses. **READING STRATEGY**

OPEN-ENDED RESPONSE
Write a letter to Alejandro from one of the larger animals in the story. Explain why the second water hole is better, and tell him how his gift helps you.

And in these moments when Alejandro sat quietly listening to the sounds of his desert neighbors, he knew that the gift was not so much a gift that he had given, but a gift he had received.

THINK AND RESPOND

1 What gift does Alejandro give, and what gift does he receive?

2 What kind of person is Alejandro? How do you know?

3 Why is Alejandro's first water hole **shunned** by the animals?

4 Would you enjoy a visit to Alejandro's home? Explain your answer.

5 What strategies did you use to help you understand "Alejandro's Gift"? When did you use them?

340

COMPREHENSION

End-of-Selection Test
To evaluate comprehension, see *Practice Book* pages A45–A48.

MEET THE AUTHOR
Richard E. Albert

Richard E. Albert spent most of his life working as an engineer for a gas company. He wrote some Western stories, as well as stories for children's magazines. Then, when he was eighty-three, he wrote *Alejandro's Gift*. It was the first book he had written for children.

MEET THE ILLUSTRATOR
Sylvia Long

Drawing and horses were always on Sylvia Long's mind when she was a child. Her favorite birthday presents were crayons, paints, and pencils. She also wished for a horse on every birthday. Finally she got her own horse after she was married.

Today Sylvia Long lives in Arizona and draws pictures for magazines and picture books. She says that she feels "so lucky to be able to draw and call it work."

Visit *The Learning Site!*
www.harcourtschool.com

▲ Practice Book, page A45

▲ Practice Book, page A48

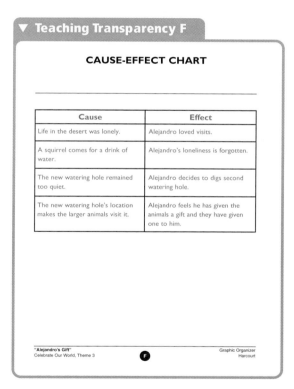
WRITTEN SUMMARY
Have students use their completed cause-effect charts to write a summary telling why Alejandro gave his gift to the desert animals. PERFORMANCE ASSESSMENT

Reading Across Texts

Genre Study Explain that students are going to read a science article called "Seeds Can Sleep." Ask what they think the article will be about. (seeds not growing for a long time)

Have students read the article silently to find out how seeds can "sleep." Then ask:

❶ (Focus Skill) **CAUSE-EFFECT** **What helped the lotus seed survive for so long?** (Possible response: The seed's hard shell protected it and held in water, and it was somehow able to repair itself.)

Think and Respond

Possible response: If scientists can learn how the lotus seed protected itself, then maybe they can find ways to protect other plants and crops.

Scientific Information Have students form small groups and read "Seeds Can Sleep" as if they were teachers instructing a class. Encourage students to focus on tone and pacing, reading the selection clearly and slowly.

Genre
Expository Nonfiction

Seeds Can Sleep
by Mary Brown

Each bump in the pod contains one fruit. A fruit is about the size and shape of a peanut, and it holds one seed.

Like animals, plants need water to live. Some plants have structures that let them live for a long time without water. The lotus is such a plant. Its seed can be kept dry for many years before it is germinated, or made to grow. In fact, one scientist in California germinated a seed that was more than 1,000 years old! This is the oldest seed ever reported to sprout.

In 1982, Dr. Jane Shen-Miller was given seven lotus fruits as a gift. The fruits had been found deep underground by scientists in Beijing, China. Because they were far beneath the earth, Dr. Shen-Miller knew that the fruits must have fallen a very long time ago.

342

So she and a team of scientists studied the seeds of the fruits to find out how old they were. The oldest seed was about 1,288 years old. The youngest was about 95 years old.

Next, Dr. Shen-Miller began the process of germination. She carefully cut a hole in the outer shell of the oldest seed. After a thousand-year sleep, the ancient seed was given air and water. It grew a little green shoot in only four days.

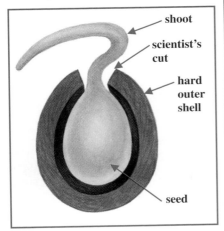

Cross-section of the lotus seed

How could a seed lie dormant, alive but not growing, for so many years? Research shows several reasons for the lotus seed's survival.

Most important was the hard shell of the seed. The shell protected the seed  from changes in the weather and from harmful bacteria. Plus, the shell held in just the right amount of water for the seed. Another reason the seed could sprout after a thousand years is that it was somehow able to repair itself. Scientists are trying to find out how.

Research on this amazing plant continues today. Scientists hope that their research will help them find ways to protect and store useful crops, such as corn and wheat. If we find a way to keep crops alive longer, how will this affect the way we share food with the rest of the world?

The mature seed pod on the right shows how the fruit are exposed.

Think and Respond

Why is the lotus seed important to scientists?

343

related books

You may want to recommend to students interested in this subject that they locate these titles.

LIBRARY BOOKS COLLECTION

Jordi's Star
by Alma Flor Ada.

ADDITIONAL READING

- *Jimmy's Boa Bounces Back*
  by Trinka Hakes Noble. Dutton, 1992. **EASY**

- *Dick King-Smith's Animal Friends: Thirty-One True Life Stories*
  by Dick King-Smith. Candlewick, 1996. **AVERAGE**

- *Deserts*
  by Neil Morris. Raintree Steck-Vaughn, 1997. **CHALLENGING**

LITERARY ANALYSIS

Scientific Terms   Point out that scientific articles often discuss information familiar only to scientists. Because of this, authors of science articles sometimes include definitions in their writing so that non-scientists can more easily understand the topic. Point out the words *germinated* (p. 342) and *dormant* (p. 343). Explain that the author immediately tells readers what these words mean. Once they have read the definitions, readers are more comfortable when they encounter the words later in the article.

Making Connections

COMPARE TEXTS

Answers:

1 Possible response: Alejandro loves the creatures of the desert around him and does his best to help them. **THEME**

2 Possible response: Birds and small animals come to drink water from the furrows in Alejandro's garden. The larger animals are more cautious and will not come out where they can be seen. **COMPARE AND CONTRAST**

3 Possible response: "Alejandro's Gift" is a story. The author's purpose is to entertain readers and create images in their minds. "Seeds Can Sleep" is a nonfiction article. The author's purpose is to inform readers about a topic. **AUTHOR'S CRAFT/LANGUAGE USE**

4 Responses will vary. **USE PRIOR KNOWLEDGE/MAKE JUDGMENTS**

5 Responses will vary. **EXPRESS PERSONAL OPINIONS**

▲ Alejandro's Gift

Making Connections

Compare Texts

1 How is "Alejandro's Gift" related to the theme Celebrate Our World?

2 How do the birds and small animals in the story behave differently from the larger animals?

3 Why does the author of "Alejandro's Gift" use more colorful language than the author of "Seeds Can Sleep"?

4 What is another realistic fiction story you have read that tells about wildlife? Which story is better at showing how people should treat wild animals? Explain your answer.

5 Which of the animals in "Alejandro's Gift" would you most like to learn more about? Tell why.

Write a Journal Entry

The first day the animals start coming to the new water hole is special for Alejandro. Think about what Alejandro would say if he wrote about it in his journal. Write to express Alejandro's thoughts and feelings.

Use a graphic organizer like this one to plan Alejandro's journal entry.

Writing CONNECTION

When and where did the events take place?	What happened?	How do I (Alejandro) feel about it?

344

Investigate Windmills

Alejandro in "Alejandro's Gift" has a windmill for pumping water from his well. Windmills have been used for hundreds of years to pump water and grind grain. Do research to find out how a windmill uses wind energy to do work. Show the results of your research in a picture or diagram with labels and captions, or by constructing a model and explaining how it works.

Science CONNECTION

Give an Oral Presentation

Alejandro planted a variety of vegetables in his desert garden. The kinds of plants that grow in a region depend on the soil and climate. How did Native Americans get food from the land long ago? What foods did they have? How did the climate and resources in the region affect the way they got their food? Research these questions, and prepare an oral presentation to share your information.

Social Studies CONNECTION

345

Making Connections

HOMEWORK FOR THE WEEK

Students and family members can work together to complete the activities on page T97. You may want to assign some or all of the activities as homework for each day of the week.

technology
Visit *The Learning Site:*
www.harcourtschool.com
See Resources for Parents and Teachers:
Homework Helper.

Teacher's Edition, p. T97 ▶

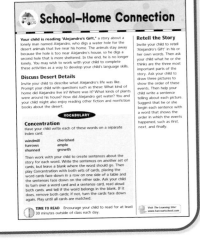

🏠 **School–Home Connection**

Your child is reading "Alejandro's Gift," a story about a lonely man named Alejandro, who digs a water hole for the desert animals that live near his home. The animals stay away because the hole is too near Alejandro's house, so he digs a second hole that is more sheltered. In the end, he is no longer lonely. You may wish to work with your child to complete these activities as a way to develop your child's language skills.

Discuss Desert Details
Invite your child to describe what Alejandro's life was like. Prompt your child with questions such as these: What kind of home did Alejandro live in? Where was it? What kinds of plants were around his house? How did Alejandro get water? You and your child might also enjoy reading other fiction and nonfiction books about the desert.

Retell the Story
Invite your child to retell "Alejandro's Gift" in his or her own words. Then ask your child what he or she thinks are the three most important parts of the story. Ask your child to draw three pictures to show the order of these events. Then help your child write a sentence telling about each picture. Suggest that he or she begin each sentence with a word that shows the order in which the events happened, such as *first, next,* and *finally.*

VOCABULARY

Concentration
Have your child write each of these words on a separate index card:

windmill   cherished
furrows   ample
shunned   growth

Then work with your child to create sentences about the story for each word. Write the sentences on another set of cards, but leave a blank where the word should go. Then play Concentration with both sets of cards, placing the word cards face down in a row on one side of a table and the sentence cards face down on the other side. Ask your child to turn over a word card and a sentence card, read aloud both cards, and tell if the word belongs in the blank. If it does, remove both cards; if not, turn the cards face down again. Play until all cards are matched.

⏱ **TIME TO READ** Encourage your child to read for at least 30 minutes outside of class each day.

Visit The Learning Site!
www.harcourtschool.com

WRITING

Write a Journal Entry Remind students to write their journal entries from the first person point of view. Elicit that this means using such words as *I, me,* and *my* to tell about Alejandro's actions and give opinions.

📁 **PORTFOLIO OPPORTUNITY**
Students may choose to place their journal entries in their working portfolios.

SCIENCE

Investigate Windmills Have different students research the different kinds of windmills and their uses. One or more students could research the history of the windmill. Then create a "windmill gallery" that shows the different types. Invite students to explain each type.

SOCIAL STUDIES

Give an Oral Presentation
Have students work in groups. Group members can divide research tasks and then collaborate on planning their presentations. Each group member should deliver part of the presentation. Remind students who use notes to project their voices and make eye contact with the audience periodically.

Cause and Effect

SKILL TRACE
CAUSE AND EFFECT

Introduce	p. 324I
Reteach	pp. S74, S86, T71
Review	**pp. 346, 369D, 370I, 398**
Test	Theme 3 Vol. 2

RETURN TO THE SKILL

Have students read page 346 in the *Pupil Edition*. You may wish to use this model with the sentence about the squirrel to determine cause and effect:

MODEL When I read this sentence, I ask myself, "What happened?" The answer is: Alejandro hoped the squirrel would come again. *Because he felt less lonely* was the cause. The word *because* helped me figure that out.

Have students explain how identifying causes and effects helped them understand "Alejandro's Gift."

PRACTICE/APPLY

Students can work in pairs to identify several cause-effect relationships between events in a selection they have read previously, such as "Leah's Pony" or "Boom Town."

PERFORMANCE ASSESSMENT

Visit *The Learning Site:*
www.harcourtschool.com
See Skill Activities and Test Tutors: Cause and Effect.

▲ Alejandro's Gift

Cause and Effect

Focus Skill

In stories, one event often leads to another. The reason an event happens is the **cause**. What happens is the **effect**. Here are some examples from "Alejandro's Gift."

Cause		Effect
Animals needed water.	→	They came to Alejandro's garden.
The water hole was too close to the house and road.	→	Animals didn't come to the water hole.

Authors often use signal words for causes and effects.

And <u>because</u> he felt less lonely, Alejandro found himself hoping the squirrel would come again.

<u>Because</u> signals that the author is telling about a cause and effect. Other signal words and phrases include <u>so that</u>, <u>since</u>, <u>as a result</u>, <u>therefore</u>, <u>for this reason</u>, <u>in order to</u>, and <u>so</u>.

Often you will need to use your own knowledge to figure out causes and effects in stories. You can also ask yourself questions. To find an effect, ask "What happened?" To find a cause, ask "Why did it happen?"

Visit *The Learning Site!*
www.harcourtschool.com
See *Skills* and *Activities*

346

Below · On-Level · Advanced · ELL

REACHING ALL LEARNERS

Diagnostic Check: Comprehension and Skills

If . . . students are having difficulty identifying cause-effect relationships,

Then . . . make a cause-effect chart starting with the first action of the plot (cause) and the outcome of that action (effect). Model the first few for them.

ADDITIONAL SUPPORT ACTIVITIES

BELOW-LEVEL	Reteach, p. S74
ADVANCED	Extend, p. S75
ENGLISH-LANGUAGE LEARNERS	Reteach, p. S75

Focus Skill

Test Prep
Cause and Effect

▶ **Read the paragraphs.**

> Betsy was lonely. She couldn't have a pet because pets were not allowed in her building. Then one day Betsy saw an advertisement in the newspaper. "If I had a bird feeder like the one in the ad," Betsy said, "then I wouldn't be lonely anymore."
>
> Betsy was right. Soon many birds began to come to her feeder. She loved to sit and watch them.

1. **What caused Betsy to be lonely?**

   A   She lived in an apartment building.

   B   She saw an advertisement in the newspaper.

   C   She could not have a pet.

   D   She wanted a bird feeder.

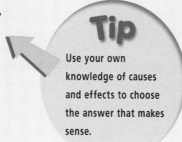

Tip

Use your own knowledge of causes and effects to choose the answer that makes sense.

2. **What was the effect of Betsy's seeing the advertisement?**

   F   She could not have a pet.

   G   She got a bird feeder.

   H   She was lonely.

   J   She lived in an apartment building.

Tip

Keep in mind that the effect happens after the cause.

347

Test Prep

Cause and Effect   Have students read the passage carefully, looking for cause-effect relationships between the events described. Use the Tips to reinforce good test-taking strategies. (I.C; 2.G)

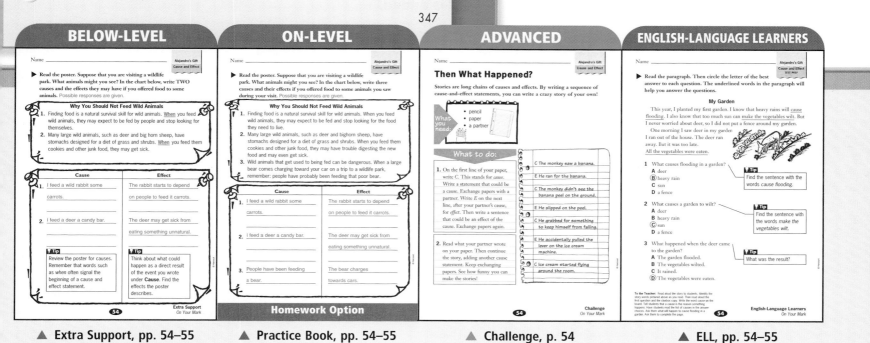

BELOW-LEVEL

▲ Extra Support, pp. 54–55

ON-LEVEL

▲ Practice Book, pp. 54–55

ADVANCED

▲ Challenge, p. 54

ENGLISH-LANGUAGE LEARNERS

▲ ELL, pp. 54–55

Phonics

OBJECTIVE

To decode and understand words with inflected endings

SKILL TRACE

**WORD STRUCTURE:
ROOT WORD + INFLECTION**

Introduce	Grade 2
Maintain	**p. 347A**

ONGOING ASSESSMENT

If students are not able to fluently read approximately 114 words per minute, **then** they require phonics instruction and will also benefit from fluency practice.

NOTE: For assessment of oral reading practice and fluency, see pages T78–T80.

Phonics Practice Book, *Intermediate*, pp. 250–264

Decoding/Phonics

Word Structure: Root Word + Inflection

REVIEW THE SKILL

Discuss inflected endings. Write this sentence on the board:

Animals perched on the branches of a mesquite bush.

Read the sentence aloud. Point to the words *animals, perched, and branches*, and ask students to identify the endings. (*-s, -ed, and -es*) Then have students read these words aloud. Review with them that recognizing endings such as *-s, -es, -ed*, and *-ing* can help them decode and understand longer words. Review these points:

- Adding *-s* and *-es* forms the plural of many words. The letter *s* is added to most words to name more than one. The letters *-es* are added to words that end in *s, x, sh*, or *ch*. If a word ends in *f* or *fe*, the *f* is often changed to *v* before *-es* is added.

- Adding *-ed* forms the past tense of many words. When *-ed* or *-ing* is added to a word that ends with *e*, the *e* is dropped before the ending is added. If a root word has a short vowel sound and ends with a single consonant, the consonant is doubled before the ending is added.

- When a base word ends in *y*, the *y* is changed to *i* before *-es* or *-ed* is added.

PRACTICE/APPLY

Decode words with inflected endings. Write these word equations on the board. Have students break each word into a root word and inflected ending.

> approached = _____ + _____
> surrounding = _____ + _____
> carried = _____ + _____
> thieves = _____ + _____

To check understanding, have students read aloud these words: *gathering* and *scampered*. **PERFORMANCE ASSESSMENT**

Paraphrase

Comprehension

REVIEW THE SKILL

Understand paraphrasing. Review with students that paraphrasing is retelling information in their own words without changing the meaning. When you paraphrase, you use about the same number of words. Have students reread page 334 in "Alejandro's Gift." Model paraphrasing the important ideas.

> **MODEL** I can restate this information in my own words this way: "Alejandro figured out that the animals came for water, not company. He worried about the animals that didn't come. He could use his windmill to get water to them."

PRACTICE/APPLY

Paraphrase information. Have students paraphrase in writing the first paragraph on *Pupil Edition* page 338. After students have prepared their paraphrases, call on volunteers to read the paragraph from page 338 aloud and then present their paraphrased versions. Encourage listeners to tell whether the same information is presented in both versions. **PERFORMANCE ASSESSMENT**

Summarize. Have a volunteer summarize what he or she knows about paraphrasing. (Possible response: Paraphrasing is retelling information in your own words. Each person does it differently.)

OBJECTIVE

To restate information presented in a text without changing the meaning

SKILL TRACE
PARAPHRASE

| Introduce | pp. 261A–B |
| Review | p. 347B |

BELOW-LEVEL

You may want to give students the following tips about paraphrasing:

- Keep the same meaning.
- Make it shorter and easier.
- Use synonyms.

Writer's Craft

Thank-You Letter

Writer's Craft: Word Choice

TRAITS OF GOOD WRITING

	INTRODUCE AND PRACTICE	APPLY TO LONGER WRITING FORMS
Focus/Ideas	329E–F (3-1)	355E–F, 387E–F (3-1)
Organization	167C–D, 193E–F (3-2)	221E–F, 261E–F (3-2)
Voice	41C–D, 67E–F (3-1)	99E–F, 129C–D (3-1)
Word Choice	**323C–D, 347C–D (3-2)**	**369E–F, 399E–F (3-2)**
Development	303E–F, 329E–F (3-1)	355E–F, 387E–F (3-1)
Effective Sentences	35E–F, 59E–F (3-2)	93E–F, 117C–D (3-2)
Effective Paragraphs	181E–F, 205E–F (3-1)	223E–F, 255C–D (3-1)
Conventions	(See Grammar and Spelling Lessons.)	(Applied to all Writing lessons.)

technology

***Writing Express™* CD-ROM**

Visit *The Learning Site:*
www.harcourtschool.com
See Writing Detective, Proofreading
Makes Perfect.

TRAITS OF GOOD WRITING

- **Focus/Ideas:** Max has a clear purpose and audience.
- **Organization/Paragraphs:** The first paragraph makes the purpose clear. The next one gives details. The last one says "thank you" again.
- **Voice:** The writing is respectful.
- **Development:** Max sticks to the topic.
- **Word Choice:** Max is writing to an adult, so he uses her title (*Ms.*) and signs "sincerely."
- **Effective Sentences:** The sentences are logically connected.

DAY 1 — TEACH/MODEL

CONNECT READING TO WRITING
Ask students what people could do if they wanted to thank Alejandro for letting them drink water from his well. (Possible response: write him a thank-you letter) Explain that in this lesson, students will write a thank-you letter.

WORD CHOICE Display Transparency 246, and analyze the model with students. Point out to students that when they write a letter to an adult they do not know well, they need to include a title such as *Ms.* Discuss the appropriateness of different ways of closing a letter, such as *Love, Your friend,* or *Sincerely.*

▼ **Teaching Transparency 246**

STUDENT MODEL: THANK-YOU LETTER

A thank-you letter is one kind of friendly letter. It thanks a person for giving a gift or doing something. Here is a thank-you letter that a student wrote to Sylvia Long, the illustrator of "Alejandro's Gift."

Heading (address and date)
123 Desert Lane
Anytown, AZ 44556
February 26, 20—

Greeting *Dear Ms. Long,*

Our class just read "Alejandro's Gift." Thank you for drawing such wonderful pictures. The pictures you drew of the plants in Alejandro's garden were very life-like. I especially enjoyed the red chili peppers, yellow squash, and tomatoes. They looked good enough to eat!

Body
The desert landscape also looks very natural. When I look at the hills and rocks and sand, I can almost feel the dirt beneath my feet and the sun on my face.

The illustrations I liked the most are of the animals. My two favorite animals are the desert gray fox that is leaping in the brush and the raccoon that is climbing up in the tree. Thank you again for the wonderful illustrations.

Closing *Sincerely,*

Signature *Max Silver*

"Alejandro's Gift"
Celebrate Our World, Theme 3   **246**   Writing Harcourt

DAY 2 — WRITER'S CRAFT

WORD CHOICE Point out that good writers use colorful, vivid language in order to show the reader exactly what they mean. Explain that one way to make language more colorful is to use vivid verbs and specific nouns.

Display Transparency 247A. Read the introduction aloud. Have volunteers read aloud the directions and take turns completing the sentences.

APPLY TO WRITING Ask pairs of students to complete the activity on Transparency 247B. You may want to have them use a thesaurus.

▼ **Teaching Transparency 247 A–B**

VIVID VERBS

Read each sentence frame below. Look at the verbs in parentheses ( ). Then choose a more vivid verb from the box to complete the sentence.

1. The coyote slowly _____crept_____ through the desert. (moved)
2. A hawk _____soared_____ through the air. (flew)
3. The wind _____roared_____ through the canyon. (blew)
4. The squirrel _____raced_____ up the tree. (went)
5. Deer _____nibbled_____ the bushes near the water hole. (ate)
6. The leaves _____danced_____ in the wind. (turned)

raced	roared	crept
nibbled	soared	danced

"Alejandro's Gift"
Celebrate Our World, Theme 3   **247A**   Writing Harcourt

5 Day Plan

DAY 3 · PREWRITE

APPLY TO LITERATURE Have students look at the paragraph on page 330. Ask them to make a list of all the vivid verbs the writer uses to describe the movement of the animal. (*crept, hesitated, looked, approached, ran, drank, scampered*)

PREWRITE Ask students to use the prompt or brainstorm their own ideas for a thank-you letter:

WRITING PROMPT *Write a letter to a relative or friend thanking that person for giving a gift or for doing something. Include vivid verbs and specific nouns in your letter.*

Have students list things they are thanking someone for.

DAY 4 · DRAFT

DRAFT Have students use the steps below to draft their letters:

1. **Write** the address, date, and greeting.

2. **Begin** the body by stating what you are thanking the person for. Restate the thank you at the end.

3. **Provide** supporting examples. Include vivid verbs and specific nouns to add detail.

4. **Conclude** the letter.

5. **Write** the closing, and sign the letter.

DAY 5 · REVISE AND REFLECT

REVISION FOCUS: CLARIFYING WORDS Explain that when writers revise, they check that their words are vivid and specific. Write this sentence on the board: *The dog went across the yard*. Invite students to revise the sentence to include a more vivid verb and specific nouns. For example: *The dog bolted across the yard*.

PEER CONFERENCE CHECKLIST Have partners use this checklist to discuss and revise their letters:

✓ **Does the letter include all the parts: heading, greeting, closing, and signature?**

✓ **Does the body state what I am thanking the person for? Do I include supporting details?**

✓ **Do I use vivid verbs and specific nouns to describe things clearly?**

Have students revise their letters. They may want to keep their revised thank-you letters in their work portfolios.

 **Language Handbook, pp. 18–21, 74**

SCORING RUBRIC

	4	3	2	1
FOCUS/IDEAS	Completely focused, purposeful.	Generally focused on task and purpose.	Somewhat focused on task and purpose.	Lacks focus and purpose.
ORGANIZATION/ PARAGRAPHS	Ideas progress logically; transitions make the relationships among ideas clear.	Organization mostly clear, but some lapses occur; some transitions are used.	Some sense of organization but inconsistent or unclear in places.	Little or no sense of organization.
DEVELOPMENT	Central idea supported by strong, specific details.	Central idea with adequate support, mostly relevant details.	Unclear central idea; limited supporting details.	Unclear central idea; little or no development.
VOICE	Viewpoint clear; original expressions used where appropriate.	Viewpoint somewhat clear; few original expressions.	Viewpoint unclear or inconsistent.	Writer seems detached and unconcerned.
WORD CHOICE	Clear, exact language; freshness of expression.	Clear language; some interesting word choices.	Word choice unclear or inappropriate in places.	Word choice often unclear or inappropriate.
SENTENCES	Variety of sentence structures; flows smoothly.	Some variety in sentence structures.	Little variety; choppy or run-on sentences.	Little or no variety; sentences unclear.
CONVENTIONS	Few, if any, errors.	Few errors.	Some errors.	Many errors.

REPRODUCIBLE STUDENT RUBRICS for specific writing purposes and presentations are available on pages T90–T92.

Grammar

The Verb Be

DAY 1 — TEACH/MODEL

DAILY LANGUAGE PRACTICE

1. **Alejandro and his burro. Lived alone in the desert** (burro lived; desert.)
2. **He planted a garden, and wateried it every day.** (garden and; watered)

INTRODUCE THE CONCEPT Use Transparency 248 to discuss these points:

- The verb *be* links the subject to the predicate.
- Forms of *be* tell *what* or *where*.

Ask which words are linked in sentences 1–3. Then ask whether each sentence tells *what* or *where*. Students can complete sentences 4 and 5.

▼ Teaching Transparency 248

THE VERB BE

1. The house is in the desert. The house—in the desert; where
2. Alejandro is alone. Alejandro—alone; what
3. I am Alejandro's friend. I—Alejandro's friend; what
4. Today I am _____.
5. Yesterday I was _____.

Forms of Be

Pronoun Subjects	Present	Past
Singular		
I	am	was
you	are	were
he, she, it	is	was
Plural		
we	are	were
you	are	were
they	are	were

6. He _____ in the desert. is, was
7. They _____ in the desert. are, were
8. I _____ in the desert. am, was

"Alejandro's Gift"
Celebrate Our World, Theme 3
248
Grammar
Harcourt

DAY 2 — EXTEND THE CONCEPT

DAILY LANGUAGE PRACTICE

1. **all kinds of animals appeared near the garden?** (All; garden.)
2. **They was thirsty and wanted the water in the puddles** (were; puddles.)

DEVELOP THE CONCEPT Refer to the chart on Transparency 248 as you discuss the following point:

- The subject of the sentence and the form of the verb *be* must agree.

Point out which pronoun subjects use the same forms of *be*. Then have volunteers supply the present-tense and past-tense forms of *be* that would complete sentences 6–8. **PERFORMANCE ASSESSMENT**

Name _____

Alejandro's Gift
Grammar:
The Verb Be

Skill Reminder • Forms of the verb *be* link the subject of a sentence to the predicate.
• The subject of the sentence and the form of *be* must agree. When the subject is one person or thing, use *am, is,* or *was*. When the subject is more than one, use *are* and *were*.

▶ Underline the forms of the verb *be*. Write whether each is *present* or *past* tense.

1. Alejandro was a kind man. _____ past
2. The animals were pleased with his gift. _____ past
3. Now he is less lonely. _____ present
4. The animals are happier, too. _____ present
5. I am glad for all of them. _____ present

▶ Rewrite each sentence, using the form of *be* given in the parentheses ( ).

6. You _____ are _____ rarely alone. (present)
   You are rarely alone.
7. He _____ is _____ with his friends. (present)
   He is with his friends.
8. I _____ am _____ a friendly person. (present)
   I am a friendly person.
9. He _____ was _____ lonely for his family. (past)
   He was lonely for his family.
10. They _____ are _____ far away. (present)
    They are far away.

Homework Option

▲ Practice Book, p. 56

SKILL TRACE

THE VERB *BE*

Introduce	pp. 347E–F
Review	p. 347F, 369H, S77, T72
Test	Theme 3, Vol. 2

REACHING ALL LEARNERS

Diagnostic Check: Grammar and Writing

If . . . students have difficulty using the verb *be*,

Then . . . use sentence frames such as I _____ here. You _____ there. He _____ here.

ADDITIONAL SUPPORT ACTIVITIES

BELOW-LEVEL	Reteach, p. S76
ADVANCED	Extend, p. S77
ENGLISH-LANGUAGE LEARNERS	Reteach, p. S77

technology

Grammar Jingles™ CD,
Intermediate: Track 8
Visit *The Learning Site:*
www.harcourtschool.com
See Grammar Practice Park, Multimedia Grammar Glossary.

DAILY LANGUAGE PRACTICE

1. **Alejandro made a watering hole for the animals but they didnt come** (animals, but; didn't; come.)

2. **It was to close to the house, and the animals was afraid.** (too; were)

WHAT WAS HE? Have students say sentences about Alejandro that begin with *He was* and about the animals that begin with *They were.*

Test Prep Tip

"Remember this about subject-verb agreement:

- In the present tense, plural subjects go with the form *are*. *Am* goes with *I*. Other singular subjects go with *is*."

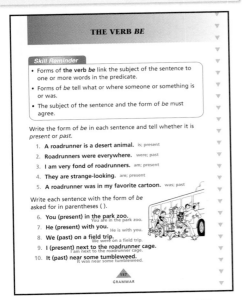

▲ Language Handbook, p. 157

DAILY LANGUAGE PRACTICE

1. **Alejandro digged another holes and put plants around it.** (dug; hole)

2. **He waited soon the animals came again to drink.** (waited. Soon OR waited, and)

CHANGING TENSE Have students use this sentence as a model:

He <u>was</u> lonely, but he <u>is</u> not lonely now.

Ask students to write similar sentences that use past- and present-tense forms of *be* with the pronouns *I, you, she, we,* and *they.*

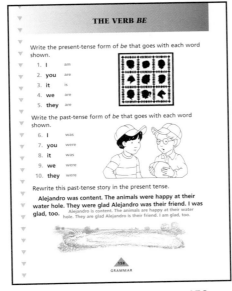

▲ Language Handbook, p. 158

DAILY LANGUAGE PRACTICE

1. **Alejandro gived the animals a usefull gift.** (gave; useful)

2. **He was'nt lonly anymore.** (wasn't; lonely)

IRREGULAR VERB ROUNDUP

Have students copy and complete the chart.

Present	Past
1. you have	you _had_
2. he _is_	he was
3. she does	she _did_
4. we ride	we _rode_
5. they _go_	they went

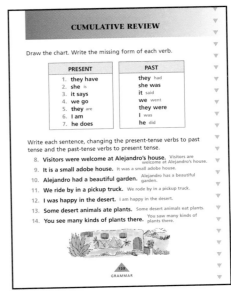

▲ Language Handbook, p. 159

Alejandro's Gift **347F**

Spelling Words

1. pennies
2. buried
3. replied
4. candies
5. emptied
6. stories
7. married
8. copies
9. parties
10. studied
11. mysteries
12. discoveries
13. worries
14. families
15. ponies

Challenge Words

16. adobe*
17. marble
18. brick
19. building
20. material

* Selection Words

Spelling

Changing y to i

DAY 1 — PRETEST/SELF-CHECK

ADMINISTER THE PRETEST Use the Dictation Sentences under Day 5. Help students self-check their pretests using Transparency 249.

ADVANCED

Use the Challenge Words in these Dictation Sentences:

16. You may find **adobe** houses in the desert.
17. There is a **marble** statue in the garden.
18. This is the only **brick** house in town.
19. When will the new **building** be finished?
20. This cotton **material** feels light and soft.

DAY 2 — TEACH/MODEL

WORD SORT Display Transparency 249. Make sure students know the meanings of the words. Then ask students to copy the chart and to write each Spelling Word where it belongs.

Point to and read the word *pennies*. Ask students to tell what the last three letters in the word are. (*-ies*) Have a volunteer circle them. Repeat the procedure with the word *buried*. Ask students what change was made in the words before the endings were added. (The *y* was changed to *i*.) Have students read the generalization to confirm their conclusion.

HANDWRITING Remind students to always dot the *i* when they write.

i

▼ Teaching Transparency 249

CHANGING y TO i

Spelling Words

1. pennies	6. stories	11. mysteries
2. buried	7. married	12. discoveries
3. replied	8. copies	13. worries
4. candies	9. parties	14. families
5. emptied	10. studied	15. ponies

- When a word ends in a consonant and *y*, change *y* to *i* before adding *-es* or *-ed*.

Words that end with *-es*	Words that end with *-ed*
pennies	buried
candies	replied
stories	emptied
copies	married
parties	studied
mysteries	
discoveries	
worries	
families	
ponies	

"Alejandro's Gift"
Celebrate Our World, Theme 3
249
Spelling
Harcourt

▲ Practice Book, p. 57

▲ Spelling Practice Book, p. 98

5 Day Plan

SPELLING RULES   Write the words *candy* and *candies* on the board. Ask a volunteer to tell what change was made before adding *-es*. (The *y* was changed to *i*.) Repeat the procedure with the words *reply* and *replied*. Challenge students to explain the spelling rule for a word that ends with a consonant and *y*. Change *y* to *i* before adding *-es* or *-ed*.

Apply to Writing

Have students think about the "*y* to *i*" spelling rule as they proofread their writing. Have them look for words that end with *-ies* and *-ied* to be sure they have spelled them correctly.

THINK AND SPELL   Organize students into small groups to play this game. The person who is "It" thinks of a Spelling Word. He or she writes it on a slip of paper and gives it to another student. The other students in the group have to guess the word by spelling it within a given number of turns. They start by guessing the first letter, the second, and so on. The student who is "It" writes the correct letters on a piece of paper as they are guessed. The student who completes the word becomes "It."

WRITING HEADLINES   Have students write a newspaper headline that uses one of the Spelling Words and then write a brief news story to go with it. Ask volunteers to share their stories.

DICTATION SENTENCES

1. How many **pennies** make a dollar?
2. That dog **buried** a bone in our yard.
3. She **replied** to the question quickly.
4. My mother makes several kinds of **candies**.
5. The baby **emptied** her toy box on the floor.
6. We are going to read two **stories** about horses.
7. My sister was **married** last month.
8. Please make **copies** of the picture.
9. It is fun to go to birthday **parties**.
10. I **studied** for the spelling test.
11. Who enjoys reading **mysteries**?
12. He wrote his **discoveries** down in a notebook.
13. Dad **worries** about our old car.
14. There were many **families** at the park.
15. We fed the **ponies** cubes of sugar.

▲ Spelling Practice Book, p. 99

▲ Spelling Practice Book, p. 100

Alejandro's Gift   **347H**

Word Study

MULTIPLE-MEANING WORDS

Determining Meanings

OBJECTIVE

To distinguish and interpret words with multiple meanings

Write the word *furrow* on the board. Explain that in "Alejandro's Gift," this word is a noun meaning "a groove dug into soil for farming." However, it can also be a verb that means "to crease." Ask students which meaning *furrows* has in the sentence *The doctor furrows his forehead when he's upset* and how they know.

Write the following multiple-meaning words on the board: *squash, well, company*. Have pairs of students work together to write a sentence using two possible meanings for each word. Have them use a dictionary if they are having trouble.

 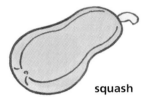

squash

ADVANCED

Divide students into two groups. Tell each group to think of ten words that have more than one meaning. They should make a list of the words and their meanings. They can play a game where they can challenge each other to make up sentences using as many meanings as possible. The team that uses the most word meanings wins.

ANALOGIES

Word Relationships

OBJECTIVE

To use knowledge of word relationships to determine analogies

Review with students that an analogy is a statement showing how two words in a pair are related in the same way as two words in another pair. Read aloud the following analogy frames. Ask students to complete each one. (Possible responses are shown.)

1. A *wood rat* is to *desert* as a *polar bear* is to _____. (*arctic*)
2. *Screwdriver* is to a *screw* as *hammer* is to a _____. (*nail*)
3. *Shunned* is to *hated* as *cherished* is to _____. (*loved*)
4. *Farming* is to *water* as *dancing* is to _____. (*music*)

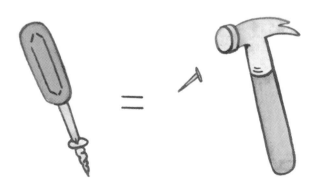

Speaking and Listening

Give an Oral Presentation

OBJECTIVE
To use an oral presentation to express feelings of thanks

Students may wish to publish their thank-you letters by presenting them orally to the class.

Organization   Share the following **organizational tips** with students.

- List important points on note cards.
- Highlight or underline parts of the letter you want to emphasize.

Delivery   Share the following **tips** with students.

- Practice presenting your letter so that you sound like you're speaking, not reading.
- Adjust the way you speak when expressing your feelings.

Students can give their presentations in small groups or in front of the whole class. After the speaker has finished, the audience can ask questions about the speaker's message.

Ask a Speaker Questions

OBJECTIVE
To formulate questions relating to the presentation

Encourage students to think about questions to ask as they listen to speakers.

GIVING GOOD RESPONSES   Have students develop a list of appropriate responses for listening to presentations, such as:

- Laugh if the speaker tells a joke.
- Nod if you agree with the speaker.
- Clap at the end of the presentation.

Listening Tips

- Listen to hear how the speaker expresses his or her message.
- Ask questions one at a time, and wait for an answer.
- Save questions until the presentation is over.

Viewing Photography

OBJECTIVE
To compare and contrast photography and illustration

Desert Landscape
Provide students with a photograph from the southwestern United States.

Have them consider the following:

- **What do the story illustrations show that the photograph does not show?**
- **How is the photograph different from the illustrations in "Alejandro's Gift"? How is it similar?**

Books for All Learners

Reinforcing Skills and Strategies

■ BELOW-LEVEL

☑ **Focus Skill: Cause and Effect**

☑ **Focus Strategy: Read Ahead**

☑ **Vocabulary: *windmill, cherished, furrows, ample, shunned, growth***

Genre: Realistic Fiction
Science Connection: Animal Populations and Limited Resources

SUMMARY   A shy burro who has spent her life wandering the desert and avoiding people is tamed by a gentle gold miner. After a year, the miner's work is done. He gives the burro to a family. Meanwhile, the desert's wild burro population decreases as their habitat becomes increasingly populated by humans.

 Visit *The Learning Site:*
www.harcourtschool.com
See Resources for Parents and Teachers: Books for All Learners.

BEFORE READING

Preview/Set Purpose   Read the title aloud and ask students to preview the pictures and predict what the book will be about. Guide them to set a purpose for reading.

Reinforce Cause and Effect   Help students create a cause-and-effect chart to help them keep track of story events and the reasons why they happen. **CAUSE AND EFFECT/GRAPHIC AIDS**

Causes		Effects
	→	

Reinforce Vocabulary   Use illustrations to review key vocabulary. Ask questions such as these: How are *windmills* and *furrows* signs that people live nearby?

READING THE BOOK

Pages 2–5   What big change took place in the burro's life? (After a lifetime of wandering freely and avoiding people, the burro is caught by a miner.) Was this a good change or a bad one? (Possible responses: good, because the miner was kind; bad, because the burro lost her freedom) **MAKE JUDGMENTS**

Pages 10–13   What caused the wild burro population to get smaller? (More and more people moved to the desert, so the burros' home got smaller; burros were rounded up and sold.) **CAUSE AND EFFECT**

Reread for Fluency   Have students reread their favorite parts of the story aloud to you.

RESPONDING

Cause-and-Effect Chart   Guide students to use the completed cause-and-effect chart to retell the story's main events.

Oral Reading Fluency

Use Books for All Learners to promote oral reading fluency.

See **Fluency Routine Cards,** pp. T80a–T80b.

■ ON-LEVEL

 Focus Skill: Cause and Effect

 Focus Strategy: Read Ahead

 Vocabulary: *windmill, cherished, furrows, ample, shunned, growth*

Genre: Fiction
Science Connection: Continuity and Change

SUMMARY   In the 1940s a girl named Lisa loans her favorite book to a classmate named Miguel. The book is filled with notes Lisa has written about the book. When Miguel's father is suddenly transferred to another Army base, Lisa thinks she will never see her cherished book again. Sixty years later, Lisa is delighted when she receives her book in the mail. It is stuffed with notes and reflections written by three generations of Miguel's family.

 Visit *The Learning Site:*
www.harcourtschool.com
See Resources for Parents and Teachers: Books for All Learners.

BEFORE READING

Preview/Set Purpose   Have students preview the book. Point out the dates on the notes and ask students when the first and last notes were written. Then ask students to predict what might happen to the girl and the book, and help them set a purpose for reading.

Reinforce Cause and Effect   Help students create a cause-and-effect chain to help them keep track of important story events and their causes.

Causes		Effects
	→	

READING THE BOOK

Pages 2–11   What happened to Lisa's favorite book? (She loaned it to a friend named Miguel; Miguel's father was transferred to another base, and Miguel didn't have time to return it.) **SUMMARIZE**

Pages 12–16   What happened to the book over the next 60 years? (Miguel read it; he gave it to his children and grandchildren. Everyone who read it added a note to it.)

Page 15   Why did people add notes to the book? (It was a tradition Lisa had started; the book was powerful and touched many people.) What effect did the return of the book have on Lisa? (She was happy to get it, and glad so many people had enjoyed it.) **CAUSE AND EFFECT**

Rereading for Fluency   Have pairs of students reread their favorite parts of the book aloud.

RESPONDING

Cause-and-Effect Chain   Guide students to retell the important events in the story using their completed cause-and-effect chains.

Guided Reading
OPTIONS

Books for All Learners

Reinforcing Skills and Strategies

■ ADVANCED

 Focus Skill: Cause and Effect

 Focus Strategy: Read Ahead

 Vocabulary: *underbrush, mesquite, saguaro, clearing, sheltered, freedom, sculptor*

Genre: Nonfiction
Social Studies Connection: Citizenship and Freedom

SUMMARY The Statue of Liberty, created by sculptor Frédéric Bartholdi, was given as a gift from France to the United States to honor friendship and a mutual commitment to freedom. The statue has been painstakingly repaired and maintained for more than 100 years, and today it remains a symbol of freedom for America and the world.

 Visit *The Learning Site:*
www.harcourtschool.com
See Resources for Parents and Teachers: Books for All Learners.

BEFORE READING

Preview/Set Purpose Have students read the title and the table of contents and preview the illustrations. Ask them to predict what the book is about and set a purpose for reading it.

Reinforce Cause and Effect Remind students that paying attention to what causes events to happen can help them understand what they read. Create a cause-effect chart on the board and have students use it to record the causes and effects they read about in the book.

Causes		Effects

Expand Vocabulary Write the words *freedom* and *sculptor* on the board and discuss their meanings. Ask students how a sculptor might celebrate freedom through his or her art.

READING THE BOOK

Pages 2–5 What led to the idea of the Statue of Liberty? (France had helped America win freedom from Great Britain in the American Revolution, and were inspired to fight for their own freedom. In 1865 a French teacher had the idea of giving a huge statue to the United States as a gift from France.) CAUSE AND EFFECT

Pages 6–12 Why was building the Statue of Liberty such a difficult job? (It was huge. It had to be built in pieces. It took a long time.) SYNTHESIZE

Pages 13–16 Why does the author call the Statue of Liberty a gift that keeps on giving? (because it still stands as a symbol of hope and freedom for people) INTERPRET FIGURATIVE LANGUAGE

Rereading for Fluency Have students reread sections of the book aloud as if they were presenting a tour of the Statue of Liberty.

RESPONDING

Chart Ask students to summarize the book orally or use the completed cause-effect chart to explain the Statue of Liberty's history.

Managing Small Groups

While you work with small groups, have other students do the following:
- **Self-Selected Reading**
- **Practice Pages**
- **Cross-Curricular Centers**
- **Journal Writing**

▲ **page 347K**   ▲ **page 347L**

■ ENGLISH-LANGUAGE LEARNERS

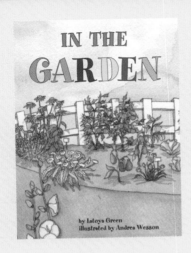

 Focus Skill: Cause and Effect

 Focus Strategy: Read Ahead

 Concept Vocabulary:
vegetables, garden, dig, shovel, rake, rows

Genre: Realistic Fiction
Science Connection: Processes of Life

SUMMARY   A young girl and her grandfather plant a vegetable garden in spring. They tend it carefully so that each plant receives the right amount of water and sunlight, and in the summer they pick the ripe vegetables. As with many gardens, they find that some vegetables have grown better than others.

   Visit *The Learning Site:*
www.harcourtschool.com
See Resources for Parents and Teachers: Books for All Learners.

BEFORE READING

Tap Prior Knowledge   Write the word *garden* on the board and invite students to describe any experiences they have had planting, tending, or harvesting vegetables from a home garden.

Total Physical Response   Ask students to pantomime along with you these actions: digging soil; planting a seed in the soil; covering the seed with soil; watering the plants; picking and eating the ripe vegetables.

Display Vocabulary/Concept Words   Display the vocabulary words on the board. Explain each word using story illustrations to help you.

Preview the Book   Conduct a picture walk through the story and have students predict what the girl and her grandfather will do, using sentence frames such as: "I think the girl and her grandfather will (plant a garden). I think they will grow ____(vegetables)____."

READING THE BOOK

Pages 3–4   What does the girl do before she plants the seeds? (She picks a good spot for the garden, gets the soil ready by pulling out the weeds, and digs up 12 inches of soil.) **SEQUENCE**

Page 9   What do the seeds need in order to grow? (sunlight and water) **NOTE DETAILS**

Page 14   What happened in summer? (The ripe vegetables are picked.) Why did some vegetables grow better than others? (Some vegetables got everything they needed; others, like the carrots, got too little water and sun.) **CAUSE AND EFFECT**

Rereading   Have students reread portions of the book aloud after hearing you read them.

RESPONDING

Diagrams   Have students retell the story using simple diagrams that show a seed, a sprout, a half-grown plant, and a mature plant with vegetables on it.

Teacher Notes

Teacher Notes

348BB

THEME CONNECTION:
Celebrate Our World

GENRE:
Expository Nonfiction

SUMMARY:

This selection describes the four layers of Earth, and explains how Earth's plates can shift to cause earthquakes or tsunamis, or push together to form mountains. The selection also explains the role wind and water play in shaping Earth's features.

 All selections available on *Audiotext 6*

Books for
All Learners

Lesson Plans on pages 369M–369P

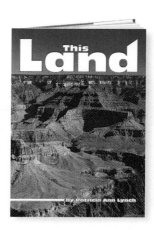

BELOW-LEVEL	ON-LEVEL	ADVANCED	ELL
• Lesson Vocabulary • Focus Skill: Locate Information	• Lesson Vocabulary • Focus Skill: Locate Information	• Challenge Vocabulary • Focus Skill: Locate Information	• Concept Vocabulary • Focus Skill: Locate Information

MULTI-LEVEL PRACTICE

Extra Support, pp. 58–61

Practice Book, pp. 58–63

Challenge, pp. 58–61

English-Language Learners, pp. 58–61

ADDITIONAL RESOURCES

Spelling Practice Book, pp. 101–103

Language Handbook, pp. 160–162

Audiotext 6

Intervention Resource Kit, Lesson 28
- Intervention Reader, *Included in Intervention Resource Kit*

English-Language Learners Resource Kit, Lesson 28

Technology

- *Writing Express*™ **CD-ROM**

- *Grammar Jingles*™ **CD**

- *Media Literacy and Communication Skills Package* (Video)

- *Reading and Language Skills Assessment* **CD-ROM**

- *The Learning Site:*
  www.harcourtschool.com

	Day 1	**Day 2**
5-15 Minutes **ORAL LANGUAGE** • Question of the Day • Sharing Literature	**Question of the Day,** p. 348H *What word names something you eat from and also names something that can collide to make things shake?* **Literature Read-Aloud,** pp. 348G–H	**Question of the Day,** p. 348H *Where might you see examples of erosion?* **Think and Respond,** p. 364

15-30 Minutes **SKILLS & STRATEGIES**
• Comprehension
• Vocabulary

Day 1

Comprehension:
 (Skill) Locate Information, p. 348I **T**
(Strategy) Adjust Reading Rate, p. 348J

Vocabulary, p. 348L

Day 2

Comprehension:
(Skill) Locate Information, pp. 350–365 **T**

Decoding/Phonics:
Syllable Patterns: Schwa, p. 369C

30-45 Minutes **READING**
• Guided Comprehension
• Independent Reading
• Cross-Curricular Connections

Day 1

Read: Vocabulary Power, pp. 348–349
Vocabulary Power Words:
edges, range, peak, epicenter, magma, coast

 Independent Reading
Books for All Learners

SCIENCE Wave Action

Day 2

Reading the Selection, pp. 350–365
Vocabulary Power Words

 Independent Reading
Books for All Learners

SCIENCE Earth in the Making
SCIENCE Forms of Matter

45-90 Minutes **LANGUAGE ARTS**
• Writing
  Daily Writing Prompt
• Grammar
  Daily Language Practice
• Spelling

Daily Routines
• Question of the Day
• Daily Language Practice
• Daily Writing Prompt

Day 1

Writing: Writing Process, p. 369E

✏ **Writing Prompt:**
Geology is the study of the earth. Other branches of science study the oceans, plant and animal life, and outer space. Write a paragraph explaining which branch of science is most interesting to you and why.

Grammar:
Contractions, p. 369G **T**

Daily Language Practice
1. i just found this map. It were in a bag with forty pennys. (I; was; pennies)
2. The map show mountains. All over the world. (shows; mountains all)

Spelling:
Contractions, p. 369I **T**

Day 2

Writing: Writing Process, p. 369E

✏ **Writing Prompt:**
Before scientists learned the real causes of earthquakes, storytellers told legends about why earthquakes happen. Write your own legend about why earthquakes happen.

Grammar:
Extend the Concept, p. 369G **T**

Daily Language Practice
1. Look at this mountain. Its the most highest in the world. (It's; the highest)
2. It is called Mount Everest. And its' in the Himalayas. (Everest, and; it's)

Spelling:
Word Sort, p. 369I **T**

Focus Skill

Locate Information

Objectives of the Week:

- To use book parts to locate information
- To read and understand a nonfiction selection
- To write contractions correctly
- To write a play with a beginning, a middle, and an ending

Day 3

Question of the Day, p. 348H
In what state might you see a volcanic eruption and a tsunami on the same day?

Oral Grammar, p. 369H

Comprehension:
 Locate Information, pp. 368–369 **T**
Test Prep

Word Study:
Homographs, p. 369K

Rereading for Fluency, p. 363

 Independent Reading
Books for All Learners

SCIENCE Interpret Sketches and Diagrams
SCIENCE Use Numerical Data to Compare

Writing: Writing Process, p. 369F

Writing Prompt:
Is the earth more like an onion or more like an orange? Write a paragraph that answers this question and explains why. (Hint: Think about the layers of earth.)

Grammar:
Contraction Q & A, p. 369H **T**

Daily Language Practice

1. No person has ever went to the center of our planet (gone; planet.)
2. Youd burn up before you got there (You'd; there.)

Spelling:
Contractions, p. 369J **T**

Day 4

Question of the Day, p. 348H
You know what causes volcanoes. What effects do you think volcanoes have on plants, animals, land, and people?

Graphic Aids, pp. 369A–B **T**

Cause and Effect, p. 369D **T**

Self-Selected Reading, p. 348F

 Independent Reading
Books for All Learners

SCIENCE Wave Energy
SCIENCE Responding to Change

Writing: Writing Process, p. 369F

Writing Prompt:
A tsunami is on the way, and you are the only one who knows it. Think about how you could warn people of the tsunami and help them escape the giant wave. Now write a story about how you saved the day.

Grammar:
Flash Cards, p. 369H **T**

Daily Language Practice

1. Can you believe it The inner core of the planet is solid? (it? The; solid.)
2. Thats because the other layers pushes down on it. (That's; push)

Spelling:
Word Constructions, p. 369J **T**

Day 5

Question of the Day, p. 348H
If you could drill a hole from the North Pole straight through the earth's core to the South Pole, about how long would the hole you drilled be?

Listening and Speaking
Explanation, p. 369L

Comprehension:
 Locate Information, pp. 369M–O

Word Study:
Borrowed Words, p. 369K

Self-Selected Reading, pp. 363, T101

Independent Reading
Books for All Learners

SCIENCE Write a Report
MATH Estimate Distances

Writing: Writing Process, p. 369F

Writing Prompt:
Many powerful events occur in nature, including earthquakes, tsunamis, hurricanes, tornadoes, and floods. Think of a powerful natural event that you have seen or have seen pictures of. Now write about the event and its effects.

Grammar:
Proofread, p. 369H **T**

Daily Language Practice

1. how hot is the center. i think its 9000°F. (How; center? I; it's)
2. Im reading about tsunamis. But Iv'e never seen one. (I'm; tsunamis, but; I've)

Spelling:
Posttest, p. 369J **T**

Cross-Curricular Stations

Materials

- shallow pan
- water
- two leaves
- a pebble
- notebook and pencil

SCIENCE

Wave Action

OBJECTIVE: To predict and then determine how an earthquake's force moves outward from its epicenter

Use this activity to predict and then show how shock waves from an earthquake move outward from its epicenter.

- Fill a large, shallow pan with water.
- Float two small leaves in the water.
- Predict where the leaves will move if you drop a pebble into the middle of the pan. Write your prediction. Then drop a pebble into the center of the pan.
- Compare your prediction about the leaves with what really happens.

Materials

- research materials
- pencils, crayons
- poster paper

SCIENCE

Earth in the Making

OBJECTIVE: To research how land forms change over time

Work in a group to show how wind, water, and the movement of the earth's plates can form and change the land.

Ruby Falls, TN

- Look in an encyclopedia, a library book, or on the Internet to find a picture of an unusual natural feature or landscape.
- Research the natural forces that shaped that feature.
- Draw a picture of the feature. Write a caption telling how it was shaped.
- Post the pictures and captions on a bulletin board.

 Search for information using a CD-ROM encyclopedia.

LIBRARY CENTER

Self-Selected Reading

OBJECTIVE: To independently select and read books

Read more about forces that shape Earth in these books:

- *What Happens When Volcanoes Erupt?* by Daphne Butler. Raintree Steck-Vaughn, 1996. **NONFICTION**
- *The Magic School Bus: Inside the Earth* by Joanna Cole. Scholastic, 1989. **NONFICTION**
- *Earthquakes* by Seymour Simon. Mulberry, 1995. **NONFICTION**

Remember to

- keep track in your Reading Log of what you read each day.

Materials

- self-selected book
- *My Reading Log* copying master, p. R42

INQUIRY PROJECT

Extending the Selection

OBJECTIVE: To research a self-selected topic

What other topics might "Rocking and Rolling" lead you to learn more about? Write your ideas inside a volcano shape. Or, use these books to get ideas:

- *Ring of Fire*
- *The Perfect Ending*
- *Rock Hounds*
- *This Land*

Materials

- research materials
- paper
- pencils

TECHNOLOGY

Information Search

OBJECTIVE: To learn about earthquakes and volcanoes that are happening now

Volcanoes erupt and earthquakes happen every day. Find out more about how the earth "rocks and rolls." Find and visit a website that keeps track of earthquakes and volcanoes.

Remember to

- mark the locations by putting self-stick notes on a world map.
- use the rules for Internet safety.

Materials

- computer with Internet access
- paper
- pencil
- world map or globe

Read Aloud

SET A PURPOSE
Listen to Gain Information
Have students listen carefully to how the poet explains what science is. Read the poem aloud, using the rhyming words to guide the rhythm and pacing.

LISTENING STRATEGY
Concentrate on the Speaker
Encourage students to listen carefully to the speaker's explanation and examples. Explain that concentrating on the speaker will help students understand the poet's view about science.

What Is Science?

by Rebecca Kai Dotlich

What is science?
So many things.

The study of stars—
Saturn's rings.
The study of rocks—
geodes and stones—
dinosaur fossils,
old-chipped bones.
The study of soil,
oil, and gas.
Of sea and sky,
of seed and grass.
Of wind
and hurricanes
that blow;
volcanoes,
tornadoes,
earthquakes,
snow.

What is science?
the study of trees.
Of butterflies
and killer bees.
Glaciers, geysers,
clay, and sand;
mighty mountains,
the rolling land.
The power of trains—
planes that soar.
Science is this
and so much more.
So into the earth
and into the sky;
we question
the how
the where
when
and
why.

- **What is the purpose of this poem?** (Possible response: to try to explain what science is) AUTHOR'S PURPOSE

- **How does the poet describe what science is about?** (Possible response: She gives many examples of the kinds of things that can be studied. She lists the types of questions a scientist might ask.) AUTHOR'S CRAFT

- **How do you think the poet feels about science?** (Possible response: She probably enjoys science, because she says that it is so much more than what she is able to explain in her poem.) AUTHOR'S VIEWPOINT

Question of the Day

DEVELOP ORAL LANGUAGE

- Display the first question on Transparency 252 or write it on the board. Ask a volunteer to read it aloud.

 - **Response Journal** Explain to students that they should think about the question throughout the day and write their responses in their journals. Tell students to be prepared to discuss the answer or answers to it by the end of the day or at another time you choose.

- You may want to repeat this process daily for each of the five discussion questions.

▼ **Teaching Transparency 252**

QUESTION OF THE DAY

DAY 1: What word names something you eat from and also names something that can collide to make things shake? Possible response: a plate.

DAY 2: Where might you see examples of erosion? Possible responses: You can see erosion on a hillside or a cliff; in a mountain that has been worn down; in a riverbed or canyon.

DAY 3: In what state might you see a volcanic eruption and a tsunami on the same day? Possible response: Hawaii

DAY 4: You know what causes volcanoes. What effects do you think volcanoes have on plants, animals, land, and people? Possible responses: A volcano could destroy animal's and people's homes and possibly kill them; it could burn trees; it could change the shape of land; it could create islands in the sea.

DAY 5: If you could drill a hole from the North Pole straight through the earth's core to the South Pole, about how long would the hole you drilled be? The hole would be about 7,920 miles long. If it is 3,960 miles from Earth's surface to its center, it would be double that number from Earth's center to the opposite surface.

"Rocking and Rolling"
Celebrate Our World, Theme 3

 252

Question of the Day
Harcourt

Focus Skill — Locate Information

OBJECTIVE

To use book parts to locate information

SKILL TRACE

LOCATE INFORMATION

Introduce	p. 348I
Reteach	pp. S80, S92, T73
Review	pp. 368, 399B, 400I, 416
Test	Theme 3 Vol. 2

▼ **Teaching Transparency 253**

LOCATE INFORMATION

You can use the parts of a book to locate, or find, information.

- The **title** is the name of a unit, book, or chapter.
- The **table of contents** is a list of the titles of all the units, chapters, or stories in a book.
- A **chapter heading** is a title that comes before each new part of a chapter.
- A **glossary** is a dictionary of important words used in a book. It appears at the back of a book.
- An **index** is an alphabetical list of topics with page numbers where facts about each topic can be found.

What parts of a book would you look at if you wanted to answer these questions? Write the question number next to the book part where you would find the answer.

1. What does the word *magma* mean?   **title** (3)
2. Where can I find facts about   **table of contents** (5)
   volcanoes in this book?
3. What is the whole book about?   **chapter heading** (4)
4. What is the next part of this   **glossary** (1)
   chapter about?
5. What chapters are in this book?   **index** (2)

"Rocking and Rolling"
Celebrate Our World, Theme 3   **253**   Focus Skill
                                                    Harcourt

BELOW-LEVEL

Additional Support
- *Intervention Teacher's Guide,* p. 280

ENGLISH-LANGUAGE LEARNERS

Additional Support
- *English-Language Learners Teacher's Guide,* p. 165

INTRODUCE THE SKILL

Access prior knowledge.   Display a science or social studies textbook. Invite volunteers to name the different parts of the book, such as the title, table of contents, and index. Ask students who have used these book parts to tell how they use them.

TEACH/MODEL

Tell students that understanding the different parts of a book can help them find information quickly. Display Transparency 253.

- **Call on volunteers to read aloud the bulleted items in the box.**

- **Then have volunteers read and answer the questions. Work with students to identify each book part and tell what type of information it contains.**

Text Structure   Tell students that the next selection has headings that will signal each main idea.

PRACTICE/APPLY

As students read, they can use headings, captions, and other parts of "Rocking and Rolling" to help them answer the questions they write in their K-W-L charts.

K-W-L Chart		
What I Know	What I Want to Know	What I Learned

For opportunities to apply and reinforce the skills, see the following pages:

During reading: pages 354, 360, and 362
After reading: *Pupil Edition* pages 368–369

 **Focus Strategy**

Adjust Reading Rate

OBJECTIVE

To read factual material more slowly and carefully than fiction

REVIEW THE STRATEGY

Point out to students that the next selection is expository nonfiction. Review with students that expository nonfiction often provides information about several topics and in different forms. Ask students why it might be necessary to adjust their reading rate when reading this type of material.

TEACH/MODEL

Remind students that they may need to change the rate, or speed, of their reading to match the text they are reading. Often, reading complicated passages more slowly will help them understand new words and ideas. Read aloud the first page of "Rocking and Rolling" and model the strategy.

> **MODEL** This selection is about a topic that is new to me. To better understand what the author says about the earth, I'll try reading parts that contain new words and ideas more slowly. I'll also read the captions and diagrams carefully.

SKILL ⟷ STRATEGY CONNECTION

Tell students that if they have difficulty **locating information** in one part of the selection, they can adjust their **reading rate** and try reading it more slowly.

PRACTICE/APPLY

For opportunities to apply and reinforce the strategy **during reading**, see pages 353 and 361.

Strategies Good Readers Use

- Use Decoding/Phonics
- Make and Confirm Predictions
- Create Mental Images
- Self-Question
- Summarize
- Read Ahead
- Reread to Clarify
- Use Context to Confirm Meaning
- Use Text Structure and Format
- **Adjust Reading Rate** **Focus Strategy**

Building Background

ACCESS PRIOR KNOWLEDGE

Ask students to think about how forces of nature change things in nature. Ask: **How does wind change mountains? What do heavy waves do to the shoreline?**

Help students begin a K-W-L chart listing some things they already know about how natural forces can change the earth's features.

K-W-L Chart		
What I Know	**What I Want to Know**	**What I Learned**
Rain and wind wear down sharp mountain peaks. Waves wash away the edges of the coast.		

 technology

Visit *The Learning Site:*
www.harcourtschool.com
See Building Background.

DEVELOP CONCEPTS

Help students further develop selection concepts by asking questions such as these:

• **Have you ever seen a tsunami? If so, how high was it? Where were you?** (Responses will vary.)

• **How frequently do earthquakes occur? Can scientists predict earthquakes?** (Possible responses: They occur somewhere in the world every day; No, scientists cannot predict them.)

• **Where are the most active volcanoes? Will one erupt soon?** (Possible response: in Hawaii, in Sicily)

Tell students that some of these questions will be answered in the next selection.

REACHING ALL LEARNERS

Diagnostic Check: Vocabulary

If . . . students have not mastered at least five of the six vocabulary words . . .

Then . . . have them write original sentences for the vocabulary words and share them with the class.

ADDITIONAL SUPPORT ACTIVITIES

BELOW-LEVEL	Reteach, p. S78
ADVANCED	Extend, p. S79
ENGLISH-LANGUAGE LEARNERS	Reteach, p. S79

Vocabulary

Vocabulary

edges places where something ends

range a line of mountains

peak the top of a mountain

epicenter the place on the earth's surface just above the center of an earthquake

magma melted rock inside the earth

coast land along the sea

TEACH VOCABULARY STRATEGIES

Use familiar letter patterns. Display Transparency 254. Ask volunteers to read the sentences aloud. Remind students that they can often use familiar letter patterns to decode an unfamiliar word. Model decoding the word *coast:*

> **MODEL** I see that the vowels *o* and *a* appear together in this word. I know that this pair often has a long *o* sound, as in *boat* and *coat*. I can blend the beginning /k/ sound with /ō/ and then see if it is a word I know.

Tell students to read the transparency silently. Work with them to use the strategy to decode the vocabulary words. Then discuss the meanings of the vocabulary.

Remind students that when they use familiar letter patterns to decode unfamiliar words, they should confirm meanings and pronunciations by checking a glossary or a dictionary and asking themselves whether each word makes sense in the sentence.

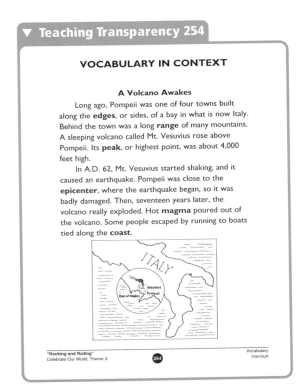

▼ Teaching Transparency 254

VOCABULARY IN CONTEXT

A Volcano Awakes

Long ago, Pompeii was one of four towns built along the **edges**, or sides, of a bay in what is now Italy. Behind the town was a long **range** of many mountains. A sleeping volcano called Mt. Vesuvius rose above Pompeii. Its **peak**, or highest point, was about 4,000 feet high.

In A.D. 62, Mt. Vesuvius started shaking, and it caused an earthquake. Pompeii was close to the **epicenter**, where the earthquake began, so it was badly damaged. Then, seventeen years later, the volcano really exploded. Hot **magma** poured out of the volcano. Some people escaped by running to boats tied along the **coast**.

"Rocking and Rolling" Celebrate Our World, Theme 3 — 254 — Vocabulary Harcourt

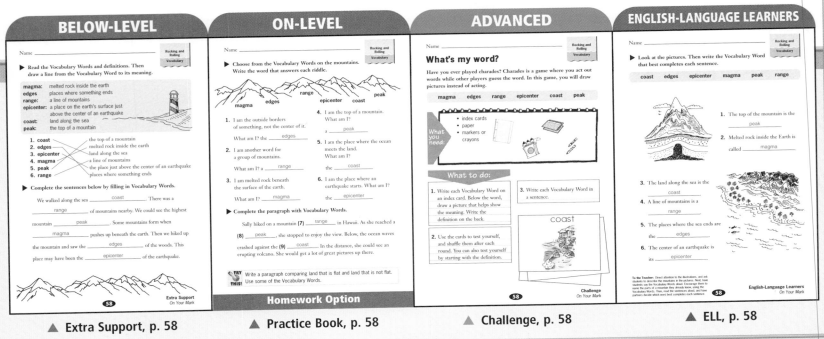

BELOW-LEVEL

▲ Extra Support, p. 58

ON-LEVEL

Homework Option

▲ Practice Book, p. 58

ADVANCED

▲ Challenge, p. 58

ENGLISH-LANGUAGE LEARNERS

▲ ELL, p. 58

Rocking and Rolling **348L**

Vocabulary Power

APPLY STRATEGIES

Ask a volunteer to read aloud the headline on page 348. Ask another volunteer to read the caption. Then have students read the news article silently. Remind them to use familiar letter patterns to help them decode words they do not know.

EXTEND WORD KNOWLEDGE

Practice other vocabulary strategies. Have students answer questions with sentences that show they understand what the vocabulary words mean. MEANINGFUL SENTENCES

• What is *magma* like? **DESCRIPTION**

• What are some *edges* that small children should stay away from? **EXAMPLE**

• During an earthquake, is a building in greater danger if it is close to the *epicenter* or far away? **DESCRIPTION**

• What might you see along a *coast* ? **PRIOR KNOWLEDGE**

• What is the opposite of a *peak* ? **ANTONYM**

• What does it mean if someone says they live near a mountain *range* ? **EXPLANATION**

▲ Rocking and Rolling

coast

edges

epicenter

range

magma

peak

348

Vocabulary Power

The selection "Rocking and Rolling" tells about some of the mighty forces that shape Earth. Read this newspaper article about earthshaking events.

Quake shakes town

Yesterday's earthquake caused damage to this house.

A small earthquake was felt yesterday on the **coast**. People living in towns near the sea were surprised, but no one was hurt. The only damage reported was to the **edges** of a roof. An old tree fell against the corner of the house and broke tiles on two sides of the roof.

The **epicenter** of yesterday's earthquake is one hundred miles from here. This place on the earth's surface is just above the center of the earthquake. It is located in a mountain **range** that includes an active volcano.

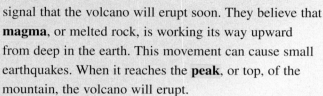

NEVADA

CALIFORNIA

epicenter

PACIFIC OCEAN

Scientists think this earthquake may be a signal that the volcano will erupt soon. They believe that **magma**, or melted rock, is working its way upward from deep in the earth. This movement can cause small earthquakes. When it reaches the **peak**, or top, of the mountain, the volcano will erupt.

Scientists will watch closely to see what happens. They stated that they are sure no one is in any danger.

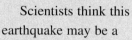

Vocabulary-Writing
CONNECTION

Would you like to live along a sea **coast** or near a mountain **range**? Write a paragraph that explains the reasons for your choice.

349

 QUICKWRITE

VOCABULARY-WRITING CONNECTION

Invite students who have lived on a coast or in the mountains to describe what these environments are like. Encourage students to support their answers with details. Students should add the Vocabulary Power words to their Word Bank for use in future writing assignments.

Prereading Strategies

PREVIEW AND PREDICT

Have students read the **genre** information on page 350. Then have them preview the selection. Ask them what they think this selection is about, based on their preview and the characteristics of expository nonfiction. Then have them write in the second column of the K-W-L chart some questions they have about the forces that shape the earth. See *Transparency* G.

K-W-L Chart		
What I Know	What I Want to Know	What I Learned
Rain and wind wear down sharp mountain peaks. Waves wash away the edges of the coast.		

Genre

Expository Nonfiction

Expository nonfiction explains information and ideas.

In this selection, look for

● text divided into sections with headings.

● information and diagrams about a topic.

350

BELOW-LEVEL	ON-LEVEL	ADVANCED	ENGLISH-LANGUAGE LEARNERS
Have students read the title and discuss the first two pages. Discuss these story words: *crust, mantle, core, plates, faults.* Help students set a purpose for reading through page 355. **SMALL GROUP**	Have students read the selection with a partner. Use the Guided Comprehension questions and Ongoing Assessments to gauge students' understanding. **PARTNER/WHOLE CLASS**	Have students read the selection silently. Then have pairs ask and answer each other's questions. **INDEPENDENT/PARTNER**	Read aloud the selection or have students listen to it on *Audiotext 6.* Then have students read aloud selected sections as a group to develop oral fluency. **SMALL GROUP**

BELOW-LEVEL ADDITIONAL SUPPORT

Intervention Reader: Bright Surprises Intervention Teacher's Guide, pp. 280–283

ENGLISH-LANGUAGE LEARNERS ADDITIONAL SUPPORT

See *English-Language Learners Resource Kit,* Lesson 28. *English-Language Learners Teacher's Guide,* pp. 165–166

ROCKING AND ROLLING

by Philip Steele

Read to find out. Tell students that one purpose for reading is to learn about a topic. Ask students to set their own purposes. Offer this suggestion:

MODEL I want to learn what causes earthquakes. I'll read to find out why earthquakes happen and how they can change the land.

(Focus Strategy) Adjust Reading Rate Have students use the strategy to understand the selection.

 "Rocking and Rolling" is available on *Audiotext 6.*

COMPREHENSION CARD 28

Questioning The Author Use the Questioning the Author strategy to help students understand the key points of the text.

Comprehension Card 28,
Page T83 ▶

▶ **Questioning the Author**   COMPREHENSION CARD **28**

Rocking and Rolling
Key Understanding: The earth has been formed and continues to be formed by forces such as water, wind, and the movement of plates

1. p. 352, line 10: To establish how very deep the earth is and how extremely hot it is: **What's the author trying to tell us about our earth?** (Possible response: The author is letting know that it's a very long distance (3,960 miles) from the crust of the earth inside to its center. The center is almost as hot as the sun.)

2. p. 353, line 15: To establish the characteristics of the four layers of the earth: **How does what the author tells us about the earth's layers connect to the picture?** (Possible response: The author describes the four layers. The crust is made of rock. The mantle is also rock, but it's so hot that some of it has melted. There are an inner and an outer core that are made of metal, and they are both very hot.)

3. p. 354, line 4: To clarify that the earth is made up of "pieces," Draw students' attention to the big picture on page 354 and ask: **What is the author trying to tell us about the earth when he says that it is like a jigsaw puzzle?** (Possible response: The earth is made up of big pieces, called plates, that fit together.)

4. p. 354, line 15: To establish one of the consequences of the movement of the earth's plates: **The author says that gooey magma sometimes comes up through the earth. What makes that happen?** (Possible response: When the

earth's plates move apart, the magma comes up to fill the space between the cracks.)

5. p. 355, line 5: To clarify the picture: **The illustrator is trying to show that the land on our planet is moving.**

6. p. 355, line 13: To establish another consequence of plates movement: **Before we learned that sometimes when plates move gooey magma comes up between them. Now what else has the author told us might happen when plates move?** (Possible response: If plates push into each other, a range of mountains can form.)

7. p. 356, line 13: To clarify why an earthquake occurs: Here the author is telling us that sometimes part of a plate can break away all of a sudden and that makes an earthquake.

8. p. 357, line 5: To help students understand the "ripples in a pond" analogy: **The author talks about "the ripples from a stone thrown into a pond. What does that mean?** (Possible response: When you throw a stone into water, waves move out from it in circles.)

9. p. 357, line 5: To help students understand the motion set off by an earthquake: **How do "ripples from a pond" connect with feeling an earthquake?** (Possible response: Circles

Guided Comprehension

1 **NOTE DETAILS** **What are the four layers of the earth?** (crust, mantle, outer core, inner core)

2 **COMPARE AND CONTRAST** **In what ways are the outer core and the inner core the same? In what ways are they different?** (Possible responses: They are both deep inside the earth; they are both very hot. The outer core is liquid, but the inner core is solid; the inner core is hotter than the outer core.)

3 **SPECULATE** **Do you think people will ever explore the center of the earth? Why or why not?** (Possible response: No; the heat is too great for people to survive.)

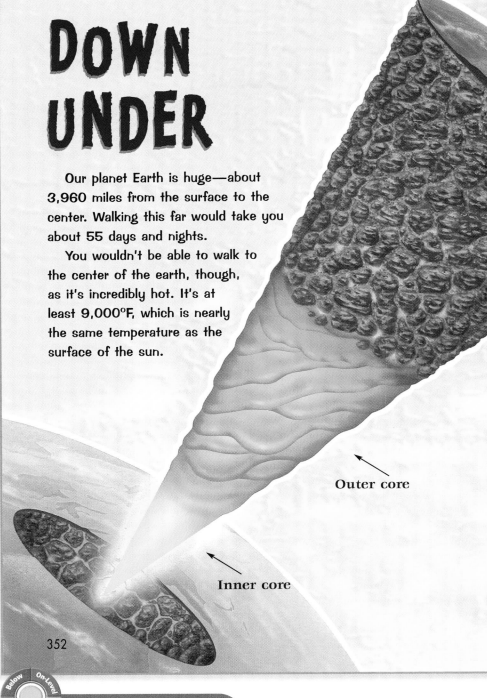

DOWN UNDER

Our planet Earth is huge—about 3,960 miles from the surface to the center. Walking this far would take you about 55 days and nights.

You wouldn't be able to walk to the center of the earth, though, as it's incredibly hot. It's at least 9,000°F, which is nearly the same temperature as the surface of the sun.

Outer core

Inner core

352

ENGLISH-LANGUAGE LEARNERS

Ask students to picture a rock and a bowl of cooked instant oatmeal cooled to room temperature. Have students briefly describe each substance. Explain that inside the earth, it is so hot that part of the rocky mantle melts and becomes mushy, like oatmeal. Remind students that when they read scientific topics, it helps to make comparisons to everyday objects to help them picture what is being described.

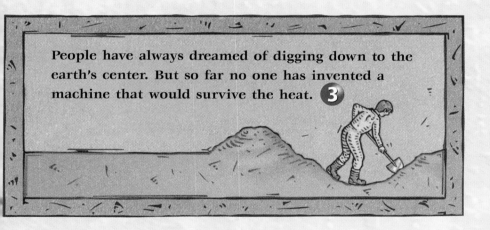

Earth has four layers. The top one is called the crust and it's made of rock. It's about 25 miles thick under the land, but only about 5 miles thick beneath the ocean.

The mantle is next. It's also made of rock, but it's so hot that some parts have melted into magma and are as gooey as oatmeal.

Beneath the mantle is Earth's core. This is made of metal and has two layers—an outer and an inner core. **1**

The outer core is runny because it's so hot. But although the inner core is even hotter, it's solid. Why? Because the other three layers are pressing down on it and the weight is enough to squash it solid! **2**

Crust

Mantle

People have always dreamed of digging down to the earth's center. But so far no one has invented a machine that would survive the heat. **3**

353

Monitor Progress

(Focus Strategy) **Adjust Reading Rate**

What could you do if you had trouble understanding the facts and vocabulary words on pages 352-353? (Possible response: Try reading more slowly to understand the details.)

Ask volunteers to tell why readers might want to read these pages at a slower rate.

If students have difficulty answering, use this model:

MODEL Page 352 contains some facts about the size of earth and the temperature of the earth's core. I will read this page and the next one more slowly to make sure I understand the facts.

SCIENCE

Forms of Matter Remind students that matter has three forms: solid, liquid, and gas. Also point out that when an object or a substance is heated, it evaporates or melts. Ask:

- **What forms of matter do the Earth's four layers have?** (solid and liquid)

- **What causes solid rock to become liquid in form?** (heat)

Ask students to find out at what temperature rocks can melt, and to share their findings in a chart or graph.

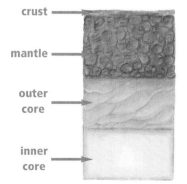

crust

mantle

outer core

inner core

Guided Comprehension

4 **USE PRIOR KNOWLEDGE** **In what way is the earth's surface like a puzzle?** (It is made up of separate pieces that fit together.)

5 **DRAW CONCLUSIONS** **Why might scientists study the movements of the earth's plates?** (Possible responses: to learn how land and mountains are formed and change; to predict how the earth's surface will look in the future)

6 (Focus Skill) **LOCATE INFORMATION** **Where on pages 354–355 would you find information about how the earth might look in millions of years?** (in the box at the top of page 355)

CRACKING UP

If all the oceans disappeared, Earth would look just like a jigsaw puzzle made up of lots of big pieces. **4**

The pieces are called plates, and there are about 20 of them. They float on the lower part of the earth's mantle, moving very, very slowly—between 1 and 8 inches per year.

Sometimes the plates move apart and gooey magma rises up from the mantle to fill the gap. The magma cools and hardens to form new land or ocean floor.

354

REACHING ALL LEARNERS

Diagnostic Check: Comprehension and Skills

If . . . students are having difficulty understanding how to use book parts,

Then . . . have small groups of students create questions for each other. Finding the answer should require students to use different book parts.

ADDITIONAL SUPPORT ACTIVITIES

BELOW-LEVEL Reteach, p. S80

ADVANCED Extend, p. S81

ENGLISH-LANGUAGE LEARNERS Reteach, p. S81

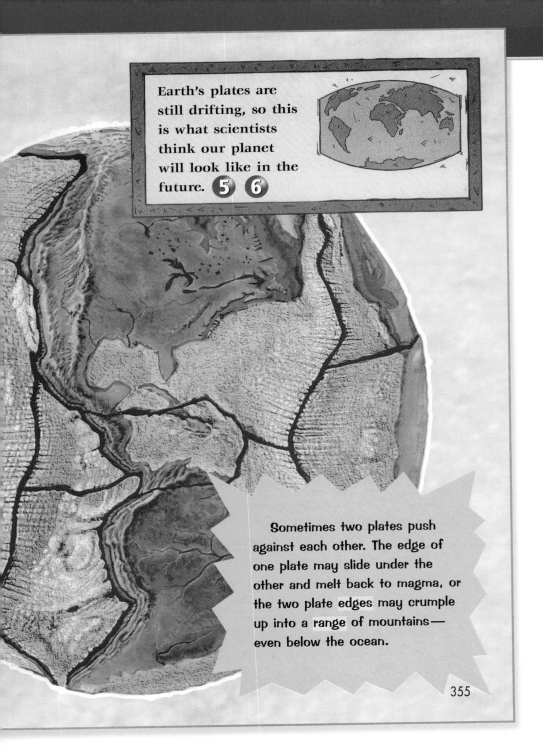

Earth's plates are still drifting, so this is what scientists think our planet will look like in the future. **5** **6**

Sometimes two plates push against each other. The edge of one plate may slide under the other and melt back to magma, or the two plate edges may crumple up into a range of mountains— even below the ocean.

355

Monitor Progress

Use Decoding/ Phonics

Ask students reading below level to read aloud the first paragraph on page 354. Listen for their pronunciation of the word *jigsaw*. If students mispronounce or cannot decode the word, model using letter sounds and word structure.

MODEL This word has the vowel-consonant-consonant-vowel pattern, so I think it has two syllables. I'll divide it between the two consonants, the *g* and the *s*. The first syllable is /jig/. The second syllable is a word I know—*saw*. The whole word is *jigsaw*, which is a type of puzzle. That makes sense.

SCIENCE

Interpret Sketches and Diagrams

Guide students to use the sketches and diagrams on pages 354–355 to understand the text. Ask:

- **What does the larger picture on these pages show?**
  (It shows the plates on the earth's surface.)

- **What does the smaller sketch on page 355 show?** (It shows how the earth's continents might look in the future as the plates continue to drift.)

Have pairs of students look through a science textbook or nature magazine and find a sketch or a diagram that shows a pattern of change. Ask partners to display the graphic and explain what it shows.

Rocking and Rolling **355**

Guided Comprehension

7 MAIN IDEA When an earthquake happens, does its force move in one direction or in all directions? (all directions)

8 AUTHOR'S CRAFT/INTERPRET IMAGERY Why do you think the author compares the movement of an earthquake's force to the movement of ripples on a pond? (Possible responses: Maybe he thinks most people have seen ripples move; he wants to help readers picture the force of the earthquake.)

QUAKE AND

Just a few minutes ago this truck was speeding along the road. Then, suddenly, there was a terrifying roar, and the ground opened up— an earthquake!

The most serious earthquakes happen deep underground, along the edges of the earth's plates.

Usually, the plates stay jammed close together. But from time to time a plate breaks away.

This makes the ground shudder and shake. Sometimes it can even split wide open.

356

ENGLISH-LANGUAGE LEARNERS

Help students understand the relationship between the earth's plates and earthquakes by placing the edges of two thick books side-by-side. Press the two books together until one slips over or under the other. Explain that the jolt that results from this kind of shift is an earthquake. If necessary, clarify other concepts by using an illustration.

SHAKE

These shudders can be felt thousands of miles away because they spread out from the earthquake's epicenter like the ripples from a stone thrown into a pond. **7** **8**

Every year, there are 40,000 to 50,000 earthquakes that are strong enough to be felt. However, only about 40 of them are big enough to cause any damage.

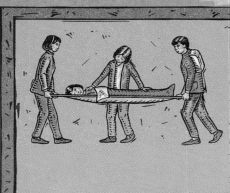

In Japan there's a National Disaster Prevention Day each year, when everyone practices what to do during an earthquake. Volunteers spend the day learning how to rescue people from fallen buildings.

357

Monitor Progress

Read Ahead

If you did not understand how the ground could open up and swallow a truck, what could you do to clear up your confusion?
(Possible response: I could keep reading. When I read ahead I find out that when the earth's plates break apart, the ground above them can split wide open.)

If students are unable to answer the question, model the strategy:

MODEL What could possibly make the earth split apart? I can try reading ahead to see if I find the answer. The next three paragraphs explain that the earth can split open when the plates break apart.

SCIENCE

Use Numerical Data to Compare Display a diagram like this one that shows the width of each layer of Earth. Have students use the measurements to compare the four layers of Earth. They should answer these questions: **Which layer is thickest? Which is thinnest? About how much thicker is the mantle than the outer core?**

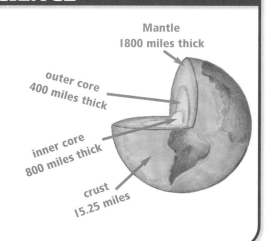

Mantle
1800 miles thick

outer core
400 miles thick

inner core
800 miles thick

crust
15.25 miles

Guided Comprehension

9 **CAUSE-EFFECT** **What causes tsunamis?** (They are caused by the force of an underwater earthquake.)

10 **MAKE COMPARISONS** **Why is a tsunami more dangerous than an ordinary wave?** (Possible responses: It is much bigger; it washes much farther onto the land; it hits with more force.)

WALLS OF

Most waves are made by the wind blowing over the sea. This is no ordinary wave, though. It's called a tsunami, and it was started by an earthquake.

A big earthquake is a lot like a huge bomb going off. The force of the explosion can create a tsunami that travels thousands of miles through the ocean. **9**

When the tsunami is in deep ocean water, its top may be only 8–12 inches above the surface.

But as it rolls on into shallower water near the **coast**, the tsunami is forced upward into a gigantic wall of water— sometimes it can be even higher than an apartment building! **10**

358

BELOW-LEVEL

Guide students to summarize what they have read by asking:

• **What can happen on land when two plates push together?** (earthquakes)

• **What can happen at sea when an earthquake occurs?** (The force of the earthquake can cause a giant wave called a tsunami to form.)

Have students read the rest of the selection to find out what other effects shifting plates can have on the earth.

WATER

359

Monitor Progress

Summarize

What are the most important ideas you have learned about earthquakes so far?
(Possible response: Earthquakes happen when the earth's plates shift or break away. An earthquake spreads outward from its epicenter. Earthquakes can cause the ground to shake or to split open. They can also cause giant waves called tsunamis.)

If students were unable to answer the question, use this model:

MODEL To summarize what I've learned about earthquakes, I restate the most important ideas in my own words. Earthquakes are caused by movement of the earth's plates. Earthquakes can cause the earth to shake or split, and they can cause giant waves called tsunamis.

SCIENCE

Wave Energy Tell students that energy can be carried from one place to another by waves, including water waves, sound waves, and electrical currents. A tsunami carries the energy released by an earthquake. Have pairs of students learn more about how a tsunami wave travels through the ocean. Have each pair create a three-panel illustration that shows a tsunami from the moment it forms until the moment it hits land.

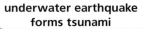

underwater earthquake forms tsunami

tsunami travels at sea 8–12 inches above surface

tsunami hits land

Guided Comprehension

11 **SUMMARIZE** **What kinds of underground movements form mountains?** (Plates crunch into one another and push up layers of crust. Magma bulges up beneath the crust to raise domes. A part of the crust is pushed up between two faults.)

12 **NOTE DETAILS** **Which type of mountain range are the Himalayas?** (fold mountains)

13 **CAUSE-EFFECT** **Why does Mount Everest keep growing?** (The plate carrying India keeps pushing against the rest of Asia, forcing the edges to continue to crumple and rise higher.)

14 (Focus Skill) **LOCATE INFORMATION** **Where on pages 360–361 would you look to find out where Mount Everest is in relation to other places?** (the map on page 361)

HIGHER AND HIGHER

Dome mountains happen when magma bulges up beneath the crust. This forces the crust up into a large rounded hump—much like the back of an elephant!

There are three main kinds of mountains. Fold mountains, like the Himalayas, form when the earth's plates crunch into one another, and layers of the crust are pushed up into loops and bumps.

360

ADVANCED

Have students find the name and height of the tallest mountain in North America (Mount McKinley), Africa (Kilimanjaro), South America (Aconcagua), and Europe (Mount El'brus). They can share what they learn in the form of a graph or pictograph. Have them include Mount Everest in the graph, too. For an additional challenge, have students find out how each mountain in their graph was formed.

El'brus	Kilimanjaro	McKinley	Aconcagua	Everest
18,510	19,341	20,320	22,834	29,035

Block mountains are made when part of the crust is forced up between two cracks in a plate. These cracks are called faults. **11**

Welcome to the top of the world. The Himalayas are the highest mountain ranges on Earth, and the tallest Himalayan peak is Mount Everest.

Everest already soars to a height of 29,029 feet. But next year it will be a tiny bit higher—it's still growing.

The Himalayas started forming around 53 million years ago when the earth's plate carrying the land that is now India began crunching upward into the rest of Asia.

Inch by inch, India pushed northward. And over tens of millions of years, the plate edges crumpled into the huge ridges, peaks, and valleys we see today. **13**

361

ONGOING ASSESSMENT

Monitor Progress

(Focus Strategy) **Adjust Reading Rate**

Which parts of pages 360–361 should you read more slowly? Why? (Possible responses: the information in the boxes; the map; These sections explain ideas that are new. I would read them more slowly in order to understand them.)

If students are unable to answer, ask: **Which parts of these pages explain how different kinds of mountains are formed? How do the words and pictures work together? If necessary, use this model:**

MODEL The words and pictures in the boxes work together to show how each kind of mountain is formed. I'll read the information slowly and then carefully study each picture to make sure I understand.

SCIENCE

Responding to Change Tell students that when an environment changes, some plants and animals that live there survive and reproduce, while others die or move to new locations. Ask students how the plant and animal population probably changed over time as the Himalayan region became more mountainous. (Possible response: Plants and animals moved to warmer regions; some might have adapted to the changes.) Invite interested students to research how the animal population in their region has changed as the environment has changed.

Guided Comprehension

15 DRAW CONCLUSIONS **What might this area look like if the river had flowed for hundreds of thousands more years? How do you know?** (The pillars might not be there; the selection says the river slowly wore the hard rock away.)

16 CAUSE-EFFECT **Why is erosion still going on today in dry, sandy places like this one?** (The wind picks up grit and sand and blasts the rocks with it.)

17 CAUSE-EFFECT/DRAW CONCLUSIONS **Where do you think small rocks come from? How do you know?** (Possible response: Small rocks come from big rocks that were chipped or broken into smaller pieces. The facts about erosion help me figure this out.)

18 (Focus Skill) LOCATE INFORMATION **Why does the heading "Going, Going, Gone" appear on these pages?** (Possible response: It tells readers that the author is about to explain a new idea—how Earth is worn down by erosion.)

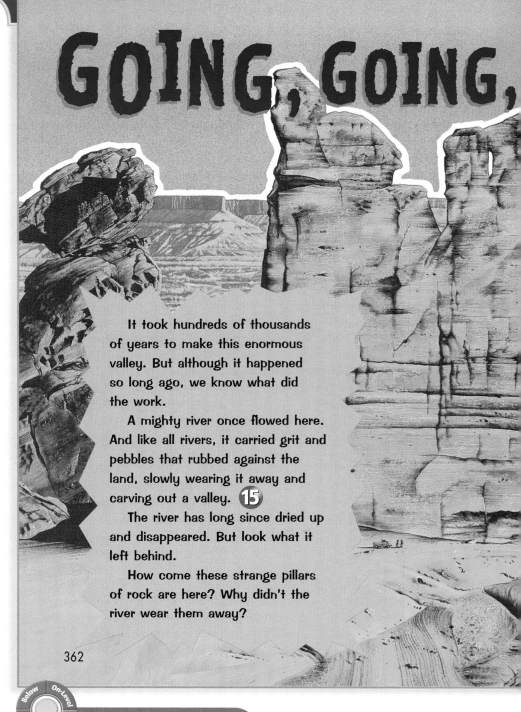

GOING, GOING,

It took hundreds of thousands of years to make this enormous valley. But although it happened so long ago, we know what did the work.

A mighty river once flowed here. And like all rivers, it carried grit and pebbles that rubbed against the land, slowly wearing it away and carving out a valley. **15**

The river has long since dried up and disappeared. But look what it left behind.

How come these strange pillars of rock are here? Why didn't the river wear them away?

362

ENGLISH-LANGUAGE LEARNERS

You may wish to explain these terms and phrases:

- **how come** ("why")
- **grit** ("tiny bits of sand or dirt")
- **wear away** ("rub against and break down")

Also, make sure students understand that when the author says the answer to what causes erosion is "blowing in the wind," he means that bits of grit and sand are being carried by the wind, and they, in turn, continue wearing away the rock.

GONE! 18

Well, some rocks are harder than others, and hard rocks break down more slowly than soft ones. 17 The river dried up before it had time to wear these pillars away.

The wearing away of the land is called erosion, and it's still going on today. But water isn't doing the work now—so what is?

The answer is blowing in the wind. Day after day it whistles through the valley, picking up grit and sand and blasting everything it touches. 16

363

related books

You may want to recommend to students these titles.

LIBRARY BOOKS COLLECTION

Jordi's Star
by Alma Flor Ada

ADDITIONAL READING

• ***What Happens When Volcanoes Erupt?***
by Daphne Butler. Raintree Steck-Vaughn, 1996. **EASY**

• ***The Earth***
by Anne Welsbacher. Abdo & Daughters, 1997.
AVERAGE

• ***The Egyptians and the Valley of the Kings***
by Philip Steele. Dillon, 1994. **CHALLENGING**

REREADING FOR FLUENCY

Readers Theatre   Have small groups choose a section of the main text of "Rocking and Rolling" to read aloud as if they were providing the voice-over for a documentary film. Discuss the use of careful phrasing, reading rate, and volume for the audience, purpose, and occasion. Circulate among students as they practice their reading.

For support, see Fluency Routine Cards in Theme Resources, pp. T80a–T80b.

Note: For assessment of oral reading accuracy and fluency, see pages T78–T80.

Guided Comprehension

RETURN TO THE PREDICTIONS/PURPOSE

Did you find the answers to your questions? Discuss with students whether their purposes for reading were met. Have them fill in the third column of the K-W-L chart.

Think and Respond

Answers:

1 Possible response: No. The plates of the earth will continue to move, forming mountains and causing earthquakes. Water and wind will continue to wear the land away. **CAUSE AND EFFECT**

2 Possible response: Pictures, captions, and diagrams explain ideas in the main text. **GRAPHIC AIDS**

3 Possible response: It builds up land and mountains when it flows out of the ground; it causes dome mountains to form. **NOTE DETAILS**

4 Answers will vary. **PERSONAL RESPONSE**

5 Possible response: Reading more slowly helped me understand new words and ideas. **READING STRATEGY**

OPEN-ENDED RESPONSE

Write a description of what you think a tsunami, a volcano, or an earthquake is like. Tell what you might see and hear before, during, and after the event.

The wind works like sandpaper, slowly wearing the rocks down and grinding them into weird and wonderful shapes.

Rock is much harder than wind and water—yet given time, wind and water are powerful enough to shape the land we live on.

Think and Respond

1 Will Earth look the same in one million years as it does now? How do you know?

2 Why is certain information placed in boxes or frames?

3 How does *magma* change the shape of Earth's surface?

4 What is one fact you learned from "Rocking and Rolling" that you did not know before?

5 How did using a reading strategy help you as you read this selection?

364

COMPREHENSION

End-of-Selection Test
To evaluate comprehension, see *Practice Book*, pages A49–A52.

MEET THE AUTHOR PHILIP STEELE

Philip Steele would make an interesting employee. Look over this application. What information might tell you that he is a good writer? Would you hire him to write for you?

Application for Employment

Name	Philip Steele	Job Desired	Author

Address Ynys Môn, Wales, United Kingdom

Education University College, Durham

Work History
English teacher, Germany
Editor for educational books, London, England
Writer and editor, North Wales

Hobbies Traveling, backpacking
Other Languages Welsh

Special Skills and Interests
I am curious and want to learn new things.
I enjoy history and nature. I also visit local schools to keep in touch with children's interests.

Published Works
The Greek News
The Blue Whale
The People Atlas

(Do you have another sheet of paper so that I can list all of them?)

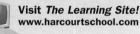

Visit *The Learning Site!*
www.harcourtschool.com

365

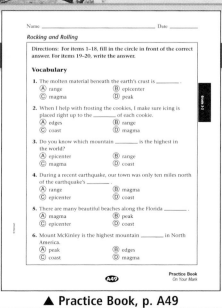

▲ Practice Book, p. A49

▲ Practice Book, p. A52

RETELL

Use these questions to guide students as they retell "Rocking and Rolling."
- What layers is the earth made up of? What is each layer like?
- How can the earth's plates change the land over time?
- What part do wind and water have in shaping the earth?

SUMMARIZE

Encourage students to summarize the selection using their completed K-W-L chart. See *Transparency* G on p. T88.

▼ Teaching Transparency G

What I Know	What I Want to Know	What I Learned
Rain and wind wear down mountain peaks. Waves wash away the edges of the coast.	This is called erosion. Is erosion still going on today?	Today, the wind is mostly responsible for erosion.

"Rocking and Rolling"
Celebrate Our World, Theme 3   **G**   Graphic Organizers Harcourt

WRITTEN SUMMARY

Have students create a written summary of the selection by answering the questions above in writing. PERFORMANCE ASSESSMENT

Making Connections

COMPARE TEXTS

Answers:

1 Possible response: by explaining the forces that shape and change Earth **THEME**

2 Possible response: Each section tells about a different topic. **TEXT STRUCTURE AND FORMAT**

3 Possible response: You need to know the information in each section in order to understand the next section. For example, the section called "Cracking Up" tells about the movement of plates on Earth's surface. The next section is about earthquakes, which are caused by the movements of the plates. The next section tells about tsunamis, which are caused by earthquakes. **TEXT STRUCTURE AND FORMAT**

4 Responses will vary. **MAKE COMPARISONS**

5 Responses will vary. **EXPRESS PERSONAL OPINIONS**

▲ Rocking and Rolling

Making Connections

Compare Texts

1 How does "Rocking and Rolling" give readers a better understanding of our world?

2 Why does the author divide the text into sections?

3 Why do you think the author put the sections in the order that he did? Explain your answer.

4 Name another nonfiction selection you have read that also includes diagrams. Which did you find easier to understand, "Rocking and Rolling" or the other selection? Tell why.

5 What topic or topics that the author tells about in "Rocking and Rolling" would you be most interested in exploring further?

Write a News Story

In "Rocking and Rolling," you read about earthquakes and tsunamis. Think about what might happen during and after an earthquake or a tsunami and how a news reporter would write about it. Then write a news story to inform the newspaper readers.

Use a graphic organizer like this one to plan your news story. Make up realistic details based on information from "Rocking and Rolling."

Writing CONNECTION

What?	
When?	
Where?	
Who?	
Why?	

366

Write a Report

In "Rocking and Rolling," you learned that some rocks are harder than others. The Earth's crust is made up of three types of rock. Do research to find out what they are and how they are different.

Write a report with three sections, one for each type of rock. Be sure to write a heading for each section. Include illustrations and diagrams if you wish. You might also want to collect some rock samples and decide what types of rock they might be.

Science CONNECTION

THE THREE TYPES OF ROCK

Estimate Distances

The distance from the surface of the Earth to its center is almost 4,000 miles. Suppose you traveled 4,000 miles north, south, east, or west from your home, on the Earth's surface. Look at a world map and estimate where you might be at the end of your journey. Then use the scale on the map to measure exactly where you would be.

Math CONNECTION

Estimated Location from Home	Actual Location from Home

367

HOMEWORK FOR THE WEEK

Students and family members can work together to complete the activities on page T98. You may want to assign some or all of the activities as homework for each day of the week.

technology
Visit *The Learning Site:*
www.harcourtschool.com
See Resources for Parents and Teachers: Homework Helper.

Teacher's Edition, p. T98 ▶

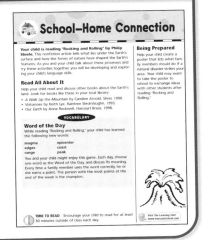

🏫 **School–Home Connection**

Your child is reading "Rocking and Rolling" by Philip Steele. This nonfiction article tells what lies under the Earth's surface and how the forces of nature have shaped the Earth's features. As you and your child talk about these processes and try these activities together, you will be developing and exploring your child's language skills.

Read All About It
Help your child read and discuss other books about the Earth's land. Look for books like these in your local library:
• *A Walk Up the Mountain* by Caroline Arnold. Silver, 1990.
• *Volcanoes* by Keith Lye. Raintree Steck-Vaughn, 1993.
• *Our Earth* by Anne Rockwell. Harcourt Brace, 1998.

VOCABULARY
Word of the Day
While reading "Rocking and Rolling," your child has learned the following new words:
magma   epicenter
edges   coast
range   peak
You and your child might enjoy this game. Each day, choose one word as the Word of the Day, and discuss its meaning. Every time a family member uses the word correctly, he or she earns a point. The person with the most points at the end of the week is the champion.

Being Prepared
Help your child create a poster that lists what family members should do if a natural disaster strikes your area. Your child may want to take the poster to school to exchange ideas with other students after reading "Rocking and Rolling."

TIME TO READ Encourage your child to read for at least 30 minutes outside of class each day.

Write a News Story
Help students create two concept webs—one for earthquakes and one for tsunamis. Encourage them to add descriptive words and vivid verbs to each web, and to use these in their articles. Ask them to think of a headline for their articles.

📁 **PORTFOLIO OPPORTUNITY**
Students may choose to place their newspaper articles in their working portfolios.

Write a Report
Bring in different types of rock and have students try to identify what kinds they are. Have students conduct their research and then return to the same rocks with their new knowledge. Have students categorize the rocks by type and explain the features of each.

Estimate Distances
If necessary, guide students in how to use the scale on a map to tell distances, as well as how to use a compass rose to tell direction. Invite them to try estimating several different distances and then checking their estimates. Interested students may want to read about one or more of the places they "landed on."

Locate Information

RETURN TO THE SKILL

Have students read page 368 in the *Pupil Edition*. You may wish to use this model:

MODEL In order to find a section about earthquakes, I'd look in the table of contents. "Quake and Shake" on page 356 looks like the right place to start looking. To find out information about the earth's mantle, I'd look in the index. That points me to page 353.

Ask students to explain how their knowledge of the parts of a book helped them to understand the information presented in "Rocking and Rolling."

PRACTICE/APPLY

Call on students to explain and demonstrate how to use the table of contents, glossary, and index to locate information in their science or social studies textbooks. PERFORMANCE ASSESSMENT

TECHNOLOGY ■ *Mission: Comprehension*™ *Skills Practice CD-ROM* provides additional practice with reading comprehension and focus skills.

Visit *The Learning Site:* www.harcourtschool.com
See Skill Actitvities and Test Tutors: Locate Information.

▲ Rocking and Rolling

Locate Information

Focus Skill

Imagine how the selection "Rocking and Rolling" would look as a book. What parts might the nonfiction book have? How could you use these parts of the book to find information?

Part of Book	Description	Example
title	• the name of a book, unit, chapter, or story	**Rocking and Rolling**
table of contents	• a list of the titles with the page numbers • near the front of a book	**Table of Contents** Down Under 35 Cracking Up 35 Quake and Shake 35
chapter heading	• title at the beginning of each new chapter	**Down Under** (on page 352)
glossary	• dictionary of terms used in the book • in the back of the book	**Glossary** **range** [rānj] *n.* A row or line of mountains
index	• alphabetical list of topics and page numbers • in the back of a book	**Index** magma 353, 354, 36 mantle 35 mountains 360–36

Visit *The Learning Site!*
www.harcourtschool.com

See Skills and Activities

368

REACHING ALL LEARNERS

Diagnostic Check: Comprehension and Skills

If . . . students are unable to identify information found in an index or a table of contents,

Then . . . conduct a scavenger hunt for information in a science or social studies textbook, having them use the table of contents and the index.

ADDITIONAL SUPPORT ACTIVITIES

BELOW-LEVEL	Reteach, p. S80
ADVANCED	Extend, p. S81
ENGLISH-LANGUAGE LEARNERS	Reteach, p. S81

Test Prep
Locate Information

▶ Here is the table of contents for a book about volcanoes.

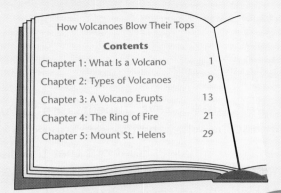

How Volcanoes Blow Their Tops

Contents

1. "A Volcano Erupts" is—

   A a book title

   B a chapter title

   C a story title

   D listed alphabetically

Tip

Look carefully at the information that the table of contents gives you.

2. **You could use this table of contents to find out—**

   F the meaning of the word *erupts*

   G which pages tell about lava

   H on what pages you can read about the Ring of Fire

   J why scientists study volcanoes

Tip

Look at the table of contents provided. Which of the answer choices matches a chapter title?

369

Focus Skill

Test Prep

Locate Information Have students read the passage carefully and think about the information it provides. Use the Tips to reinforce good test-taking strategies. (1.B; 2.H)

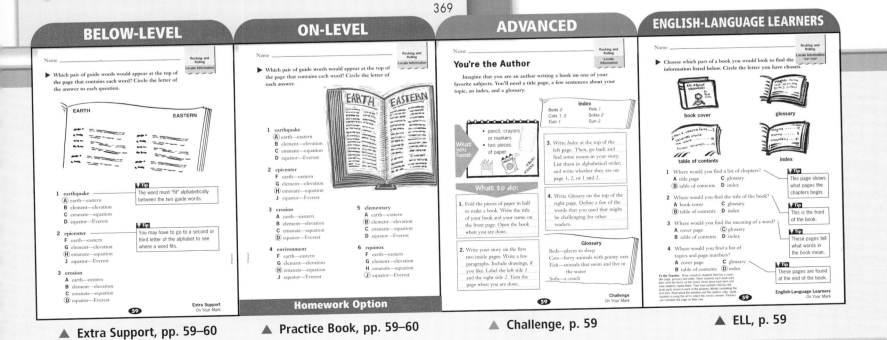

BELOW-LEVEL — ▲ Extra Support, pp. 59–60

ON-LEVEL — ▲ Practice Book, pp. 59–60

ADVANCED — ▲ Challenge, p. 59

ENGLISH-LANGUAGE LEARNERS — ▲ ELL, p. 59

OBJECTIVE

To interpret information on graphic aids

SKILL TRACE	
GRAPHIC AIDS	
Introduce	**pp. 369A–369B**
Reteach	p. T74
Review	pp. 399C, 417B
Test	Theme 3 Vol. 2

Graphic Aids

Research and Information Skills

INTRODUCE THE SKILL

Discuss using graphic aids. Have students turn to *Pupil Edition* pages 352–353 and describe what the diagram shows. (a view of what the earth's four layers are like) Point out that the diagram helps them understand the text. Explain that diagrams are one kind of graphic aid; other kinds include maps, charts, and graphs.

TEACH/MODEL

Model how to use a graphic aid. Have students turn to pages 360–361 in the *Pupil Edition*. Model using a diagram and a map to locate information.

MODEL The diagrams help me understand how fold mountains, dome mountains, and block mountains are formed. The map helps me see where Mount Everest is in relation to other places.

Display Transparency 255. Guide students in interpreting the flowchart and the bar graph. Ask:

- **What does the flow chart show?** (how a tsunami forms)

- **What is the last step in the process?** (The wave grows taller when it gets closer to land.)

- **Which country in the bar graph has the greatest number of active volcanoes?** (Costa Rica)

- **Which country has the fewest active volcanoes?** (Greece)

Make a flowchart. Have pairs of students make a flowchart that shows how the valleys and canyons pictured on pages 362–363 were formed. **PERFORMANCE ASSESSMENT**

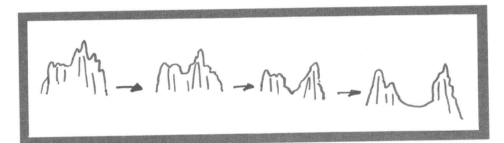

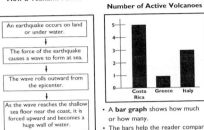

▼ **Teaching Transparency 255**

GRAPHIC AIDS

- Graphic aids include maps, charts, graphs, and diagrams.
- Graphic aids can help readers understand the words and ideas in stories and articles.

How a Tsunami Forms

| An earthquake occurs on land or under water. |
| The force of the earthquake causes a wave to form at sea. |
| The wave rolls outward from the epicenter. |
| As the wave reaches the shallow sea floor near the coast, it is forced upward and becomes a huge wall of water. |

Number of Active Volcanoes

- A **bar graph** shows how much or how many.
- The bars help the reader compare numbers in a group.

- A **flowchart** shows a sequence of steps that explains how something happens, or how to do or make something.

"Rocking and Rolling"
Celebrate Our World, Theme 3   255   Graphic Aids
Harcourt

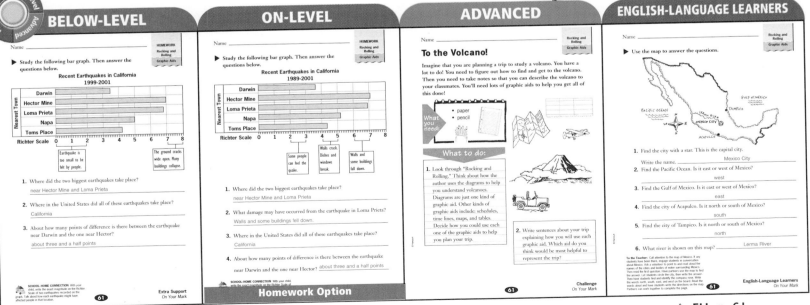

| ▲ Extra Support, p. 61 | ▲ Practice Book, p. 61 | ▲ Challenge, p. 61 | ▲ ELL, p. 61 |

Rocking and Rolling **369B**

Phonics

Decoding/Phonics

Syllable Patterns: Schwa

OBJECTIVE

To recognize the schwa sound in unstressed syllables

SKILL TRACE

SYLLABLE PATTERNS: SCHWA

Introduce	Grade 2
Maintain	**p. 369C**

ONGOING ASSESSMENT

If students are not able to fluently read approximately 114 words per minute, **then** they require phonics instruction and will also benefit from fluency practice.

NOTE: For assessment of oral reading practice and fluency, see pages T78–T80.

REVIEW THE SKILL

Discuss the schwa sound.   Write this sentence on the board:

• I wish I had a hundred dollars!

Review with students that in words with more than one syllable, one syllable is stressed more than the others. Point to the word *hundred* and pronounce it with stress on the last syllable. Ask students if this sounds correct. (no) Then try pronouncing it with the stress on the first syllable. Ask students if this sounds like a word they know. (yes) Explain that the final vowel sound in this word is a *schwa sound.* Point out that in a two-syllable word, the vowel sound in the unstressed syllable is often a schwa sound. Remind students that:

• The schwa sound is not long or short.
• The schwa sound has many different spellings.

PRACTICE/APPLY

Decode unfamiliar words.   Write these sentences on the board and have students underline the words with the schwa sound. Then, have students identify the syllables that have the schwa sound in the word.

• The dog appears to have run away! (<u>a</u>ppears, <u>a</u>way)
• Breakfast is the best meal. (break<u>fast</u>)
• The arithmetic problem is too hard! (arith<u>me</u>tic, prob<u>lem</u>)

Then have students read the sentences out loud to a partner.

To check understanding, have students read these words aloud. Have them identify the syllables that have the schwa sound: *label, calendar, senator, magazine,* and *another.* PERFORMANCE ASSESSMENT

Cause and Effect

Comprehension

REVIEW THE SKILL

Discuss cause and effect. Remind students that a *cause* makes something happen; an *effect* is what happens as a result of a cause. To figure out causes and effects, readers can look for clue words such as *because* or *so* and can use what they know from real life.

Model using a clue word to identify a cause and an effect.

> **MODEL** On page 362, the author asks: "How come these strange pillars of rock are here? Why didn't the river wear them away?" The words *how come* and *why* are clues that the author is about to state a cause. Some rocks are harder than others—that is what causes the strange pillars of rock.

PRACTICE/APPLY

Make a cause-effect chart. Have students identify two cause-and-effect relationships and two clue words in the last paragraph of selection text on page 353. Students should fill in charts like the ones below to show the events. PERFORMANCE ASSESSMENT

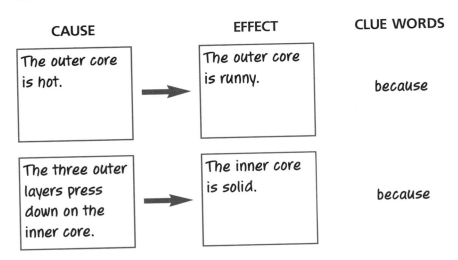

CAUSE	EFFECT	CLUE WORDS
The outer core is hot.	→ The outer core is runny.	because
The three outer layers press down on the inner core.	→ The inner core is solid.	because

Summarize. Ask students to tell what a cause-and-effect relationship is.

OBJECTIVE

To recognize cause-and-effect relationships

SKILL TRACE

CAUSE AND EFFECT

Introduce	p. 324I
Reteach	pp. S74, S86, T71
Review	**pp. 346, 369D, 370I, 398**
Test	Theme 3 Vol. 2

BELOW-LEVEL

Tell students that in the last paragraph on page 353, the effects are given before the causes. Help students rephrase the sentences by stating the causes first. (Because the outer core is hot, the outer core is runny.) Then have them complete the charts.

Writing Process

Play

Writing Process: Expressive Writing

TRAITS OF GOOD WRITING

	INTRODUCE AND PRACTICE	APPLY TO LONGER WRITING FORMS
Focus/Ideas	329E–F (3-1)	355E–F, 387E–F (3-1)
Organization	167C–D, 193E–F (3-2)	221E–F, 261E–F (3-2)
Voice	41C–D, 67E–F (3-1)	99E–F, 129C–D (3-1)
Word Choice	323C–D, 347C–D (3-2)	369E–F, 399E–F (3-2)
Development	303E–F, 329E–F (3-1)	355E–F, 387E–F (3-1)
Effective Sentences	35E–F, 59E–F (3-2)	93E–F, 117C–D (3-2)
Effective Paragraphs	181E–F, 205E–F (3-1)	223E–F, 255C–D (3-1)
Conventions	(See Grammar and Spelling Lessons.)	(Applied to all writing lessons.)

technology

Writing Express™ CD-ROM
Visit *The Learning Site:*
www.harcourtschool.com
See Writing Detective,
Proofreading Makes Perfect.

TRAITS OF GOOD WRITING

- **Focus/Ideas:** The writer of the play tells a story that focuses on one main problem or situation. The play has a beginning, middle, and ending.

- **Organization:** The writer describes the setting at the beginning. The names of the characters are given along with their dialogue. Stage directions tell how the characters move and act.

- **Voice:** The writer uses dialogue that sounds like speech.

- **Word Choice:** The writer uses vivid verbs to tell what happens.

- **Development:** The writer uses dialogue to provide details that are important to the play.

- **Effective Sentences:** The writer uses a variety of sentence types—statements, exclamations, questions, and commands.

369E   Celebrate Our World

DAY 1 — TEACH/MODEL

CONNECT READING TO WRITING
Ask students if they have ever felt an earthquake. Remind them that there are ways to prepare for an earthquake. Explain that one way to show what a family does during an earthquake is to write a story or a play about it. Inform students that in this lesson they will write plays.

REVIEW WRITER'S CRAFT Display Transparencies 256A and B. Explain that the play is about a family that survives an earthquake. Then, have volunteers read the model aloud. Point out how the author uses vivid verbs and specific nouns to keep the writing interesting.

▼ Teaching Transparency 256A&B

STUDENT MODEL: PLAY

In a play, the writer tells about one main problem or idea. At the beginning of a play, the writer describes the setting. Then the writer lists each character that speaks, and writes the words that each character says. Stage directions, which tell the actors what to do, appear in parentheses. Here is a play that a student wrote about a family that survives an earthquake.

title	**Shaken Up but Fine**
setting	*(The living room of a family home after an earthquake. A 9-year-old boy walks into the room. Soon after that his parents rush in through the front door and give him a hug.)*
characters and their dialogue	**Dad:** *Are you OK, son?*
	Ben: *Fine, Dad. Boy, that quake was something!*
	Mom: *We were worried about you! We were just walking up the street when the quake hit. Good thing we were just out for a walk and not driving on the freeway…Where were you when it hit, honey?*
events and details of the plot	**Ben:** *I was in the kitchen getting a snack and suddenly Ollie started barking like crazy. The dishes started rattling and I thought maybe there was a big truck driving by. Then I saw the light swinging back and forth, and the floor started rolling up and down like a big wave.*

"Rocking and Rolling"
Celebrate Our World, Theme 3
Writing Harcourt

DAY 2 — ANALYZE AND PREWRITE

ANALYZE THE WRITING PROMPT
Have students use the following prompt or brainstorm their own ideas for a play.

WRITING PROMPT: *Write a play for your classmates about a family that survives an emergency such as an earthquake or a flood. Be sure to include a beginning, a middle, and an ending.*

ASK THE FOLLOWING QUESTIONS:

- **Who is your audience and what is your purpose for writing?**
- **What is the setting? Who are the characters?**
- **What is the problem that they face?**
- **What is the solution to the problem?**

▼ Teaching Transparency 257

STORY MAP

Setting:	Characters:

Problem:

Beginning

Middle
Main Events/Details

Ending
Solution to Problem

"Rocking and Rolling"
Celebrate Our World, Theme 3
257
Writing Harcourt

5 Day Plan

DAY 3 — DRAFT

Display Transparency 257. Have students use it as a graphic organizer to plan their plays. They can include details about the characters, setting, and plot. Then have students use the steps below to draft their plays:

1. **Draft the Beginning** Use the ideas in your story map to introduce the setting and characters.

2. **Introduce Problem** Describe what problem or situation your characters are facing.

3. **Develop the Play** Write about the events that happen. Use details to make the events interesting to read. Remember to use the proper format for writing a play.

4. **Conclude the Play** Write an ending which gives some kind of solution to the problem.

DAY 4 — EDIT

REVISE Have students work in pairs or small groups to discuss their plays. Encourage them to ask themselves the following questions while editing:

- **Is it always clear which character is speaking?**

- **Is the sequence of events in the play clear and easy to follow?**

- **Do the stage directions make sense?**

Ask students to make sure that they introduce the setting and characters in the beginning of their plays, and that their plot also includes a middle and an ending.

PROOFREAD Have students use the questions below as they proofread:

✓ **Did I correctly use capital letters and punctuation marks?**

✓ **Did I correctly form contractions?**

✓ **Did I use correct forms of the verb *be*?**

✓ **Did I spell words correctly?**

DAY 5 — PUBLISH AND ASSESS

PUBLISH Students may want to use a computer to publish their plays. Then, if they wish, they might work in groups to perform some or all of the plays for the class.

ASSESS Have students make up criteria on which to evaluate their own and each other's work. They should add their plays and their evaluations to their portfolios.

 Language Handbook, pp. 18–21, 160–162.

Grammar

Contractions

SKILL TRACE
CONTRACTIONS

Introduce	pp. 369G–369H
Reteach	pp. S83, T75
Review	pp. 369H, 399H
Test	Theme 3 Vol. 2

REACHING ALL LEARNERS

Diagnostic Check: Grammar and Writing

If . . . students are unable to form contractions,

Then . . . have them work in pairs and use flash cards with the contraction on one side and the two words from which the contraction is formed on the other side.

ADDITIONAL SUPPORT ACTIVITIES

BELOW-LEVEL Reteach, p. S82
ADVANCED Extend, p. S83
ENGLISH-LANGUAGE LEARNERS Reteach, p. S83

technology

Grammar Jingles™ CD,
Intermediate: Track 20
Visit *The Learning Site:*
www.harcourtschool.com
See Grammar Practice Park,
Multimedia Grammar Glossary.

DAY 1 — TEACH/MODEL

DAILY LANGUAGE PRACTICE

1. i just found this map. It were in a bag with forty pennys. (I; was; pennies)
2. The map show mountains. All over the world. (shows; mountains all)

INTRODUCE THE CONCEPT   Use Transparency 258 to make these points:

• A **contraction** is a short way to write two words. In a contraction, an apostrophe (') takes the place of the missing letters.

Have students name the missing letters in the contractions in sentences 2 and 4. Then, write sentences using the contractions from items 5 and 6.

▼ **Teaching Transparency 258**

CONTRACTIONS

1. It is called a tsunami.
2. It's called a tsunami. The missing letter in *it's* is *i*.
3. A tsunami is not ordinary.
4. A tsunami isn't ordinary. The missing letter in *isn't* is *o*.
5. you + are = you're
6. are + not = aren't

CONTRACTIONS WITH PRONOUNS

Pronoun	Form of *be*	Contraction
I	am	I'm
you	are	you're
he, she, it	is	he's, she's, it's
we	are	we're
they	are	they're

CONTRACTIONS WITH NOT

Verb	+ not	Contraction
can	not	can't
could	not	couldn't
do, does, did	not	don't, doesn't, didn't
have, has, had	not	haven't, hasn't, hadn't
is, are, was, were	not	isn't, aren't, wasn't, weren't
should	not	shouldn't

"Rocking and Rolling"
Celebrate Our World, Theme 3   258   Grammar
Harcourt

DAY 2 — EXTEND THE CONCEPT

DAILY LANGUAGE PRACTICE

1. Look at this mountain. Its the most highest in the world. (It's; the highest)
2. It is called Mount Everest. And its' in the Himalayas. (Everest, and; it's)

DEVELOP THE CONCEPT   Use the charts on Transparency 258 to make these points:

• Subject pronouns are often used in contractions.

• The negative *not* is often used in a contraction with a verb.

Ask students to identify the missing letters in the contractions. Point out that the *o* in *not* is left out in contractions with *not*. Discuss the verb *were* and the contraction *we're*. **PERFORMANCE ASSESSMENT**

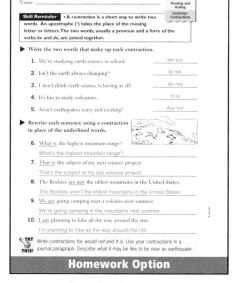

Name _____

Skill Reminder • A contraction is a short way to write two words. An apostrophe (') takes the place of the missing letter or letters. The two words, usually a pronoun and a form of the verbs be and do, are joined together.

▶ Write the two words that make up each contraction.

1. We're studying earth science in school. ___ we are
2. Isn't the earth always changing? ___ is not
3. I don't think earth science is boring at all! ___ do not
4. It's fun to study volcanoes. ___ It is
5. Aren't earthquakes scary and exciting? ___ Are not

▶ Rewrite each sentence using a contraction in place of the underlined words.

6. **What is** the highest mountain range?
   What's the highest mountain range?
7. **That is** the subject of my next science project.
   That's the subject of my last science project.
8. The Rockies **are not** the oldest mountains in the United States.
   The Rockies aren't the oldest mountains in the United States.
9. **We are** going camping near a volcano next summer.
   We're going camping in the mountains next summer.
10. **I am** planning to hike all the way around the rim.
    I'm planning to hike all the way around the rim.

TRY THIS! Write contractions for *would not* and *it is*. Use your contractions in a journal paragraph. Describe what it may be like to be near an earthquake.

Homework Option

▲ Practice Book, p. 62

5 Day Plan

DAY 3 — ORAL REVIEW/PRACTICE

DAILY LANGUAGE PRACTICE

1. No person has ever went to the center of our planet (gone; planet.)

2. Youd burn up before you got there (You'd; there.)

CONTRACTION Q & A   Ask a question about the selection; for example—*Don't earthquakes cause tsunamis?* Have students identify the contraction and reply in a complete sentence—*Yes, earthquakes do cause tsunamis.*

Test Prep Tip

"To help you on language tests, always remember that:

• often the apostrophe in a pronoun-verb contraction replaces the first letter or letters of the verb."

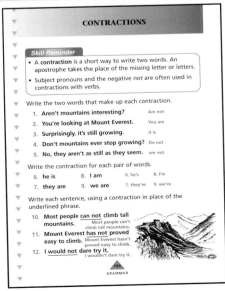

▲ Language Handbook, p. 160

DAY 4 — APPLY TO WRITING

DAILY LANGUAGE PRACTICE

1. Can you believe it The inner core of the planet is solid? (it? The; solid.)

2. Thats because the other layers pushes down on it. (That's; push)

FLASH CARDS   Have students make a set of flash cards for studying contractions. One side of each card should have a sentence that uses a contraction, and the other side should have the two words from which the contraction is formed. Ask students to study the contractions and then work together to test themselves. After they finish, have students write story scenes with dialogue that uses contractions.

▲ Language Handbook, p. 161

DAY 5 — CUMULATIVE REVIEW

DAILY LANGUAGE PRACTICE

1. how hot is the center. i think its 9000°F. (How; center? I; it's)

2. Im reading about tsunamis. But Iv'e never seen one. (I'm; tsunamis, but; I've)

PROOFREAD   Display the following sentences. Ask students to proofread them for errors in spelling, punctuation, and grammar. Then have them rewrite each sentence correctly.

1. He coulnd't join we for lunch. (couldn't; join us)

2. Paul and Scott hasn't arrived yet. (haven't)

3. Were going to an concert tonight. (We're; a)

4. Their studying earthquake. (They're; earthquakes)

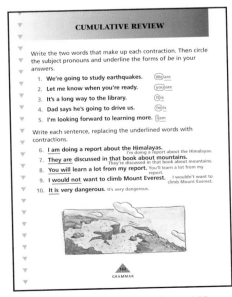

▲ Language Handbook, p. 162

Rocking and Rolling   **369H**

Spelling Words

1. it's*
2. isn't*
3. you've
4. we'd
5. didn't
6. she's
7. we've
8. haven't
9. he'd
10. they'd
11. there's*
12. don't
13. we'll
14. won't
15. he's

Challenge Words

16. temperature*
17. depth
18. width
19. weight*
20. height

* Selection Words

Spelling

Contractions

DAY 1 — PRETEST/SELF-CHECK

ADMINISTER THE PRETEST   Use the Dictation Sentences under Day 5. Help students self-check their pretests using Transparency 259.

ADVANCED

Use the Challenge Words in these Dictation Sentences:

16. My **temperature** is normal.
17. What is the **depth** of the ocean?
18. I used my ruler to find the **width** of the rectangle.
19. The nurse wrote down my **weight**.
20. The doctor measured my **height**.

DAY 2 — TEACH/MODEL

WORD SORT   Display Transparency 259. Make sure students know the meanings of the words. Then ask students to copy the chart and to write each Spelling Word where it belongs.

Next, point to and read the word *it's*. Ask students what two words make up the contraction. (it is) Repeat with the word *we've*. (we have) Ask students what takes the place of the missing letters. (an apostrophe)

HANDWRITING   Advise students not to join the letter before the apostrophe to the letter after it.

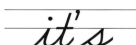

▼ Teaching Transparency 259

CONTRACTIONS

Spelling Words

1. *it's*	6. *she's*	11. *there's*
2. *isn't*	7. *we've*	12. *don't*
3. *you've*	8. *haven't*	13. *we'll*
4. *we'd*	9. *he'd*	14. *won't*
5. *didn't*	10. *they'd*	15. *he's*

- A contraction is a short way to write two words.
- An apostrophe replaces any missing letters.

with *not*	with *is*	with *have*	with *would*	with *will*
isn't	it's	you've	we'd	we'll
didn't	she's	we've	he'd	
haven't	there's		they'd	
don't	he's			
won't				

"Rocking and Rolling"
Celebrate Our World, Theme 3
259
Spelling
Harcourt

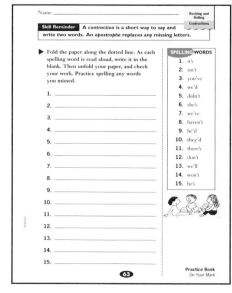

▲ Practice Book, page 63

▲ Spelling Practice Book, page 101

5 Day Plan

DAY 3 — SPELLING STRATEGIES

CONTRACTIONS Ask students what kinds of words can be written together as a contraction. (*a pronoun and a verb; a verb and not*) Write the following sentence on the board: *They would like to go with you.* Have students read the sentence. Ask them which two words can be replaced by a contraction, and have them tell what the contraction would be. (*they would; they'd*)

✏️ Apply to Writing

Have students proofread their writing, looking for contractions to be sure they have spelled them correctly.

▲ Spelling Practice Book, page 102

DAY 4 — SPELLING ACTIVITIES

WORD CONSTRUCTIONS Write the following words on the board:

does	would
she	not
have	is
we	

Have students work in pairs to see how many contractions they can make by combining two words and adding an apostrophe. When they have finished, make a master list of words on the board to see how many contractions were formed.

doesn't	haven't
she's	we'd
we've	she'd
wouldn't	

▲ Spelling Practice Book, page 103

DAY 5 — POSTTEST

DICTATION SENTENCES

1. **It's** a sunny day.
2. He **isn't** my brother.
3. It has been a long time since **you've** been absent.
4. They know that **we'd** like to go swimming with them.
5. I **didn't** like that board game.
6. I wonder if **she's** ready to go.
7. **We've** been waiting for you for an hour.
8. You **haven't** told us your name.
9. He said that **he'd** like to go with us to the zoo.
10. Do you think **they'd** like to help with the puppet show?
11. **There's** more food in the kitchen.
12. I **don't** feel sleepy yet.
13. **We'll** go fishing on Sunday.
14. Dad **won't** let me go to the party.
15. **He's** waiting for us at the park.

Rocking and Rolling **369J**

Word Study

Homographs

OBJECTIVE

To use knowledge of homographs to determine word meaning

Write the word *coast* on the board. Ask students if they can think of two meanings for this word. ("land along the sea"; "to glide downhill") Remind students that words that are spelled alike but have different meanings are called **homographs.**

Work with students to find out how each word in the left-hand column of the chart below is used in the selection. Then have pairs of students find the meaning for each word and its homograph in a dictionary, and add them to the chart.

Selection Word and Meaning	Homograph and Meaning
felt (p. 357) (noticed)	felt (soft cloth made of wool or cotton)
rolls (p. 358) (turns over and over)	rolls (small, rolled pieces of bread)
faults (p. 361) (cracks in the earth's plates)	faults (weaknesses)
top (p. 361) (highest part of something)	top (a toy that spins)

ADVANCED

Have students brainstorm a list of homographs. Then have them write sentences using both meanings of the word in each sentence. Encourage students to rewrite their sentences, omitting the homographs. Have them exchange their sentence frames with a partner. Partners should use context to determine the words in each sentence.

Borrowed Words

OBJECTIVE

To determine word origins

Inform students that the word *tsunami* is a Japanese word meaning "harbor wave"—a wave that rolls into a harbor. Explain that English has borrowed this word. Invite students to speculate on why the Japanese created a word for this type of wave. (Possible response: They probably had many of these waves come ashore and cause damage.)

Have students work in small groups. Each group can look in a dictionary to find what language the following words are from.

plaza	(Spanish)
karate	(Japanese)
kayak	(Inuit)
spaghetti	(Italian)
yogurt	(Turkish)

Encourage groups to think of other words that have been borrowed and to look in a student dictionary to see if they are correct.

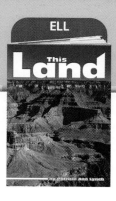
Managing Small Groups

While you work with small groups, have other students do the following:
- Self-Selected Reading
- Practice Pages
- Cross-Curricular Centers
- Journal Writing

▲ page 369M   ▲ page 369N

■ ENGLISH-LANGUAGE LEARNERS

 Focus Skill: Locate Information

 Focus Strategy: Adjust Reading Rate

 Concept Vocabulary: *island, lake, canyon, desert, forest*

Genre: Narrative Nonfiction
Social Studies: Physical Geography

SUMMARY   The author invites readers to take an imaginary hot-air balloon trip across the United States. She describes the West Coast mountain ranges, the western deserts, the Rocky Mountains, the Great Plains, the Mississippi River, the Great Lakes, the Smoky Mountains, and Florida's Everglades. The journey ends with side trips over Alaska and Hawaii.

 Visit *The Learning Site:*
www.harcourtschool.com
See Resources for Parents and
Teachers: Books for All Learners.

BEFORE READING

Tap Prior Knowledge   Write the word *geography* on the board and tell students that geography is the study of *mountains, rivers,* and other features of the earth. Ask students to name some different land forms they know of. Sketch and label each feature as students name it.

Total Physical Response   Say the names of the geographic features students listed and have them use hand movements to depict each one. (For *mountain,* students might form a peak using two hands.)

Display Vocabulary/Concept Words   Write vocabulary words that have not been discussed on the board. Use the picture on pages 2–3 to explain the directional words *north, south, east,* and *west.*

Preview the Book   Have students preview the book by looking at the map and illustrations. Tell students what this selection is about.

READING THE BOOK

Pages 2–3   Where in this book can you find the names of all 50 U.S. states? (The map on pages 2–3 shows the states' names and locations.) **LOCATE INFORMATION**

Pages 2–8   What parts of the United States have we seen so far? (the West Coast mountain ranges, the desert sand dunes and mesas, the Colorado River, the Grand Canyon, and the Rocky Mountains) Is the land the same everywhere? (No, it is different in different places.) **MAIN IDEA**

Pages 9–11   What are the Great Plains like? (They are wide, flat, and grassy.) Describe the Great Lakes. (They are five huge freshwater lakes.) **NOTE DETAILS**

Rereading   Invite students to name some places in the selection they would like to visit someday. Read aloud the description of each place with students.

RESPONDING

Map Tour   Display a map of the United States. Have students point to one state, river, or landform and tell what they learned about it.

Teacher Notes

Teacher Notes

THEME CONNECTION:
Celebrate Our World

GENRE:
Informational Narrative

Award-Winning Author/Illustrator

Comparing Informational Narrative and Expository Nonfiction

▲ **READING ACROSS TEXTS:** "Mapping the World," by Barbara Taylor
GENRE: Expository Nonfiction

SUMMARY:

To find out where in the world his home is, Armadillo leaves the Texas woods, crosses prairies, rides on an eagle's back, and then boards a space shuttle. From space he sees that his state, Texas, is in the United States on the North American continent, on planet Earth.

 All selections available on *Audiotext 6*.

Books for All Learners

Lesson Plans on pages 399M–399P

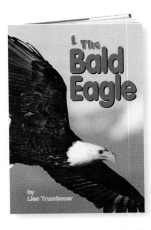

BELOW-LEVEL	ON-LEVEL	ADVANCED	ELL
• Lesson Vocabulary	• Lesson Vocabulary	• Challenge Vocabulary	• Concept Vocabulary
• Focus Skill: Cause and Effect	• Focus Skill: Cause and Effect	• Focus Skill: Cause and Effect	• Focus Skill: Cause and Effect

MULTI-LEVEL PRACTICE

Extra Support, pp. 64–65

Practice Book, pp. 64–67

Challenge, pp. 64–65

English-Language Learners, pp. 64–65

ADDITIONAL RESOURCES

Spelling Practice Book, pp. 104–106

Language Handbook, pp. 73, 163–165

Audiotext 6

Intervention Resource Kit, Lesson 29
  • Intervention Reader, *Included in Intervention Resource Kit*

English-Language Learners Resource Kit, Lesson 29

Technology

• *Writing Express*™ **CD-ROM**

• *Grammar Jingles*™ **CD**

• *Media Literacy and Communication Skills Package* (Video)

• *Reading and Language Skills Assessment* **CD-ROM**

• *The Learning Site:* **www.harcourtschool.com**

5–15 Minutes

ORAL LANGUAGE

- Question of the Day
- Sharing Literature

15–30 Minutes

SKILLS & STRATEGIES

- Comprehension

- Vocabulary

30–45 Minutes

READING

- Guided Comprehension

- Independent Reading

- Cross-Curricular Connections

45–90 Minutes

LANGUAGE ARTS

- Writing

  Daily Writing Prompt

- Grammar

  Daily Language Practice

- Spelling

Daily Routines
- Question of the Day
- Daily Language Practice
- Daily Writing Prompt

Day 1

Question of the Day, p. 370H
Where in the world are you?

Literature Read-Aloud, pp. 370G–H

Comprehension:
 (Skill) Cause and Effect, p. 370I **T**
 (Strategy) Reread to Clarify, p. 370J

Vocabulary, p. 370L

Read: Vocabulary Power, pp. 370–371
Vocabulary Power Words:
eventually, converse, continent, sphere, universe, homeward

 Independent Reading
Books for All Learners

SCIENCE Map Vegetation Areas

Writing: Writing Process, p. 399E

Writing Prompt:
The plates on an armadillo's body protect it from animals that may want to eat it. Think of another animal that has a built-in defense. Now write about that animal and how it protects itself from enemies.

Grammar:
Adverbs, p. 399G **T**

Daily Language Practice

1. what kind of animal is a armadillo. (What; an; armadillo?)
2. Its an animal with bony plates. All over its body and head. (It's; plates all)

Spelling:
Words That End Like *ever*, p. 399I **T**

Day 2

Question of the Day, p. 370H
What parts of our state have you explored? What parts would you like to explore?

Think and Respond, p. 390

Comprehension:
 (Skill) Cause and Effect, pp. 372–393 **T**

Decoding/Phonics:
Syllables: Unaccented Syllables, p. 399A

Reading the Selection, pp. 372–393
Vocabulary Power Words

 Independent Reading
Books for All Learners

SOCIAL STUDIES Draw State Symbols
SCIENCE Nine-Banded Armadillos

Writing: Writing Process, p. 399E

Writing Prompt:
Imagine that you could take a rocket trip into space. Think about what you would see and do in space. Now write a postcard telling about your journey.

Grammar:
Extend the Concept, p. 399G **T**

Daily Language Practice

1. i've just read a story about an curious armadillo. (I've; a)
2. The armadillo left home and gone out. To see the world. (went; out to)

Spelling:
Word Sort, p. 399I **T**

370C Celebrate Our World

T = tested skill

Objectives of the Week:
- To recognize cause and effect relationships
- To read and understand an informational narrative and expository nonfiction
- To recognize adverbs and use them correctly in speaking and writing
- To write an invitation

Day 3

Question of the Day, p. 370H
What do you need to know to use a map?

Oral Grammar, p. 399H

Comprehension:
 Cause and Effect, pp. 398–399 **T**
Test Prep

Word Study:
Prefixes, p. 399K

Reading Across Texts
Genre: Expository Nonfiction

Rereading for Fluency, p. 389

 Independent Reading
Books for All Learners

SOCIAL STUDIES The Grand Canyon of Texas
SOCIAL STUDIES Spanish Heritage of the Southwest

Writing: Writing Process, p. 399F

Writing Prompt:
One day a huge eagle lands in front of your house and asks you if you would like a ride. Think about where you would go and what you would see. Now write a story about the day you flew with an eagle.

Grammar:
Where? When? How?, p. 399H **T**

Daily Language Practice
1. The armadillo met a eagle and was no longer lonley. (an; lonely)
2. They could see the erth but the air were thin up there. (earth, but; was thin)

Spelling:
Word Shapes, p. 399J **T**

Day 4

Question of the Day, p. 370H
If you were planning a trip to another state, how would you go about getting information?

Locate Information, p. 399B **T**

Graphic Aids, p. 399C **T**

Make Inferences, p. 399D

Self-Selected Reading, p. 370F

 Independent Reading
Books for All Learners

SCIENCE The Solar System
SCIENCE Phases of the Moon

Writing: Writing Process, p. 399F

Writing Prompt:
Where in the world do you live? Write a paragraph that answers this question. Tell the name of your community, state, region, and country. Also include any other facts you know about your location.

Grammar:
Lively Verbs and Adverbs, p. 399H **T**

Daily Language Practice
1. the eagle had a brilliant thoughts (The; thought.)
2. what if her and the armadillo could travel out in space (What; she; space?)

Spelling:
Word Book, Writing Book Titles, p. 399J **T**

Day 5

Question of the Day, p. 370H
Why do different places have different kinds of plant life?

Listening and Speaking
Invitation, p. 399L

Comprehension:
 Cause and Effect, pp. 399M–O **T**

Word Study:
Rhyming Words, p. 399K

Self-Selected Reading, pp. 395, T101

 Independent Reading
Books for All Learners

SCIENCE Create a Diagram or Model
SOCIAL STUDIES Design Postcards

Writing: Writing Process, p. 399F

Writing Prompt:
If you could design a postcard of your community, what picture would you put on the front of it? Think of a scene that gives a feeling for what your community is like. Now write about the picture your postcard would show.

Grammar:
Not Is an Adverb, p. 399H **T**

Daily Language Practice
1. suddenly a space shuttle came along. it take them aboard. (Suddenly; It; took)
2. The eagle and the armadillo seen the earth from space (saw, space.)

Spelling:
Posttest, p. 399J **T**

Cross-Curricular Stations

MANAGING THE CLASSROOM   While you provide direct instruction to individuals or small groups, other students can work on ongoing activities such as the ones below.

SCIENCE

Map Vegetation Areas

OBJECTIVE: To compare places and their environments

With a partner, choose a state, and draw a map showing its vegetation areas.

- Use an encyclopedia or the Internet to find an article about the state. Draw an outline of the state.
- Color each vegetation area a different color.
- Make a map key that tells what each color stands for.

 Students can go online to find a vegetation map of the state they are researching.

Materials

- encyclopedia or computer with Internet access
- paper
- pencils
- crayons, colored pencils, markers

SOCIAL STUDIES

Draw State Symbols

OBJECTIVE: To learn the history and significance of state symbols

Each state has its own flag, official state flower, and other symbols that represent it. Work with a group to make a display of the symbols of your state.

- Use an almanac or other reference source to find out about your state's flower, bird, tree, flag, and state seal. Find out why each one was chosen to represent your state.
- Draw each symbol.
- Display your drawings in the classroom.

You can expand your celebration of your state's symbols by learning the official state song and singing it with the class.

Materials

- almanac
- encyclopedia or computer with Internet access (optional)
- paper
- pencils, markers

LIBRARY CENTER

Self-Selected Reading

OBJECTIVE: To independently select and read books

Look for these books about wild animals and their habitats:

- *Our Earth* by Anne Rockwell. Harcourt Brace, 1998. FICTION
- *Armadillos Sleep in Dugouts & Other Places Animals Live* by Pam Muñoz Ryan. Disney, 1997. NONFICTION
- *A River Ran Wild* by Lynne Cherry. Harcourt Brace, 1997. NONFICTION

Remember to

- review several books to get an idea of what they are about.

Materials

- Self-selected book
- *My Reading Log* copying master, p. R42

20 Minutes a day

INQUIRY PROJECT

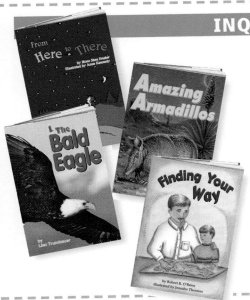

Extending the Selection

OBJECTIVE: To select a focus for an inquiry project

Use the ideas in "The Armadillo from Amarillo" to brainstorm with a partner related topics to explore. Organize your ideas into a web. Use one of these books to begin your project.

- *From Here to There*
- *Amazing Armadillos*
- *The Bald Eagle*
- *Finding Your Way*

Materials

- research materials
- paper
- pencils

30 Minutes

TECHNOLOGY

Information Search

OBJECTIVE: To use technology resources to research an animal

Use the Internet or a CD-ROM encyclopedia to find out more about armadillos or another unusual animal.

Remember to

- describe the natural environment the animal lives in.
- use the rules for Internet safety.

Materials

- computer with Internet access or CD-ROM encyclopedia
- paper
- pencils

60 Minutes

Read Aloud

SET A PURPOSE
Listen to Understand
Tell students that some poems, including the one they are about to hear, express dreams and fantasies. Read the poem aloud with energy and enthusiasm.

LISTENING STRATEGY
Keep an Open Mind
Encourage students to keep an open mind as they listen to the poem. Explain that often what seems difficult to believe at first may in time make sense to those who keep an open mind.

I Am Flying!
by Jack Prelutsky

I am flying! I am flying!
I am riding on the breeze,
I am soaring over meadows,
I am sailing over seas,
I ascend above the cities
where the people, small as ants,
cannot sense the keen precision
of my aerobatic dance.

I am flying! I am flying!
I am climbing unconfined,
I am swifter than the falcon,
and I leave the wind behind,
I am swooping, I am swirling
in a jubilant display,
I am brilliant as a comet
blazing through the Milky Way.

I am flying! I am flying!
I am higher than the moon,
still, I think I'd best be landing,
and it cannot be too soon,
for some nasty information
has lit up my little brain—
I am flying! I am flying!
but I fly without a plane.

- **Who do you think is the speaker in the poem?** (Possible responses: a person; an animal that normally can't fly)
POINT OF VIEW

- **Do you think this poem describes a real or an imaginary event? Why?** (Possible response: The event is imagined. No one can really fly without some kind of plane.) FANTASY/REALITY

- **What do you think this poem is really about?** (Possible response: It's about one person's dream of flying.) MAIN IDEA

Question of the Day

DEVELOP ORAL LANGUAGE

- Display the first question on Transparency 262 or write it on the board. Ask a volunteer to read it aloud.

- **Response Journal** Explain to students that they should think about the question throughout the day and write their responses in their journals. Tell students to be prepared to discuss the answer or answers to it by the end of the day or at another time you choose.

- You may want to repeat this process daily for each of the five discussion questions.

▼ **Teaching Transparency 262**

QUESTION OF THE DAY

DAY 1: Where in the world are you? Response should reflect the community's location within the state, nation, and world.

DAY 2: What parts of our state have you explored? What parts would you like to explore? Responses will vary.

DAY 3: What do you need to know to use a map? Possible responses: Where you are and where you want to go.

DAY 4: If you were planning a trip to another state, how would you go about getting information? Possible response: look in an atlas for a map; look in the library for a tour book and travel magazines; go on the Internet to find places to stay

DAY 5: Why do different places have different kinds of plant life? Possible response: They have different climates and different soils.

"The Armadillo from Amarillo"
Celebrate Our World, Theme 3   262   Question of the Day
Harcourt

OBJECTIVE

To recognize cause-and-effect relationships

SKILL TRACE

CAUSE AND EFFECT	
Introduce	p. 324I
Reteach	pp. S74, S86, T7I
Review	**pp. 346, 369D, 370I, 398**
Test	Theme 3 Vol. 2

▼ **Teaching Transparency 263**

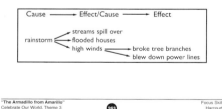

CAUSE AND EFFECT

A **cause** is something that makes something happen.

An **effect** is what happens.

Sometimes a cause has more than one effect.

Sometimes there is more than one cause for an effect.

EXAMPLE:

A huge rainstorm hit our state this week. It caused small streams to spill over their banks. Houses in low-lying areas were flooded. The high winds that the storm brought with it broke branches off trees. They also blew down power lines.

Cause ——→ Effect/Cause ——→ Effect

rainstorm { streams spill over / flooded houses / high winds } ——→ broke tree branches / blew down power lines

"The Armadillo from Amarillo" 263 Focus Skill
Celebrate Our World, Theme 3 Harcourt

BELOW-LEVEL

Additional Support
• *Intervention Teacher's Guide*, p. 290

ENGLISH-LANGUAGE LEARNERS

Additional Support
• *English-Language Learners Teacher's Guide*, p. 171

370I   **Celebrate Our World**

Focus Skill — Cause and Effect

REVIEW THE SKILL

Access prior knowledge. Turn off the lights in the classroom. Ask students to identify the **cause** of the darkness (flipping the switch) and the **effect** (the room is darker).

TEACH/MODEL

Display Transparency 263. Tell students that understanding cause-and-effect relationships can help them understand how and why things happen.

• **Have volunteers read the information in the boxes.**

• **Then have a volunteer read aloud the paragraph. Help students determine multiple causes and effects. Discuss how cause and effect can become a chain reaction.**

Finally, have students read the events in the diagram. Point out that the rainstorm caused several effects and that one of the effects, in turn, caused an effect.

PRACTICE/APPLY

Students can use a cause/effect chart to record important events in "The Armadillo from Amarillo" and note what caused each one to happen.

Cause	Effect

For opportunities to apply and reinforce the skill, see the following pages:

During reading: pages 376, 382, 384, 386, and 388
After reading: *Pupil Edition* pages 398–399

Reread to Clarify

Focus Strategy

Strategies Good Readers Use

- Use Decoding/Phonics
- Make and Confirm Predictions
- Create Mental Images
- Self-Question
- Summarize
- Read Ahead
- **Reread to Clarify** (Focus Strategy)
- Use Context to Confirm Meaning
- Use Text Structure and Format
- Adjust Reading Rate

REVIEW THE STRATEGY

Explain to students that they will read a poem that is a fantasy. Ask students why fantasy might be difficult to understand. What might they do to help them understand what is going on in a fantasy?

TEACH/MODEL

Point out that the rereading strategy is one of the most helpful strategies to use when events in a story seem confusing. Good readers pay attention to whether they understand what is happening in a story, and then reread if they need to clear up confusion.

Read aloud the first two verses of the poem on page 370G. Then model the strategy.

MODEL In the first verse the poet says that people are small as ants. I'm confused. Why would people be as small as ants? I'd better reread the first verse. Oh, now I see. The people are small as ants because the poet is flying. He is over meadows, over seas, and over cities.

SKILL ⟷ STRATEGY CONNECTION

Explain to students that if the **cause** or the **effect** of a story event is unclear, they can reread parts of the story to help them figure it out.

PRACTICE/APPLY

Remind students to use the Reread to Clarify strategy if they are having difficulty understanding part of the story. For opportunities to apply and reinforce the strategy **during reading**, see pages 383 and 385.

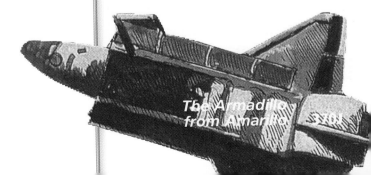

Building Background

ACCESS PRIOR KNOWLEDGE

Ask students if they have visited other parts of their state or traveled to other states or countries. Ask: **Where have you gone and what do you remember most about the place?** Ask students what other ways there are to learn about a place. Have them explore this question using a web.

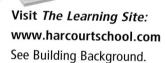

Visit *The Learning Site:*
www.harcourtschool.com
See Building Background.

DEVELOP CONCEPTS

Help students further develop the concepts by asking questions such as these:

- **What would you like to see that you can't see in your home state?** (Responses will vary.)

- **What does it mean to have a "birds-eye view" of the world?** (It means to see things from above, the way a bird would see it.)

- **Why is it important to find our place in the universe?** (Possible responses: It gives us a sense of the order of things; it helps us understand what else exists besides people in our part of the world.)

REACHING ALL LEARNERS

Diagnostic Check: Vocabulary

If . . . students have not mastered at least five of the six vocabulary words . . .

Then . . . have them play a matching game in pairs using word cards and blank cards on which the definitions are written.

ADDITIONAL SUPPORT ACTIVITIES

BELOW-LEVEL	Reteach, p. S84
ADVANCED	Extend, p. S85
ENGLISH-LANGUAGE LEARNERS	Reteach, p. S85

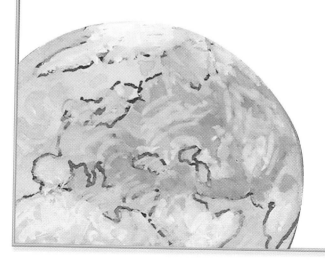

Vocabulary

TEACH VOCABULARY STRATEGIES

Use multiple-meaning words. Display Transparency 264, and ask volunteers to read the first paragraph aloud. Remind students that some words have more than one meaning. Model using the strategy to determine the correct meaning of *converse*.

MODEL I know there are two words with this spelling. /kon' vûrs/ means "opposite." /kən • vûrs'/ means "talk to one another." To figure out which pronunciation to use, I have to look at how the word is used. The word *told* is a clue. I think the word here is /kən • vûrs'/. That would make sense in the sentence.

Have students use this strategy and others as they read the rest of the passage. Point out the remaining vocabulary words on the transparency, and discuss the meaning of each word.

Remind students to use this strategy when they come across other multiple-meaning words as they read.

Vocabulary

eventually sometime in the future, finally

converse talk to one another

continent one of the seven large land areas on Earth

sphere a round object like a ball; a planet

universe everything that exists, including the sun, stars, all the planets, and outer space

homeward toward home

▼ Teaching Transparency 264

VOCABULARY IN CONTEXT

Feebee's Fantastic Flights

Have you told your friends that **eventually**, you will take an exciting vacation? Don't just **converse**. Take action! We will take you where few have dared to go!

- Zoom into space. Find out what your **continent** looks like from above. See the shape of the land you live on.
- Rocket farther into space! Explore a round **sphere** other than Earth!
- See as much of the **universe** as you can! Go beyond Pluto!
- Spend four days and three nights in space. Then travel **homeward** at the speed of light.

Take an adventure that's truly out of this world! Call Feebee's Fantastic Flights!

"The Armadillo from Amarillo"
Celebrate Our World, Theme 3   264   Vocabulary Harcourt

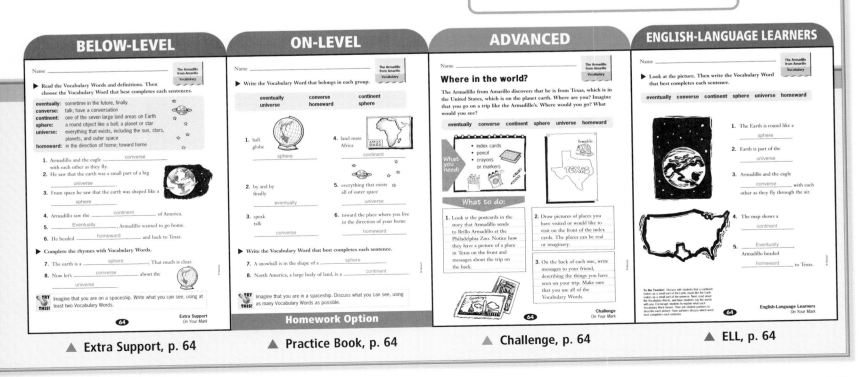

| BELOW-LEVEL | ON-LEVEL | ADVANCED | ENGLISH-LANGUAGE LEARNERS |

▲ Extra Support, p. 64   ▲ Practice Book, p. 64   ▲ Challenge, p. 64   ▲ ELL, p. 64

Homework Option

Vocabulary Power

Vocabulary Power

APPLY STRATEGIES

Have a volunteer read aloud the first paragraph on page 370. Then ask students to read the remaining text silently. Remind them to apply the strategy of looking at how multiple-meaning words are used.

EXTEND WORD KNOWLEDGE

Practice other vocabulary strategies.
Ask students to respond to questions with sentences that show what the vocabulary words mean. **MEANINGFUL SENTENCES**

- **When do you *converse* with your friends? EXAMPLE**

- **What is one *sphere* used at recess? EXAMPLE**

- **What is the opposite of *eventually*? ANTONYM**

- **Which direction is *homeward* for you? DESCRIPTION**

- **What is one instrument used to study the *universe*? PRIOR KNOWLEDGE**

- **On which *continent* is the United States? PRIOR KNOWLEDGE**

▲ The Armadillo from Amarillo

eventually
universe
sphere
continent
converse
homeward

370

Do you ever wonder what lies beyond your own city or town, your country, or your own planet Earth? It's natural to be curious.

DANNY: Dad, will people ever travel to other planets?

DAD: Maybe they will **eventually**, but not very soon.

DANNY: How big is the **universe**, Dad?

DAD: It's too big to measure. The universe contains everything that exists—all the stars you see in the sky, the moon, the sun, the planets, and all of space.

DANNY: Wow, that's bigger than I thought! (*He is silent for a moment.*) Dad, why does the moon change its shape?

DAD: It doesn't really change shape. The moon is a **sphere**. It is round like a ball, but we see only part of it. The part we see changes as the moon moves around the earth.

DANNY: Dad, my teacher said we live on the **continent** of North America. She said a continent is a large area of land. How many continents are there?

DAD: There are seven continents, Danny. We can find them on our map of the world when we get home. We could **converse** about this for hours. I've enjoyed our talk. (*He looks at his watch.*) It's getting late. We'd better head **homeward**.

DANNY: Okay, I'm ready to start toward home now.

Vocabulary–Writing CONNECTION

A circle is a flat shape, but a **sphere** is round like a ball. Write a list of objects that are like spheres and a list of objects that are like circles.

371

 QUICKWRITE

VOCABULARY-WRITING CONNECTION

To help students distinguish objects that are like spheres and objects that are like circles, display a spherical object such as an orange and a circular object such as a plate. Suggest that students try to think of other objects that have each shape. Students should add the Vocabulary Power words to their Word Banks to use in future writing assignments.

Prereading Strategies

PREVIEW AND PREDICT

Have students read the **genre** information on page 372. Then have them preview the selection. Ask them what they think this selection is about, based on their preview and the characteristics of informational narrative. Then have them record predictions about where Armadillo will go and what he will learn by going there. They can begin a cause/effect chart. See Transparency F.

Cause	Effect
Armadillo wants to find out where in the world he is.	He leaves his home to explore a nearby area.

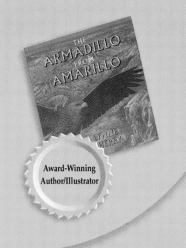

Genre

Informational Narrative

An informational narrative is a story that presents information and facts.

In this selection, look for

● elements of fiction and nonfiction.

● information about a topic.

372

TEXAS ARMADILLO
This burrowing mammal is covered with a bony shell. When attacked, the armadillo may roll up like a ball and defend upon its own armor for protection. Armadillos feed on fruits, roots, and insects.

Dear Brillo,
I've lately had the urge to go and visit San Antonio, a city I've not seen before that my friends tell me I'd adore.
Sasparillo

BLUEBONNETS
SAN ANTONIO
TEXAS

Dear Brillo,
Hi and warm rega from your cousi Sasparillo. I la my head and sle today on a blue bluebonnet pillow
Love,
Sasparillo

BELOW-LEVEL	ON-LEVEL	ADVANCED	ENGLISH-LANGUAGE LEARNERS
Guide students as they preview the selection. Discuss the meaning of these words: *city, county, explore, state, wondered, world.* Help students set a purpose for reading through page 377. **SMALL GROUP**	Students can read the selection with a partner. Use the Guided Comprehension questions and Ongoing Assessments to check students' understanding. **PARTNER**	Let students who are reading on or above level read independently at their own pace. Then suggest that they work with other independent readers to discuss the questions at the end of the selection. **INDEPENDENT/SMALL GROUP**	Read aloud the selection or have students listen to it on *Audiotext 6.* Then have students read aloud selected pages as a group to develop oral fluency. **SMALL GROUP**

BELOW-LEVEL — **ADDITIONAL SUPPORT**

Intervention Reader: Bright Surprises Intervention Teacher's Guide, pp. 290–293

ENGLISH-LANGUAGE LEARNERS — **ADDITIONAL SUPPORT**

See *English-Language Learners Resource Kit,* Lesson 29. *English-Language Learners Teacher's Guide,* pp. 171–172

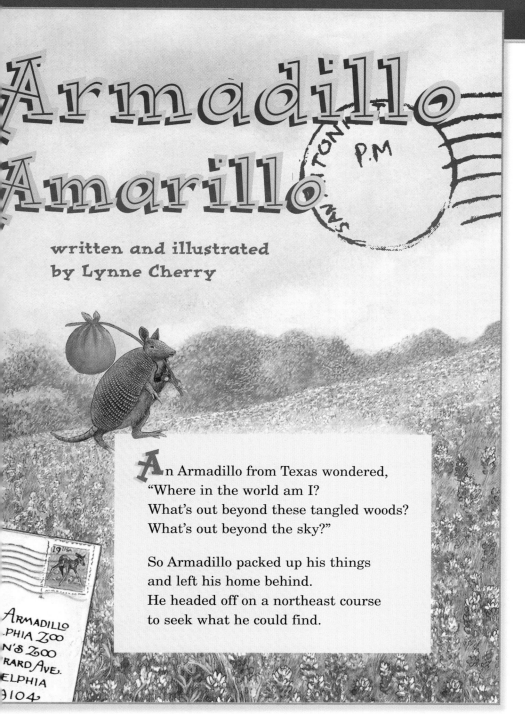

Armadillo Amarillo

written and illustrated
by Lynne Cherry

An Armadillo from Texas wondered,
"Where in the world am I?
What's out beyond these tangled woods?
What's out beyond the sky?"

So Armadillo packed up his things
and left his home behind.
He headed off on a northeast course
to seek what he could find.

ARMADILLO
-PHIA ZOO
N'S ZOO
RARD AVE.
ELPHIA
9104

SET PURPOSE

Read to be entertained and informed.
Remind students that they can read for enjoyment and information at the same time. Ask students to set their own purposes. Offer this suggestion:

MODEL As I previewed this informational narrative, I saw maps and illustrations of the environment. I will use my imagination as I read this selection. I also expect to learn some facts about the world.

Focus Strategy **Reread to Clarify** Have students use this strategy to help them understand what they read.

 "The Armadillo from Amarillo" is available on *Audiotext 6*.

COMPREHENSION CARD 29

Author's Purpose Have students use Comprehension Card 29 to discuss author's purpose in "The Armadillo from Amarillo."

► **Author's Purpose**   COMPREHENSION CARD **29**

During Reading
1. Do you think the author wrote this selection
   ■ to inform?
   ■ to entertain?
   ■ to explain?
   ■ to persuade?
2. What clues from the story helped you decide the author's purpose?

Comprehension Card 29,
Page T84 ►

Guided Comprehension

1 **SPECULATE** Armadillo knows he is in San Antonio. Why does he ask, "Where in the world am I"? (Possible response: He knows where he is standing, but he does not know where he is in the whole world.)

2 **DRAW CONCLUSIONS** What does Armadillo do after he leaves the tower in San Antonio? (Possible response: He keeps on traveling.)

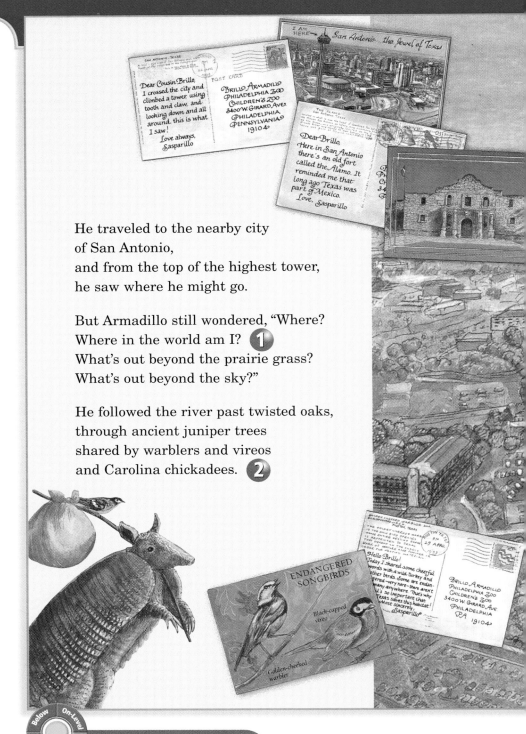

He traveled to the nearby city
of San Antonio,
and from the top of the highest tower,
he saw where he might go.

But Armadillo still wondered, "Where?
Where in the world am I? **1**
What's out beyond the prairie grass?
What's out beyond the sky?"

He followed the river past twisted oaks,
through ancient juniper trees
shared by warblers and vireos
and Carolina chickadees. **2**

 ENGLISH-LANGUAGE LEARNERS

Teach position words as antonym pairs to help students visualize relative locations, such as *top* and *bottom*. Draw on the board a tower similar to the one in San Antonio. Point to the top and bottom of the building, and say *top* and then *bottom*. Then tell students to use a coin or other object to represent the armadillo. Have them place the coin at the top of the tower in the picture on *Pupil Edition* page 375. Say, "Armadillo is at the *top* of the tower." Repeat with the word *bottom*.

Visit *The Learning Site:* **www.harcourtschool.com** See Language Support.

375

Monitor Progress

Use Text Structure and Format

Which of the birds the author mentions in the poem on page 374 are endangered?

(the vireo and the warbler)

If students are unable to answer, use this model:

MODEL I have to read both the text and the postcards to understand what the author is telling about. When I read the postcard near the bottom of the page, I see that two birds mentioned in the poem are endangered.

SCIENCE

Nine-Banded Armadillos Explain to students that the main character, Armadillo, is a nine-banded armadillo, the only kind of armadillo found in the United States. (Students can count the bands on the close-up illustration of Armadillo on page 379.) *Nine-banded* means nine narrow bands of very tough skin slide over one another to form the shell. This shell is the armadillo's main defense. When threatened, a nine-banded armadillo digs a hole to hide in or scuttles away using its tough shell as its armor.

Guided Comprehension

3 **SYNTHESIZE** **What is Armadillo learning about the world as he walks through Texas?** (Possible response: Different regions have different landscapes and different vegetation.)

4 **MAKE COMPARISONS** **What is a difference between the canyons and the plains near Amarillo?** (Possible response: The plains are higher than the canyons and have lots of flowers.)

5 (Focus Skill) **CAUSE/EFFECT** **What is the effect of Armadillo's climbing up to higher ground?** (Possible responses: He can see farther. He stops walking and looks around.)

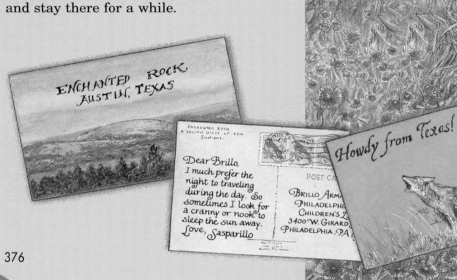

The landscape changed dramatically **3**
through woodland, towns, and plains.
Armadillo explored canyons
and walked through heavy rains.

He walked for weeks and came to Austin,
continued west and north
to Abilene and Lubbock,
he hiked and sallied forth.

Armadillo often along the way
climbed up to higher ground.
He scurried up the canyon walls
and stopped to look around.

How different were the plains above— **4 5**
flowers went on for a mile!
Armadillo decided to settle down
and stay there for a while.

Dear Brillo,
I much prefer the
night to traveling
during the day. So
sometimes I look for
a cranny or nook to
sleep the sun away.
Love, Sasparillo

376

REACHING ALL LEARNERS

Diagnostic Check: Comprehension and Skills

If . . . students are having difficulty understanding a character's motivation,

Then . . . ask them to write a series of "why" questions about the character's actions. Have students put the questions and answers together into cause-and-effect statements.

ADDITIONAL SUPPORT ACTIVITIES

BELOW-LEVEL Reteach, p. S86

ADVANCED Extend, p. S87

ENGLISH-LANGUAGE LEARNERS Reteach, p. S87

Dear Brillo,
n near Amarillo.
his land is cool and
at! It's definitely
a inadequate
madillo habitat!
be the only
madillo who lives
the city of
arillo!
Sasparillo

POST CARD

BRILLO ARMADILLO
PHILADELPHIA ZOO
CHILDREN'S ZOO
3400 W. GIRARD AVE.
PHILADELPHIA, PA
19104

ONGOING ASSESSMENT

Monitor Progress

Create Mental Images

Which city is farther north—Austin or Abilene? How do you know? (Possible response: Abilene; Armadillo gets to Austin and then travels northwest to Abilene.)

If students have difficulty answering the question, provide this model:

MODEL This is the story of a journey. I want to understand where the main character is traveling. I pay attention to direction words and use those to picture places on a map. The words *west* and *north* help me picture the location of Abilene, which is to the northwest of Austin on a map of Texas.

LITERARY ANALYSIS

Accuracy in Words and Pictures Inform students that to prepare to write and illustrate this book, Lynne Cherry did a great deal of research about Texas. She traveled within Texas, studied maps and photographs, took photographs, and talked with environmental experts. While her pictures show what different areas look like, she also found a clever way to add interesting information about Texas through Armadillo's postcards to Brillo. Have students select one fact or drawing in the story and speculate on where the author-illustrator got information to make it accurate.

The Armadillo from Amarillo **377**

Guided Comprehension

6 **FANTASY/REALITY** **What parts of the story so far are factual?** (Possible response: the description of the geography, landscape, and vegetation of Texas)

7 **FANTASY/REALITY** **What things in the story make it a fantasy?** (Possible response: things that could not happen in real life, such as an armadillo talking and writing postcards, and an eagle letting an armadillo ride on its back)

8 **MAKE AND CONFIRM PREDICTIONS** **Have your predictions about the selection turned out to be correct so far?** (Responses will vary.) **What do you think will happen in the next part?** (Possible response: Armadillo will see all of Texas as he flies with the eagle.)

But Armadillo still wondered, "Where?
Where in the world *am* I?
Perhaps I'd have a better idea
if I could somehow fly." **6**

One day he asked the golden eagle
as she came breezing by,
"What can I do for a bird's-eye view
from up in the big blue sky?"

"Hop on my back," said the eagle. **7**
"I'll fly you wide and far.
And then you'll see, eventually,
where in the world we are."

Upward and upward the eagle flew.
Armadillo held on tight.
"With my tail-tip curled I'll explore the world
from morning until night!" **8**

Palo Duro Canyon
Amarillo, TEXAS

Dear Brillo,
Except for the canyons like this one here, this land is flat, flat, flat! And an Armadillo near Amarillo should wear a scarf and hat!
Love,
Sasparillo

POST CARD

BRILLO ARMADILLO
PHILADELPHIA ZOO
CHILDREN'S ZOO
3400 W. GIRARD AVE.
PHILADELPHIA, PA
19104

378

ENGLISH-LANGUAGE LEARNERS

Remind students that a contraction is a shortened way of saying two separate words together. Most contractions are made in one of two ways:

- with pronouns and verbs as in *I'm* for *I am*
- with verbs and *not* as in *aren't* for *are not*

Point out the contractions *I'd, I'll* (twice), and *you'll* on page 378. Help students recognize that these are shortened forms of *I would, I will,* and *you will.*

ONGOING ASSESSMENT

Monitor Progress

Self-Question

Think about Armadillo's experiences on his trip. Why might he think that flying would give him a better idea of where he is? (Possible response: He saw a lot of San Antonio from the top of the tower.)

If students are unable to answer the question, model the strategy:

MODEL How could flying help Armadillo know about the world? If he were flying, he would be up high. That might help. When he was on top of a tower in San Antonio, he saw a lot of the city. That's probably why he thinks flying will help him.

SOCIAL STUDIES

The Grand Canyon of Texas   Tell students that the postcard on page 378 shows a picture of Palo Duro Canyon. This canyon, cut by a fork of the Red River, is located just south of Amarillo. The canyon drops approximately 1,200 feet into the Earth. In 1876 Charles Goodnight established the first ranch in the Texas panhandle here. The canyon is now part of a state park, and visitors can actually drive to the floor of the canyon on paved road. Ask students whether they would like to visit Palo Duro Canyon, and why or why not.

The Armadillo from Amarillo   **379**

Guided Comprehension

9 **NOTE DETAILS** **Why does the town of Amarillo have that name?** (Possible response: *Amarillo* means "yellow." The prairie around the town is yellow and brown.)

10 **COMPARE AND CONTRAST** **Who has a better idea of where he or she is in the world—Armadillo or Eagle? What makes you think so?** (Possible response: Eagle, because she is teaching Armadillo about the world)

Armadillo looked down below and asked,
"Where in the world *are* we?"
"We're over a prairie, and in the distance,
that's Amarillo you see.

"We've flown over the prairie.
We've flown over a town.
Amarillo means yellow, my dear little fellow, **9**
and the prairie's all yellow and brown!"

"I see Amarillo," said Armadillo.
"Could we see all Texas, though?
And if we fly *higher* up into the sky,
could we see New Mexico?

"Or if we fly *higher* up into the sky,
could we see the entire earth?"
"Well, certainly, surely, if you hold on securely,
we'll try!" cried the eagle with mirth.

"*Amarillo*'s a *city?*" asked Armadillo.
To this the eagle replied,
"Yes, Amarillo's a city in *Texas*,
the *state* where we reside.

"And Texas is in the *United States*,
our *country* wide and dear,
on the *North American continent*,
which is on the *earth*, a sphere. **10**

380

BELOW-LEVEL

Have students use their cause/effect charts to summarize the story so far.

- Because Armadillo wants to know where he is in the world, he takes a journey.
- Because he walks a long way, he discovers that different places have different landforms, wildlife, and vegetation.
- Because he wants to see a larger part of the world, he asks an eagle to take him flying.
- Because the eagle wants to help the armadillo, the eagle shows and tells Armadillo about the United States, North America, and planet Earth.

Have students read to the end of the story to find out what else Armadillo discovers about the world.

SOCIAL STUDIES

Spanish Heritage of the Southwest   Remind students that Eagle says that *amarillo* means "yellow." Ask students what language they think the word *amarillo* is from, and why they think so. (Possible responses: Spanish: Texas and the Southwest have many Spanish place names.) If necessary, point out that the first European settlers in Texas were Spanish.

The Armadillo from Amarillo   **381**

Guided Comprehension

11 (Focus Skill) **CAUSE/EFFECT** **What causes Armadillo to hold tightly to Eagle's neck?** (Possible response: Armadillo is afraid of falling to Earth.)

12 **SYNTHESIZE** **What does Eagle mean when she says "these planets turn round the sun"?** (Possible response: The planets have a path that they follow around the sun.)

13 **DETERMINE CHARACTERS' EMOTIONS** **How does Armadillo feel on this flight? Why do you think that?** (Possible responses: Armadillo is excited and scared. He talks about curling his tail up around him while he explores the world. That sounds like he wants to do it. He also talks about it being hard to breathe and wanting to leave. That sounds like he is scared.)

382

ADVANCED

Point out that as Armadillo is flying high above Earth, he complains about being cold and having problems breathing. Ask volunteers to find out why Armadillo is having these difficulties and report back to their classmates.

stratosphere
troposphere
Earth

"This sphere is called a *planet*,
of nine we are just one,
and as we converse, in the *universe*,
these planets turn round the sun." **12**

Armadillo held tightly to Eagle's neck,
afraid of a long, long fall. **11**
From over his shoulder, with the air getting colder,
this is what he saw.

They flew so high up into the sky
that Texas they saw below—
the part they call the Panhandle—
and the state of New Mexico.

"With my tail-tip curled I'll explore the world!"
Armadillo said to his friend.
Through the clouds they twirled, in the wind
they whirled, and up they were hurled again!

And when they looked up they could see into space.
They'd flown up into thin air.
"It's hard to breathe here! I'd like to leave here! **13**
Eagle, homeward let's repair!"

383

ONGOING ASSESSMENT

Monitor Progress

(Focus Strategy) **Reread to Clarify**

Why does Armadillo want to go home now?
(Possible response: He and the eagle are so high up that the air is thin and he can't breathe.)

Ask volunteers to model how they could use the Reread to Clarify strategy to answer the question.

If students have difficulty, provide this model:

MODEL To find out why Armadillo suddenly wants to go home, I can reread the last two stanzas on page 383. I see that Armadillo and the eagle have been hurled up into thin air by the wind, and that Armadillo has trouble breathing there. That is why Armadillo wants to go home.

SCIENCE

The Solar System Ask volunteers to explain how the planets move around the sun. Have them point out that Earth is one of nine planets that orbit, or have a path around, the sun. All these planets also revolve, or spin, as they follow this path. Have students draw a labeled diagram of the planets in relation to the sun. Interested students might look in an encyclopedia to find facts about Mercury, Venus, Earth, and Mars, and add these to the diagram.

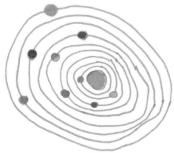

The Armadillo from Amarillo **383**

Guided Comprehension

14 **(Focus Skill)** **CAUSE/EFFECT** **Why does Eagle suggest that she and Armadillo ride on the rocket ship?** (Possible response: because it can fly to the moon)

15 **FANTASY/REALITY** **How does Eagle and Armadillo's ride on the rocket ship show you that this story is a fantasy?** (Possible response: This could not really happen, and stories about things that can't really happen are called fantasy stories.)

"We're very high now," said Eagle,
"on the edge of air and space.
The atmosphere's ending, we should be descending,
but what a remarkable place!

"There must be a way to fly higher up,
bringing some air aboard.
Perhaps we should travel to Cape Canaveral,"
Eagle said as she soared.

As they spoke of Cape Canaveral—
the rocket-launching place—
a shuttle took off with a roar of fire
and headed out toward space.

Eagle had a brilliant thought
and whistled a happy tune.
"Let's hitch a trip on this rocket ship
and fly up to the moon!" **14**

With a burst of speed the eagle flew
in the path of the rocket ship.
It took her and Armadillo aboard
and continued on its trip. **15**

384

REACHING ALL LEARNERS

Diagnostic Check: Comprehension and Skills

If . . . students are having difficulty identifying cause-and-effect relationships,

Then . . . have them make a cause-and-effect chart starting with the first action (cause) and the outcome of that action (effect). Model the first few for them.

ADDITIONAL SUPPORT ACTIVITIES

BELOW-LEVEL Reteach, p. S86

ADVANCED Extend, p. S87

ENGLISH-LANGUAGE LEARNERS Reteach, p. S87

385

ONGOING ASSESSMENT

Monitor Progress

(Focus Strategy) Reread to Clarify

Why might Eagle be more willing than Armadillo to continue flying so high?
(Possible response: Eagle is used to it. She knows what to do.)

If students are unable to answer the question, ask: How could you find the answer to this question? If necessary, use this model:

MODEL I see on page 383 that Armadillo has trouble breathing. He isn't used to being up so high. Then I see on page 384 that Eagle knows where they are—at the edge of the atmosphere—and thinks it's a remarkable place. Because Eagle is used to being high in the sky, she is happy to keep flying.

SCIENCE

Phases of the Moon Explain to students that the moon revolves around the Earth, and that it appears bright to us because it reflects the light of the sun. Display or draw on the board the phases of the moon. Explain to students that each phase appears about every 28 days; for example, we see a full moon about every 28 days. Have students predict which phase of the moon Armadillo will see.

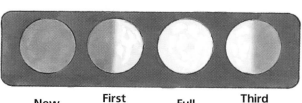

| New | First quarter | Full | Third quarter |

The Armadillo from Amarillo **385**

Guided Comprehension

16 (Focus Skill) **CAUSE/EFFECT** What happens as Armadillo and Eagle fly higher and higher into the sky? (Possible response: They see more and more of Earth.)

17 **DRAW CONCLUSIONS** What does Eagle mean when she says, "We're *out* of this world"? (Possible response: that they are so far out in space that not even Earth's atmosphere touches them anymore)

18 **SPECULATE** What do you think is the deep blue background behind the white clouds that astronauts see when they look at Earth from the moon? (Possible response: Earth's oceans)

19 **MAKE/CONFIRM PREDICTIONS** Has this part of Armadillo's journey turned out as you expected? (Responses will vary.) **How do you predict the journey will end?** (Possible response: Armadillo will return to Amarillo.)

The higher they flew, the farther they saw—
Louisiana and Arkansas!
And there were some other countries below—
they could see Cuba and Mexico! **16**

The spaceship then zoomed so high up
that Armadillo could not tell
where a country began or ended,
or where its borders fell.

The earth was now so far away—
so very, very far.
"I'm wondering," said Armadillo,
"where in the world we are."

"We're *out* of this world," said the eagle **17**
to the armadillo, her friend.
"Ten miles from earth starts the universe
right at the atmosphere's end."

From space the earth was a big round ball,
with swirling clouds of white
against a deep-blue background, **18**
like the blue-black sky at night.

Planets shone around them,
reflecting starlike light.
In that silent room floating in the dark,
they traveled through the night.
19

386

BELOW-LEVEL

To help students understand the last stanza on page 386, set up a demonstration to show that the planets, including Earth, have no light of their own, but only reflect the light of the sun. In a darkened room, have one student shine a flashlight on a globe.

Explain that the flashlight represents the sun, and the Earth is reflecting its light. Point out that without the sun there would be no life as we know it on Earth. Ask volunteers to speculate why.

387

LITERARY ANALYSIS

Metaphor Have students reread the fifth stanza on page 386. Ask what the Earth is being compared to. (a big round ball) Next, ask whether the author says the Earth is *like* a ball or *is* a ball. (*is* a ball) Tell students that comparisons in which the author says something is another thing are called *metaphors*.

The Armadillo from Amarillo   **387**

Guided Comprehension

20 IDENTIFY WITH CHARACTERS
Imagine you are Armadillo looking at Earth. What does this view make you realize about the world? (Possible responses: how big the world is compared to Amarillo; how small the world is compared to all of space)

21 (Focus Skill) CAUSE/EFFECT Why does Armadillo get homesick? (Possible response: He sees how far he is from home, and this makes him sad.)

22 PROBLEM/SOLUTION How do you know that Armadillo answered his question, "Where in the world am I?" (Possible response: He says to Eagle, "I know where . . . I am, Eagle, thanks to you!")

388

BELOW-LEVEL

Have students summarize Armadillo's journey. Ask them to identify the places he visits and what he learns.

- Armadillo climbs a high tower in San Antonio and sees prairie and sky.
- From there, he travels through woods, plains, and canyons to Austin, and then on to Abilene and Lubbock.

- He flies with an eagle and learns that Texas is a state in the United States, on the North American continent, on the planet Earth.
- To see more of the universe, they board a space shuttle, go to the moon, see Earth and other planets, and return home.

Before them was earth's silver moon—
a white and glowing sphere.
They hovered there, floating in thin air,
over craters, with no fear. **20**

And as they watched in wonder,
the earth rose on the horizon.
They sat and gazed at their far-off home—
watched earth-set and earth-risin'.

Armadillo said, "I'm homesick. **21**
Hey, Eagle, let's go back.
Let's go back down to our yellow town,
away from this blue and black."

The rocket began a downward arc,
then flew over land and sea.
The adventurous pair flew through the air
to their home by the yellow prairie.

He'd wondered where in the world he was,
and now Armadillo knew.
He said, "I know where, in the scheme of things,
I am, Eagle, thanks to you! **22**

389

REREADING FOR FLUENCY

Choral Reading Read aloud at least one full page of "The Armadillo from Amarillo," modeling for students fluent reading. Remind students to pay attention to punctuation and phrasing. Then have students read chorally with you. For variety, you may choose to divide the class into two or three groups and have them alternate reading while the others follow along silently in their books.

For support, see Fluency Routine Cards in Theme Resources, pp. T80a–T80b.

Note: For assessment of oral reading accuracy and fluency, see pages T78–T80.

Guided Comprehension

Were your predictions about Armadillo's journey correct? Explain your answer. Discuss with students whether their purposes for reading were met.

Think and Respond

Answers:

1 Possible response: He wants to find out where in the world he is. He learns that Amarillo is a city in Texas in the United States, which is on the continent of North America on Earth. **SUMMARIZE**

2 Possible response: She could give the same information in sentences, but it might not be as much fun to read. **LITERARY ANALYSIS**

3 Possible response: They add information about the places Armadillo visits and what he sees. **CAUSE/EFFECT**

4 Responses should be similar to the response to Question 1. **PERSONAL RESPONSE**

5 Accept reasonable responses. **READING STRATEGIES**

OPEN-ENDED RESPONSE

Take the role of Armadillo and write a thank-you letter to Eagle, telling her what you learned from your adventures.

"I now live near Amarillo,
a city that's rather small,
which is in the state of Texas,
one of fifty states in all,

"in the United States of America,
the country of my birth,
on the North American continent,
in the world, on planet earth.

"In all, there are nine planets,
and earth is only one,
and as we converse, in the universe,
eight planets besides this one
warmly, hotly, coldly, cooly
revolve around the sun."

390

COMPREHENSION

End-of-Selection Test
To evaluate comprehension, see *Practice Book*, pages A53–A56.

Think and Respond

1 Why does Armadillo go on his journey? What does he learn?

2 How would the story be different if the author, Lynne Cherry, had not used rhyming words?

3 How do the postcard illustrations add to the story?

4 On the last page of the story, Armadillo tells exactly where he is in the **universe**. Where are you? Give your location exactly, beginning with your school.

5 Give an example of a reading strategy you used as you read this selection. How was it helpful?

DEAR SASPARILLO,
I'M GLAD YOU FOUND
YOUR WAY BACK TO
YOUR NEW HOME. YOUR
POSTCARDS FROM ALL
OVER THE PLACE HAVE
INSPIRED ME TO ROAM.
LOVE,
BRILLO

SASPARILLO ARMA
GENERAL DELIVE
AMARILLO, TX
79104

DEAR SASPARILLO,
HELLO, DEAR COUSIN!
I'VE JUST ESCAPED FROM
THE PHILADELPHIA ZOO, AND
NOW I'M OFF TO SEE THE
WORLD FROM A DIFFERENT
CITY THAN YOU. I'M LEAVING
PHILADELPHIA, PENNSYLVANIA
IS MY STATE. WITH MY TAIL-TIP
CURLED, I'LL EXPLORE THE
WORLD! I CAN HARDLY
WAIT! LOVE, BRILLO

SASPARILLO ARMA
GENERAL DELIVE
AMARILLO, TX
79109

▲ Practice Book, p. A53

▲ Practice Book, p. A56

Meet the Author
and Illustrator
Lynne Cherry

Lynne Cherry enjoys watching animals and nature. Her art shows the beauty she sees in life. By traveling and learning about other places, authors can get new ideas. Here is a passport with more information about Lynne Cherry.

PASSPORT
Lynne Cherry

Number: J00932A09 Armadillo
Name: Lynne Cherry
Address: Washington, D.C., and Maryland
Country of birth: United States of America
Place of birth: Philadelphia, PA, U.S.A.
Date of birth: January 5, 1952
Profession: Author and illustrator of children's picture books

Visit *The Learning Site!*
www.harcourtschool.com

393

ABOUT THE AUTHOR AND ILLUSTRATOR

Lynne Cherry does a lot of research for her books. For *The Armadillo from Amarillo*, she talked with astronauts about how Earth looks from space. She even visited a real armadillo named Brillo at the Philadelphia Children's Zoo and had him pose for her illustrations.

Discuss with students what the author means when she says that through her stories, she tries to make the world better. (Possible response: She tries to get people to appreciate and protect nature.)

TECHNOLOGY Additional author information can be found on *The Learning Site* at **www.harcourtschool.com.**

Reading Across Texts

INTRODUCING THE ARTICLE

Genre Study   Have students read the title and look at the pictures. Ask what the article is about. (Possible response: what old maps were like)

READING THE ARTICLE

Have students read the first page silently, paying attention to the reasons why globes are better representations of Earth than maps. Next, have students read the two sections on page 395. Ask:

1 MAIN IDEA   Why is a globe more accurate than a map of the earth?
(Possible response: A globe is the same shape as Earth, so it can show the true sizes and shapes of land areas.)

2 DRAW CONCLUSIONS   Why do continents look different on old maps from how they look on new maps?
(Possible response: People knew less about the world and its land areas long ago than we know today.)

Think and Respond

Possible responses: when you want to look at details such as small towns, roads, and landforms

REREADING FOR A PURPOSE

Preparing for an Experiment   Have students reread "Try This!" aloud, identify the materials needed, the steps to follow, and the expected outcome. Then have them work in pairs to carry out the experiment.

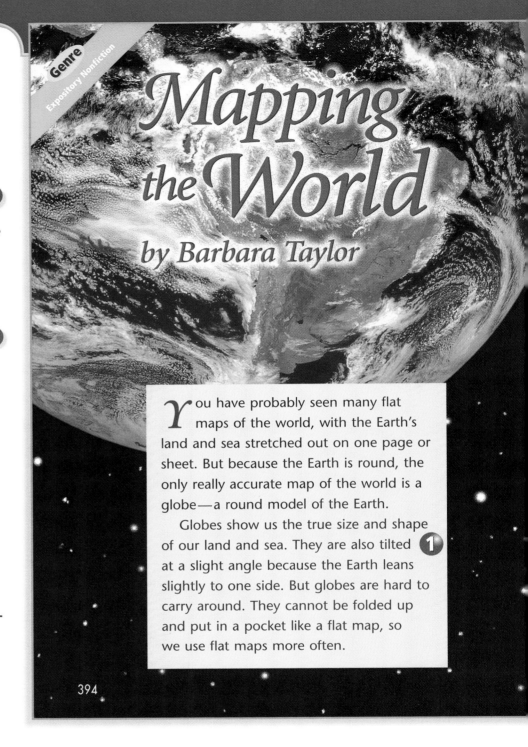

Genre
Expository Nonfiction

Mapping the World
by Barbara Taylor

You have probably seen many flat maps of the world, with the Earth's land and sea stretched out on one page or sheet. But because the Earth is round, the only really accurate map of the world is a globe—a round model of the Earth.

Globes show us the true size and shape of our land and sea. They are also tilted **1** at a slight angle because the Earth leans slightly to one side. But globes are hard to carry around. They cannot be folded up and put in a pocket like a flat map, so we use flat maps more often.

394

Old Maps

Hundreds of years ago most people believed that the Earth was flat, like a giant tabletop. They thought they would fall off the edge if they sailed far enough out to sea. This map was drawn about 500 years ago.

Although it is not accurate, it is easy to recognize the shapes of the different land areas. Can you recognize parts of Europe and Africa?

Try This!

Have you ever had to wrap up a round birthday present? Try covering a ball with a single sheet of paper and not leaving any gaps. You can see how hard it is to make a flat map of the Earth.

Think and Respond

When is a flat map better than a globe?

395

related books

You may want to recommend to students interested in this subject that they locate these titles.

LIBRARY BOOKS COLLECTION

Earth: Our Planet in Space
by Seymour Simon

ADDITIONAL READING

- *Our Earth*
  by Anne Rockwell. Harcourt Brace, 1998. **EASY**

- *Armadillo Rodeo*
  by Jan Brett. Putnam, 1995. **AVERAGE**

- *Exploring Land Habitats*
  by Margaret Yatsevitch Phinney. Mondo, 1994. **CHALLENGING**

LITERARY ANALYSIS

Comparing Texts   Have students fill in a chart similar to the following to compare this article with "The Armadillo from Amarillo."

	The Armadillo from Amarillo	**Mapping the World**
Genre	informational narrative	nonfiction
Characters	Armadillo, Eagle	none
Maps	yes	yes
Topic	seeing the world	seeing the world

The Armadillo from Amarillo   **395**

Making Connections

COMPARE TEXTS

Answers:

1. Possible response: He may appreciate it more because he understands it better. **THEME**

2. Possible response: fantasy—talking animals, armadillos sending postcards and riding on an eagle's back, hitching a ride on a rocket ship; fact—names and locations of places on Earth, what Earth looks like from space, facts about the solar system **FANTASY/REALITY**

3. Possible response: Both are about seeing the world. Both have illustrations that show maps, globes, and photographs of Earth. "The Armadillo from Amarillo" is a fantasy story with animal characters. "Mapping the World" is a nonfiction article. **COMPARE AND CONTRAST**

4. Responses will vary. **USE PRIOR KNOWLEDGE**

5. Responses will vary. **EXPRESS PERSONAL OPINIONS**

▲ The Armadillo from Amarillo

Making Connections

Compare Texts

1. How might Armadillo feel differently about earth after his journey? Tell why.

2. Give examples of fantasy and fact from "The Armadillo from Amarillo."

3. In what ways are "The Armadillo from Amarillo" and "Mapping the World" alike and unlike?

4. Think of another fantasy story you have read. Does that story also give information, as "The Armadillo from Amarillo" does? Explain.

5. Which topic would you rather research to learn more about—your city, your state, your country, your continent, or the universe? Explain the reasons for your choice.

Write a Poem

"The Armadillo from Amarillo" is written in rhyme. Think about a subject you would like to write a rhyming poem about, such as a favorite place or animal. Write to express your thoughts and feelings in rhyme and rhythmic language.

Jot down rhyming words for your poem in a graphic organizer like this one.

Writing CONNECTION

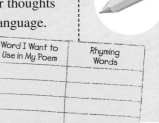

Word I Want to Use in My Poem	Rhyming Words

396

Create a Diagram or Model

Science CONNECTION

In "The Armadillo from Amarillo," Armadillo learns that Earth is one of nine planets that revolve around the sun. Find out the names of all nine planets, their order from nearest to farthest away from the sun, and their order from smallest to largest. Show the information by drawing a diagram or constructing a model. Include a brief written explanation of your diagram or model.

Design Postcards

Social Studies CONNECTION

Armadillo sends many postcards to his cousin Brillo. Design at least one postcard that someone who lived long ago in your community might have sent to a friend. On one side, draw a picture that shows something about your area at a time in the past. You might use your social studies text or sources such as old photographs and newspapers. On the other side of the card, write a brief description of the picture and the time period it shows.

Making Connections

397

HOMEWORK FOR THE WEEK

Students and family members can work together to complete the activities on page T99. You may want to assign some or all of the activities as homework for each day of the week.

technology
Visit *The Learning Site:*
www.harcourtschool.com
See Resources for Parents and Teachers: Homework Helper.

Teacher's Edition, p. T99 ▶

School–Home Connection

Your child is reading "The Armadillo from Amarillo" by Lynne Cherry. This fantasy is about an armadillo named Sasparillo, who wonders how big the world is and where his place is in it. The story teaches children about geography. You may enjoy discussing the story and doing these activities with your child. Together you and your child can enrich his or her language skills.

Reading Together
Your child may enjoy reading with you other award-winning books written and illustrated by Lynne Cherry. You may be able to find the following books and several others in your local library:
• *A River Ran Wild.* Harcourt Brace, 1992.
• *The Great Kapok Tree.* Harcourt Brace, 1990.
• *Flute's Journey.* Harcourt Brace, 1997.

VOCABULARY

Vocabulary Practice
The following words are new vocabulary your child has learned while reading "The Armadillo from Amarillo":

eventually / entire
continent / sphere
universe / homeward

Discuss when you might use or hear these words. During the week, to encourage your child to use the words, ask questions such as these: Where in the universe would you travel if you were an astronaut? What could you do with an entire room of straw?

Let's Take a Trip
Talk with your child about a trip you have taken or would like to take. Tell him or her what you learned about the place, why you wanted to go there, how you got there, and what happened on your journey. If you have mementos or photographs of your trip, share them with your child. Encourage your child to ask you questions and to share his or her ideas for a trip.

TIME TO READ Encourage your child to read for at least 30 minutes outside of class each day.

Visit The Learning Site!
www.harcourtschool.com

SCIENCE

Create a Diagram or Model You might have students 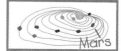 use what they have learned to make a human model of the solar system. First, ten students can be chosen by height corresponding to the size of the planets and the sun. Then the "planets" can stand in order of distance from the "sun." Each "planet" can tell a fact about itself.

SOCIAL STUDIES

Design Postcards
Students may want to interview an elder from the community about an important event from the past. Provide old postcards that have been mailed to show correct format, as well as index cards and markers for creating new postcards.

(Focus Skill) # Cause and Effect

 ▲ The Armadillo from Amarillo

Cause and Effect **(Focus Skill)**

SKILL TRACE

CAUSE AND EFFECT

Introduce	p. 324I
Reteach	pp. S74, S86, T7I
Review	**pp. 346, 369D, 370I, 398**
Test	Theme 3 Vol. 2

RETURN TO THE SKILL

Have students read page 398 in the *Pupil Edition*. You may wish to use this model with the first diagram:

MODEL To begin with, **Armadillo wonders where in the world he is. As a result of that** *cause*, **he leaves home, asks the eagle for a ride, and flies on a rocket ship. All of these events are effects.**

Have students share how identifying cause and effect relationships in "The Armadillo from Amarillo" helped them understand the reasons why certain events occurred in the story.

PRACTICE/APPLY

Students can create cause/effect diagrams to explain volcanoes and earthquakes as they are described in "Rocking and Rolling."
PERFORMANCE ASSESSMENT

Visit *The Learning Site:* **www.harcourtschool.com**
See Skill Activities and Test Tutors: Cause and Effect.

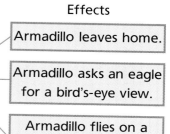
▲ The Armadillo from Amarillo

Cause and Effect **(Focus Skill)**

You know that a **cause** is the reason something happens. An **effect** is the result of an action or event.

Sometimes a cause has more than one effect.

Cause

Armadillo wonders where in the world he is.

Effects

Armadillo leaves home.
Armadillo asks an eagle for a bird's-eye view.
Armadillo flies on a rocket ship.

Sometimes there is more than one cause for an effect.

Causes

Armadillo walks for weeks and sees different places.
Armadillo sees the world from an eagle's back.
Armadillo sees the earth from a rocket ship.

Effect

Armadillo finds out where in the world he is.

Visit *The Learning Site!*
www.harcourtschool.com
See Skills and Activities

398

REACHING ALL LEARNERS

Diagnostic Check: Comprehension and Skills

If . . . students have not completed *Practice Book* page 65 correctly,

Then . . . have pairs of students take turns writing simple cause-and-effect statements such as "I overslept, so I missed the bus and was late for school."

ADDITIONAL SUPPORT ACTIVITIES

BELOW-LEVEL Reteach, p. S86
ADVANCED Extend, p. S87
ENGLISH-LANGUAGE LEARNERS Reteach, p. S87

Focus Skill

Test Prep
Cause and Effect

One day a traveling lizard came upon a rabbit who looked very sad. The rabbit told the lizard, "Usually the crops in the farmer's fields grow well. The soil is rich, and there has always been enough sunshine and enough rain. But now there has been no rain for many weeks. Soon the crops will turn brown and dry up."

Just then, the lizard felt a drop hit her head. It began to rain. The lizard got wet, but she was glad that the crops would be saved.

1. The story states three reasons that—

   A the lizard is traveling

   B the rabbit looks sad

   C the crops usually grow well

   D the lizard got wet

Tip
Look back at the story to see how many reasons it gives for each of the choices.

2. What does the rabbit say the effect will be since there has been no rain for many weeks?

   F It will begin to rain. The crops will be saved.

   G The crops will get enough sun. They will grow well.

   H The soil will be rich. There will be plenty to eat.

   J The crops will turn brown. The crops will dry up.

Tip
Be sure that both of the effects in the answer you choose are caused by not having rain.

399

Test Prep

Cause and Effect Have students read the passage carefully, paying careful attention to effects and their causes. Use the Tips to reinforce good test-taking strategies. (1.C; 2.J)

BELOW-LEVEL   **ON-LEVEL**   **ADVANCED**   **ENGLISH-LANGUAGE LEARNERS**

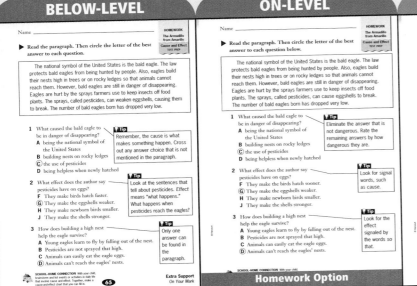

▲ Extra Support, p. 65   ▲ Practice Book, p. 65   ▲ Challenge, p. 65   ▲ ELL, p. 65

Phonics

Phonics

OBJECTIVE

To decode words with unaccented syllables

SKILL TRACE

SYLLABLES: UNACCENTED SYLLABLES

Introduce	Grade 2
Maintain	**p. 399A**

ONGOING ASSESSMENT

If students are not able to fluently read approximately 114 words per minute, **then** they require phonics instruction and will also benefit from fluency practice.

NOTE: For assessment of oral reading accuracy and fluency, see pages T78–T80.

Decoding/Phonics

Syllables: Unaccented Syllables

REVIEW THE SKILL

Discuss unaccented syllables. Write this sentence on the board:

• **The sun rose on the horizon.**

Review with students that in words with more than one syllable, one syllable has more stress than the others. Point to the word *horizon*. Explain that you will try pronouncing it in different ways. Stress the first syllable, and ask students if this sounds like a word they know. (no) Stress the second syllable and ask students if this is a word they know. (yes) Explain that while one syllable is stressed, the others may be unstressed or unaccented. Make sure students know that

• **in two-syllable words, the first syllable usually is stressed.**

• **in words with three or more syllables, two syllables may be stressed. This is called primary and secondary stress.**

• **unaccented syllables often have the schwa sound.**

PRACTICE/APPLY

Decode longer words. Write these words on the board. Have students draw an accent mark over the stressed syllable, and circle the unstressed syllable or syllables.

golden   exploring   remarkable
distance   powerful   dramatically

Then have students pronounce the words with a partner.

To check understanding, have students check their answers in a dictionary and pronounce these words: *decided, landscape, dramatically*. PERFORMANCE ASSESSMENT

Locate Information

Research and Information Skills

REVIEW THE SKILL

Discuss parts of a book. Remind students that understanding the different parts of a nonfiction book can help them find facts and other useful information. Model looking in a nonfiction book about nature for information on armadillos.

MODEL The title tells me what this whole book is about. The table of contents tells me what each chapter is about. I skim the chapter titles to see if any mention armadillos. Next, I check to see if the book has an index. If it does, I look under *a* for the word *armadillo*.

PRACTICE/APPLY

Find a topic. Have students work with partners to find a topic. Give each pair a nonfiction book. Have one partner skim the book and find a topic it focuses on. That student should then hand the book to the partner, say the topic, and tell the partner to use the parts of the book to find information on that topic. After finding the information, the partner should tell what parts of the book he or she used to locate it. Have students then trade roles and repeat the process. **PERFORMANCE ASSESSMENT**

Summarize. Have a volunteer summarize what the different parts of a book list or contain, and tell how each part can be helpful in locating information.

BELOW-LEVEL

Have students prepare self-sticking labels to mark each part of the nonfiction book (title page, table of contents, index) before they begin the Practice/Apply activity.

Graphic Aids

Research and Information Skills

OBJECTIVE

To use book parts to locate information

SKILL TRACE	
GRAPHIC AIDS	
Introduce	pp. 369A–369B
Reteach	p. T74
Review	**pp. 399C, 417B**
Test	Theme 3 Vol. 2

BELOW-LEVEL

Have students work in heterogeneous groups. If possible, provide materials that promote tourism in your state. Have one student take the role of Armadillo. The other group members can take turns presenting travel ideas to him, showing and explaining the graphic aids in the publications.

REVIEW THE SKILL

Discuss using graphic aids. Point out that the author/illustrator of "The Armadillo from Amarillo" helped readers picture the places Armadillo saw. She created accurate illustrations and also included picture postcards, a globe, and a map. Model using the globe and map (*Pupil Edition* pages 390–391) to better understand the events in the poem.

MODEL The globe shows where Texas is located in the United States and North America. Seeing Texas on the globe helps me understand where in the world Armadillo's home is. The map shows vegetational zones of Texas. On it I see the high plains region that Armadillo crossed. Now I understand where and how large that region is.

PRACTICE/APPLY

Use graphic aids. Have students imagine that Armadillo is about to take a journey across your state. Ask them to look in almanacs, newspapers, magazines, encyclopedias, or nonfiction books to find graphic aids that would give Armadillo some important information about your state. Have students display these graphic aids and tell what information each provides. PERFORMANCE ASSESSMENT

Summarize. Ask students why authors sometimes include maps, charts, and other graphic sources in stories.

Make Inferences

Comprehension

REVIEW THE SKILL

Discuss making inferences. Remind students that authors do not explain everything in a story; readers must figure out some things for themselves. Tell students that when readers use text clues and what they know from their own experiences to make sense of story events, they are making inferences. Model the skill:

> **MODEL** The author doesn't say that Armadillo is happy by the end of the story, but I can make an inference that he is. The author says Armadillo accomplished his goal: "He'd wondered where in the world he was/and now Armadillo knew." I know that when people accomplish a goal, they feel happy.

PRACTICE/APPLY

Make inferences about the story. Guide students to complete inference charts like the ones below. **PERFORMANCE ASSESSMENT** (Sample responses are given.)

Text Clues		What I Know		Inference
The grass around Amarillo is yellow.	+	Grass turns yellow when it starts to dry out.	=	(Amarillo is in a fairly dry region.)
Armadillo sends many postcards to his cousin Brillo.	+	People send postcards to people they like.	=	(Armadillo really likes his cousin Brillo.)
Eagle takes Armadillo for a long ride.	+	It's nice to give someone a ride when he or she wants or needs one.	=	(Eagle is a kind creature.)

Summarize. Ask students how making inferences can help readers understand and enjoy fantasy stories such as "The Armadillo from Amarillo."

OBJECTIVE

To make inferences about texts, using text ideas, prior knowledge, and experience

SKILL TRACE	
MAKE INFERENCES	
Introduce	pp. 153A–153B Vol. 1
Review	**pp. 93C, 399D Vol. 2**

BELOW-LEVEL

Copy or duplicate all nine squares in the Making Inferences chart. Have students first find the three squares that give facts from the story. Then, have them identify the three squares that tell things people know, and put each one beside the story fact it relates to. Finally, have students complete each row by placing the inference square at the end.

Writing Process

Invitation

Writing Process: Expository Writing

TRAITS OF GOOD WRITING

	INTRODUCE AND PRACTICE	APPLY TO LONGER WRITING FORMS
Focus/Ideas	329E–F (3-1)	355E–F, 387E–F (3-1)
Organization	167C–D, 193E–F (3-2)	221E–F, 261E–F (3-2)
Voice	41C–D, 67E–F (3-1)	99E–F, 129C–D (3-1)
Word Choice	323C–D, 347C–D (3-2)	369E–F, 399E–F (3-2)
Development	303E–F, 329E–F (3-1)	355E–F, 387E–F (3-1)
Effective Sentences	35E–F, 59E–F (3-2)	93E–F, 117C–D (3-1)
Effective Paragraphs	181E–F, 205E–F (3-1)	223E–F, 255C–D (3-1)
Conventions	(See Grammar and Spelling Lessons.)	(Applied to all writing lessons.)

technology

Writing Express™ CD-ROM
Visit *The Learning Site:*
www.harcourtschool.com
See Writing Detective,
Proofreading Makes Perfect.

TRAITS OF GOOD WRITING

- **Focus/Ideas:** The writer focuses on one event and on details that will encourage the reader to attend.

- **Organization/Paragraphs:** The writer groups ideas in a way that makes sense: first she introduces the event, then she describes the event, and finally she provides time and place.

- **Voice:** The writer uses a friendly, lively tone.

- **Development:** The writing includes details that make the event sound fun and interesting. The day, date, time, place, and address of the event are given.

- **Word Choice:** The writer uses exact words to make ideas clear.

- **Effective Sentences:** The sentences vary in length and structure.

DAY 1 — TEACH/MODEL

CONNECT READING TO WRITING

Tell students that in "The Armadillo from Amarillo," an eagle kindly invites Armadillo to hop on her back to see the world. Ask students to imagine that they are writing a letter to Armadillo to invite him to visit their town. Explain that students will write invitations in this lesson.

REVIEW WRITER'S CRAFT
Display Transparency 265. Have a volunteer read the model aloud, and instruct the students to pay attention to the author's word choice. Then ask volunteers to give examples of descriptive language, vivid verbs, and specific nouns.

▼ **Teaching Transparency 265**

STUDENT MODEL: INVITATION LETTER

An invitation is one kind of friendly letter. It invites someone to do something. Here is an invitation letter that a student wrote to invite Armadillo to come to an event at her school.

Heading
(address and date)

567 Rose Drive
Clearmont, CA 90000
March 2, 20___

Greeting

Dear Armadillo,

Body

I know how much you like to see the world, so I would like to invite you to visit my school in Clearmont. In April, we are having our annual World Community Festival. There will be people there from all over the neighborhood...and the world!

There will be lots of fun activities. You can try all kinds of food, such as Chinese dim sum, Mexican tamales, and pad thai from Thailand. There will be performers putting on skits and musicians singing folk songs in many different languages. Arts and crafts by local artists will be on display, and there will be workshops where you can do your own art projects.

Time and Place

It will be a day full of fun, so please join us! The festival will be held on Saturday, April 14th, from 10 a.m. to 4 p.m. at Rosa Parks Elementary School at 1501 Arbor St. in Clearmont. I hope you can make it.

Closing
Signature

Your friend,
Wen-Yee Chang

"The Armadillo from Amarillo"
Celebrate Our World, Theme 3
265
Writing
Harcourt

DAY 2 — ANALYZE AND PREWRITE

ANALYZE THE WRITING PROMPT

Have students use the following prompt, or brainstorm their own ideas for an invitation.

WRITING PROMPT: *Think of an event that you would like to invite someone to. Write an invitation letter to that person in which you explain what the event is, and where and when it will be held. Encourage the person to attend. Remember to include all parts of a friendly letter.*

ASK THE FOLLOWING QUESTIONS:

- **Who is your audience,** and what is your purpose for writing?

- **What details should you include to describe the event?**

- **Where and when will the event be held?**

5 Day Plan

DAY 3 DRAFT

Have students follow these steps to draft their invitations:

1. WRITE A HEADING AND GREETING Write your address, the date, and a greeting for your invitation.

2. DRAFT THE OPENING Introduce the topic of your invitation.

3. DEVELOP THE TOPIC Include main ideas and details to describe the topic of your invitation.

4. CONCLUDE Remember to include details about when and where the event will take place. Close and sign your letter.

DAY 4 EDIT

REVISE Have students work in pairs or small groups to discuss their invitations. They can use the student rubric on page T91 as they revise. Ask them to make sure that the sentences they write clearly explain the event.

PROOFREAD Have students use the questions below:

 Did I include adverbs that tell _where, when,_ or _how_ to make my writing more colorful?

 Did I correctly write the plural forms of nouns?

 Did I correctly use capital letters and punctuation marks?

DAY 5 PUBLISH AND ASSESS

PUBLISH Students may want to decorate or illustrate their invitations as they publish them. If appropriate, have students mail their invitations.

ASSESS Have students use the rubric to evaluate their own and each other's work. They should add their invitations and their evaluations to their portfolios.

 Language Handbook, pp. 73, 163–165, 238–239

SCORING RUBRIC

	4	3	2	1
FOCUS/IDEAS	Completely focused, purposeful.	Generally focused on task and purpose.	Somewhat focused on task and purpose.	Lacks focus and purpose.
ORGANIZATION/ PARAGRAPHS	Ideas progress logically; transitions make the relationships among ideas clear.	Organization mostly clear, but some lapses occur; some transitions are used.	Some sense of organization but inconsistent or unclear in places.	Little or no sense of organization.
DEVELOPMENT	Central idea supported by strong, specific details.	Central idea with adequate support, mostly relevant details.	Unclear central idea; limited supporting details.	Unclear central idea; little or no development.
VOICE	Viewpoint clear; original expressions used where appropriate.	Viewpoint somewhat clear; few original expressions.	Viewpoint unclear or inconsistent.	Writer seems detached and unconcerned.
WORD CHOICE	Clear, exact language; freshness of expression.	Clear language; some interesting word choices.	Word choice unclear or inappropriate in places.	Word choice often unclear or inappropriate.
SENTENCES	Variety of sentence structures; flows smoothly.	Some variety in sentence structures.	Little variety; choppy or run-on sentences.	Little or no variety; sentences unclear.
CONVENTIONS	Few, if any, errors.	Few errors.	Some errors.	Many errors.

REPRODUCIBLE STUDENT RUBRICS for specific writing purposes and presentations are available on pages T90-T92.

Grammar

Adverbs

SKILL TRACE
ADVERBS

Introduce	pp. 399G–399H
Reteach	pp. S89, T76
Review	pp. 399H, 417F
Test	Theme 3 Vol. 2

REACHING ALL LEARNERS

Diagnostic Check: Grammar and Writing

If . . . students are having difficulty identifying adverbs,

Then . . . write a simple sentence on the board with an action verb. Ask students to add words to tell *where, when,* and *how* the action took place.

ADDITIONAL SUPPORT ACTIVITIES

BELOW-LEVEL	Reteach, p. S88
ADVANCED	Reteach, p. S89
ENGLISH-LANGUAGE LEARNERS	Reteach, p. S89

technology

Grammar Jingles™ CD,
Intermediate: Track 18
Visit *The Learning Site:*
www.harcourtschool.com
See Grammar Practice Park,
Go for Grammar Gold,
Multimedia Grammar Glossary.

DAY 1 — TEACH/MODEL

DAILY LANGUAGE PRACTICE
1. what kind of animal is a armadillo. (What; an; armadillo?)
2. Its an animal with bony plates. All over its body and head. (It's; plates all)

INTRODUCE THE CONCEPT
Display Transparency 266.

- An **adverb** describes a verb. It can tell *where, when,* or *how* an action happens.

Have students decide whether each adverb in sentences 2–4 tells *where, when,* or *how* about *revolve.* Then have them rewrite #5, telling *where, when,* and *how* about a verb.

▼ Teaching Transparency 266

ADVERBS

1. The planets revolve.
2. The planets revolve here. here—where
3. The planets revolve constantly. constantly—when
4. The planets revolve slowly. slowly—how
5. The armadillo scurried _____. Possible responses:
   (1) away, (2) again, (3) nervously; the verb is scurried.

What Adverbs Tell

Where	When	How
there	often	politely
outside	finally	joyfully
everywhere	soon	neatly
ahead	yesterday	quickly
upstairs	now	silently

"The Armadillo from Amarillo"
Celebrate Our World, Theme 3   266   Grammar
Harcourt

DAY 2 — EXTEND THE CONCEPT

DAILY LANGUAGE PRACTICE
1. i've just read a story about an curious armadillo. (I've; a)
2. The armadillo left home and gone out. To see the world. (went; out to)

BUILD ORAL LANGUAGE   Display
the chart on Transparency 266, and have volunteers read the adverbs in each column. Ask students to supply additional examples of each kind of adverb.

Go around the room, asking volunteers to supply adverbs to complete the sentences below. Encourage creative thinking.

The armadillo climbed _____.

The eagle soared _____.

The cat howled _____.

PERFORMANCE ASSESSMENT

Name _____

The Armadillo from Amarillo
Grammar
Adverbs

Skill Reminder • An adverb is a word that describes a verb.
• An adverb may tell *how, when,* or *where.*

▶ Underline the verb. Circle the adverb that describes it.
1. The armadillo lands (shakily.)
2. He sits (down) with a sigh.
3. The eagle flaps his beautiful wings (again.)
4. The armadillo waves (sleepily.)
5. (Then) he closes his eyes.

▶ Write what each underlined adverb tells: *where, when,* or *how.*
6. Together we fly into the sky. ___ how
7. We see all of Texas below. ___ where
8. Now I can see Mexico. ___ when
9. It shines brightly in the sun. ___ how
10. We return to earth afterward. ___ when

▶ Choose two sentences from 1–10. Rewrite each sentence, using a different adverb. Answers will vary.
11. _____
12. _____

Homework Option

▲ Practice Book, p. 66

5 Day Plan

DAY 3 — ORAL REVIEW/PRACTICE

DAILY LANGUAGE PRACTICE
1. **The armadillo met a eagle and was no longer lonley.** (an; lonely)
2. **They could see the erth but the air were thin up there.** (earth, but; was thin)

WHERE? WHEN? HOW?
Write *inside*, *later*, and *politely* on the board. Have students say a sentence for each adverb. Ask them to identify the verb in the sentence.

Test Prep Tip

"This strategy will help you on a language test:

- To identify adverbs in a sentence, look for words that tell *where*, *when*, or *how* an action occurs."

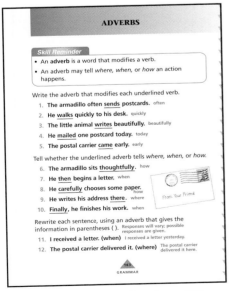

▲ Language Handbook, p. 163

DAY 4 — APPLY TO WRITING

DAILY LANGUAGE PRACTICE
1. **the eagle had a brilliant thoughts** (The; thought.)
2. **what if her and the armadillo could travel out in space** (What; she; space?)

LIVELY VERBS AND ADVERBS
Have students work in pairs to list five action verbs. Then have them brainstorm adverbs that could tell *where*, *when*, or *how* about the verbs they wrote. Ask students to pick their favorite adverbs of the ones they brainstormed and use them in sentences with the five verbs. Discuss how the adverbs help show the action.

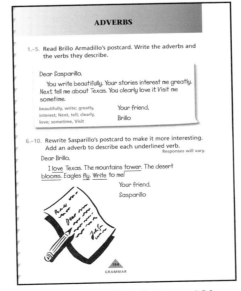

▲ Language Handbook, p. 164

DAY 5 — CUMULATIVE REVIEW

DAILY LANGUAGE PRACTICE
1. **suddenly a space shuttle came along. it take them aboard.** (Suddenly; It; took)
2. **The eagle and the armadillo seen the earth from space** (saw; space.)

NOT IS AN ADVERB
Tell students that *not* is an adverb. Have students underline verbs and circle adverbs in each sentence given. Then have them rewrite each sentence, changing each verb + *not* to a contraction.
1. He <u>is</u> ⬭not⬭ a native Texan. (isn't)
2. They <u>are</u> ⬭not⬭ in Abilene. (aren't)
3. She <u>was</u> ⬭not⬭ from Dallas. (wasn't)
4. They <u>stood</u> ⬭proudly⬭.
5. They <u>greeted</u> us ⬭again⬭.

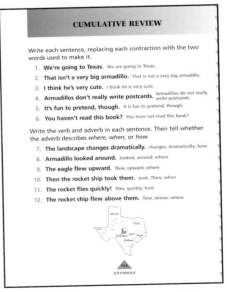

▲ Language Handbook, p. 165

The Armadillo from Amarillo **399H**

Spelling Words

1. water
2. over*
3. never
4. under
5. river
6. number
7. wonder*
8. tower*
9. rather*
10. finger
11. center
12. prefer
13. better*
14. border*
15. fever

* Selection Words

Challenge Words
16. mirth*
17. laughter
18. chuckle
19. humor
20. giggle

Spelling

Words That End Like ever

DAY 1 — PRETEST/SELF-CHECK

ADMINISTER THE PRETEST Use the Dictation Sentences under Day 5. Help students self-check their pretests using Transparency 267.

ADVANCED

Use the Challenge Words in these Dictation Sentences:

16. We heard sounds of **mirth** from the people watching the cartoon.
17. The humorous speech caused much **laughter**.
18. Dad let out a **chuckle** when I told him what had happened.
19. The storyteller had a wonderful sense of **humor** and made us laugh often.
20. My brothers **giggle** when they tell jokes.

DAY 2 — TEACH/MODEL

WORD SORT Display Transparency 267. Make sure students know the meanings of the words. Then ask students to copy the chart and to write each Spelling Word where it belongs.

Point to and read the word *never*. Ask students to name the last two letters in the word (*er*). Have a volunteer circle them. Repeat the procedure with the word *tower*. Ask students what is the same about the two words. (Both end with *er*.) Have them read the generalization to confirm their conclusion.

HANDWRITING When you write an *r*, make sure it does not look like a *v*.

▼ Teaching Transparency 267

WORDS THAT END LIKE EVER

Spelling Words

1. *water*	6. *number*	11. *center*
2. *over*	7. *wonder*	12. *prefer*
3. *never*	8. *tower*	13. *better*
4. *under*	9. *rather*	14. *border*
5. *river*	10. *finger*	15. *fever*

The ending sound you hear in *ever* is usually spelled *er*.

Sort the Spelling Words by the vowel in the first syllable.

a
water   rather

e
never   center   prefer   better   fever

i
river   finger

o
over   wonder   tower   border

u
under   number

"The Armadillo from Amarillo"
Celebrate Our World, Theme 3   **267**   Spelling Harcourt

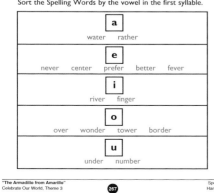

▲ Practice Book, page 67

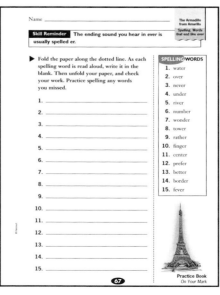

▲ Spelling Practice Book, page 104

DAY
3 SPELLING STRATEGIES

WORD SHAPES Have students look at the list of Spelling Words and tell which words have the same word shapes. (water/under, river/never, number/wonder/center, tower/fever) Have them draw the word shapes on the board to show how they are the same for each group of words.

Apply to Writing

Have students use the word shapes strategy as they proofread their writing. Suggest that they draw word shapes if they are unsure of how to spell a word.

DAY
4 SPELLING ACTIVITIES

WORD BOOK Ask students to write sentences using Spelling Words, one sentence per sheet of paper. (They should use both sides of the paper.) Then have them illustrate their sentences. When they are finished, have them make a cover for the "*ER* Book" and then assemble the pages. Allow time for students to exchange books with others.

WRITING BOOK TITLES Have students write imaginary book titles using Spelling Words. Allow volunteers to share their titles.

DAY
5 POSTTEST

DICTATION SENTENCES

1. Please turn on the **water** in the bathtub.
2. When will the storm be **over**?
3. I **never** go to scary movies.
4. My pencil rolled **under** my desk.
5. The **river** has many kinds of fish.
6. What **number** comes after eight?
7. I **wonder** where I left my coat.
8. There is a flag on the top of the **tower**.
9. I would **rather** have milk with my lunch.
10. How did you hurt your **finger**?
11. Draw a circle in the **center** of the paper.
12. I **prefer** juice over milk.
13. Are you feeling **better** today?
14. She put a **border** around the picture.
15. I had a **fever** last night.

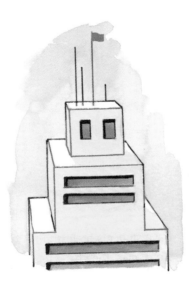

▲ Spelling Practice Book, page 105

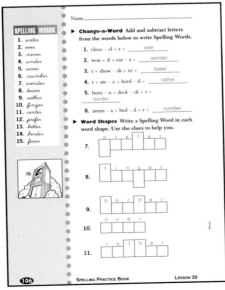

▲ Spelling Practice Book, page 106

The Armadillo from Amarillo **399J**

Word Study

Prefixes

OBJECTIVE

To use knowledge of prefixes to determine the meanings of words

Write on the board *converse* and *universe*. Circle *con-* in *converse*. Explain to students that *converse* contains the prefix *con-*, also spelled *com-*, which means "with" or "together." Write the following words beneath *converse*: *convey, compatriot, confine, conform.* Explain that each word begins with the same prefix, meaning "with." Have students find the meaning for each word in a dictionary. Follow the same procedure for *universe*. (prefix *uni-*, meaning "single" or "one"; other words with the prefix: *unicycle, uniform, unify, unison*)

converse
universe

ADVANCED

Have students brainstorm a list of additional rhyming word pairs. Then have them write sentences for each pair of words. The sentences should be related and, together, relate some kind of story. For example:

This story was about an armadillo who traveled to a town called Amarillo.

Rhyming Words

OBJECTIVE

To identify and properly use rhyming elements of language

Write on the board *trees* and *chickadees*. Ask students what makes these words rhyme. (They have the same vowel and consonant sounds at the end: long *e* and /z/). Have students work in pairs to play a game of Rhyming Word Concentration by doing the following:

- Find ten pairs of rhyming words in "The Armadillo from Amarillo."
- Write each word on a card.
- Turn all twenty cards face down.
- Take turns turning over two cards. If the words on the cards match, the player keeps the cards and goes again. Challenge groups to think of other words that rhyme with the words on the cards and add those to the game.

Speaking and Listening

Extending an Invitation

OBJECTIVE

To convey important information in a telephone call

Tell students they will role-play using a telephone to invite a friend to an event.

Organization   Share these **organizational tips** with students.

- Prepare an outline to invite your friend by telephone. List the name of the event, the date and time, the location, and any other important details.

Delivery   Share the following **practice tips** with students.

- When someone answers the phone, identify yourself by name and ask to speak with your friend.

- Speak slowly and clearly. Name the date, time, and place so that your friend can understand them and write them down.

Have students work in pairs to role-play giving and receiving an invitation by telephone.
PERFORMANCE ASSESSMENT

Responding

OBJECTIVE

To respond politely to an invitation

Have students listen to note details and respond appropriately.

PHONE TIPS   Have students write a list of listening tips to use when taking telephone messages:

- Keep a notepad and pencil by the telephone.
- Write down the caller's name and phone number.

Listening Tips

- Listen carefully to what, when, where, and what time the event will take place.

- Ask a parent or other adult whether you can accept the invitation.

- Thank the caller for inviting you. Say whether you will be able to go.

Physical Maps

OBJECTIVE

To use a map and a map key to gain information about the geography of a region

Display a physical map of the United States, and have students point out the landforms and bodies of water. Also, refer students to their science books for physical features and land formations. Next, tell students to use the illustrations as guides for creating clay models of one land formation in their state.

Guided Reading OPTIONS

Books for
All Learners
Reinforcing Skills and Strategies

■ BELOW-LEVEL

From
Here to There
by Mona Shea Frazier
Illustrated by Anne Kennedy

 Focus Skill: Cause and Effect

 Focus Strategy: Reread to Clarify

 Vocabulary: *eventually, converse, continent, sphere, universe, homeward*

Genre: Fiction
Social Studies Connection: Spatial Understanding of Location

SUMMARY Jill tells her dad that she feels small when she thinks about the stars in the sky. He responds by explaining that small things are part of bigger things. He goes on to explain Jill's place in her home, neighborhood, community, county, region, state, country, continent, planet, and solar system, and helps her see that she has a special place in the universe.

 Visit *The Learning Site:*
www.harcourtschool.com
See Resources for Parents and Teachers: Books for All Learners.

BEFORE READING

Preview/Set Purpose Have students preview the story and predict what it is about. Invite them to set a purpose for reading.

Reinforce Cause and Effect Guide students to complete a series of cause-effect sentence frames to help them understand why the story characters feel and speak as they do. CAUSE AND EFFECT/GRAPHIC AIDS

Cause	Effect

Reinforce Vocabulary To review vocabulary, write the words on the board one at a time, use each in an oral sentence, and call on students to do the same.

READING THE BOOK

Pages 2–8 What does Jill's dad mean when he tells her that small things are part of bigger things? (He means that everything, including atoms and people, is part of a bigger world.) What is Jill's place? (Her place is her room, inside her house, in her neighborhood, in Summit County.) NOTE DETAILS

Pages 9–16 Why does Jill's dad keep saying, "But there's more"? (He keeps going on to tell her about bigger and bigger parts of the world that she is also part of.) CAUSE AND EFFECT

Reread for Fluency Invite pairs of students to reread favorite parts of the book aloud to you.

RESPONDING

Retell Have students complete the cause-effect sentence frames. They can use the sentence frames to help them retell the story.

▲ page 399O   ▲ page 399P

Oral Reading Fluency

Use Books for All Learners to promote oral reading fluency.

See Fluency Routine Cards, pp. T80a–T80b.

■ ON-LEVEL

 Focus Skill: Cause and Effect

 Focus Strategy: Reread to Clarify

 Vocabulary: *eventually, converse, continent, sphere, universe, homeward*

Genre: Nonfiction
Science Connection: Living Things Interact

SUMMARY This informational book about armadillos begins with a legend about how armadillos come to be. It goes on to explain how long armadillos have been on the earth, how their unusual bodies are constructed, how they build homes and protect themselves, and where these small armored survivors live today.

 Visit *The Learning Site:*
www.harcourtschool.com
See Resources for Parents and Teachers: Books for All Learners.

BEFORE READING

Preview/Set Purpose Have students read the title and table of contents, preview the illustrations, and predict what they will learn. Guide them to set a purpose for reading.

Reinforce Cause and Effect Remind students that paying attention to causes and effects can help them understand what they read. Students can fill in a cause-and-effect chart as they read the book. CAUSE AND EFFECT/GRAPHIC AIDS

READING THE BOOK

Pages 2–6 What explanation does this folktale give for how armadillos came to be? (It says armadillos were tricksters who were turned to stone as punishment for their misbehavior.) CAUSE AND EFFECT

Pages 7–13 What makes armadillos unique? (They have bony plates covering their bodies; they can roll up into a ball; they can walk under water.) NOTE DETAILS

Pages 14–16 Where did the armadillos in North America come from? (South America) Do you agree that armadillos are "true survivors"? Explain. (Possible response: yes, because in 200 years they have migrated over a very wide area and survived in many different environments) MAKE JUDGMENTS

Rereading for Fluency Invite students to choose a page, passage, or paragraph from the book to read aloud.

RESPONDING

Armadillo Fact Chart Ask students to complete the fact chart and use it to retell the important information they learned about armadillos.

The Armadillo from Amarillo   **399N**

Books for All Learners

Reinforcing Skills and Strategies

■ ADVANCED

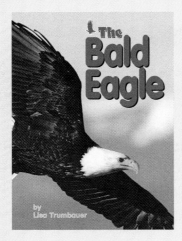

 Focus Skill: Cause and Effect

 Focus Strategy: Reread to Clarify

☑ **Vocabulary: *eventually, converse, continent, sphere, universe, homeward, symbol, national***

Genre: Nonfiction
Social Studies Connection: National Symbols

SUMMARY   The bald eagle was chosen as America's national bird by Congress in 1782. In the wild, bald eagles are powerful birds of prey, excellent flyers, and attentive parents. Hunting and chemicals once threatened the bald eagles' survival, but today they thrive in many parts of North America. The bald eagle has appeared as a symbol on coins, stamps, and flags, and has become an emblem for many groups who admire its freedom and strength.

 Visit *The Learning Site:*
www.harcourtschool.com
See Resources for Parents and Teachers: Books for All Learners.

BEFORE READING

Preview/Set Purpose   Ask students to preview the book, predict what it will tell readers about the bald eagle, and decide why they will read the book.

Reinforce Cause and Effect   As students read, suggest that they look for reasons why the bald eagle has become a symbol for so many people. Remind them to also look for other cause-effect relationships. They can fill in a chart like the one below. CAUSE AND EFFECT/GRAPHIC AIDS

Causes	Effects

Expand Vocabulary   Write the term *national symbol* on the board and discuss its meaning. Ask students to name some national symbols they know of, such as the bald eagle, the stars and stripes, and Uncle Sam. Discuss the ideas these symbols stand for.

READING THE BOOK

Pages 2–4   Why was the bald eagle chosen as America's national bird? (Congress chose it because it is powerful and is native to North America.) CAUSE AND EFFECT

Pages 7–10   How would you describe bald eagles in the wild? (They are powerful predators, strong flyers, and good parents.) MAKE GENERALIZATIONS

Rereading for Fluency   Have students take turns asking questions about bald eagles that are answered in the book and then reading aloud the sections that provide the answers.

RESPONDING

All About Eagles   Ask students to complete the cause-effect chart. They can use it to help them explain why the bald eagle has become such an important symbol in America.

Managing Small Groups

While you work with small groups, have other students do the following:

- Self-Selected Reading
- Practice Pages
- Cross-Curricular Centers
- Journal Writing

■ ENGLISH-LANGUAGE LEARNERS

Finding Your Way

by Robert R. O'Brien
illustrated by Jennifer Thermes

 Focus Skill: Cause and Effect

 Focus Strategy: Reread to Clarify

Concept Vocabulary: *north, south, east, west, landmark, compass*

Genre: Fiction
Social Studies Connection: Map Skills

SUMMARY When a boy receives an invitation to a birthday party in the mail, along with a list of directions for how to get there, he and his father use a street map and the directions to help them find the address. In the process, the boy learns map skills such as how to use a compass rose, identify landmarks, and determine whether to turn left or right at intersections.

 Visit *The Learning Site:*
www.harcourtschool.com
See Resources for Parents and Teachers: Books for All Learners.

BEFORE READING

Tap Prior Knowledge Ask students if they have ever used a map or a set of directions to help them find a place. If possible, display a map of your community and have students find the location of their homes, their school, or other places they know well.

Total Physical Response Have students stand and follow these directions: *Turn* to the *right*. *Turn* to the *left*. *Point straight* ahead of you. Touch the *top* of your head.

Display Vocabulary/Concept Words Write the words on the board. Use the story illustrations and gestures to explain their meanings.

Preview the Book Guide students to preview the book by reading page 2 and viewing the illustrations.

READING THE BOOK

Page 5 How does finding your house or street on the map before you start your trip help you get where you want to go? (Knowing where you are starting from will help you figure out which way to go.) CAUSE AND EFFECT

Pages 10–16 What are some other things you need to pay attention to when you are following directions? (the names of streets; landmarks the directions tell you to look for; where to turn; whether to turn right or left) If a direction confused you, what could you do? (You could reread it.) REREAD TO CLARIFY

Rereading Reread the directions aloud with students, pausing after each page to have students pantomime following the directions.

RESPONDING

Have small groups create a simple map of the classroom, designating one spot as a "landmark." Each group should create a set of directions telling how to get from the classroom door to another location in the room, using the landmark as a guide.

Teacher Notes

Teacher Notes

THEME CONNECTION:
Celebrate Our World

GENRE:
Expository Nonfiction

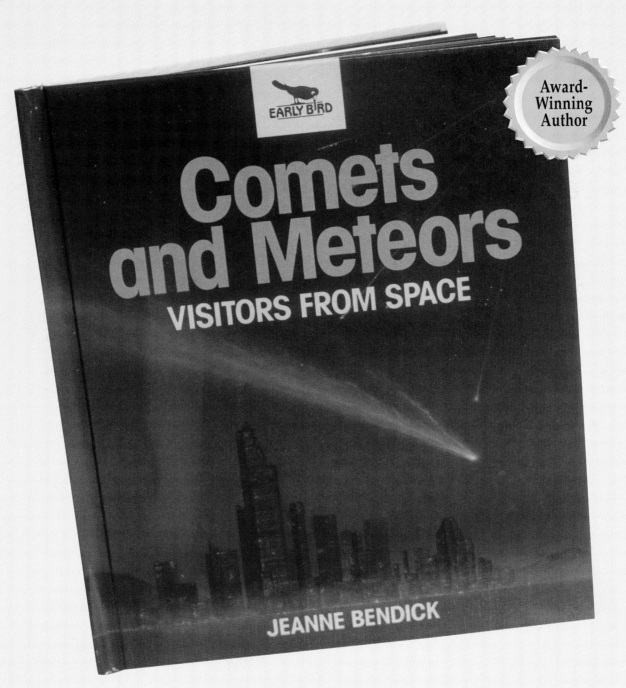

Award-Winning Author

EARLY BIRD

Comets and Meteors
VISITORS FROM SPACE

JEANNE BENDICK

SUMMARY:

We see comets when the Sun's gravity pulls them past Earth. Comets may look like bright, fuzzy balls or long-haired stars, but they are really made of rock, dust, and ice.

 All selections available on *Audiotext 6.*

Books for All Learners

Lesson Plans on pages 417K–417N

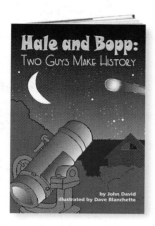

BELOW-LEVEL	ON-LEVEL	ADVANCED	ELL
• Lesson Vocabulary	• Lesson Vocabulary	• Challenge Vocabulary	• Concept Vocabulary
• Focus Skill: Locate Information	• Focus Skill: Locate Information	• Focus Skill: Locate Information	• Focus Skill: Locate Information

MULTI-LEVEL PRACTICE

Extra Support, pp. 68–69

Practice Book, pp. 68–71

Challenge, pp. 68–69

English-Language Learners, pp. 68–69

ADDITIONAL RESOURCES

Spelling Practice Book, pp. 107–109

Language Handbook, pp. 56–57, 166–168

Audiotext 6

Intervention Resource Kit, Lesson 30
  • Intervention Reader, *Included in Intervention Resource Kit*

English-Language Learners Resource Kit, Lesson 30

 # Technology

• *Writing Express*™ **CD-ROM**

• *Grammar Jingles*™ **CD**

• *Media Literacy and Communication Skills Package* (Video)

• *Reading and Language Skills Assessment* **CD-ROM**

• *The Learning Site:* **www.harcourtschool.com**

5-15 Minutes

ORAL LANGUAGE

- **Question of the Day**

- **Sharing Literature**

15-30 Minutes

SKILLS & STRATEGIES

- **Comprehension**

- **Vocabulary**

30-45 Minutes

READING

- **Guided Comprehension**

- **Independent Reading**

- **Cross-Curricular Connections**

45-90 Minutes

LANGUAGE ARTS

- **Writing**

  Daily Writing Prompt

- **Grammar**

  Daily Language Practice

- **Spelling**

Daily Routines
- Question of the Day
- Daily Language Practice
- Daily Writing Prompt

Day 1

Question of the Day, p. 400H
What is the most interesting thing you have seen in the night sky? Why was it interesting?

Literature Read-Aloud, pp. 400G–H

Comprehension:
 (Skill) Locate Information, p. 400I **T**
(Strategy) Use Text Structure and Format, p. 400J
Vocabulary, p. 400L

Read: Vocabulary Power, pp. 400–401
Vocabulary Power Words:
fluorescent, force, loops, nucleus, particles, solar wind

 Independent Reading
Books for All Learners

SCIENCE Research Constellations of Stars

Writing: Writing Process, p. 417C

🖊 **Writing Prompt:**
There are plenty of things to see in the night sky. Think about the most interesting or unusual thing you have seen in the night sky. Now write about what you saw.

Grammar:
Comparing with Adverbs, p. 417E **T**

Daily Language Practice
1. i wunder what that bright light are. (I; wonder; is)
2. how far away is the planet mars. (How; Mars?)

Spelling:
Words Ending with -*le* or -*al*, p. 417G **T**

Day 2

Question of the Day, p. 400H
What does solar mean? Why do you think the earth's part of the universe is called a "solar system"?

Think and Respond, p. 410

Comprehension:
 (Skill) Locate Information, pp. 402–413 **T**

Decoding/Phonics:
Syllables: Consonant -*le* Syllable Pattern, p. 417A

Reading the Selection, pp. 402–413
Vocabulary Power Words

 Independent Reading
Books for All Learners

SCIENCE Create a Solar System Map
SCIENCE Telescopes

Writing: Writing Process, p. 417C

🖊 **Writing Prompt:**
Imagine that one night a meteor lands in your yard. Think about how the meteorite looks and sounds as it speeds toward the ground. Now write a story about the night a meteorite landed in your yard.

Grammar:
Extend the Concept, p. 417E **T**

Daily Language Practice
1. comets are ball of frozen gassies (Comets; balls; gases.)
2. Have you ever saw a comet in the sky. (seen; sky?)

Spelling:
Word Sort, p. 417G **T**

- **Does this passage describe a real event that takes place on Mars? How do you know?** (Possible response: No, it takes place in a museum exhibit on Earth. The second paragraph explains that the passage is about a simulation of a mission to Mars.) FANTASY/REALITY

- **What is the main purpose of the exhibit?** (Possible response: to teach kids about space exploration) MAIN IDEA

- **Is this an exhibit you would like to see? Why or why not?** (Responses will vary.) EXPRESS PERSONAL OPINIONS

Question of the Day

DEVELOP ORAL LANGUAGE

- Display Transparency 270 and ask a volunteer to read the first question aloud.

- **Response Journal** Explain to students that they should think about the question throughout the day and write their responses in their journals. Tell students to be prepared to discuss the answer or answers to it by the end of the day or at another time you choose.

- You may want to repeat this process daily for each of the five discussion questions.

OBJECTIVE

To use book parts to locate information and find answers to questions in text

SKILL TRACE
LOCATE INFORMATION

Introduce	p. 348I
Reteach	pp. S80, S92, T73
Review	**pp. 368, 399B, 400I, 416**
Test	Theme 3 Vol. 2

▼ **Teaching Transparency 271**

LOCATE INFORMATION

- You can use **parts of a book** to find information.
- When you want to find specific information or find an answer to a question, **chapter headings** can help you.

BOOK PART	INFORMATION FOUND THERE
Cover	title and author
Table of Contents	the sections or chapters in order
Glossary	definitions of terms used in the book, listed in alphabetical order
Index	alphabetical listing of topics covered in the book
Chapter Headings	what the different parts of a chapter or story are about

EXAMPLE:
Stars look like tiny glowing points in the night sky, but stars are not tiny. They are large balls of burning gas far out in space.

"Visitors From Space"
Celebrate Our World, Theme 3   271   Focus Skill
Harcourt

BELOW-LEVEL

Additional Support
- *Intervention Teacher's Guide*, p. 300

ENGLISH-LANGUAGE LEARNERS

Additional Support
- *English-Language Learners Teacher's Guide*, p. 177

Focus Skill   Locate Information

REVIEW THE SKILL

Access prior knowledge.   Display a copy of a science or social studies textbook. Ask students to identify the book part they would use to find out the chapter titles. (the table of contents) What book part would they use to find the definition of a particular word in the book? (the glossary)

TEACH/MODEL

Display Transparency 271.

- Tell students that good readers use book parts to locate information. Have a volunteer read aloud the bulleted items.

- Read the name of each book part and the kind of information it contains. Hold up a science textbook and turn to the book part as it is discussed.

- Read the example sentences to students and ask them to list appropriate chapter headings. (stars)

Text Structure   Point out that headings, captions, and chapter titles can help readers locate information.

PRACTICE/APPLY

Students can use a SQR chart like this to record what they learn in "Visitors from Space."

S-Q-R Chart		
Survey	Question	Review

For opportunities to apply and reinforce the skill, see the following pages:

During reading: pages 404 and 406
After reading: *Pupil Edition* pages 416–417

Use Text Structure and Format

REVIEW THE STRATEGY

Remind students that good readers **use text structure and format** to understand what they read. Good readers are active readers, and they pay attention to how an author has organized information in a selection.

TEACH/MODEL

Review with students that many nonfiction selections include headings and captions. Explain that major ideas are organized under headings, and that captions give information about illustrations or photographs.

Ask students to preview pages 404 and 405 of "Visitors from Space." Point out the headings, illustrations, and captions. Then model the strategy.

> **MODEL** **These pages have headings, illustrations and a caption. As I read, I can refer back to this information to help me understand this part of the selection.**

SKILL ⟷ STRATEGY CONNECTION

Explain to students that **text structure and format** will help them **locate information** in a selection.

PRACTICE/APPLY

Remind students to use text structure and format if they have trouble locating information in a text. For opportunities to apply and reinforce the strategy **during reading**, see pages 405 and 409.

Strategies
Good Readers Use

- Use Decoding/Phonics
- Make and Confirm Predictions
- Create Mental Images
- Self-Question
- Summarize
- Read Ahead
- Reread to Clarify
- Use Context to Confirm Meaning
- **Use Text Structure and Format**
- Adjust Reading Rate

Building Background

ACCESS PRIOR KNOWLEDGE

Ask students to describe the Solar System. Ask: **What makes up the Solar System?** Guide students to use a web to organize their ideas.

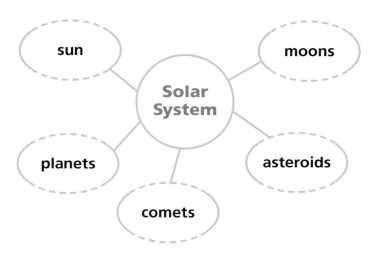

 technology

Visit *The Learning Site:*
www.harcourtschool.com
See Building Background.

DEVELOP CONCEPTS

Help students use prior knowledge to develop concepts by asking the following questions:

- **What is the difference between a comet and a star?** (Possible responses: Comets are rock, ice, gas; a star is made up of hot gas.)

- **What do astronomers do? Do you think it would be fun to be an astronomer?** (Possible responses: They study objects in the sky; Responses will vary.)

- **If you could name something in the sky after you, what would it be?** (Responses will vary.)

Tell students that they will be reading an expository nonfiction selection about comets.

REACHING ALL LEARNERS

Diagnostic Check: Vocabulary

If . . . students do not understand at least five of the six vocabulary words,

Then . . . have them use the glossary or a dictionary to find synonyms for the words to help reinforce the meanings.

ADDITIONAL SUPPORT ACTIVITIES

BELOW-LEVEL	Reteach, p. S90
ADVANCED	Extend, p. S91
ENGLISH-LANGUAGE LEARNERS	Reteach, p. S91

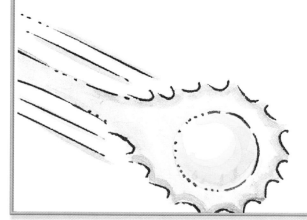

Vocabulary

Vocabulary

fluorescent bright and glowing
force power that causes motion or change
loops moves in a circling way
nucleus center of a comet
particles tiny pieces
solar wind continuous flow of gases from the Sun

TEACH VOCABULARY STRATEGIES

Use context to confirm meaning. Display Transparency 272. Choose three volunteers to play the roles of Maria, Arnold, and Professor Stella. Before they begin reading, remind students to use context to help them determine meanings of unfamiliar words. Model using context to determine the meaning of *fluorescent*.

MODEL The words *glowing* and *light* tell me that *fluorescent* must be an adjective that means "glowing" or "bright." When I read the dictionary definition of *fluorescent*, I find out that fluorescent light bulbs use a special gas to glow the way they do.

Have students read the play silently. Ask volunteers to identify the context clues they used to determine the meanings of the remaining vocabulary words.

Tell students to use context to determine the meaning of other unfamiliar words when they read. Remind them to use dictionaries, glossaries, or electronic reference sources to check a word's meaning and pronunciation.

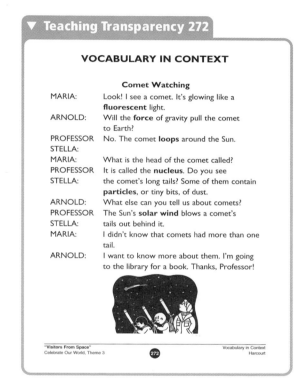

▼ **Teaching Transparency 272**

VOCABULARY IN CONTEXT

Comet Watching

MARIA: Look! I see a comet. It's glowing like a **fluorescent** light.

ARNOLD: Will the **force** of gravity pull the comet to Earth?

PROFESSOR STELLA: No. The comet **loops** around the Sun.

MARIA: What is the head of the comet called?

PROFESSOR STELLA: It is called the **nucleus**. Do you see the comet's long tails? Some of them contain **particles**, or tiny bits, of dust.

ARNOLD: What else can you tell us about comets?

PROFESSOR STELLA: The Sun's **solar wind** blows a comet's tails out behind it.

MARIA: I didn't know that comets had more than one tail.

ARNOLD: I want to know more about them. I'm going to the library for a book. Thanks, Professor!

"Visitors From Space"
Celebrate Our World, Theme 3   272   Vocabulary in Context
                                                    Harcourt

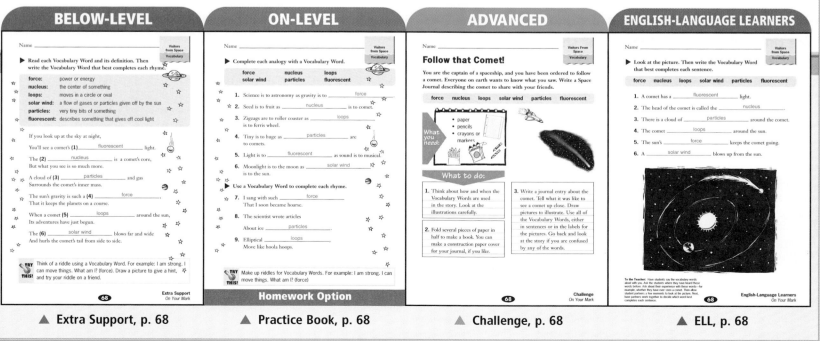

BELOW-LEVEL	ON-LEVEL	ADVANCED	ENGLISH-LANGUAGE LEARNERS

▲ Extra Support, p. 68   ▲ Practice Book, p. 68   ▲ Challenge, p. 68   ▲ ELL, p. 68

Homework Option (ON-LEVEL)

Vocabulary Power

Vocabulary Power

APPLY STRATEGIES

Ask a volunteer to read aloud the first paragraph on page 400. Then have students read the remaining text silently. Remind them to apply the strategy of using context clues to confirm the meanings of any unfamiliar words.

EXTEND WORD KNOWLEDGE

Practice other vocabulary strategies.
Ask students to answer questions with sentences that show what the Vocabulary Words mean. MEANINGFUL SENTENCES

- On what might *fluorescent* paint be used? **PRIOR KNOWLEDGE**

- On Earth, does the *force* of gravity pull things up or down? **PRIOR KNOWLEDGE**

- Are *particles* large or small? **DESCRIPTION**

- The *nucleus* is what part of a comet? **EXPLANATION**

- If an ice skater skates *loops* around an ice rink, what shape does he or she make? **EXAMPLE**

- Where does *solar wind* come from? **EXPLANATION**

▲ **Visitors from Space**

| solar wind |
| particles |
| force |
| fluorescent |
| nucleus |
| loops |

400

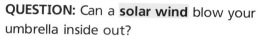

What are comets? Where do they come from? These questions were like riddles to people long ago. Here are some other science questions and riddles you can try to answer.

QUESTION: Can a **solar wind** blow your umbrella inside out?

ANSWER: No. The solar wind is magnetic material that flows from the sun. It is a stream of tiny **particles**, or bits too small to see or feel. The **force**, or energy, of the solar wind doesn't reach the ground on Earth. However, it is a very strong wind, causing comets' tails to move and change shape.

QUESTION: How is a TV screen like a firefly?

ANSWER: Both are **fluorescent**, or bright and glowing. TV screens are coated with a special material that glows. Fireflies glow because of something natural that takes place in their bodies.

QUESTION: How is the head of a comet like the center of a raindrop?

ANSWER: Both can be called a **nucleus**. The head of a comet is the nucleus that is pulled in a huge oval as it **loops** around the sun. When water gathers around a particle to form a raindrop, the particle is also called a nucleus.

Vocabulary–Writing CONNECTION

At school crossings, traffic signs are often painted **fluorescent** yellow. Write a paragraph telling what you think of this, and where else fluorescent paint could be useful.

401

 QUICKWRITE

VOCABULARY-WRITING CONNECTION

Encourage students to think about how fluorescent paint is different from ordinary paint and how this would make it more useful. Students should add the Vocabulary Power words to their Word Banks to use in future writing assignments.

Prereading Strategies

PREVIEW AND PREDICT

Have students read the **genre** information on page 402. Then have them preview the selection. Ask them what they think this selection is about, based on their preview and the characteristics of expository nonfiction. Then have them record predictions about what they might learn. They can begin a SQR chart like this. See Transparency G.

Survey	Question	Review
Look! A comet!	What is a comet?	

Genre

Expository Nonfiction

Expository nonfiction explains information and ideas.

In this selection, look for

- **illustrations with captions and labels.**

- **sections divided by headings.**

402

BELOW-LEVEL	**ON-LEVEL**	**ADVANCED**	**ENGLISH-LANGUAGE LEARNERS**
As you preview the selection with students, discuss the meanings of the following words: *gases, glow, orbit, thirsty, visitors,* and *water.* Help students set a purpose for reading through page 408. **SMALL GROUP**	Students can read the selection with a partner. Use the Guided Comprehension questions and Ongoing Assessments to measure students' understanding. **PARTNER**	Pairs of students who need little teacher support may want to read silently, pausing after several pages to discuss the selection. Encourage pairs to share new information that they found interesting. **INDEPENDENT PARTNER**	Read aloud the selection or have students listen to it on *Audiotext 6.* Then have students read aloud selected pages as a group to develop oral fluency. **SMALL GROUP**

BELOW-LEVEL (continued):
ADDITIONAL SUPPORT
Intervention Reader: Bright Surprises
Intervention Teacher's Guide, pp. 300–303

ENGLISH-LANGUAGE LEARNERS (continued):
ADDITIONAL SUPPORT
See *English-Language Learners Resource Kit,* Lesson 30.
English-Language Learners Teacher's Guide, pp. 177–178

VISITORS FROM SPACE

by Jeanne Bendick
illustrated by David Schleinkofer

403

SET PURPOSE

Locate information. Tell students that one purpose for reading is to locate information. Ask students to set their own purposes. Offer this suggestion:

MODEL I want to find out the answers to the questions in my SQR chart.

Focus Strategy **Use Text Structure and Format** Have students use this strategy to help them understand the selection.

 "Visitors from Space" is available on *Audiotext 6.*

COMPREHENSION CARD 30

Reading Nonfiction Students may use Comprehension Card 30 to discuss Reading Nonfiction in "Visitors from Space."

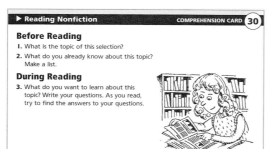

▶ **Reading Nonfiction**   COMPREHENSION CARD **30**

Before Reading
1. What is the topic of this selection?
2. What do you already know about this topic? Make a list.

During Reading
3. What do you want to learn about this topic? Write your questions. As you read, try to find the answers to your questions.

Comprehension Card 30,
Page T85 ▶

Guided Comprehension

1 **COMPARE AND CONTRAST** How are our ideas about comets today different from people's ideas about comets long ago? (Possible response: Long ago, people thought comets were magical signs that meant something bad was going to happen. Today we know that comets are made of rock, dust, ice, and gas, and travel through space.)

2 **NOTE DETAILS** Who are *astronomers?* (scientists who study the planets and stars)

3 (Focus Skill) **LOCATE INFORMATION** Where on these pages would you look to find out where comets come from? Explain your answer. (Possible response: I would read page 404. The heading asks, "Where do comets come from?", so I think that's where I'd find the answer.)

Look! A Comet

This is what a big, bright comet looks like in the sky. (top right).

Long ago, people thought a comet was a warning that something terrible was going to happen on Earth. It might be an earthquake, a flood, or maybe a war. Why else would a flaming ball suddenly appear in the sky?

Today we know much more about comets. A comet is not a warning of bad things to come. And we know that comets do not appear suddenly. We just don't notice them until they are near the Sun. **1**

Where Do Comets Come From? **3**

Astronomers are scientists who study the planets and stars. They think that comets are made of bits **2** of rock, dust, ice, and gas that were left over when the *Solar System* formed about $4\frac{1}{2}$ billion years ago. The Solar System is the Sun and its family of planets and moons.

Scientists think that far out in space, out past the farthest planet from our Sun, there is a huge cloud of comets wrapped around our Solar System. There may be billions of comets there, moving around like a giant swarm of bees.

404

REACHING ALL LEARNERS

Diagnostic Check: Comprehension and Skills

If . . . students are having difficulty understanding how to use an index, a table of contents, or other book parts,

Then . . . have small groups of students create questions for each other. Finding the answer should require students to use book parts.

ADDITIONAL SUPPORT ACTIVITIES

BELOW-LEVEL Reteach, p. S92

ADVANCED Extend, p. S93

ENGLISH-LANGUAGE LEARNERS Reteach, p. S93

The Oort cloud may be like a giant shell around the Solar System. It was named after a Dutch astronomer, Jan H. Oort.

405

ONGOING ASSESSMENT

Monitor Progress

(Focus Strategy) Use Text Structure and Format

What information does the caption on page 405 give? (It explains that the illustration shows a comet cloud, and it tells how the comet cloud got its name.)

Ask volunteers to model how they could use text structure and format to answer the question. If students have difficulty, provide this model:

MODEL **A caption gives information about an illustration. This illustration shows the Solar System with a ring of comets around it. The caption explains what this ring is and how it got its name.**

SCIENCE

Telescopes Explain to students that in order to study faraway objects such as planets and stars, astronomers look through *telescopes*. A reflecting telescope uses mirrors to detect light from objects in space. Explain that:

1. Starlight enters the telescope and hits a bowl-shaped mirror.

2. The bowl-shaped mirror reflects the light onto a small flat mirror.

3. The small mirror reflects the light onto the focus, where it can be viewed or photographed.

If possible, have students use a telescope to view distant objects.

Guided Comprehension

4 CAUSE-EFFECT/SUMMARIZE How does a comet begin its travels?
(Possible response: A distant star gives a sudden push or pull that moves the comet out of the comet cloud. Then the comet may shoot off into space or move toward the Sun as it is attracted by the Sun's gravity.)

5 SUMMARIZE How does a comet change as it gets closer to the Sun?
(Possible response: It begins to melt and forms a coma, or cloud, around its nucleus. Solar wind blows its tails away from the nucleus. The tails point away from the Sun.)

6 (Focus Skill) LOCATE INFORMATION
What is *solar wind*? Where else in the book could you find the meaning of this term? (Possible response: the continuous flow of gases from the Sun; in the book's Glossary)

7 COMPARE AND CONTRAST How are a comet's tails different? How are they alike? (Possible responses: One tail is made of gas and is straight and long; the other tails are made of dust and are shorter and curved. All the tails always point away from the Sun.)

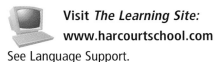
**Visit *The Learning Site:*
www.harcourtschool.com**
See Language Support.

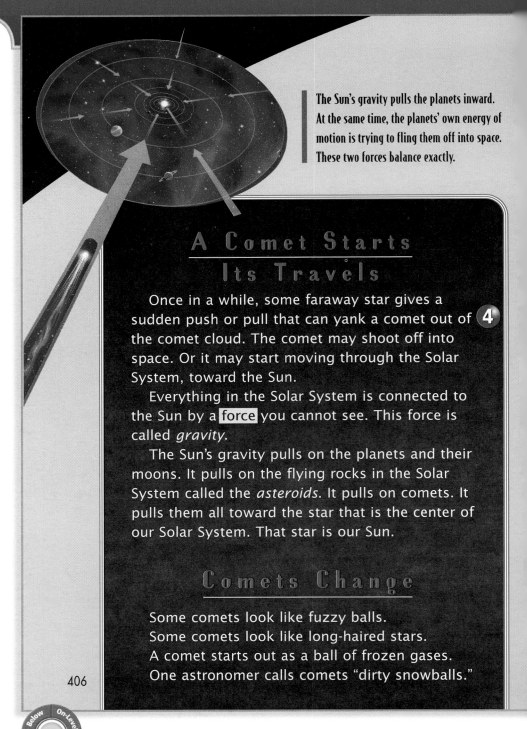

The Sun's gravity pulls the planets inward. At the same time, the planets' own energy of motion is trying to fling them off into space. These two forces balance exactly.

A Comet Starts Its Travels

Once in a while, some faraway star gives a sudden push or pull that can yank a comet out of **4** the comet cloud. The comet may shoot off into space. Or it may start moving through the Solar System, toward the Sun.

Everything in the Solar System is connected to the Sun by a force you cannot see. This force is called *gravity*.

The Sun's gravity pulls on the planets and their moons. It pulls on the flying rocks in the Solar System called the *asteroids*. It pulls on comets. It pulls them all toward the star that is the center of our Solar System. That star is our Sun.

Comets Change

Some comets look like fuzzy balls.
Some comets look like long-haired stars.
A comet starts out as a ball of frozen gases.
One astronomer calls comets "dirty snowballs."

406

ENGLISH-LANGUAGE LEARNERS

If students are having trouble forming mental images of the movement words *yank, shoot off, moving through,* and *pulls them all toward,* use pantomime or draw sketches on the board to communicate the meaning of each term.

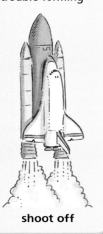
shoot off

That dirty snowball is the nucleus of the comet. It is the seed around which the rest of the comet grows. It may be a big seed—a mile or even a few miles wide.

As the comet comes closer to the hot Sun, the ice begins to melt. The frozen gases spread into a misty cloud around the nucleus. That cloud is called the *coma*. The coma may be half a million miles across. **5**

Part of the coma is pushed behind the comet. A force from the Sun called the solar wind blows this *tail* out behind the comet. **6**

Most comets grow two tails or more. One tail is gas. It is straight and long—maybe 10 million miles long.

The other tails are shorter and curved. They are made of dust. **7**

The tails of a comet always point away from the Sun. After the comet loops around the Sun, the solar wind blows the tail out in front of the comet.

The coma is blown away from the Sun, forming gas tails and dust tails.

dust tail

gas tail

407

ONGOING ASSESSMENT

Monitor Progress

Use Decoding/ Phonics

Have students reading below level read aloud the first sentence on page 406. Listen for their pronunciation of the word *comet*. If students do not pronounce it correctly, model the strategy:

MODEL I can break this word into two syllables, *com* and *et*. Since it has more than one syllable, I know that one syllable has more stress than the other. I'll try pronouncing it in different ways. If I stress *com*, the word sounds familiar, but when I stress *et*, the word sounds confusing. The stressed syllable in *comet* must be the first one, *com*.

SCIENCE

Asteroid Landing   On February 12, 2001, NASA's NEAR spacecraft landed on the surface of a large asteroid named Eros. It was the first time a human-made craft has ever landed on an asteroid! Built to orbit and study the slow-moving rock from a distance, the car-sized NEAR wasn't designed to handle a landing. It finished its main mission successfully, so scientists decided to give a landing a try. During its descent onto the asteroid 196 million miles from Earth, the NEAR snapped 69 photographs—the most detailed asteroid pictures ever taken. After landing, the NEAR continued to send information to NASA for several days.

Guided Comprehension

8 **CAUSE-EFFECT** **Why don't comets glow when they are far from the Sun?** (Possible response: They do not have their own light; they reflect the Sun's light. The farther a comet is from the Sun, the less it glows.)

9 **MAKE PREDICTIONS** **Has the selection discussed what you predicted it would discuss?** (Responses will vary.) **What do you predict the author will tell you about next?** (Possible response: how comets move through the Solar System)

10 **COMPARE AND CONTRAST** **How are comets' orbits different from planets' orbits? How are they alike?** (Possible responses: A comet's orbit is usually an ellipse, while a planet's orbit is almost round. Comets' and planets' orbits both go around the Sun, and sometimes their orbits crisscross.)

11 **AUTHOR'S CRAFT** **Why do you think the author compares the Moon's movements to a comet's movements?** (Possible response: She is trying to explain something that may be hard for readers to understand–that a fast-moving comet seems to stand still. She uses the Moon as an example because readers have seen the Moon.)

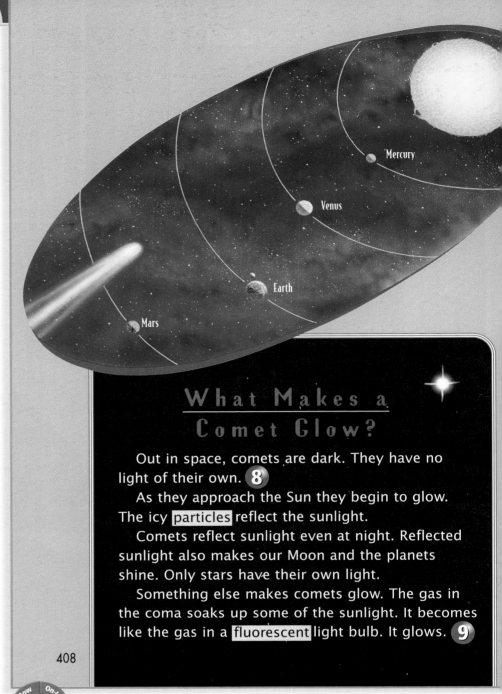

Mercury

Venus

Earth

Mars

What Makes a Comet Glow?

Out in space, comets are dark. They have no light of their own. **8**

As they approach the Sun they begin to glow. The icy particles reflect the sunlight.

Comets reflect sunlight even at night. Reflected sunlight also makes our Moon and the planets shine. Only stars have their own light.

Something else makes comets glow. The gas in the coma soaks up some of the sunlight. It becomes like the gas in a fluorescent light bulb. It glows. **9**

408

BELOW-LEVEL

Work with students to summarize what they have read so far.

- A comet is a bright moving object in the sky.
- Comets are made of bits of rock, dust, ice, and gas.
- The Sun's gravity pulls a comet.
- Comets change as they get closer to the Sun.
- Comets have no light of their own.

Have students set a purpose for reading through page 411.

About Orbits

The planets move around the Sun in regular paths, called *orbits*. The orbit of a planet is almost round. When a planet orbits the Sun once, it is a *year* on that planet.

Comets also move in orbits around the Sun. Their orbits are shaped more like eggs. These orbits are called *ellipses* [i•lip´sēz]. Comet orbits may be really long, if the comet starts far out in space.

Some comets take thousands or even millions of years to complete their orbits. Other comets take only a few years. Their orbits might crisscross the orbits of the planets. The time it takes a comet to complete its orbit is called the comet's *period*. **10**

Comets move fast. But they seem to almost stand still in the sky for many nights in a row. They do not seem to move because they are so far away. Doesn't the Moon seem to stand still, too? You have to watch it for a long time to see that it is moving. **11**

A comet's orbit is usually an ellipse.

409

ONGOING ASSESSMENT

Monitor Progress

(Focus Strategy) **Use Text Structure and Format**

How do the heading, the illustration, and the caption work together on page 409?
(The heading tells what the section is about—orbits. The caption describes a comet's orbit—usually an ellipse. The illustration shows a comet orbiting the Sun.)

If students are unable to answer, ask: How could you find an answer to this question? If necessary, use this model:

MODEL The headings tell me that the author is moving on to a new subject. The illustrations and captions give me more specific information about the heading's subject.

REREADING FOR FLUENCY

Tape-Assisted Reading Have students listen to all or part of "Visitors from Space" on *Audiotext* 6 as they follow along in their *Pupil Edition*. Students may listen to a section of the text, then replay it as they read aloud with the recording. They may then reread the same section aloud to you or to an audience of peers.

For support, see Fluency Routine Cards in Theme Resources, pp. T80a–T80b.

Note: For assessment of oral reading accuracy and fluency, see pages T78–T80.

Guided Comprehension

Were you able to find the answers to your questions? Discuss with students whether their purposes for reading were met. Have students complete their SQR charts.

Think and Respond

Answers:

1 Possible response: A comet's orbit is oval; a planet's is almost round. Comets have tails; planets do not. Comets move fast; planets do not. Some planets have moons; comets do not. **SUMMARIZE/TEXT STRUCTURE**

2 Possible response: They signal a new topic and what that topic will be. **STRATEGY**

3 Possible response: It pushes part of the coma out behind the comet to form one or more tails. **LITERARY ANALYSIS/TEXT STRUCTURE**

4 Possible response: What made you decide to study comets? **PERSONAL RESPONSE**

5 Accept reasonable responses. **READING STRATEGY**

OPEN-ENDED RESPONSE

Choose one object from the Solar System. Write a paragraph about why it was interesting to you.

TIMED WRITING OPTION Allow 15 minutes for students to write their paragraphs.

The Most Famous Comet

Certain comets appear in the sky again and again. We can predict when they will come. These comets are usually given names. Comets are usually named for the people who saw them first.

The most famous comet is called Halley's Comet. We see it about every 76 years, when it comes closest to the Sun. Its period is 76 years.

Halley's Comet passed us in 1985–86. It will come again in 2060. How old will you be then?

This scientist uses a huge dirty snowball to teach students about comets.

What Happens to Comets?

When comets come close to the Sun, the Sun boils away some of the gas in the coma and tail. Bits of dust and rock are blown away from the nucleus. This leaves a trail of comet matter along the comet's orbit. Those pieces, called *meteoroids*, keep on orbiting.

410

COMPREHENSION

End-of-Selection Test

To evaluate comprehension, see *Practice Book*, pages A57–A60.

When the Earth passes through their orbit, the meteoroids glow. That's because the Earth is wrapped in a blanket of air called the *atmosphere*. When the meteoroids enter the atmosphere, air particles rub against them. The meteoroids get hotter and hotter until they start to burn. Then they are called *meteors*.

Some people call meteors "shooting starts" or "falling stars." They are not shooting or falling stars. Stars don't fall. You are seeing meteors.

Think and Respond

1 How are comets different from planets?

2 What is the purpose of the words in red letters at the tops of some pages?

3 What effect does the solar wind have on comets?

4 If you could talk with the author, what question would you ask her? Why would you ask this question?

5 What reading strategies did you use to help you understand information in "Visitors from Space"?

411

ONGOING ASSESSMENT

RETELL

Use these questions to guide students as they retell "Visitors from Space."

- What is a comet?
- Where do comets come from?
- How do comets travel through the Solar System?

SUMMARIZE

Encourage students to summarize the selection using their completed SQR charts. See Transparency G on page T88.

▼ **Teaching Transparency G**

Survey	Question	Review
Look! A Comet!	What is a comet?	It's a big, bright object in the sky.
Where do Comets Come From?	What are comets made of?	They're made of bits of rock, dust, ice, and gas left over when the Solar System was formed.
A Comet Starts Its Travels	How do comets break away?	A star gives a push or pull that puts a comet into motion. It may move into space or be pulled toward the Sun.
Comets Change	What do comets look like?	Comets start out as frozen gases. As they get closer to the Sun, they begin to melt. The gases spread into a cloud called the coma.
What Makes a Comet Glow?	Do comets glow all the time?	In space, comets are dark. When they get closer to the Sun, they reflect sunlight.
About Orbits	Are comet orbits the same as planet orbits?	Planet orbits are round. Comet orbits are egg-shaped. The length of a comet orbit depends on how far it is out in space.

"Visitors From Space" Celebrate Our World, Theme 3   **G**   Graphic Organizer Harcourt

WRITTEN SUMMARY

Have students use their completed SQR charts to write a summary describing comets and their place in the Solar System.
PERFORMANCE ASSESSMENT

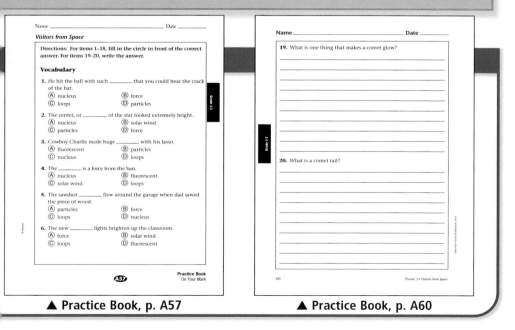

▲ Practice Book, p. A57 ▲ Practice Book, p. A60

412

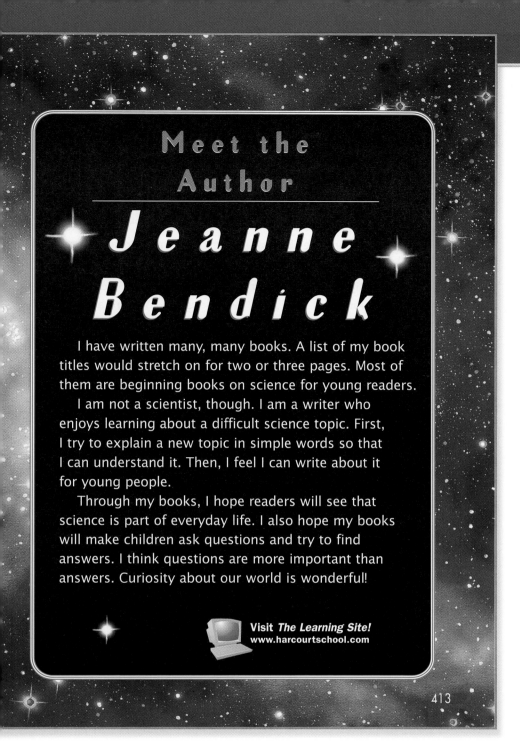

Meet the Author
Jeanne Bendick

I have written many, many books. A list of my book titles would stretch on for two or three pages. Most of them are beginning books on science for young readers.

I am not a scientist, though. I am a writer who enjoys learning about a difficult science topic. First, I try to explain a new topic in simple words so that I can understand it. Then, I feel I can write about it for young people.

Through my books, I hope readers will see that science is part of everyday life. I also hope my books will make children ask questions and try to find answers. I think questions are more important than answers. Curiosity about our world is wonderful!

Visit *The Learning Site!*
www.harcourtschool.com

413

related books

You may want to recommend to students these titles.

LIBRARY BOOKS COLLECTION

Earth: Our Planet in Space
by Seymour Simon

ADDITIONAL READING

• ***So That's How the Moon Changes Shape***
by Allan Fowler. Children's Press, 1991. **EASY**

• ***Moons and Rings: Companions to the Planets***
by Jeanne Bendick et al. Millbrook, 1991.
AVERAGE

• ***Comets, Meteors, and Asteroids***
by Seymour Simon. Mulberry, 1994.
CHALLENGING

ABOUT THE AUTHOR

Jeanne Bendick explains why she writes for young people: "Everything they learn is another piece they can fit into a giant puzzle. Where does each piece fit to make the picture clearer? One part of the job I set for myself is to make those young readers see that everything is connected to everything."

Ask students why they think Jeanne Bendick wants readers to see that science is a part of everyday life. (Possible response: She hopes that readers will then love science as she does.)

Making Connections

COMPARE TEXTS

Answers:

1 Possible response: because our world is part of the universe, and learning about it is a way of exploring **THEME**

2 Possible response: Much of the information would be difficult or impossible to show in photographs. **SPECULATE**

3 Possible response: She helps readers understand things that are unfamiliar by telling how they are like things that readers have seen for themselves. **AUTHOR'S PURPOSE**

4 Possible responses: Both are nonfiction selections that give information on scientific topics. Both are divided into sections with headings. "Visitors from Space" is about comets. "Rocking and Rolling" is about forces that shape and change Earth. **COMPARE AND CONTRAST**

5 Responses will vary. **SYNTHESIZE**

▲ **Visitors from Space**

Making Connections

Compare Texts

1 Why does the selection "Visitors from Space" belong in a theme about exploring and celebrating our world?

2 Why are the illustrations for this nonfiction selection mostly diagrams and drawings instead of photographs?

3 Why does the author compare the glow of a coma to a fluorescent light bulb? Why does she compare a comet's movement with the moon's?

4 Compare and contrast "Visitors from Space" with "Rocking and Rolling."

5 After reading "Visitors from Space," what other questions do you have about our solar system?

Write a Song

"**V**isitors from Space" tells how a comet forms and begins its journey around the sun. Think about what you would like to say in the form of a song about a comet. Write to express your thoughts, and set them to music.

Plan your song in a web like this one. You may write a poem and make up your own tune, or write new words for a song you know, such as "Twinkle, Twinkle, Little Star."

Writing CONNECTION

COMET

414

Give a Demonstration

"Visitors from Space" describes how comets and the moon seem to stand still in the sky, even though they are moving. When we observe the sun over the period of a day, it appears to move across the sky, rising in the east and setting in the west. Do research to find out if the sun is actually moving. Give a demonstration with models of the sun and Earth to show your research.

Science CONNECTION

Make an Internet Guide

In "Visitors from Space," you learned that Halley's Comet last passed Earth in 1985–1986. Photographs of the comet were taken from the spacecraft *Giotto* and from Earth. Do an Internet search to find photographs of Halley's Comet. Take notes on the photographs you find, and record the addresses of the websites. Then write an Internet guide that lists the addresses and describes each site.

Social Studies/Science CONNECTION

415

HOMEWORK FOR THE WEEK

Students and family members can work together to complete the activities on page T100. You may want to assign some or all of the activities as homework for each day of the week.

technology
Visit *The Learning Site:*
www.harcourtschool.com
See Resources for Parents and Teachers: Homework Helper.

Teacher's Edition, p. T100 ▶

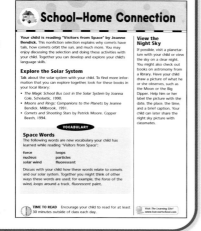

School–Home Connection

Your child is reading "Visitors from Space" by Jeanne Bendick. This nonfiction selection explains why comets have tails, how comets orbit the sun, and much more. You may enjoy discussing the selection and doing these activities with your child. Together you can develop and explore your child's language skills.

Explore the Solar System
Talk about the solar system with your child. To find more information that you can explore together, look for these books in your local library:
• *The Magic School Bus Lost in the Solar System* by Joanna Cole. Scholastic, 1990.
• *Moons and Rings: Companions to the Planets* by Jeanne Bendick. Millbrook, 1991.
• *Comets and Shooting Stars* by Patrick Moore. Copper Beech, 1994.

VOCABULARY

Space Words
The following words are new vocabulary your child has learned while reading "Visitors from Space":
force   loops
nucleus   particles
solar wind   fluorescent
Discuss with your child how these words relate to comets and our solar system. Together you might think of other ways these words are used, for example, the *force* of the wind, *loops* around a track, *fluorescent* paint.

View the Night Sky
If possible, visit a planetarium with your child or view the sky on a clear night. You might also check out books on astronomy from a library. Have your child draw a picture of what he or she observes, such as the Moon or the Big Dipper. Help him or her label the picture with the date, the place, the time, and a brief caption. Your child can later share the night sky picture with classmates.

TIME TO READ Encourage your child to read for at least 30 minutes outside of class each day.

Visit The Learning Site! www.harcourtschool.com

Write a Song Have students form pairs after writing a draft of their songs and ask their partner for feedback. Allow students to sing their songs for the class if they wish to.

PORTFOLIO OPPORTUNITY
Students may choose to place their songs in their working portfolios.

Make an Internet Guide Guide students by asking questions such as: Who is the sponsor or creator of this site? Is that person or group an authority on the subject? Is the website easy to use? Students might devise their own rating system for Web sites, and put a star beside the sites they think are best.

Internet Guide to Halley's Comet

Give a Demonstration
Provide students with an encyclopedia or science book about the Earth's solar system. Encourage students to be imaginative when they choose objects to use in their demonstration. Instead of balls to represent planets, they might use pieces of round fruit, coins on a tabletop, or balloons suspended from strings.

Locate Information

SKILL TRACE

LOCATE INFORMATION

Introduce	p. 348I
Reteach	pp. S80, S92, T73
Review	**pp. 368, 399B, 400I, 416**
Test	Theme 3 Vol. 2

RETURN TO THE SKILL

Have students read page 416 in the *Pupil Edition*. You may wish to use this model:

MODEL The book's table of contents helps me find the selection. Headings help me find the section about why comets glow. When I find the information I'm looking for, it contains the word *particles*, which I don't recognize. I can look up this word in the glossary.

Ask students to explain how they can use the section headings to locate information on another topic in "Visitors from Space."

PRACTICE/APPLY

Students can work in pairs to create a set of steps like those on page 416 to find a piece of information in a science textbook. When partners have finished, ask them to exchange their work with another pair and follow the steps to find the requested information. PERFORMANCE ASSESSMENT

Visit *The Learning Site:*
www.harcourtschool.com
See Skill Activities and Test
Tutors: Locate Information.

▲ Visitors from Space

Locate Information

Focus Skill

How does ice cause a comet to glow? You can find the answer in "Visitors from Space." Follow these steps to practice **locating information** in textbooks and other nonfiction books.

> Look at the table of contents. Locate the number of the page that "Visitors from Space" begins on. Turn to that page.

> The selection is divided into sections that are short chapters. Read all of the headings. In which section might you find the answer?

> Under the heading "What Makes a Comet Glow?" look for information about ice.

Visit *The Learning Site!*
www.harcourtschool.com

See *Skills* and *Activities*

> You've found this sentence: "The icy particles reflect the sunlight." Use the glossary to check the pronunciation and meaning of *particles*.

416

REACHING ALL LEARNERS

Diagnostic Check:
Comprehension and Skills

If . . . students do not know how to locate information using an index, a table of contents, or other book parts,

Then . . . review with students the purpose of each book part. Guide them to use the table of contents to find chapter titles and an index to locate topics.

ADDITIONAL SUPPORT ACTIVITIES

BELOW-LEVEL	Reteach, p. S92
ADVANCED	Extend, p. S93
ENGLISH-LANGUAGE LEARNERS	Reteach, p. S93

Test Prep
Locate Information

► This is an index from a book about comets. Use this to answer Numbers 1 and 2.

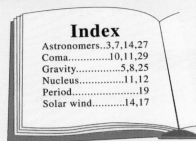

Index
Astronomers..3,7,14,27
Coma..............10,11,29
Gravity...............5,8,25
Nucleus...............11,12
Period.....................19
Solar wind...........14,17

1. **You can find information about solar wind on pages—**

   A   26 and 30

   B   11 and 12

   C   1, 4, 9, 24, and 28

   D   14 and 17

Tip

Look up *solar wind* in the index to locate the correct page numbers.

2. **Where should a listing be added for orbit?**

   F   before astronomers

   G   between gravity and nucleus

   H   between nucleus and period

   J   after solar wind

Tip

Remember that an index is arranged alphabetically.

Focus Skill

417

Test Prep

Locate Information   Have students review the index carefully and then use what they know about book parts to answer the questions. Use the Tips to reinforce good test-taking strategies.

(I.D; 2.H)

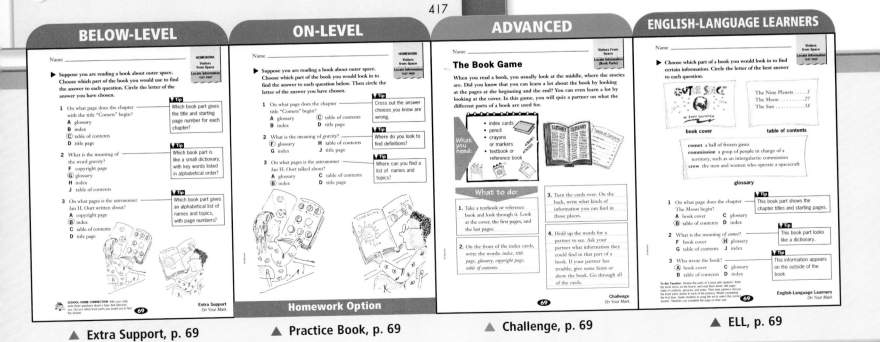

▲ Extra Support, p. 69   ▲ Practice Book, p. 69   ▲ Challenge, p. 69   ▲ ELL, p. 69

![Phonics]

Decoding/Phonics

Syllables: Consonant -le Syllable Pattern

OBJECTIVE

To decode words with the Consonant -le syllable pattern

SKILL TRACE

SYLLABLES: CONSONANT -*LE* SYLLABLE PATTERN	
Introduce	Grade 2
Maintain	p. 417A

ONGOING ASSESSMENT

If students are not able to read approximately 114 words per minute fluently, **then** they require phonics instruction and will also benefit from fluency practice.

NOTE: For assessment of oral reading accuracy and fluency, see pages T78–T80.

REVIEW THE SKILL

Discuss the consonant -*le* syllable pattern. Write this sentence on the board:

Put the map on the table.

Read the sentence aloud. Then point to the word *table*. Ask students which letters in the word *table* stand for the /bəl/ sound. Review with students that if the last syllable of a word ends in consonant -*le*, the consonant before -*le* usually begins the last syllable.

Then ask students to identify the letters that stand for the /bəl/ sound (*ble*). Have students blend the word parts to say the word *table*. Repeat the procedure to break *puzzle* into syllables and to blend them to read the word.

PRACTICE/APPLY

Decode longer words. Write these words on the board. Have students pronounce them, using what they know about the consonant -*le* syllable pattern.

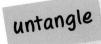 untangle 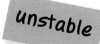 unstable 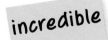 incredible recircle

Have students draw a line between syllables. To check understanding, have students pronounce these words aloud: *humble*, *fable*, *scramble*, and *cradle*. **PERFORMANCE ASSESSMENT**

Graphic Aids

Research and Information Skills

REVIEW THE SKILL

Discuss using graphic aids. Explain to students that the illustrator of "Visitors from Space" created illustrations and captions to help readers better understand the Solar System. Model using the illustration and caption on *Pupil Edition* page 406 to better understand the Sun's gravity and the orbits of the planets.

MODEL The illustration uses arrows to show that the Sun is always pulling objects toward it. The caption tells me that the planets have their own energy of motion that is pulling them off into space. This energy balances with the Sun's gravity exactly. The orbits that are shown in the illustration must result from this exact balance.

PRACTICE/APPLY

Create a diagram and caption. Have pairs of students work together to create a diagram of a comet that shows its nucleus, its dust tail, and its gas tail. Tell them to include a caption that tells what the diagram shows.

PERFORMANCE ASSESSMENT

Summarize. Ask a volunteer to explain why an author would include a map, chart, or other graphic aid in a nonfiction selection.

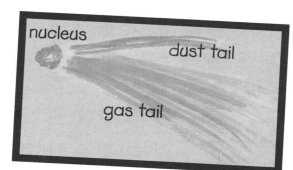

OBJECTIVE

To interpret information on graphic aids

SKILL TRACE

GRAPHIC AIDS

Introduce	pp. 369A–369B
Reteach	p. T74
Review	**pp. 399C, 417B**
Test	Theme 3 Vol. 2

BELOW-LEVEL

You may want to remind students that graphic aids can be maps, charts, globes, labeled illustrations, or anything else that is used to *show* an idea or information to readers. Common graphic aids for the Solar System include models, diagrams, and photographs.

Writing Process

Story

Writing Process: Expressive Writing

CONNECT READING TO WRITING

Remind students that the information in "Visitors from Space" is true. Ask them to name something that the class has read recently that was a made-up story. (Possible response: "Alejandro's Gift") Explain that they will be writing stories in this lesson.

REVIEW WRITER'S CRAFT

Display Transparency 273 and explain that the story is one a student wrote to entertain his classmates. Have volunteers read the model aloud. Then have students give examples of the writer's use of descriptive language, vivid verbs, and specific nouns.

ANALYZE THE WRITING PROMPT

Have students use the following prompt or brainstorm their own ideas for a story.

WRITING PROMPT: *Imagine one or more characters is traveling through space. Write a story for your classmates about what happens to the characters and what they discover in their travels. Be sure to include a beginning, middle, and ending.*

ASK THE FOLLOWING QUESTIONS:

- Who is your audience, and what is your purpose for writing?
- What is the setting? Who are the characters?
- What is the problem they face?
- What is the solution to the problem?

TRAITS OF GOOD WRITING

	INTRODUCE AND PRACTICE	APPLY TO LONGER WRITING FORMS
Focus/Ideas	329E–F (3-1)	355E–F, 387E–F (3-1)
Organization	167C–D, 193E–F (3-2)	221E–F, 261E–F (3-2)
Voice	41C–D, 67E–F (3-1)	99E–F, 129C–D (3-1)
Word Choice	323C–D, 347C–D (3-2)	369E–F, 399E–F (3-2)
Development	303E–F, 329E–F (3-1)	355E–F, 387E–F (3-1)
Effective Sentences	35E–F, 59E–F (3-2)	93E–F, 117C–D (3-2)
Effective Paragraphs	181E–F, 205E–F (3-1)	223E–F, 255C–D (3-1)
Conventions	(See Grammar and Spelling Lessons.)	(Applied to all writing lessons.)

technology

Writing Express™ CD-ROM
Visit *The Learning Site:*
www.harcourtschool.com
See Writing Detective,
Proofreading Makes Perfect.

TRAITS OF GOOD WRITING

- **Ideas:** The writer tells a story that focuses on one main event. The story has a beginning, a middle, and an ending.
- **Organization/Paragraphs:** The beginning introduces the setting, characters, and main event. The middle includes details that are easy to follow. The end presents a resolution.
- **Voice:** The writer includes details about the setting, characters, and events that will interest his audience. The writer uses dialogue to bring the characters to life.
- **Word Choice:** The writer uses exact words to make ideas clear.
- **Effective Sentences:** The writer uses sentences that vary in length and structure.

▼ Teaching Transparency 273

STUDENT MODEL: STORY

In a story, the writer tells about one main problem or idea. A story has characters, a setting, and a plot. The plot has a beginning, a middle, and an ending. Here is a story that one student wrote.

title — Hitching a Ride in Space

character and setting introduced — Engineer Johnson was worried as he went to tell the captain the bad news. In the recreation room the captain was busy losing another game of Martian Checkers to his old friend, First Mate Zormaxx. Johnson had just learned that the spaceship's fuel supply was dangerously low.

the characters' problem explained — Their ship had recently lost a couple of tanks in a battle with the Gorloggs. The radio was also badly damaged so they could not signal for help.

Gathering up his courage, Johnson told the captain the bad news. The captain listened with a frown.

events and details of the plot — "I figure that we have just enough fuel to get back into our solar system, Captain," Johnson said. "Then we will be stranded near Jupiter," he added.

"Perfect!" interrupted First Mate Zormaxx. "Halley's Comet is due to zoom past Jupiter next week. We can lock the tractor beam on the comet and hitch a ride as far as Mars. Then we can refuel for the rest of the trip to Earth."

problem solved — "Good idea, Zormaxx!" agreed the Captain. "It will take the comet about a year to pull us as far as Mars, but fortunately, we have enough food and water to last that long. And there are plenty of repairs to make that will keep us busy."

"Yes, Captain," Zormaxx replied. "And maybe by then you might be able to beat me in a game of Martian Checkers!"

"Visitors From Space"
Celebrate Our World, Theme 3
 273
Writing
Harcourt

▼ Teaching Transparency 274

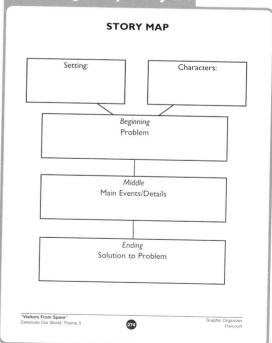

STORY MAP

Setting: ___

Characters: ___

Beginning
Problem

Middle
Main Events/Details

Ending
Solution to Problem

"Visitors From Space"
Celebrate Our World, Theme 3
274
Graphic Organizer
Harcourt

5 Day Plan

DAY 3 DRAFT

Have students use the steps below to draft their stories:

1. **DRAFT THE BEGINNING** Use the ideas in your story map to introduce the setting and characters.

2. **INTRODUCE THE PROBLEM** Describe what problem or situation your character(s) are facing.

3. **DEVELOP THE STORY** Write about the events that happen. Use details to make the events interesting to read. Use time-order words to make the order of events clear. Include dialogue to bring characters to life.

4. **CONCLUDE THE STORY** Write an ending which gives some kind of solution to the problem.

DAY 4 EDIT

REVISE Have students work in pairs or small groups to discuss their stories. They can use the rubric on page T91 as they revise. Ask them to make sure that they introduce the setting and characters in the beginning of their stories, and that their plot also includes a middle and an ending.

PROOFREAD Have students use the questions below:

 Did I correctly use capital letters and punctuation marks?

 Did I form contractions in dialogue correctly?

 Did I spell words correctly?

DAY 5 PUBLISH AND ASSESS

PUBLISH Allow volunteers to read their stories to the class. Students may enjoy illustrating their stories as they publish them.

ASSESS Have students use the student rubric to evaluate their own and each other's work. They should add their stories and their evaluations to their portfolios.

SCORING RUBRIC

	4	3	2	1
FOCUS/IDEAS	Completely focused, purposeful.	Generally focused on task and purpose.	Somewhat focused on task and purpose.	Lacks focus and purpose.
ORGANIZATION/ PARAGRAPHS	Ideas progress logically; transitions make the relationships among ideas clear.	Organization mostly clear, but some lapses occur; some transitions are used.	Some sense of organization but inconsistent or unclear in places.	Little or no sense of organization.
DEVELOPMENT	Central idea supported by strong, specific details.	Central idea with adequate support, mostly relevant details.	Unclear central idea; limited supporting details.	Unclear central idea; little or no development.
VOICE	Viewpoint clear; original expressions used where appropriate.	Viewpoint somewhat clear; few original expressions.	Viewpoint unclear or inconsistent.	Writer seems detached and unconcerned.
WORD CHOICE	Clear, exact language; freshness of expression.	Clear language; some interesting word choices.	Word choice unclear or inappropriate in places.	Word choice often unclear or inappropriate.
SENTENCES	Variety of sentence structures; flows smoothly.	Some variety in sentence structures.	Little variety; choppy or run-on sentences.	Little or no variety; sentences unclear.
CONVENTIONS	Few, if any, errors.	Few errors.	Some errors.	Many errors.

REPRODUCIBLE STUDENT RUBRICS for specific writing purposes and presentations are available on pages T90-T92.

 **Language Handbook,** pp. 18–21, 56–57, 166–168

Grammar

Comparing with Adverbs

SKILL TRACE

COMPARING WITH ADVERBS	
Introduce	pp. 417E–417F
Review I	p. 417F
Test	Theme 06

REACHING ALL LEARNERS

Diagnostic Check: Grammar and Writing

If . . . students are unable to understand how to use comparative forms of adverbs,

Then . . . have them create a three-column chart labeled *adverb, more/er,* and *most/est.*

ADDITIONAL SUPPORT ACTIVITIES

BELOW-LEVEL	Reteach, p. S94
ADVANCED	Extend, p. S95
ENGLISH-LANGUAGE LEARNERS	Reteach, p. S95

technology

Visit *The Learning Site:*
www.harcourtschool.com
See Grammar Practice Park,
Multimedia Grammar Glossary.

DAY 1 — TEACH/MODEL

DAILY LANGUAGE PRACTICE

1. **i wunder what that bright light are.** (I; wonder; is)
2. **how far away is the planet mars.** (How; Mars?)

INTRODUCE THE CONCEPT Display sentences 1–3 on Transparency 275.

- Adverbs can be used to compare two or more actions.
- When you compare two actions, add -*er* to most short adverbs.
- When you compare one action with two or more other actions, add -*est* to most short adverbs.

Have students rewrite sentences 4–6, using the correct form of the adverb *late.*

▼ Teaching Transparency 275

COMPARING WITH ADVERBS

1. Earth moves fast.
2. That rocket ship moves faster than Earth does.
3. The comet moves fastest of all.
4. John stayed up _____ to watch the comet. late
5. Sue stayed up _____ than John. later
6. Mike stayed up _____ of all. latest
7. A star shines on us more brightly than a comet does.
8. The sun shines on us most brightly of all.

Adverb	Comparing Two Things	Comparing More Than Two Things
hard	harder	hardest
quickly	more quickly	most quickly
carefully	more carefully	most carefully

"Visitors From Space"
Celebrate Our World, Theme 3   **275**   Grammar Harcourt

DAY 2 — EXTEND THE CONCEPT

DAILY LANGUAGE PRACTICE

1. **comets are ball of frozen gassies** (Comets; balls; gases.)
2. **Have you ever saw a comet in the sky.** (seen; sky?)

DEVELOP THE CONCEPT Display sentences 7–8 on Transparency 275.

- Use *more* or *most* before most adverbs that have two or more syllables.
- Do not use both -*er* and *more* or both -*est* and *most* when you make comparisons.

Explain that *more* and *most* are often used with adverbs that end in -*ly*. Display the chart on Transparency 275, and have students supply the missing adverbs.

PERFORMANCE ASSESSMENT

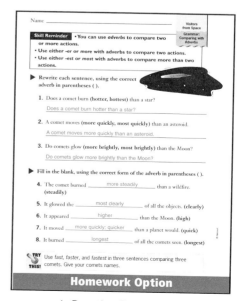

Name _____

Skill Reminder • You can use *adverbs* to compare two or more actions.
• Use either -*er* or *more* with adverbs to compare two actions.
• Use either -*est* or *most* with adverbs to compare more than two actions.

▶ Rewrite each sentence, using the correct adverb in parentheses ( ).

1. Does a comet burn (hotter, hottest) than a star?
   Does a comet burn hotter than a star?
2. A comet moves (more quickly, most quickly) than an asteroid.
   A comet moves more quickly than an asteroid.
3. Do comets glow (more brightly, most brightly) than the Moon?
   Do comets glow more brightly than the Moon?

▶ Fill in the blank, using the correct form of the adverb in parentheses ( ).

4. The comet burned _____ more steadily _____ than a wildfire. (steadily)
5. It glowed the _____ most clearly _____ of all the objects. (clearly)
6. It appeared _____ higher _____ than the Moon. (high)
7. It moved _____ more quickly; quicker _____ than a planet would. (quick)
8. It burned _____ longest _____ of all the comets seen. (longest)

TRY THIS! Use *fast, faster,* and *fastest* in three sentences comparing three comets. Give your comets names.

Homework Option

▲ Practice Book, p. 70

DAILY LANGUAGE PRACTICE

1. some comets melt more faster than others. (Some; melt faster)
2. what a long tail that comet have. (What; has!)

ER, EST, MORE, MOST Write adverbs on the board. Have students take turns supplying a form of comparison and use each one in a sentence.

slowly	(more slowly, most slowly)
softly	(more softly, most softly)
soon	(sooner, soonest)
early	(earlier, earliest)

Test Prep Tip

"This tip for using adverbs that compare can help you on language tests:

- Do not use both *-er* and *more*, or both *-est* and *most*, to compare with adverbs."

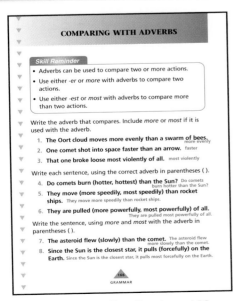

▲ Language Handbook, p. 166

DAILY LANGUAGE PRACTICE

1. Is the tail of a comet make out of watter. (made; water?)
2. the tail stretch out longer than you think. (The; stretches)

COMPARE THE WAYS Have students list five adverbs that tell how they do an activity, such as study for a test or clean their rooms. Then ask them to write a paragraph in which they use several of the adverbs. Tell them to make at least two comparisons. They can compare the way they do the activity at two different times, or they can compare the way they do the activity with the way someone else does it.

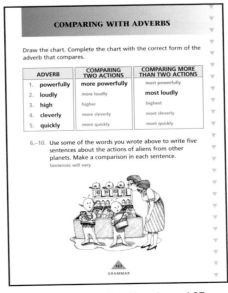

▲ Language Handbook, p. 167

DAILY LANGUAGE PRACTICE

1. Does a comet really travel more fast than a planet! (faster; planet?)
2. One famous comet appear every 76 year. (appears; years)

PROOFREAD FOR ADVERBS

Display the following sentences. Ask students to proofread for errors in adverb use, punctuation and grammar. Then have them rewrite each sentence correctly.

1. Baby's are more messily than third graders. (Babies; are messier)
2. The dog sat quiet beside I in the car. (quietly; me)
3. Who jumped more high than James. (jumped higher; James?)

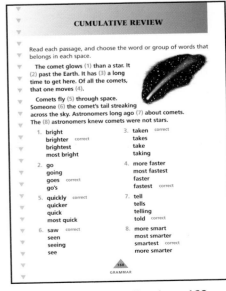

▲ Language Handbook, p. 168

Spelling Words

1. simple
2. total
3. apple
4. title
5. central
6. purple
7. signal
8. normal
9. middle
10. able
11. terrible*
12. people
13. medal
14. handle
15. single

* Selection Words

Challenge Words

16. explore*
17. discovery
18. astronaut
19. visible
20. scientist

Spelling

Words ending with -le or -al

DAY 1 — PRETEST/SELF-CHECK

ADMINISTER THE PRETEST Use the Dictation Sentences under Day 5. Help students self-check their pretests using Transparency 276.

ADVANCED

Use the Challenge Words in these Dictation Sentences:

16. We wanted to **explore** the cave.
17. The doctor made an exciting **discovery**.
18. An **astronaut** came to speak at our school.
19. The stars are **visible** on clear nights.
20. Molly's sister is a **scientist**.

DAY 2 — TEACH/MODEL

WORD SORT Display Transparency 276. Make sure students know the meanings of the words. Then ask them to copy the chart and to write each Spelling Word where it belongs.

Point to and read the words *apple* and *normal*. Ask students what sound they hear at the end of both words. (the /əl/ sound) Circle the last two letters in both words. Have students read the generalization to confirm their conclusion.

HANDWRITING Tell students to make sure *le* does not look like *ee*.

▼ Teaching Transparency 276

WORDS ENDING WITH *le* OR *al*

Spelling Words

1. simple	6. purple	11. terrible
2. total	7. signal	12. people
3. apple	8. normal	13. medal
4. title	9. middle	14. handle
5. central	10. able	15. single

Bottle	Final
simple	total
apple	central
title	signal
purple	normal
middle	medal
able	
terrible	
people	
handle	
single	

• The ending sound you hear in *little* can be spelled *le* or *al*.

"Visitors From Space"
Celebrate Our World, Theme 3   276   Spelling Harcourt

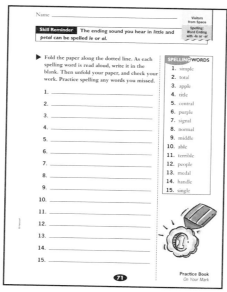

▲ Practice Book, p. 71

Name _____

Words Ending with -le or -al

SPELLING WORDS
1. simple
2. total
3. apple
4. title
5. central
6. purple
7. signal
8. normal
9. middle
10. able
11. terrible
12. people
13. medal
14. handle
15. single

▶ Write a Spelling Word for each clue.

1. center _____ middle
2. common _____ normal
3. entire _____ total
4. easy _____ simple
5. noticeable message _____ signal

▶ Write a Spelling Word to complete each sentence.

6. What is the _____ title _____ of the book?
7. The family room is in the _____ central _____ part of our house.
8. My favorite color is _____ purple
9. Carry the suitcase by its _____ handle
10. I was not _____ able _____ to lift the box.
11. The judge pinned a gold _____ medal _____ on Leon's shirt.

▶ Write the following Spelling Words: *apple*, *terrible*, *people*, and *single*. Use your best handwriting.

12. _____ apple _____   14. _____ people
13. _____ terrible _____   15. _____ single

Handwriting Tip: When you write in small spaces, be sure to keep all tall letters the same height, all short letters the same height, and all letters with tails the same length.

simple

LESSON 30   SPELLING PRACTICE BOOK   107

▲ Spelling Practice Book, p. 107

Day Plan

SPELLING STRATEGIES

USING A DICTIONARY Write the following Spelling Words on the board (some of which are misspelled): *appal*, *middle*, *signle*, *central*, *abel*, *title.*

Explain that some of the words are not spelled correctly. Have students read the words and circle the ones that they are not sure of. Have them use dictionaries to check the spellings. Point out that guide words in a dictionary can help them locate a word quickly.

Apply to Writing

Have students use a dictionary to check words they are not sure of as they proofread their writing. Have them look for words that end with *le* or *al* to be sure they have spelled them correctly.

SPELLING ACTIVITIES

PLAY CATERPILLAR Divide the group into two teams. Have the first player of one team spell a word. If the player spells it correctly, he or she draws one part of a caterpillar's body on the board. If the word is misspelled, play turns to the other team. Alternate between the two teams until one team has completed its caterpillar.

LIFE ON MARS Students can work in groups to write about what life might be like on Mars. Tell them to use as many Spelling Words as possible in their descriptions.

POSTTEST

DICTATION SENTENCES

1. It will not take long to do this **simple** homework.
2. Add the two numbers to get the **total**.
3. There is an **apple** tree in our backyard.
4. What is the **title** of that book?
5. Our school is in the **central** part of town.
6. My favorite color is **purple**.
7. He gave the **signal** that the coast was clear.
8. Her voice finally seems **normal** after her cold.
9. The workers painted a solid line down the **middle** of the road.
10. Are you **able** to carry the chair?
11. That is a **terrible** movie.
12. There were lots of **people** at the beach.
13. Did you win a **medal** in the track meet?
14. Can you **handle** all the work?
15. John got a **single** scoop of ice cream.

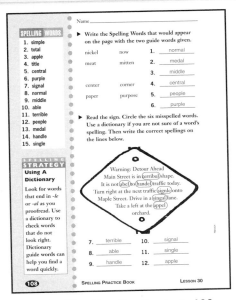

▲ Spelling Practice Book, p. 108

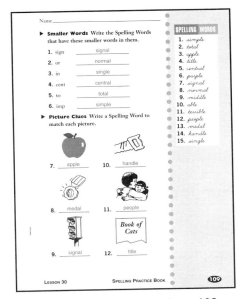

▲ Spelling Practice Book, p. 109

Visitors from Space **417H**

Word Study

Words with Latin Roots

OBJECTIVE

To find words with the root words lunar *and* solar

Tell students that many English terms related to the Sun and moon originated in Latin. Write *solar* and *lunar* on the board. Explain that *solar* comes from the Latin word for Sun; *sol.* Then, tell them that *lunar* comes from the Latin word for moon; *luna.*

Next write these compound words on the board: *solar wind, lunar year*. Explain that some compound words, like *sunshine,* are one word; others are two separate words. Have students use a dictionary to list other compound words made from *solar* or *lunar.* (lunar module; lunar month; solar battery; solar cell; solar flare)

solar   lunar

ADVANCED

Have students look through the index of their science books or an encyclopedia to compile a list of additional science words. Encourage them to use their knowledge of suffixes and root words to try to determine the meanings of the words before looking them up. Have them use their sources to check the word meanings.

Science Words

OBJECTIVE

To use knowledge of suffixes and roots to decode scientific terms

Write the words *astronomy* and *astronomer* on the board. Remind students that an astronomer is a scientist who studies space. Explain that the suffixes *-nomy* and *-logy* can mean "science of" or "study of." *Astro,* the root in *astronomy,* means "stars." Write the following chart on the board, and have students fill in the columns. They can use dictionaries to look up the definition of each branch of science.

Ask students what they think *astronomy* means. ("the study of the universe, including the stars, planets, and so on")

Branch of Science	Definition	Scientist Who Studies This Topic
biology	"the study of living things"	biologist
zoology	"the study of animals"	zoologist
botany	"the study of plants"	botanist

Speaking and Listening

Tell a Story

OBJECTIVES

To use an oral presentation to relate a story

Students may wish to publish their stories by presenting them to the class orally.

Organization   Share these **organizational tips** with students.

- Highlight or underline parts of the story that you want to emphasize.
- Choose props or background music to enhance your presentation.

Delivery   Share the following **practice tips** with students.

- Practice speaking in front of a mirror. Speak clearly. Keep your voice steady—both in pacing, pitch and tone.
- If possible, use props, music, or sound effects to enhance your story.

Students can give their oral presentations to a small group of classmates. Remind them that when telling a story, gestures will help make it more interesting.

PERFORMANCE ASSESSMENT

Listen to a Story

OBJECTIVE

To listen actively to a story and be prepared to ask questions

As groups listen to the stories, have them think about questions they would like to ask each speaker.

GIVING GOOD RESPONSES
Have students make a list of suitable responses for listening to stories.

Listening Tips

- Listen to hear how the speaker retells his or her story. Be aware of the beginning, the middle, and the ending.
- Save questions until the story is over.

Good Response Tips

Try to picture the setting, characters, and events.

Clap at the end of the story.

Scientific Film

OBJECTIVE

To compare film and illustrations

Have students view a television program or documentary film about the Solar System. Ask:

- What can a film show that the illustrations in "Visitors from Space" cannot show?
- Which shows the movements of the Solar System more accurately? Why?

Books for All Learners

Reinforcing Skills and Strategies

■ BELOW-LEVEL

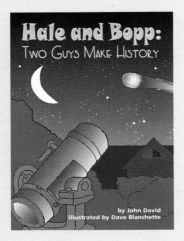

Hale and Bopp:
TWO GUYS MAKE HISTORY

by John David
illustrated by Dave Blanchette

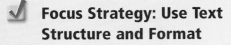

✓ **Focus Skill: Locate Information**

✓ **Focus Strategy: Use Text Structure and Format**

✓ **Vocabulary: *fluorescent, force, loops, nucleus, particles, solar wind***

Genre: Nonfiction
Science Connection: The Solar System

SUMMARY In July of 1995 two amateur astronomers, Thomas Bopp of Arizona and Alan Hale of New Mexico, noted an unusual glow in the night sky. Each reported the sighting to a comet-tracking center in Massachusetts. The center soon confirmed that they had discovered a new comet. Comet Hale-Bopp was visible for several months in 1997; it will be visible again in the year 4377.

 Visit *The Learning Site:*
www.harcourtschool.com
See Resources for Parents and Teachers: Books for All Learners.

BEFORE READING

Preview/Set Purpose Ask students to preview the selection and predict what it will be about. Guide them to set a purpose for reading.

Reinforce Locate Information Remind students that illustrations, captions, and headings can help them locate information in nonfiction text. Create an outline frame like the one below on the board and guide students to record important ideas and details as they read.

LOCATE INFORMATION/GRAPHIC AIDS

> Comet Hale-Bopp
> I. Thomas Bopp _____
>   A. _____
>   B. _____
> II. Alan Hale _____

Reinforce Vocabulary Use illustrations in the selection to review vocabulary. Ask questions such as: "What might something *fluorescent* look like against a dark background?"

READING THE BOOK

Pages 2–6 What did Alan Hale and Thomas Bopp discover one night in 1995? (a new comet) Why do you think both men contacted the center in Massachusetts? (Maybe they wanted to have an official comet–tracking center confirm what they saw.) DRAW CONCLUSIONS

Pages 8–16 Which part of the selection tells when Hale-Bopp will make its next appearance in the sky above Earth? (page 15) Which part gives facts about comets in general? (pages 8–11) LOCATE INFORMATION

Reread for Fluency Have students select and read aloud to you a page or passage they found especially interesting.

RESPONDING

Outline Help students complete the outline and use it as a guide for retelling the important ideas in the book.

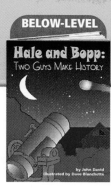

▲ page 417M ▲ page 417N

Oral Reading Fluency

Use Books for All Learners to promote oral reading fluency.

See **Fluency Routine Cards**, pp. T80a–T80b.

■ ON-LEVEL

 Focus Skill: Locate Information

 Focus Strategy: Use Text Structure and Format

 Vocabulary: *fluorescent, force, loops, nucleus, particles, solar wind*

Genre: Nonfiction
Science Connection: The Solar System

SUMMARY   The moon is our closest space neighbor. As it orbits the Earth, the moon seems to change shape as different parts of its surface reflect the sun. The moon's gravity affects ocean tides, and its surface is covered with craters and hills. Though scientists have studied the moon and astronauts have explored its surface, many questions about it remain unanswered.

 Visit *The Learning Site:*

www.harcourtschool.com

See Resources for Parents and Teachers: Books for All Learners.

BEFORE READING

Preview/Set Purpose   Ask students to read the title, preview the selection, and predict what they will learn about the moon. Guide them to set a purpose for reading.

Reinforce Locate Information   Remind students that headings, illustrations, and captions can help them locate information in nonfiction books. Help students create a chart based on the book's headings and use it to help them keep track of important facts as they are reading. LOCATE INFORMATION/GRAPHIC AIDS

READING THE BOOK

Pages 2–7   What are some reasons why the moon looks different at different times? (Its shape seems to change as it goes through its phases; an eclipse can make the moon's outline glow red; the moon looks paler during the day.) SYNTHESIZE

Pages 2–15   How do the headings in this book help you? (The headings tell readers when a new idea is about to be explained; the headings give the main ideas.) USE TEXT STRUCTURE AND FORMAT

Rereading for Fluency   Ask volunteers to ask questions about the moon that the book answers; other volunteers can reread the answers aloud.

RESPONDING

Chart   Guide students to complete the chart and use it to retell the main ideas.

Books for All Learners

Reinforcing Skills and Strategies

■ ADVANCED

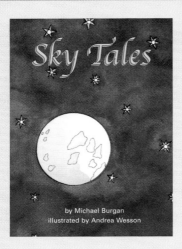

Sky Tales

by Michael Burgan
illustrated by Andrea Wesson

 Focus Skill: Locate Information

 Focus Strategy: Use Text Structure and Format

 Vocabulary: *fluorescent, force, loops, nucleus, particles, solar wind, hauled, fascinated*

Genre: Folktales
Social Studies Connection: Traditions and Customs

SUMMARY This book presents three traditional folktales about the moon. The first story explains how the moon was placed in the sky. The second tells how the stars rewarded a girl for her kindness. The third explains why the sun, the moon, and the wind have such different effects on those who experience them.

 Visit *The Learning Site:*
www.harcourtschool.com
See Resources for Parents and Teachers: Books for All Learners.

BEFORE READING

Preview/Set Purpose Ask students to preview the book by reading the introduction and the story titles. Have them predict what the book is about and set a purpose for reading.

Reinforce Locate Information
Ask students which part of the book lists the stories in the book and the pages they begin on. (the table of contents) Have students use a comparison chart like this one to record story elements as they read. LOCATE INFORMATION/GRAPHIC AIDS

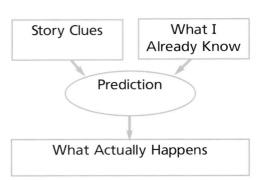

Expand Vocabulary Write *hauled* and *fascinated* on the board and discuss their meanings. You might ask: "Why have people always been *fascinated* by the moon? What might be *hauled* away by a junk collector?"

READING THE BOOK

Pages 4–7 What do you think the purpose of "Four Men and the Moon" is? (It explains how the moon came to be seen in the night sky.) AUTHOR'S PURPOSE/GENRE

Pages 8–16 Which two stories contain story elements that happen in "threes"? Explain. ("Star Money" and "How Sun, Moon, and Wind Went Out to Dinner"; in the first story the girl meets three people on the road; in the second, Star has three children.) USE TEXT STRUCTURE AND FORMAT

Rereading for Fluency Ask volunteers to select a folktale and reread it aloud as a storyteller might have told it.

RESPONDING

Purpose Have students write summaries of the folktales. They should introduce each summary with a brief statement of what its purpose is.

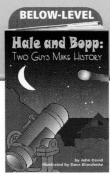   

▲ page 417K ▲ page 417L

Managing Small Groups

While you work with small groups, have other students do the following:

- Self-Selected Reading
- Practice Pages
- Cross-Curricular Centers
- Journal Writing

■ ENGLISH-LANGUAGE LEARNERS

What Shape is That?

by Anne O'Brien
Illustrated by Suydam Studios

 Focus Skill: Locate Information

 Focus Strategy: Use Text Structure and Format

 Concept Vocabulary: *circle, square, rectangle, triangle*

Genre: Nonfiction
Math Connection: Geometric Shapes

SUMMARY The world around us is full of objects that have the shape of a circle, a square, a rectangle, or a triangle. Some of these shapes can be combined to make a different shape.

 Visit *The Learning Site:*
www.harcourtschool.com
See Resources for Parents and Teachers: Books for All Learners.

BEFORE READING

Tap Prior Knowledge Draw a circle and a square on the board. Ask students if they know the names of these shapes. Have students draw and name other shapes they know.

Total Physical Response Have students draw the outlines of these shapes in the air as you name them: *circle, square, triangle, rectangle.*

Display Vocabulary/Concept Words Write the vocabulary words on the board and use simple drawings or story illustrations to explain the meanings.

Preview the Book Read the title aloud and help students preview the book. Point out and discuss the drawings and the labels, and help students name each everyday object that is pictured.

READING THE BOOK

Pages 2–4 In what part of this book might you find descriptions of different shapes? (In the first part of the book) **LOCATE INFORMATION**

Pages 7–16 What does the second part of the book tell about? (It gives examples of everyday objects that have the shapes described in the first part of the book.) **USE TEXT STRUCTURE AND FORMAT**

Rereading Reread the book aloud with students.

RESPONDING

Shapes Everywhere Ask students to give examples of other objects in the classroom that have the shape of a square, a rectangle, a circle, or a triangle. They can write the name of each object under its picture.

Theme Wrap-Up & Review

Discuss the Literature

- **Why do you think this theme is called "Celebrate Our World"?** (Possible response: The selections are about things that can be appreciated in the natural world.)

- **What different parts of our world do the selections in this theme celebrate?** (Possible responses: the planet Earth itself; animal life; outer space; deserts; exploration of the world)

- **Which selection would you recommend to someone interested in learning about earthquakes?** ("Rocking and Rolling") **About traveling?** ("Armadillo from Amarillo") **About comets?** ("Visitors from Space")

Return to the Theme Connections

Ask students to review and revise their graphic organizers to include information about all the selections they have read and listened to.

How do people celebrate the world?			
WHO	WHAT	WHEN	WHERE
my class and I	planted trees	on Arbor Day	in Liberty Park
the teacher and students	recycle paper	every day	in our classroom
the narrator	celebrates nature	all year	in the desert
Alejandro	builds a water hole for animals	during the day	in the desert
scientists	study earthquakes	every day	in the layers of the Earth
Armadillo	explored the world	from morning until night	city, state, continent
astronomers	study the stars and planets	every day	in the sky

Response Options

 REFLECT Have students reflect on what they have learned about celebrating the natural world. Students can write their reflections in their journals.

 SELF-ASSESSMENT Students can reflect on their own progress using the **My Reading Log** and the **Thinking About My Reading and Writing** blackline masters on pp. R42–R43.

THEME PROJECT

Project Presentations

An Observation Poster

Students who have completed their projects can present their work to an audience. Encourage students to demonstrate creatively what they learned. Here is an idea you may suggest:

GUESS THE IMAGE Students can display their close-up drawings without telling viewers what the subjects are. Viewers can then guess what objects are being depicted. Have students read their paragraphs after the subjects of the drawings have been identified.

Direct students to the Presenting Your Writing section of the *Writer's Handbook*, pp. 440–441.

See also the Rubric for Presentations on p. T92 of this Teacher's Edition.

Review

Comprehension

You may use the Read Aloud selection for **"Visitors from Space"** to review the tested focus skills for this theme. Reread the selection aloud. Then ask:

 LOCATE INFORMATION

Let's say you have a copy of the book this story appears in. What part of the book would you look at to find out what page the story begins on? (the table of contents)

 CAUSE AND EFFECT

What causes the red alert? (Possible response: an approaching dust storm)

 SUMMARIZE

Summarize what happens to visitors in the Mission to Mars exhibit. (Possible response: Visitors become part of a make-believe crew of scientists who arrive on Mars to study the planet. Crew members work together to collect information, but an approaching storm cuts short their stay. In order to avoid the storm, the scientists quickly leave the planet in their shuttle.)

Grammar

Have students revisit a writing assignment or choose a piece from their portfolios. Have them edit that piece of writing using the following directions:

• Add a colorful adverb to one sentence.
• Check that you have used forms of the verb *be* correctly.
• Include some contractions, especially in dialogue, to help the dialogue sound natural.

 Visit *The Learning Site:*
www.harcourtschool.com
See Go for Grammar Gold.

Vocabulary

Have students use vocabulary from the theme in a vocabulary drill. Write each word on a slip of paper. Line students up in two teams. Draw a slip and ask the first student in Team 1 to use the word in a sentence. If the student succeeds, the team gets a point. If not, the first student in Team 2 gets a chance. Continue until all the words have been used.

admiring	epicenter	particles
ample	eventually	peak
average	fluorescent	range
celebrations	force	shunned
cherished	furrows	signal
choosy	growth	solar wind
coast	homeward	sphere
continent	loops	tracks
converse	magma	universe
edges	nucleus	windmill

Spelling

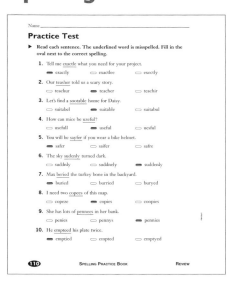

▲ Spelling Practice Book, pages 110–111

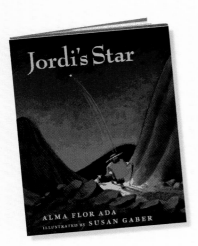

▲ *Jordi's Star*
by Alma Flor Ada

THEME: Celebrate Our World

As they read *Jordi's Star,* students will learn the power of love and faith in making the world beautiful.

GENRE: Fantasy

Summary: After a violent thunderstorm, goatherd Jordi finds a pool of water on his dry, rocky hillside. In the pool he sees the reflection of a star, which he mistakenly thinks has fallen in. He puts new-found energy into making the pool beautiful for his new friend, the star, bringing moss and rocks, and planting trees and flowers. Over time, his desolate hillside blooms, and Jordi blooms with it.

ABOUT THE AUTHOR

An accomplished translator of children's books from English to Spanish, **Alma Flor Ada** was born in Cuba and has lived in Spain, Peru, and the United States. Her original fiction often introduces children to Central and South American landscapes and cultures.

Library Book Lesson

Access Prior Knowledge

Show students the book cover and read the title aloud. Have students describe what they see on the cover. (a goatherd; a goat; a rocky, hilly place; a star) Ask a volunteer to explain a goatherd's job. (to tend and care for goats; perhaps to sell their milk)

Set Purpose / Predict

Tell students that although this book seems like a folktale, it is really an original story made up by the author. Have students read the first five text pages of the story, to the point where Jordi sees the star. Have them predict what the star will mean to Jordi based on what they have read about the character and their prior knowledge about folktales. Ask volunteers to state their purpose for reading such a book. (to be entertained)

DEVELOP VOCABULARY

Ask students to list unfamiliar words from the selection in their journals and to use a dictionary to locate definitions they could not discover from context clues. Ask them to use three new words in original sentences.

Options for Reading

Guided Comprehension

⭐ (Focus Strategy) **STRATEGY REMINDER** Although the story's pictures are vivid, tell students that they can also use their own background knowledge to **create mental images** of Jordi's landscape before and after he found the star. During reading, ask the questions at the right and help students monitor their own comprehension as they read. WHOLE CLASS/SMALL GROUP

Cooperative Reading

Have groups of three to four students use Comprehension Card 27 (Theme) to guide their discussion. INDEPENDENT/SMALL GROUP

Independent Reading

Students can write in their journals about whether their predictions were confirmed and whether they would recommend this book to a friend, and why. After reading, have students complete the self-assessment forms found on pages R42–R43 and add them to their reading portfolios. INDEPENDENT/WHOLE CLASS

Teacher Read-Aloud

Read aloud the first few pages of *Jordi's Star* as students listen responsively. Ask students to listen carefully to determine what kind of person Jordi is and how his life differs from and is similar to their own. Students may then complete the book independently. INDEPENDENT/WHOLE CLASS

Options for Responding

Personal Response

Have students respond to these questions to demonstrate understanding and share their interpretations. INDEPENDENT/WHOLE CLASS

Compare Selections

Have students compare this book to "Alejandro's Gift" by answering these questions about both.
- Who was the main character?
- What was the setting for the story as the story began?
- How did the main character make changes to his setting?
- How does the story fit the theme "Celebrate Our World"?

INDEPENDENT/ WHOLE CLASS

Discuss Author's Craft

Discuss the constructions the author uses to make the story read like a folktale. Rewrite a few as they might be said in ordinary conversation:
- "First he found a small quartz stone, white and brilliant."
- "First he found a small, white, shiny quartz stone."
- "Jordi could not understand how life had once seemed so sad and lonely to him, filled as it was with so many beautiful things to discover."
- "Jordi saw that the world was filled with beautiful things, and couldn't understand why he had felt so sad and lonely."

Read aloud the author's words and the revised words, and have students decide which sound better and why. SMALL GROUP

OPTIONS FOR READING

1 **Why would the sight of a star in his pool make Jordi feel so happy?** (Possible response: Jordi isn't used to seeing anything beautiful.) CRITICAL: IDENTIFY WITH CHARACTERS

2 **Why doesn't Jordi see the star when the sun is out?** (The star is not reflected because of the light of the sun.) INFERENTIAL: CAUSE-EFFECT

3 **How does Jordi change his own world?** (Possible response: By using soil, rocks, and seeds, he makes things grow where nothing grew before. He is no longer lonely.) INFERENTIAL: SUMMARIZE

OPTIONS FOR RESPONDING

1 **How did you feel toward Jordi at the beginning of the story? Did your opinion of him change?** (Responses will vary.) CRITICAL: EXPRESS PERSONAL OPINIONS/ IDENTIFY WITH CHARACTERS

2 **What did you like most about this story? What did you like least?** (Responses will vary.) METACOGNITIVE: EXPRESS PERSONAL OPINIONS

Below / On-Level / Advanced / ELL

ENGLISH-LANGUAGE LEARNERS

Have students retell the story by adding a sentence at a time to this story starter: "Jordi, the lonely goatherd, lived on a rocky hillside."

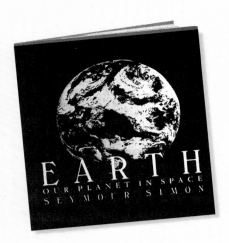

▲ *Earth: Our Planet in Space*
by Seymour Simon

THEME: Celebrate Our World

As students read *Earth: Our Planet in Space,* they will learn about the world by observing the Earth from a new point of view.

GENRE: Nonfiction

Summary: With the use of photographs taken from space, the author reveals many of the features that make the Earth unique among planets. He explores the effects of the Earth's rotation and revolution, its magnetic field, geographical features, and the ways in which human habitation has altered the planet.

ABOUT THE AUTHOR

More than half of **Seymour Simon's** 150 science books have been named Outstanding Trade Books for Children by the National Science Teachers Association. His books on the human body and the planets in our solar system are particularly admired. He is also the author of the Einstein Anderson series of scientific mysteries.

Library Book Lesson

Access Prior Knowledge

Display the book cover and read the title aloud. Have students suggest how the cover photograph might have been taken. (from space) Ask them what the photograph shows about the Earth. (its shape, the clouds and weather patterns that cover its surface, and so on)

Set Purpose / Predict

Have students read the first two pages of the book. Ask whether this is a fiction or nonfiction book about the Earth. Have students use their prior knowledge and their preview to think about what the rest of the book might tell them. Tell them to list two things they hope to learn about the Earth by reading this book. Ask students to decide the purpose for which they will read the book. (to learn something)

DEVELOP VOCABULARY

Write these words on the board, and have students record them in their journals. As they read, have them try to determine the meanings of unfamiliar words from context clues. If they cannot, tell them to use a dictionary.

planet	solar system	orbit	
atmosphere	aurora	magnetic field	eroded

Options for Reading

Guided Comprehension

STRATEGY REMINDER

Explain that this book is set up in sections. Students can **use text structure and format** to determine where one topic ends and a new one begins. They should look for large capital letters at the beginnings of paragraphs. These letters will alert them to the beginning of a new topic. During reading, ask the questions at the right and help students monitor their own comprehension as they read. WHOLE CLASS/SMALL GROUP

Cooperative Reading

Have groups of three to four students use Comprehension Card 29 (Author's Purpose) to guide their discussion. INDEPENDENT/SMALL GROUP

Independent Reading

Students can write in their journals about whether their predictions were confirmed and whether they would recommend this book to a friend, and why. After reading, have students complete the self-assessment forms found on pages R42–R43 and add them to their reading portfolios.
INDEPENDENT/WHOLE CLASS

Teacher Read-Aloud

Read aloud the first few pages of *Earth: Our Planet in Space* as students listen responsively. Have them keep their reading purpose in mind as they listen. Students may then read the whole book independently. INDEPENDENT/WHOLE CLASS

Options for Responding

Personal Response

Have students respond to these questions to demonstrate understanding and share their interpretations. INDEPENDENT/WHOLE CLASS

Compare Selections

Have students compare this book to "The Armadillo from Amarillo" by completing this chart.
INDEPENDENT/WHOLE CLASS

	Armadillo	**Earth**
genre	fiction	nonfiction
viewpoints about the Earth		

Discuss Author's Purpose

This book sticks to a single purpose: to inform. Have students discuss how the book would change if the author also intended to entertain.
SMALL GROUP/WHOLE CLASS

New Point Of View

Have students fold art paper in half and use pencils, markers, or crayons to show a single feature of Earth from two points of view. For example, they might show a mountaintop from the point of view of an airplane pilot and the point of view of an ant. INDEPENDENT

OPTIONS FOR READING

1 How did the Earth's shadow help people learn that Earth is round? (The shadow of the Earth across the moon is curved.)
INFERENTIAL: CAUSE-EFFECT

2 Why does it look as though the sun is going down at sunset? (The light side of the Earth is spinning away from the sun.)
INFERENTIAL: CAUSE-EFFECT

3 Would you expect the Earth's surface to stay the way it looks now or to change over the next several thousand years? Explain your answer. (Possible response: It will change because water, ice, and people are constantly making changes in the surface.) METACOGNITIVE: SPECULATE

OPTIONS FOR RESPONDING

1 How do the photographs add to your enjoyment of this book? (Possible response: They show the things the author is talking about from an unusual point of view.) CRITICAL: EXPRESS PERSONAL OPINIONS

2 What is the most important thing you learned from this book? Why do you feel it is important? (Responses will vary.) CRITICAL: MAKE JUDGMENTS

Celebrate Our World 417T

Assessing Student Progress
to Modify Instruction

- **End-of-Selection Test** (in Practice Book)
- **Oral Reading Fluency Assessment**

Monitoring of Progress

END-OF-SELECTION TESTS **IF** you want to monitor student progress in selection vocabulary and comprehension,	**THEN** administer the multiple-choice and short answer diagnostic **End-of-Selection Tests.**
ORAL READING FLUENCY ASSESSMENT **IF** you want to know how your students' fluency skills are progressing,	**THEN** use the **Oral Reading Fluency Assessment.**

Multiple Measures

Anecdotal Records To track the progress of an individual student's literacy development, establish procedures for keeping anecdotal records. Consider setting aside several pages in a spiral notebook for each child in the class. Focus on one to three behaviors or understandings during each week.

Checklists Use the checklists on R39–R44 to track students' progress in Listening, Speaking, Reading, and Writing.

Portfolios Have students keep copies of their works-in-progress and final drafts of writing assignments in a Working Portfolio. Encourage them to choose their best work and keep it in a Show Portfolio. Use teacher-student conferences to review student progress in writing.

Reading Notebooks To learn about students' independent or self-selected reading, have students keep a log of their reading in a Reading Notebook or use the **My Reading Log Copying Master** (page R42). Encourage them to keep lists of titles, authors, and genres that they enjoy.

- **Reading and Language Skills Assessment: Posttest**
- **Holistic Assessment**
- **End-of-Year Reading and Language Skills Assessment**

Summative Assessment

READING AND LANGUAGE SKILLS ASSESSMENT: POSTTEST **IF** you want to evaluate a student's mastery of the skills in this theme,	**THEN** administer the Reading and Language Skills Assessment.
HOLISTIC ASSESSMENT **IF** you want to know more about a student's ability to read a passage and apply literal, inferential, and critical thinking skills in a global and holistic manner, revising and editing skills in writing, and how he or she responds to multiple-choice and short and extended open ended questions,	**THEN** administer the Holistic Assessment.
END-OF-YEAR READING AND LANGUAGE SKILLS ASSESSMENT **IF** you want to evaluate students' mastery of the skills in themes 1–3,	**THEN** administer the End-of-Year Reading and Language Skills Assessment.

Additional Support Activities

Celebrate Our World

Additional Support Activities

Additional Support Activities
Vocabulary

■ BELOW-LEVEL

Reteach: Vocabulary

See the Words

Display Transparency 241. Discuss each picture as you say the word in dark type.

Hear the Words

Say these sentences aloud to reteach vocabulary.

- We always invite family and friends to my birthday **celebrations.**

- Deanna is **admiring** Tonya's pretty dress. Soon she will tell Tonya how much she likes it.

- An **average** day's walk in the woods becomes special if we find animal **tracks** in the snow.

- When leaves fall from trees, they **signal** the beginning of Fall.

- I'm **choosy** about what I eat. I only like fresh fruit and vegetables.

Say the Words

Have students read aloud the vocabulary words from the transparency.

Need More Intensive Instruction?

See Intervention Resource Kit, Lesson 26 for additional **preteach** and **reteach** activities.

▼ Teaching Transparency 241

A WINTER TREAT

"We had a fun New Year's party at my house!"

Today began as an **average** winter's day. Nothing special was happening.

At first, we talked about our New Year's **celebrations.**

Then we found deer **tracks** in the snow.

I used my hand to **signal** that the others should stop.

When food is hard to find in winter, the deer aren't **choosy** about what they eat.

We spent a long time **admiring** the deer.

"I'm in Charge of Celebrations"
Celebrate Our World, Theme 3   **241**   Reteach
Harcourt

average   tracks   signal   choosy

■ ADVANCED

Bonus Words

- **beargrass**—a plant with leaves that look like thick blades of grass
- **coyote**—a wild member of the dog family
- **quail**—small birds in the same family as turkeys
- **whirlwinds**—small, spinning windstorms
- **yuccas**—plants with long, pointed leaves

Extend: Bonus Words

Display Transparency 242. Have students look at the first illustration as you read aloud the word *quail*. Then ask students for an approximate definition of this word. Repeat the procedure for the remaining Bonus Words. Finally, have students confirm the meanings of the words in a dictionary.

▼ **Teaching Transparency 242**

BONUS WORDS

quail

coyote

beargrass

whirlwinds

yuccas

"I'm in Charge of Celebrations"
Celebrate Our World, Theme 3   242   Bonus Words
Harcourt

■ ENGLISH-LANGUAGE LEARNERS

Reteach: Background and Vocabulary

Display Transparency 241. Point to and read aloud each vocabulary word and have students repeat it after you. Next, use the following prompts to help students understand the vocabulary words.

- Point to the appropriate time on a wall clock as you say: **On an** *average* **day, school starts at _____ A.M.**

- Hold your index finger to your lips and say: **I use my hand like this to** *signal* **when it's time to be quiet.**

- Step on a piece of paper with your shoes and say: **If I have dirt on my shoes, they will leave** *tracks* **on the paper.**

- Take one book off of a bookshelf, then look at it, put it back, and take another. Say: **I'm** *choosy* **about the books I read.**

- Hold up a student's lunchbox and look at it admiringly. Then say: **I like this lunchbox. I am** *admiring* **it.**

- Hold up party decorations. Say: **We use these to decorate for** *celebrations*.

tracks

Need More Language Development?

See English-Language Learners Resource Kit, Lesson 26 for additional pre-teach and reteach activities.

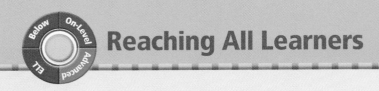
Additional Support Activities
Comprehension and Skills

**Need More
Intensive Instruction?**

**See Intervention
Resource Kit, Lesson
26** for additional **reteach**
activities.

■ **BELOW-LEVEL**

Reteach: Summarize

Remind students that to **summarize** is to tell the most important events or ideas in a selection in their own words. Create on the board a numbered web like the one below. Use it to help students summarize "I'm in Charge of Celebrations."

Work with students to add to the diagram the most important details about each celebration. Then use the chart to summarize the poem orally. The summary should begin by stating the main idea of the poem.

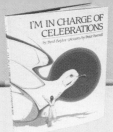

■ ADVANCED

Extend: Summarize

Have students look in science textbooks for examples of natural wonders and choose one to read about. Then have students give a summary telling what they have learned about the wonder and why it is unique. Students can share their summaries in small groups, discussing whether each one gives readers enough information about the main idea and important details.

■ ENGLISH-LANGUAGE LEARNERS

Reteach: Oral Summary

Assign each student one of the following natural wonders from the poem: seven whirlwinds, a triple rainbow, a green cloud in the shape of a parrot, a coyote, a meteor shower, several white-winged doves. Ask students to use the illustrations from the poem to help them draw a picture of their assigned element. Then read aloud the name of each celebration: Dust Devil Day, Rainbow Celebration Day, Green Cloud Day, Coyote Day, The Time of Falling Stars, New Year Celebration. Ask students who have drawn the corresponding picture to stand up, show their picture, and tell what happened on that day.

Need More Language Development?

See English-Language Learners Resource Kit, Lesson 26 for additional reteach activities.

Additional Support Activities
Writing and Grammar

■ BELOW-LEVEL

Reteach: Interactive Writing

BUILD ON PRIOR KNOWLEDGE   Work with students to choose a topic for an unrhymed poem and generate a list of thoughts and feelings about the topic. Then, as a group, have them brainstorm words and images that describe each thought or feeling. Record these ideas in a chart.

Topic:	
Thought/Feeling 1:	Thought/Feeling 2:
Images/Descriptive Words or Phrases:	Images/Descriptive Words or Phrases:

DRAFT THE POEM   "Share the pen" with students by working with them to draft the poem. Write the first stanza, introducing the topic. Then have students continue the poem in this way.

- **Write a sentence that describes the first thought or feeling from the chart. Include an image or descriptive word or phrase from the list.**

- **Repeat the process with the second thought or feeling.**

- **Think of a title that names the poem's topic.**

REVISIT THE TEXT   As you work with students to revise the poem, have volunteers reread stanzas or lines aloud to monitor how clearly they convey the thought or feeling being described.

Need More Intensive Instruction?

See Intervention Resource Kit, Lesson 26 for additional **reteach** activities.

■ ADVANCED

Extend: Writing

NATURAL WONDERS OF DAILY LIFE Ask students to take time during the day to observe what is happening in the world around them. Tell them to take notes about anything that they find particularly interesting—it might be a ladybug crawling on a leaf or raindrops splashing in a puddle. Have them write a poem, either rhymed or unrhymed, about one of the things in their notes. When they have finished, encourage them to read their poems aloud to classmates. Ask them to compare the natural wonders that they wrote about.

■ ENGLISH-LANGUAGE LEARNERS

Reteach: Grammar and Writing

IRREGULAR VERB PRACTICE Write the following verbs and their irregular past-tense forms on the board: *eat–ate, eaten, give–gave, given, go–went, gone, ride–rode, ridden, take–took, taken.* Have students fold a sheet of paper four times to create sixteen boxes, and copy one word in each box. (One box will be empty.) Then have them cut out the words to create separate word cards. Next, read these sentences aloud:

I **eat** a sandwich for lunch.
Yesterday, I **ate** a sandwich for lunch.
I have **eaten** a sandwich for lunch every day this week.

As you read each sentence, ask students to hold up the card with the correct word. Then ask volunteers to use each form of the verb *eat* in an original oral sentence. Repeat this process for the other verbs and their irregular past-tense forms.

eat	ate	eaten	give
gave	given	go	went
gone	ride	rode	ridden
take	took	taken	

Need More Language Development?

See English-Language Learners Resource Kit, Lesson 26 for additional **reteach** activities.

Additional Support Activities
Vocabulary

■ BELOW-LEVEL

Reteach: Vocabulary

See the Words

Display Transparency 250. Point to each Vocabulary Word as you say it aloud.

Hear the Words

Say these sentences aloud to reteach vocabulary.

- Matt's family moved from their farm to the city six months ago. He isn't happy. He **cherished** every day on the farm.

- Matt felt shy and out of place in the city. He **shunned** people, so he made few new friends.

- Matt thinks about his old farm chores, such as plowing **furrows** in the soil and weeding the plant **growth**.

- On the farm, there was **ample** room for everyone. In the city, Matt feels crowded.

- Matt's favorite part of the farm was its big **windmill**. He loved watching its huge arms spin in the wind.

Say the Words

Have volunteers read aloud the Vocabulary Words and their meanings. Have them decide which picture fits each word.

Need More Intensive Instruction?

See Intervention Resource Kit, Lesson 27 for additional **preteach** and **reteach** activities.

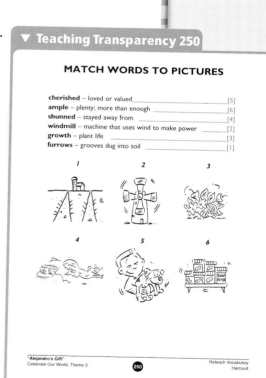

▼ **Teaching Transparency 250**

MATCH WORDS TO PICTURES

cherished – loved or valued _____ [5]
ample – plenty; more than enough _____ [6]
shunned – stayed away from _____ [4]
windmill – machine that uses wind to make power _____ [2]
growth – plant life _____ [3]
furrows – grooves dug into soil _____ [1]

"Alejandro's Gift"
Celebrate Our World, Theme 3   250   Reteach Vocabulary
Harcourt

■ ADVANCED

Bonus Words

- **clearing** — open area
- **mesquite** — thorny, low bush
- **saguaro** — large cactus
- **sheltered** — protected
- **underbrush** — small bushes or plants

Extend: Bonus Words

Display Transparency 251. Ask students to look at the illustration and listen for context clues as you read the first sentence aloud. Then ask students to discuss a possible definition for *clearing*. Have them confirm the meaning in a dictionary. Repeat this procedure for the rest of the Bonus Words.

BONUS WORDS

The Desert

The jackrabbit hopped into the **clearing** with a great burst of speed. It was time to eat!

First, it sampled a **mesquite**, but there were too many thorns.

Next, it tried a **saguaro**, but it was far too big.

At last, it spotted some low bushes with soft leaves. This **underbrush** was perfect for two reasons. First, it tasted great. Second, it **sheltered** the jackrabbit from coyotes!

"Alejandro's Gift"
Celebrate Our World, Theme 3   **251**   Bonus Words
Harcourt

■ ENGLISH-LANGUAGE LEARNERS

Reteach: Vocabulary

Display Transparency 250. Point to and read aloud each Vocabulary Word, and have students repeat the words after you.

Next, use the illustrations on the Transparency to develop students' understanding of the Vocabulary Words. Use questions and responses such as these:

Question	Response
Would you keep or throw away something that is *cherished*?	You would ___keep___ something that is *cherished*.
What is another word for *plenty*?	Another word for *plenty* is ___ample___.
What tool could you use to dig *furrows*?	You could use a ___plow___ to dig *furrows*.

Need More Language Development?

See **English-Language Learners Resource Kit, Lesson 27** for additional **preteach** and **reteach** activities.

Additional Support Activities
Comprehension and Skills

■ BELOW-LEVEL

Reteach: Cause and Effect

Review with students that a **cause** is the reason why something happens, and an **effect** is what happens. Write the following sentences on the board:

- **The animals weren't afraid to drink at the water hole.**
- **Alejandro built a second water hole that was hidden.**

Have students reread page 338 in the *Pupil Edition* and choose which sentence on the board is the cause and which is the effect. (The first sentence is the effect; the second sentence is the cause.) Then have students identify a signal word on page 338 that helps show this cause and effect relationship. (*Because*)

Have students draw a line to match each cause with its effect, and then restate the two events using a signal word such as *because* or *so*.

Alejandro is lonely.   They visit the garden.

Animals are thirsty.   They don't want to get too close to the house.

Large animals stay away from the water hole.   He plants a garden.

Need More Intensive Instruction?

See Intervention Resource Kit, Lesson 27 for additional **preteach and reteach** activities.

■ ADVANCED

Extend: Cause and Effect

Have students find and read an article about desert gardening or about the ways desert communities get the water they need. They can look for information in an encyclopedia or a social studies text-book. Have them note causes and effects as they read. They can list causes and effects they find in a cause-effect chart.

Causes		Effects
	→	
	→	

■ ENGLISH-LANGUAGE LEARNERS

Reteach: Cause and Effect/Selection Summary

Walk students through "Alejandro's Gift" page by page, and ask students to orally summarize the story. Then write the following on the board:

Cause

Alejandro built a second water hole that was hidden.

Effects

Then ask: *What happened after Alejandro dug the second hole?* Have students each work with a partner to draw a picture of an effect. When students are finished, have them place their pictures in the chalk tray below the word **Effects**. Ask them to use the words *so* or *because* to explain the events.

Need More Language Development?

See **English-Language Learners Resource Kit, Lesson 27** for additional **reteach** activities.

Additional Support Activities
Writing and Grammar

■ BELOW-LEVEL

Reteach: Writer's Craft

ANALYZE AND PREWRITE   Discuss with students the author's use of specific nouns in "Alejandro's Gift" by naming the animals the author mentions. Explain that fiction authors use specific nouns and vivid verbs such as *rustling* and *charging* to help bring the story to life. If students use vivid verbs and specific nouns in a letter, they will better express their feelings.

DRAFT   Write on the board a letter frame like the one below. Then "share the pen" with students by working together to write a thank-you letter to the illustrator for creating such beautiful pictures. Allow students to take turns being scribes. As they write, point out any inflected endings and help use them correctly.

Address:	_____
Date:	_____
Greeting:	Dear _____,
Body:	_____
	_____
	_____
Closing:	_____
Signature:	_____

REVISE   Model revising sentences to include vivid verbs and specific nouns. ("The picture of the pig helped me understand what it looks like" might be "Your drawing of the little peccary helped me understand how long its snout is and how bristly its back is.")

Need More Intensive Instruction?

See Intervention Resource Kit, Lesson **27** for additional **reteach** activities.

■ ADVANCED

Extend: Writing

LETTER TO A COMMUNITY WORKER   Have students brainstorm a list of community workers such as park rangers, health-care professionals, street cleaners, and others who keep the community safe and clean. Ask students to select one kind of worker and to thank that person for doing that job. Tell students that they should use the name of the job in their greeting (for example: *Dear Park Ranger*).

■ ENGLISH-LANGUAGE LEARNERS

Reteach: Grammar and Writing

THE VERB *BE*   Write the following sentences on the chalkboard:

He _____ angry. (is/was)
We _____ glad. (are/were)
I _____ upset. (am/was)
They _____ happy. (are/were)

Ask students to supply the correct present-tense and past-tense form of *be* for these four sentences. Remind them that:

- the subject of the sentence and the form of the verb *be* must agree.
- in the past tense, singular subjects use *was*, and plural subjects use *were*.

Have students write a short paragraph about Alejandro and the animals he helped. Tell them to include a form of the verb *be* in at least two of their sentences.

Need More Language Development?

See English-Language Learners Resource Kit, **Lesson 25** for additional **reteach** activities.

Alejandro's Gift   **S77**

Additional Support Activities
Vocabulary

■ BELOW-LEVEL

Reteach: Vocabulary

See the Words

Display Transparency 260. Then point to each word and its corresponding part of the picture as you say the words aloud.

Hear the Words

Say these sentences to reteach vocabulary.

- A mountain **range** is a group of mountains.
- The **peak** of a mountain can be sharp.
- Birds feed along the **edges** of a lake.
- **Magma** comes from deep underground.
- An earthquake is the strongest at its **epicenter**.
- The **coast** has many fine beaches.

Say the Words

Have students read aloud the words on the transparency. Then guide them to answer the questions below each picture.

▼ Teaching Transparency 260

VOLCANOES AND EARTHQUAKES

magma

peak

epicenter

range

coast

edges

- Where does the mountain **range** begin and end?
- Find another **peak**.
- What might you see along the **edges** of the bay?
- Where do you think the **magma** comes from?
- Is the volcano near the **epicenter** of the earthquake?
- Where is another part of the **coast**?

"Rocking and Rolling"
Celebrate Our World, Theme 3   260   Reteach Vocabulary
                                              Harcourt

Need More Intensive Instruction?

See Intervention Resource Kit, Lesson 28 for additional **preteach** and **reteach** activities.

range

magma

epicenter

coast

■ ADVANCED

Bonus Words

- **earthquakes**—severe earth movements
- **erosion**—the wearing away of land
- **ocean floor**—the land beneath the ocean
- **ridges**—narrow, raised strips of land
- **valleys**—low lands that lie between mountains or hills

Extend: **Bonus Words**

Display Transparency 261. Ask students to use context clues and view the illustration as you read the first sentence aloud. Ask students to write an approximate definition for *ocean floor*. Follow a similar process for the remaining Bonus Words. When finished, have students sort the words into two categories: words that name land or landforms, and words that name events.

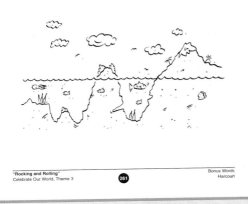

BONUS WORDS

The **ocean floor** is not flat. Like the surface of the Earth, the bottom of the ocean has **ridges** and deep **valleys**. **Earthquakes** can cause mountains to push up from the ocean floor. Some mountains push up above the ocean's surface to form islands. Wave action can cause **erosion** under water as well as on land. Undersea mountains are worn away bit by bit by the force of moving water and sand.

"Rocking and Rolling"
Celebrate Our World, Theme 3   **261**   Bonus Words
Harcourt

■ ENGLISH-LANGUAGE LEARNERS

Reteach: **Background and Vocabulary**

Display Transparency 260. Point to each word as you say it aloud. Then have students answer these questions:

- Could big waves wear away the **coast**? (yes)
- Is **magma** hot or cold? (hot)
- Which mountain in the picture does not have a **peak**? (the one with smoke coming out of it; the volcano)
- Do you think you might see birds by the **edges** of a bay? (yes)
- What happens at an **epicenter**? (an earthquake)
- Do you think a mountain **range** changes over time? (yes)

Need More Intensive Language Development?

See English-Language Learners Resource Kit, **Lesson 28** for additional preteach and reteach activities.

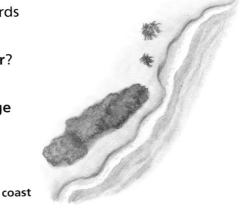

coast

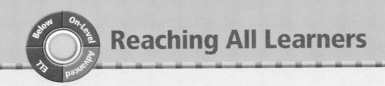
Additional Support Activities
Comprehension and Skills

Need More Intensive Instruction?

See Intervention Resource Kit, Lesson 27 for additional **reteach** activities.

■ **BELOW-LEVEL**

Reteach: Locate Information

Remind students that they can use different parts of a book or chapter to find information. Guide students in an "information scavenger hunt" using the *Pupil Edition.* Ask:

- **What pages is the table of contents on?** (pages 4–9)

- **Look at the table of contents for Theme 3 on pages 8–9. On what page does the selection "Rocking and Rolling" start?** (page 348)

- **On what page does the glossary start?** (page 442)

- **Turn to page 442. Look through the glossary to find the word** *magma.* **What page is this entry on?** (page 448)

Have pairs of students conduct a similar scavenger hunt using a science or social studies textbook or a nonfiction trade book that has a glossary and an index.

■ ADVANCED

Extend: Locate Information

Students can use the index of a science textbook, a nonfiction trade book, or an encyclopedia to find information about volcanoes, earthquakes, or rock types. Have students write down the page numbers on which this information appears, and then have them find and read the information. They can then create a bookmark with helpful hints for using an index.

Copy down all the page numbers from the index.

■ ENGLISH-LANGUAGE LEARNERS

Reteach: Locate Information

Use the *Pupil Edition* to point out the following book parts: title, table of contents, story title, glossary, index. Then have students write the name of each book part on a self-stick label and attach it to the appropriate part of the *Pupil Edition*. Finally, have students respond to the questions below by opening the *Pupil Edition* to the correct part and saying the name of that part.

- **Where can you find a list of story titles?** (the table of contents)

- **Where can you find the meaning of a word in the book?** (the glossary)

- **Where can you find a list of topics in the book, along with page numbers?** (the index)

Then have students look through "Rocking and Rolling" and tell where chapter headings can be found.

Need More Intensive Language Development?

See English-Language Learners Resource Kit, **Lesson 28** for additional reteach activities.

Additional Support Activities
Writing and Grammar

■ BELOW-LEVEL

Reteach: Writer's Process

ANALYZE AND PREWRITE   Work with a small group of students to complete a story map. Help them outline their ideas for a play about a family that survives an emergency. Discuss what each character might say and do as the play unfolds.

DRAFT   "Share the pen" with students by calling on them to say aloud lines of dialogue. Write the dialogue in play form, next to each character's name. Allow students to share the task of writing dialogue.

REVISE   Assign the characters' roles to students and have them read the dialogue aloud. Pause to revise the lines of dialogue to make them more realistic. Also, pause to insert stage directions in the appropriate places. Once the play is complete, allow students to practice and perform it as a group.

Our Class Play
centerstage: Mama
walks to table
Mama: "Children time
for dinner."

Need More Intensive Instruction?

See Intervention Resource Kit, Lesson 28 for additional **reteach** activities.

■ ADVANCED

Extend: **Locate Information/Writing**

Show Information Graphically   Have students use the index of an encyclopedia to find information about the tallest tsunamis ever recorded, or about another topic related to the selection. Have them write a paragraph that explains what they learned. They can also create a diagram or graph that provides the same information.

■ ENGLISH-LANGUAGE LEARNERS

Reteach: **Grammar-Writing**

Contractions   Write these words on the board, with their contraction form beneath them as shown.

I will	I would	I am
I'll	I'd	I'm
do not	is not	did not
don't	isn't	didn't
she is	he is	they are
she's	he's	they're

Use the words *I will* in an oral sentence, and have students restate the sentence, using *I'll*. Follow a similar procedure for the remaining words. Then have pairs of students write a short, two-character dialogue using contractions. Have them perform their dialogues for the group.

Need More Intensive Language Development?

See **English-Language Learners Resource Kit, Lesson 28** for additional **reteach** activities.

Additional Support Activities
Vocabulary

■ BELOW-LEVEL

Reteach: Vocabulary

See the Words

Display Transparency 268. Discuss the pictures. Point to each key word as you read aloud the sentences.

Hear the Words

Say these sentences aloud to reteach vocabulary:

- Our country, the United States, is big, but our **continent**, North America, is bigger.
- The **universe** includes all the stars in the sky.
- When you walk toward your house, you are heading **homeward**.
- If you keep trying, **eventually** you will succeed.
- You can **converse** with your friends on the playground.
- The globe is a **sphere**, and so is a baseball.

Say the Words

Have students read the sentences on the transparency silently and then read the vocabulary words aloud.

Need More Intensive Instruction?

See Intervention Resource Kit, Lesson 29 for additional **preteach** and **reteach** activities.

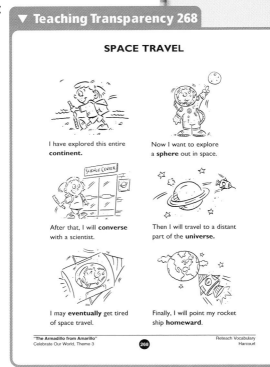

▼ **Teaching Transparency 268**

SPACE TRAVEL

I have explored this entire **continent**.

Now I want to explore a **sphere** out in space.

After that, I will **converse** with a scientist.

Then I will travel to a distant part of the **universe**.

I may **eventually** get tired of space travel.

Finally, I will point my rocket ship **homeward**.

"The Armadillo from Amarillo"
Celebrate Our World, Theme 3   268   Reteach Vocabulary
Harcourt

 continent

 homeward

 converse

sphere

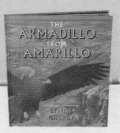

■ ADVANCED

Bonus Words

- **canyon**—a deep valley with steep walls
- **landscape**—the scenery visible from one place
- **prairie**—flat or rolling grassland
- **revolve**—to turn on an axis
- **woodland**—land with many trees

Extend: Bonus Words

Display Transparency 269. Ask students to look at the pictures and then listen for context clues as you read the sentences aloud. Ask students to suggest a definition for each word. Encourage students to check meanings in a dictionary.

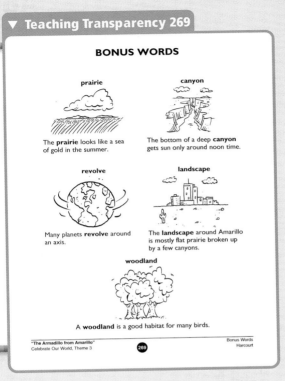

BONUS WORDS

prairie — The **prairie** looks like a sea of gold in the summer.

canyon — The bottom of a deep **canyon** gets sun only around noon time.

revolve — Many planets **revolve** around an axis.

landscape — The **landscape** around Amarillo is mostly flat prairie broken up by a few canyons.

woodland — A **woodland** is a good habitat for many birds.

"The Armadillo from Amarillo"
Celebrate Our World, Theme 3
269
Bonus Words
Harcourt

■ ENGLISH-LANGUAGE LEARNERS

Reteach: Vocabulary

Display Transparency 268. Point out and read aloud each vocabulary word. Have students say each word with you at least twice. Then ask these questions to develop knowledge of word meanings. Guide students to answer in complete sentences.

- Which is shaped like a *sphere*, a soccer ball or a football?
- Which is a *continent*, China or Asia?
- What movie is about going to a distant part of the *universe*?
- What is one thing you and your friends *converse* about?
- What is one thing you would like to do *eventually*?
- Do you head *homeward* in the morning or in the afternoon?

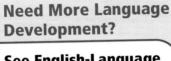

Need More Language Development?

See English-Language Learners Resource Kit, Lesson 29 for additional preteach and reteach activities.

Additional Support Activities
Comprehension and Skills

■ BELOW-LEVEL

Reteach: Cause and Effect

Remind students that a **cause** is an event that makes another event happen, and an **effect** is what happens as a result of the cause. Also remind them that many causes can lead to a single effect. Read aloud the following paragraph:

> Armadillo's Aunt Rolo lived in Austin. Her birthday was coming up. Armadillo was restless. He was in the mood to travel. He had won a free airline ticket in a contest. "I think I'll fly to Austin to surprise Aunt Rolo!" he decided.

Guide students to notice causes and effects, and list them in a diagram like the one below.

CAUSES

| Aunt Rolo lives in Austin. |
| Aunt Rolo's birthday is coming up. |
| Armadillo is feeling restless. |
| Armadillo won a free airline ticket. |

EFFECT

| Armadillo decides to fly to Austin. |

Need More Intensive Instruction?

See Intervention Resource Kit, Lesson 29 for additional **preteach and reteach** activities.

■ ADVANCED

Extend: Cause and Effect

Have students identify one cause and effect relationship described in their science textbook, and one described in their social studies textbook. Afterward, have them discuss why understanding cause and effect relationships is important in each subject.

cause   effect

■ ENGLISH-LANGUAGE LEARNERS

Reteach: Cause and Effect/Selection Summary

Write the following cloze sentences on the board. Have students copy the sentences and fill in the blanks to form a story summary. (Possible responses are shown.)

- Because Armadillo wants to know where he is in the world, he (takes a trip).

- Because he walks a long way, he discovers that different places have (different landforms and different plants).

- Because Armadillo wants to see a larger part of the world, he asks Eagle to (take him flying).

- Because Eagle wants to help Armadillo, she (takes Armadillo for a ride high into the air and teaches him about places).

- Because Armadillo and Eagle want to (fly very, very high), they go for a ride on the space shuttle.

Need More Language Development?

See English-Language Learners Resource Kit, Lesson 29 for additional preteach and reteach activities.

Additional Support Activities
Writing and Grammar

■ BELOW-LEVEL

Reteach: Writer's Process

BUILD ON PRIOR KNOWLEDGE Ask students to recall a birthday party that was held for them or which they attended. Have them fill out a chart with information about the party. Tell students that if they are not sure about a piece of information, they should make a guess.

Event:
Day and Date:
Time:
Place:

Then discuss with students how someone could have used this information to write a clear invitation to the event.

DRAFT "Share the pen" with students by collaborating on writing a draft of the invitation. Discuss words with irregular spellings.

REVISE Reread the invitation aloud with students. Work with them to check that it has a polite tone. Have them be sure all the important information is included and accurate. Help students make any necessary revisions or corrections.

**Need More
Intensive Instruction?**

**See Intervention
Resource Kit, Lesson
29** for additional **preteach
and reteach** activities.

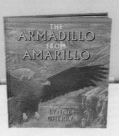

■ ADVANCED

Extend: Writing

USE ADVERBS IN A SEQUEL   Remind students that Armadillo's cousin Brillo sent him a postcard saying that he was beginning a journey of his own. Invite them to write a few paragraphs or stanzas telling about where Brillo might go and what he might see. Tell them to use at least three adverbs.

■ ENGLISH-LANGUAGE LEARNERS

Reteach: Grammar and Writing

ADVERBS AND RELATED ADJECTIVES   Inform students that many adverbs telling *how* are formed from adjectives. Write the following sentence pairs on the board, including underlines, and have students read aloud the cloze sentences, inserting the correct forms of the underlined adjectives.

Pablo is a <u>swift</u> runner.
He runs _____. (swiftly)

Marta is a <u>careful</u> driver.
She drives _____. (carefully)

Ed is a <u>humorous</u> storyteller.
He speaks _____. (humorously)

Vonda is very <u>hungry</u>.
She _____ gobbles a sandwich. (hungrily)

Have students write a short note inviting their friends to a going-away party for Armadillo. Tell them to include at least one adverb in the invitation.

Need More Language Development?

See English-Language Learners Resource Kit, Lesson 29 for additional **preteach and reteach** activities.

Additional Support Activities
Vocabulary

■ BELOW-LEVEL

Reteach: Vocabulary

See the Words

Display Transparency 277. Discuss the pictures, pointing to each word as you say it.

Hear the Words

Say these sentences aloud to reteach vocabulary.

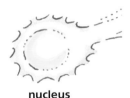

nucleus

- The ice inside a comet reflects sunlight, giving it a **fluorescent** glow.

- A comet has a head and tails. The head is the **nucleus**. The tails are made of **particles** of melted ice and dust.

- The tails are blown behind the comet by **solar wind**, a flow of gases from the Sun.

- Because of its huge size, the Sun pulls on all objects in the Solar System. This **force** makes comets circle it in large **loops**.

Say the Words

Have volunteers read aloud the Vocabulary Words from the Transparency. Then have them decide which picture fits each word.

nucleus   Particles   force   loops

Need More Intensive Instruction?

See Intervention Resource Kit, Lesson 30 for additional **preteach** and **reteach** activities.

▼ Teaching Transparency 277

VOCABULARY REVIEW

1	2	3
4	5	6

fluorescent – "bright and glowing"___5___
solar wind – "flow of gases from the Sun"___6___
particles – "tiny bits"___4___
force – "power that causes movement or change"___2___
loops – "moves in a circling way"___3___
nucleus – "center of a comet"___1___

"Visitors From Space"
Celebrate Our World, Theme 3   277   Reteach Vocabulary
Harcourt

■ ADVANCED

Bonus Words

- **gravity**—invisible force of attraction between all objects
- **moons**—rocky spheres that orbit planets
- **planets**—large spheres that orbit stars
- **Solar System**—the Sun, the nine planets, and everything else orbiting the Sun.
- **stars**—huge balls of flaming gas and energy

Extend: Bonus Words

Display Transparency 278. Ask students to listen for context clues as you read the first sentence aloud. Then ask students to discuss a possible definition for *moons*. Have them confirm the meaning in dictionaries. Repeat this procedure for the rest of the Bonus Words. Then have students create a simple diagram of the Solar System and use the Bonus Words to label it.

BONUS WORDS

Alan is an astronomer. Tonight he is working late. He is studying one of Jupiter's rockiest **moons**.

Jupiter is the largest object in our **Solar System** besides the Sun. It's bigger than all the other **planets** combined!

Jupiter's **gravity** holds 16 moons in orbit. Earth has only one moon.

Alan focuses his telescope on the distant moon. For now, he ignores the other **stars** in the night sky.

"Visitors From Space"
Celebrate Our World, Theme 3   **278**   Bonus Words
Harcourt

■ ENGLISH-LANGUAGE LEARNERS

Reteach: Background and Vocabulary

Display Transparency 277. Point to and read aloud each vocabulary word and have students repeat after you.

Then, use the art in "Visitors from Space" to show students the meanings of the Vocabulary Words.

- **Page 402 shows a comet glowing like a** *fluorescent* **light bulb.**
- **Page 406 illustrates the** *force* **of gravity.**
- **Page 407 shows the** *solar wind* **blowing a comet's tail as it** *loops* **around the Sun.**

Visit *The Learning Site:* **www.harcourtschool.com**
See Language Support.

Need More Language Development?

See English-Language Learners Resource Kit, Lesson 30 for additional preteach and reteach activities.

Additional Support Activities
Comprehension and Skills

■ BELOW-LEVEL

Reteach: Locating Information

Remind students that knowing how to use the parts of a nonfiction book can help them find the information they need quickly and easily. Write the following parts of a book on the board. Display a nonfiction trade book that contains an index and a glossary. Point to each part of the book as you review the information contained in each.

Title Page   Table of Contents   Glossary   Index

Have volunteers identify where they would look in a book about stars to answer the following questions:

- **How many chapters are in the book?** (table of contents)
- **What is the title of the book?** (cover or title page)
- **What does the word *constellation* mean?** (glossary)

Then ask students to identify where in "Visitors from Space" they could look to find answers to the questions *How do comets change?* and *What do comets do when they orbit?*

Need More Intensive Instruction?

See Intervention Resource Kit, Lesson 30 for additional **preteach** and **reteach** activities.

■ ADVANCED

Extend: Locating Information

Provide nonfiction books about stars or the Solar System for students to use. Have them locate title pages, tables of contents, glossaries, and indexes. Encourage them to use each book part to answer questions and to find information. Have students record their findings in a chart and present the information to classmates.

Book Part	Information Found
Title Page	
Table of Contents	
Glossary	
Index	
Headings, Captions, Diagrams	

■ ENGLISH-LANGUAGE LEARNERS

Reteach: Locating Information

Have students create a "parts of a book" bookmark for their *Pupil Editions*. Have them cut a piece of paper in half, and make a three-column chart containing the following information:

- **parts of the book**
- **page number or numbers where each part of the book is located**
- **information found in each part of the book**

Students can use different colors and art to personalize their bookmarks.

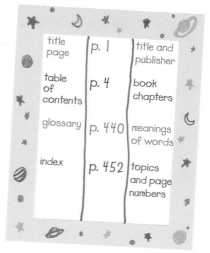

Need More Language Development?

See English-Language Learners Resource Kit, Lesson 30 for additional preteach and reteach activities.

Additional Support Activities
Writing and Grammar

■ BELOW-LEVEL

Reteach: Writer's Process

PREWRITE   Review with students that authors use dialogue to show story characters speaking to each other. Revisit *Pupil Edition* page 378 with students and point out the dialogue between the eagle and the armadillo. Explain that the words the characters say to each other are placed inside *quotation marks*, and that the speaker is usually named either before or after the quotation.

Need More Intensive Instruction?

See Intervention Resource Kit, Lesson **30** for additional **reteach** activities.

DRAFT   Have a volunteer say a simple sentence. Write what was said on the board using quotation marks, a comma, and a name. ("I like pizza," said Kevin.) Next, write sentence frames like the two below on the board. Then "share the pen" with students by working together to write a short piece of dialogue.

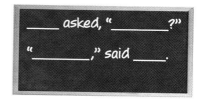

_____ asked, "_____?"

"_____," said _____.

Remind students that there are many ways to say *asked* and *said*, such as *questioned*, *wondered*, *replied*, and *answered*. Encourage students to write several lines of dialogue on their own, using other words for *said* and *asked*.

■ ADVANCED

Extend: Writing

WRITE A STORY WITH DIALOGUE   Have students picture themselves as the first-ever settlers on a large comet. Ask them to write a conversation between two settlers about life on the comet. Remind students to use quotation marks and descriptive words as they write their dialogue. When finished, ask students to present their dialogues to the class.

"Life on This Comet"

■ ENGLISH-LANGUAGE LEARNERS

Reteach: Grammar and Writing

COMPARING WITH ADVERBS   Write the following sentences on the chalkboard:

The cat moves _____, but he eats _____. (fast; slowly)

The cat moves _____ than the dog, but he eats _____. (faster; more slowly)

The cat moves _____ of all, but he eats _____. (fastest; most slowly)

Ask students to supply the correct forms of *fast* and *slowly* for these sentences. Remind them that:

- Add -er to most short adverbs when comparing two actions.

- Add -est to most short adverbs when comparing one action with two or more other actions.

- Use *more* or *most* to compare with most adverbs that end with -ly.

Once they have completed the sentences correctly, have students draw pictures of the results and present them to the group.

Need More Language Development?

See English-Language Learners Resource Kit, Lesson 30 for additional preteach and reteach activities.

Teacher Notes

Celebrate Our World
Theme Resources

More Irregular Verbs

OBJECTIVE
To identify the past-tense forms of irregular verbs

Focus
Share the following information with students:
Past-tense verbs tell about past events and actions. Most past-tense verbs are formed by adding -*d* or -*ed* to the present form of the verb. They are *regular verbs*. Verbs that do not form the past tense by adding -*d* or -*ed* to the present form are called *irregular verbs*.

Reteach the Skill
Visual Model   Copy the following chart on the board. Do not copy the past-tense forms until they are discussed in the lesson.

Regular		Irregular	
Present	**Past**	**Present**	**Past**
look	looked	get	got
walk	walked	stand	stood
explore	explored	go	went

Remind students that the past tense of regular verbs is formed by adding -*d* or -*ed* to the present-tense form. Irregular verbs are those whose past-tense form is not made in this way. Point out the present-tense form of the verb *look* on the chart and use it in an oral sentence. (Example: I look across the room.) Identify the action as happening in the present. Then repeat the sentence using the regular past-tense form. Add *looked* to the chart. Proceed in this way through the remaining regular and irregular verbs, inviting volunteers to participate in formulating sentences and writing the past-tense forms on the chart. Next, ask for examples of regular and irregular verbs and have students add them to the chart. Have students make copies of the chart for their own use later. Tell them that keeping a list of regular and irregular verbs they meet in their reading can help them learn to use verbs correctly. Then follow the suggestions in **Summarize/Assess.**

Kinesthetic Model   Display the chart from the Visual Model and read the present-tense verbs with students. Call on volunteers to act out the verbs. For example, have one student walk to the front of the classroom. Ask students to tell what their classmate did and add the word *walked* to the chart. Continue in the same way with each regular and irregular verb in the chart. When the chart is complete, have students point out the difference between regular and irregular verbs in the past form. Then follow the suggestions in **Summarize/Assess.**

Auditory Model   Ask students to listen as you say some sentences and to tell you whether the past-tense forms of the verbs are regular or irregular. Make up a sentence using *looked* and tell students that the verb is regular and takes the ending -*ed*. Follow the same procedure with *got*, pointing out that it is irregular and does not take the -*d* or -*ed* ending. Then make up additional sentences, calling on volunteers to identify the verbs as regular or irregular. Next, play a game similar to "Simon Says," as follows. Pronounce the present-tense form of a regular or irregular verb. Call on a volunteer to pronounce the past-tense form. If the verb is regular, students should stand up; if not, they should remain seated. Then follow the suggestions in **Summarize/Assess.**

Summarize/Assess
To check students' understanding of the lesson have them summarize what they have learned. (The past-tense form of regular verbs is made by adding -*d* or -*ed* to the end of the present-tense form. The past-tense form of irregular verbs is not formed in this manner.) Remind students to be careful to note the past-tense forms of irregular verbs in their reading and to use them correctly in their own writing.

Focus Skill

Cause and Effect

OBJECTIVE
To recognize cause-and-effect relationships

Focus

Share the following information with students:

The reason an event happens is the *cause*. What happens is the *effect*. To find an effect, ask *What happened?* To find a cause, ask *Why did it happen?* Authors sometimes use words such as *because, so,* and *therefore* to signal causes and effects. Being able to find causes and effects helps readers better understand what they read.

Reteach the Skill

Visual Model   Write the sentences and empty chart on the board:

An earthquake shook the city.
A tsunami reached the coast.
The weather turned very cold.
Books fell off shelves.
Ice formed on the lake.
Beach towns flooded.

Cause Why did it happen?	→	Effect What happened?
An earthquake shook the city.		Books fell off shelves.
A tsunami reached the coast.		Beach towns flooded.
The weather turned very cold.		Ice formed on the lake.

Read the sentences and the chart headings aloud with students. Then have them copy the chart on a separate sheet of paper. Have students look for cause-and-effect relationships between the first three sentences and the second three sentences. In the chart, have them write each effect directly across from its cause. When students have finished, have them work in pairs to compare their results. Then follow the suggestions in **Summarize/Assess.**

Kinesthetic Model   Have students work in pairs. Provide partners with six index cards and have them write each sentence from the Visual Model on a separate card. Then have them shuffle the cards and place them face down in preparation for playing "Cause-and-Effect Concentration." To play, one partner should turn over two cards and try to combine the sentences into a single sentence that states a cause-and-effect relationship. If the player is successful, he or she keeps the cards. If not, the cards are turned over again, and the other player takes a turn. Remind students to use signal words like *because* in their sentences. Then follow the suggestions in **Summarize/Assess.**

Auditory Model   Have students join you in a circle to play a cause-and-effect game. To begin, turn to the student on your right and say an event. (For example, *I went to the store . . .*) That student should reply by finishing the sentence with a likely cause for the event. (Example: *because I needed to buy some bread.*) The student then turns to the classmate on his or her right and restates the cause as an event. (Example: *I bought some bread.*) The next player finishes the sentence with a new cause. Play continues until all students have had a turn. Then follow the suggestions in **Summarize/Assess.**

Summarize/Assess

Ask students to summarize what they have learned. (An effect is something that happens. A cause explains why it happens. *Because, so,* and *therefore* are words that signal causes and effects.) To check students' understanding, have them write sentences that tell about two recent events and their causes.

 # The Verb *Be*

OBJECTIVE

To recognize present-tense and past-tense forms of be *and the subjects with which they agree; to recognize that* be *links the subject and predicate and tells what someone or something is*

Focus

Share the following information with students:

The verb *be* tells what someone or something is or was. In a sentence, the subject and the form of the verb should agree. The forms *am*, *is*, and *was* are used with singular subjects. The forms *are* and *were* are used with plural subjects and with the pronoun *you*.

Reteach the Skill

The Verb Be		
Pronoun	**Present-Tense**	**Past-Tense**
Singular		
I	am	was
you	are	were
he, she, it	is	was
Plural		
we	are	were
you	are	were
they	are	were

Visual Model   Display the following sentences, including the words in parentheses. Then read each sentence aloud, asking students which form of the verb *be* correctly completes the sentence, first in the present tense and then in the past. (The present-tense form is given first.) Then follow the suggestions in **Summarize/Assess**.

I (am, was) **a customer.**
You (are, were) **a customer.**
He (is, was) **a customer.**
We (are, were) **the customers.**
You (are, were) **the customers.**
They (are, were) **the customers.**

Kinesthetic Model   Use the following sentences to discuss the forms of the verb *be* in the present tense and past tense:

The man (is, are) a bank president. (is)
She (is, was) once a bank clerk. (was)
Many people (was, were) her customers. (were)
You (is, are) the best customer. (are)

Point out the subject-verb agreement. Then have each student copy one or more sentences from the Visual Model on paper strips, one sentence per strip. On one side, students should write the sentence using the present-tense form of the verb *be*. On the other side, students should write the sentence using the past-tense form. As students read their sentences aloud, classmates can identify the verb and tell whether its form shows present tense or past tense. Then follow the suggestions in **Summarize/Assess**.

Auditory Model   Read aloud each sentence from the Visual Model, having students tell you which form of the verb *be* to use to complete each of the sentences in the present tense. Then have them tell you which form of the verb to use to complete each sentence in the past tense. Then have students make up their own sentences using the verb *be*. Have volunteers read their sentences offering both choices. Have other students identify the correct form of the verb for the present tense and past tense. Then follow the suggestions in **Summarize/Assess**.

Summarize/Assess

To check understanding, have students summarize what they have learned in the lesson. (The form of the verb *be* that is used in a sentence should agree with the subject of that sentence. The forms *am*, *is*, and *was* should be used with singular subjects. The forms *are* and *were* should be used with plural subjects and with the pronoun *you*.) Remind students that knowing which form of *be* to use will help them write sentences of their own.

 **Focus Skill** **Locate Information**

OBJECTIVE
To use book parts to locate information

Focus
Share the following information with students:

Books have different parts that can help you find information. Most books have a copyright page, a table of contents, and chapter headings. Some books also have an index and a glossary.

Reteach the Skill
Visual Model   Display a textbook and explain that the parts of the book can help readers find different types of information. Display the *copyright page*. Explain that it tells when and where the book was published. Continue with the following: *table of contents* (gives the main parts of the book and where to find them); *chapter headings* (give the name of each chapter); *index* (tells where to find more information about a topic); *glossary* (gives meanings for words used in the book). Write the following on the board, omitting the information in parentheses:

1. **Where would you find out when a book was published?** (on the copyright page)
2. **Where could you find out where Chapter Six of a book begins?** (in the table of contents)
3. **Where would you find what pages had information about a topic?** (in the index)
4. **Where would you find meanings of key words used in a book?** (in the glossary)

Then follow the suggestions in **Summarize/Assess.**

Kinesthetic Model   Put several books where students can use them. On the board write a list of information to be found in them: *date of publication, name and page for Chapter One, meaning of the word _____,* and *more information about the topic _____.* Have pairs of students locate these items in the books. Then follow the suggestions in **Summarize/Assess.**

Auditory Model   Read aloud the steps below. Ask students to follow the steps to locate information in their science or social studies textbooks. Make sure the textbooks contain a copyright page, table of contents, index, and glossary. Have students write down what they find out. Then ask them to form small groups in which they can compare their findings. Then follow the suggestions in **Summarize/Assess.**

1. **Use the copyright page to find out when the book was published.**
2. **Use the table of contents to find the title of a chapter and on what page it starts.**
3. **Use the index to find a page that has information about a topic you would like to learn more about.**
4. **Find one new word in the glossary. Read the definition. Then tell a classmate what it means.**
5. **Use a chapter heading to find out the name of the chapter and what it is about.**

Summarize/Assess
Check comprehension by asking students what they have learned. (You can use book parts to find information in books.) Have students name a science or social studies topic and tell what steps they would follow to find information about it in a textbook.

Focus Skill — Graphic Aids

OBJECTIVE

To interpret information on graphic aids

Focus

Share the following information with students:

Graphic aids can help readers understand difficult ideas in stories and articles. *Graphic aids* **include maps, charts, and diagrams. A map shows where places are. A flowchart shows the steps for how to do something. A diagram is a picture with labels.**

Reteach the Skill

Visual Model Have students form groups. Display a large map of Texas. Have groups use the map to plan a road trip they would like to take. They should choose one city or town as a starting point and another as an ending point. Then they should list the main cities they will travel through on the way. Ask a student from each group to name the cities, in order. Trace the route on the map with your finger. Then write a blank flowchart on the board. Have students copy it and fill it in with the sequence of cities they will travel through. Finally, draw on the board the diagram of the suitcase shown below. Have students complete it by labeling the handle, lock, wheels, zipper and outside pocket. Then follow the suggestions in **Summarize/Assess.**

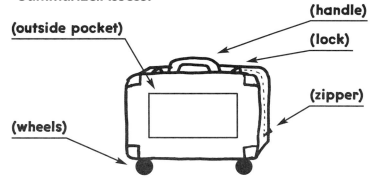

(handle)
(lock)
(outside pocket)
(zipper)
(wheels)

Kinesthetic Model Duplicate one copy of a map of Texas for each student. Help students find Corpus Christi, Houston, Austin, Dallas, and Fort Worth. Write the following directions on the board, and have students trace the route using a crayon or highlighter. *Start in Dallas. Go from Dallas*

to Fort Worth. Go from Fort Worth to Austin. Go from Austin to Houston. Go from Houston to Corpus Christi. Have students use their highlighted maps to create a flowchart showing the order of the cities they passed on the route. Finally, draw the diagram from the Visual Model on the board, putting the labels in a list to one side. Have students copy the diagram and write each label where it belongs. Then follow the suggestions in **Summarize/Assess.**

Auditory Model Duplicate one copy of a map of Texas for each student. Help students find Corpus Christi, Houston, Austin, Dallas, and Fort Worth. Then have students listen and trace the route, using crayon or highlighter, as you read the directions from the Kinesthetic Model. Then have students complete a flowchart by writing the following directions, in sequence, as you say them.

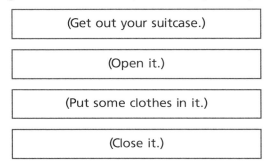

| (Get out your suitcase.) |
| (Open it.) |
| (Put some clothes in it.) |
| (Close it.) |

Finally, duplicate and display the diagram from the Visual Model, including the labels. Have students answer questions such as *What does this diagram show? How many parts of the suitcase are labeled?* Then follow the suggestions in **Summarize/Assess.**

Summarize/Assess

Ask students what maps, diagrams, and flowcharts show. (Maps show where places are. Diagrams show the parts of something. Flowcharts show sequence or steps.) To check students' understanding, have them point out maps and diagrams in their science or social studies textbooks and explain what each one shows.

Contraction

OBJECTIVE
To identify and understand contractions

Focus
Share the following information with students:

A *contraction* is a short way to write two words. When a contraction is formed, one or more letters are left out. An apostrophe (') takes the place of the missing letters. Subject pronouns, such as *I*, *you*, *he*, *she*, *it*, *we*, and *they* are often used in contractions. The negative *not* is often used in a contraction with a verb. The *o* in *not* is replaced by an apostrophe. Using contractions in your writing will make your writing seem more like the way people speak.

Reteach the Skill
Visual Model   Display the following chart:

Contraction	Two Words
he's	he is
they're	they are
it's	it is
can't	cannot

Read the chart with the students and discuss how each contraction was formed from two words. Explain that *cannot* is two words written as a single word. Then have students use each contraction in a sentence. Write their responses on the board and ask a volunteer to rewrite each sentence by replacing the contraction with the appropriate two words. Have students name more contractions, add them to the chart, and repeat the process. Then follow the suggestions in **Summarize/Assess**.

Kinesthetic Model   Have small groups write dialogue for short skits. Tell the groups to write some dialogue containing contractions and some dialogue with pairs of words that could be replaced by contractions. Have student-performers write their lines of dialogue on index cards that they can use as

prompts during their performances. Then have students act out their skits. During the performances, audience members should raise one hand when they hear a contraction and two hands when they hear two words that could be replaced by a contraction. Then follow the suggestions in **Summarize/Assess**.

Auditory Model   Have the students form pairs and ask student partners to give each other an oral quiz. Tell the first partner in each pair to name either a contraction or two words that could be replaced by a contraction. Then have the other partner explain what the contraction stands for or identify the contraction that could be used to replace the two words. Each partner should quiz the other five times and then reverse roles. Then follow the suggestions in **Summarize/Assess**.

Summarize/Assess
Ask students to summarize what they have learned. (*A contraction is a short way to write two words. When a contraction is formed, one or more letters are left out and an apostrophe (') takes the place of the missing letters.*) To reinforce the lesson, have students write a short speech that uses contractions. Ask them to read their speeches to the class.

 # Adverbs

OBJECTIVE

To recognize adverbs in sentences and identify whether they tell when, where, *or* how

Focus

Share the following information with students:

Words that describe verbs are called *adverbs*. An adverb may tell *when*, *where*, or *how* an action takes place.

Reteach the Skill

Visual Model   Display pictures from books, magazines, or catalogs that show people, animals, and objects in action. Point to a picture and have students discuss the actions taking place. Have students suggest words telling *when*, *where*, or *how* about those actions.

Write the following sentences on the board, omitting the words in parentheses:

1. **Kim really enjoys his bike.** (really; how)
2. **Ty wants to eat lunch soon.** (soon; when)
3. **Anna's friends meet there every afternoon.** (there; where)
4. **We ran quickly.** (quickly; how)

Read the first sentence aloud and point out the verb *enjoys*. Point out the adverb *really* and ask students what that adverb tells about the verb. (It tells how.) Work through the remaining examples with students. Then follow the suggestions in **Summarize/Assess**.

Kinesthetic Model   Write the headings *Where*, *When*, and *How* on the board. Write the sentences from the Visual Model and read them aloud. Call on volunteers to identify each adverb and list it under the correct heading.

When	Where	How
soon	there	really
		quickly

Have students look through reading selections, magazines, and other material to find other adverbs to add to the lists. Then follow the suggestions in **Summarize/Assess**.

Auditory Model   Read aloud the sentences from the Visual Model, having students identify the verb and adverb in each sentence. Then write these headings on the board:

Verb	When	Where	How

Ask volunteers to act out and name verbs they use every day. (*eat, run, laugh, play*) As each verb is pantomimed and named, write it on the board in the first column of the chart. Then have students suggest adverbs that could be used to describe that verb. Help students place each adverb under the appropriate heading. Then follow the suggestions in **Summarize/Assess**.

Summarize/Assess

To check students' understanding, ask them to summarize what they have learned. (Words that describe verbs are called adverbs. Adverbs may tell *when*, *where*, or *how* something happens.) Remind students that paying attention to adverbs when they are reading can help them understand and visualize what they read.

Grammar Skill

Comparing with Adverbs

OBJECTIVE

To understand the different forms of adverbs during comparison

Focus

Share the following information with students:

Adverbs **can be used to compare two or more actions. Add** *-er* **to most short adverbs when you compare two actions. Add** *-est* **to most short adverbs when you compare one action with two or more other actions. Instead of adding** *-er* **or** *-est*, **use** *more* **or** *most* **before adverbs that have two or more syllables. Do not use both** *-er* **and** *more* **or both** *-est* **and** *most* **when you compare. Knowing how to compare adverbs correctly will help readers to understand how things are alike and different.**

Reteach the Skill

Visual Model   Display these adverbs:

slow	less slowly
slower	more slowly
slowest	most slowly

Have students read each adverb and use each form in a written sentence. Help them see that *slower* also means *more slowly*, and that *slowest* also means *most slowly*. Have students name other adverbs and write all the comparative forms. Tell them to identify ways in which the same meaning can be correctly written two different ways, such as *quicker* and *more quickly*. Then follow the suggestions in **Summarize/Assess**.

Kinesthetic Model   Have students write an adverb and its two comparative forms on index cards. For example, **fast**, **faster**, **fastest** should be on one card, and each student should prepare three cards in a similar manner. Some suggestions of adverbs for cards are: *slow, loud, gracefully, high, sloppily, happily,* and *soft*. Shuffle and divide the cards among groups of three students. Invite

groups to act out sentences based on the adverb forms on their cards. Have them say their sentences as they perform the actions. Then follow the suggestions in **Summarize/Assess**.

Auditory Model   Read aloud the adverbs from the Visual Model and have students use each adverb in an oral sentence. Then have groups of three work together to create more oral sentences, with one student for each of the three comparative forms, for example: *happily, more happily, most happily.* Help students recognize that, in general, *more* and *most* are used with adverbs containing two or more syllables; *-er* and *-est* are used with shorter adverbs. Then follow the suggestions in **Summarize/Assess**.

Summarize/Assess

Ask students to summarize what they have learned. (*Adverbs* can be used to compare two or more actions. Add *-er* to most short adverbs when you compare two actions. Add *-est* to most short adverbs when you compare one action with two or more other actions. Instead of adding *-er* or *-est*, use *more* or *most* before most adverbs that have two or more syllables. Do not use both *-er* and *more* or both *-est* and *most* when you compare.) To reinforce ideas, have students write a short passage that makes comparisons between two actions and comparisons among three actions.

Oral Reading Fluency

What Is Oral Reading Fluency?

Research recognizes fluency as a strong indicator of efficient and proficient reading. A fluent reader reads orally with accuracy and expression, at a speech-like pace. Oral reading fluency is an assessment of accuracy and rate. It is expressed as the number of words read correctly per minute (WCPM).

Oral reading fluency is an important goal of reading instruction in the elementary grades. If a reader devotes most of his or her attention to pronouncing words, comprehension and meaning will suffer. Students who read fluently can devote more attention to meaning and thus increase comprehension.

The oral reading passage and recording form that follow provide a tool for gathering quantitative information about an individual's oral reading. Use the passages provided in each Teacher's Edition to collect a one-minute sample of a child's oral reading periodically throughout the school year. Track the child's progress and development on the Oral Reading Recording Forms completed and collected throughout the school year.

The passages provided were written with controlled vocabulary and progressive levels of difficulty. The originality of the passages ensures that children will not already be familiar with the content.

Administering the Oral Reading Passage

For administering the assessment you will need
- a stopwatch or a watch with a second hand
- a clean copy of the passage for the child to read
- a copy of the Recording Form version of the same passage to mark as the child reads

1. Explain the task. The child is to read the passage aloud, beginning and ending with your signals.
2. Use a stopwatch to time a one-minute interval inconspicuously. Tell the child when to begin and

when to end reading. Put a slash mark on the Recording Form after the last word the child reads.

3. As the child reads, record reading errors unobtrusively on the Recording Form. Mark mispronunciations, substitutions, omissions of a sound or word, and other errors. Do not count repetitions or self-corrections as reading errors.

Scoring the Oral Reading Fluency Rate

Complete the Oral Reading Fluency Form and save it. Use the completed forms to track growth and progress throughout the school year and to share the results with parents or guardians.

To Compute the Fluency Rate

1. Total the number of words the child read in one minute.
2. Total the number of reading errors the child made.
3. Subtract the number of reading errors from the number of words read to get the total words read correctly per minute (WCPM).

Total Words Read Per Minute _____

Number of Errors _____

Number of Words Read Correctly (WCPM)

_____

Interpreting the Oral Reading Fluency Rate

See the tables of norms provided in the *Oral Reading Fluency Assessment* to make a normative interpretation of a student's oral reading fluency score. Children who read significantly below the oral reading fluency norms will need additional word recognition instruction, more frequent monitoring of performance, and building fluency strategies such as repeated reading, echo reading, tape assisted reading, and partner reading.

Oral Reading Passage

Ants are amazing insects. They work together
to build their anthill, to get their food, and to guard
their queen ant. Each ant has its own job to do,
but they all work together. The ants even fight together
if other ants try to steal their food.

An anthill has several rooms, with tunnels leading
from one room to another. In one special room the
queen ant lays her eggs. The ants use some of the
other rooms for storing their food.

During the day the ants go out to gather food.
Picnics are one favorite place for ants to collect food.
Little morsels of food dropped by the people make
a big meal for the tiny ants. They carry the morsels
of food they find on the ground back to their anthill.
They feed the queen ant and store the rest of the
food to use later.

Oral Reading Fluency Recording Form

Child _____   Date _____

Word Count 148

Ants are amazing insects. They work together	**7**
to build their anthill, to get their food, and to guard	**18**
their queen ant. Each ant has its own job to do,	**29**
but they all work together. The ants even fight together	**39**
if other ants try to steal their food.	**47**
An anthill has several rooms, with tunnels leading	**55**
from one room to another. In one special room the	**65**
queen ant lays her eggs. The ants use some of the	**76**
other rooms for storing their food.	**82**
During the day the ants go out to gather food.	**92**
Picnics are one favorite place for ants to collect food.	**102**
Little morsels of food dropped by the people make	**111**
a big meal for the tiny ants. They carry the morsels	**122**
of food they find on the ground back to their anthill.	**133**
They feed the queen ant and store the rest of the	**144**
food to use later.	**148**

Fluency Score

Total Words Read Per Minute _____

Number of Errors _____

Number of Words Read Correctly (WCPM) _____

Fluency Routine Card 1
Echo Reading

1. Have students turn to the first page and point to the beginning of the sentence.
2. Read the sentence aloud as students track the print.
3. Then have students track the print and read the sentence aloud by themselves, matching your intonation and expression.
4. Continue through the rest of the selection.

Fluency Routine Card 2
Choral Reading

1. Tell students to track the print of the selection and read with you.
2. Remind students to use the same expression and intonation as you do.
3. Organize students into groups and assign groups alternating pages, verses, or lines.
4. Read the selection aloud, having students read their assigned parts along with you. Be sure they track the print as they read.

Fluency Routine Card 3
Partner Reading

1. Have students work with a partner.
2. As the first student reads the selected text aloud, the partner should listen actively and follow along.
3. Partners should provide word-identification assistance as needed.
4. At the end of the reading, listening partners should provide feedback on fluency behaviors.
5. Have partners switch roles and repeat the procedure.

Fluency Routine Card 4
Tape-Assisted Reading

1. Set up a listening center with headphones and a cassette or CD player, so that students may work independently.
2. As students listen to an audio recording of the selected text, they should follow along as they track the print.
3. Have students replay the recording. This time the student should subvocalize, or read aloud quietly, imitating the expression and phrasing of the recording.

Once students are confident that they can read the text fluently, have them read it orally to you. Provide feedback as needed.

Harcourt

Fluency Routine Card 5
Repeated Reading

1. Have students choose a section of the text on which to time their reading.
2. The student should read the passage aloud once, untimed.
3. The student should then use a stopwatch to time the second reading.
4. The student then sets a goal for an improved time.
5. The student then repeats the reading about three or four times until the goal is met.

Provide students with a chart on which to keep track of number of words read and time taken. You may use this information to calculate number of words per minute.

Fluency Routine Card 6
Phrase-Cued Reading

1. Select a short passage of about one hundred words at the student's independent reading level.
2. Mark with slashes the natural pauses between phrases.
3. Have students read aloud, using the slashes as guides to appropriate "chunking" or phrasing of the text.
4. Have students reread the phrase-cued text several times.
5. Provide another copy of the text, but without the slashes. Have students read aloud and compare their final reading with their first.

See also Fluency Builder pages in the *Intervention Practice Book.*

Fluency Routine Card 7
Readers Theatre

Tell students that in Readers Theatre readers use only their voices to bring text to life, and no memorization is needed. Over the course of several days, they will practice reading their parts and finally perform for an audience.

Preparing to Read   Provide each student with a copy of the script. Read the script aloud, modeling fluent and expressive reading as students follow along.

Discuss with students how a particular character might feel or act, and how the character might sound.

1. Organize students into groups and assign a role to each student in the group. You may choose to have students exchange roles for each rereading, so that they will have read the entire script by the end of the week.
2. Have students assume their roles and read the script.
3. Circulate among the groups, providing feedback and support.
4. On the assigned day, have each group perform their reading before an audience. You may choose to invite special guests, such as parents or the principal, to the reading.

16. **What do you think the narrator means when she says that she and the man spoke a language that no one else could understand?** (Possible answer: She thought they had understood each other like no one else could.)

17. **Why do you think New Year's Day is not special to the narrator?** (Possible answer: Nothing wonderful ever happened to her on that day before.)

18. **What are you thinking about now?** (Possible answer: I would like to see the beginning of spring where she is.)

---------------------------------- FOLD ----------------------------------

▶ **Think Along**   **COMPREHENSION CARD** (26)

I'm in Charge of Celebrations

You may wish to have students respond to the Think-Along questions in writing in their Response Journals.

1. **How do you think the narrator will answer the question about being lonely? Why?** (Possible answer: She will say she is not lonely, because she knows the desert.)

2. **Why does the narrator laugh?** (Possible answer: She can't understand why other people would think the desert was a lonely place.)

3. **How do you think the narrator feels about celebrations? Explain.** (Possible answer: She feels that they are important, but you have to be very excited for it to be a celebration.)

4. **What do you think is going to happen next?** (Possible answer: She is going to want to dance with the dust devil.)

5. **What are you thinking about?** (Possible answer: Seeing a dust devil would be very exciting.)

6. **Is there anything in your life that once you start you can't stop? What is it?** (Possible answer: Sometimes when I laugh I can't stop, and when I try to it makes me laugh even more.)

7. **What do you think the rabbit would do if it saw the narrator?** (Possible answer: It would probably run away.)

8. **What celebration would you like to invent? Why?** (Possible answer: Responses will vary.)

9. **Why did the narrator want to celebrate seeing the green cloud?** (Possible answer: It was very rare and beautiful.)

10. **How do you think the narrator might have met the coyote?** (Possible answer: They were walking on the same path.)

11. **What are you thinking about now?** (Possible answer: I am thinking that I would be afraid that the coyote might not be friendly.)

12. **How might meeting the coyote have changed the narrator's life?** (Possible answer: She felt really close to nature that day and wanted to keep feeling that way.)

13. **Why might the narrator think that eating in that place would make the celebration even better?** (Possible answer: Maybe she hopes the coyote will come back and eat with her.)

14, 15. **What words might describe how the narrator felt after she saw the fireball?** (Possible answer: happy, thankful, peaceful)

Harcourt

After Reading

4. What was the author's message? Which story events helped you get the message?

5. What part was
- the funniest?
- the saddest?
- the most exciting?

6. Think of another story you have read. How are the themes the same? How are they different?

----------FOLD----------

During Reading

1. From what you have read so far, what do you think the story is mostly about?

2. What point is the author trying to make? Why do you think that?

3. What do you remember most about the story so far?

Harcourt

of motion move out from the center of where an earth-quake happens.)

10. p. 358, line 4: To establish how a tsunami differs from an ordinary wave: **This picture shows a huge wave, and the author says "this is no ordinary wave." What does he mean by that?** (Possible response: The wave in the picture is a tsunami and was caused by an earthquake. Most ordinary waves, however, are caused by wind moving over water.)

11. p. 360, line 7: To establish that there are three kinds of mountains and that one was described earlier in the text: **The author says there are three kinds of mountains. The first kind, fold mountains, sound like what he told us about before: fold mountains are made when plates push into each other. Let's read to find out about the other two kinds of mountains.**

12. p. 361, line 4: To reinforce how the other two kinds of mountains are formed: **How are the two other kinds of mountains formed?** (Possible response: Magma pushes up under the crust to form dome mountains. Crust gets pushed up between cracks in a plate to form block mountains.

13. p. 361, column 2, line 10: To connect the plate's movement with Mt. Everest's growing taller: **The earth's plate where India is must still be moving and making Mt. Everest a little higher every year. That must be what the author means by "It's still growing."**

14. p. 362, line 10: To establish how a river carves a valley: **How does the author explain what rivers do to land?** (Possible response: Pebbles in the river rub against the land and wear it away.)

15. p. 363, line 5: To explain how some rocks remain: **How does the author explain why some rocks are left?** (Possible response: Some rocks are harder than others, and they don't get worn down as fast.)

16. p. 363, line 14: To establish that the wind causes erosion: **What does it mean that the answer is "blowing in the wind"?** (Possible response: Even though the river is gone, land is still being worn away by particles in the wind.)

mountains.

---FOLD---

Rocking and Rolling

Key Understanding: The earth has been formed and continues to be formed by forces such as water, wind, and the movement of plates.

1. p. 352, line 10: To establish how very deep the earth is and how extremely hot it is: **What's the author trying to tell us about our earth?** (Possible response: The author is letting us know that it's a very long distance (3,960 miles) from the crust of the earth to its center. The center is almost as hot as the sun.)

2. p. 353, line 15: To establish the characteristics of the four layers of the earth: **How does what the author tells us about the earth's layers connect to the picture?** (Possible response: The author describes the four layers. The crust is made of rock. The mantle is also rock, but it's so hot that some of it has melted. There are an inner and an outer core that are made of metal, and they are both very hot.)

3. p. 354, line 4: To clarify that the earth is made up of "pieces," draw students' attention to the big picture on page 354 and ask: **What is the author trying to tell us about the earth when he says that it is like a jigsaw puzzle?** (Possible response: The earth is made up of big pieces, called plates, that fit together.)

4. p. 354, line 15: To establish one of the consequences of the movement of the earth's plates: **The author says that gooey magma sometimes comes up through the earth. What makes that happen?** (Possible response: When the

earth's plates move apart, the magma comes up to fill the space between the cracks.)

5. p. 355, line 6: To clarify the picture: **The illustrator is trying to show that the land on our planet is moving.**

6. p. 355, line 13: To establish another consequence of plate movement: **Before we learned that sometimes when plates move, gooey magma comes up between them. Now what else has the author told us might happen when plates move?** (Possible response: If plates push into each other, a range of mountains can form.)

7. p. 356, line 13: To clarify why an earthquake occurs: **Here the author is telling us that sometimes a plate can move suddenly, and that makes an earthquake.**

8. p. 357, line 5: To help students understand the "ripples in a pond" analogy: **The author talks about "the ripples from a stone thrown into a pond." What does that mean?** (Possible response: When you throw a stone into water, waves move out from it in circles.)

9. p. 357, line 5: To help students understand the motion set off by an earthquake: **How do "ripples from a pond" connect with feeling an earthquake?** (Possible response: Circles

Harcourt

After Reading

3. Did the author do a good job of informing, entertaining, explaining, or persuading? Tell why you think as you do.

4. What question would you ask the author about his or her purpose for writing this selection?

▶ **Author's Purpose**   **COMPREHENSION CARD** 29

---FOLD---

▶ **Author's Purpose**   **COMPREHENSION CARD** 29

During Reading

1. Do you think the author wrote this selection
   - ■ to inform?
   - ■ to entertain?
   - ■ to explain?
   - ■ to persuade?

2. What clues from the story helped you decide the author's purpose?

Harcourt

After Reading

4. Look at your questions. Which ones did you find the answers to?

5. What was the most interesting thing you learned?

6. From reading this selection, what else might you want to find out about this topic? Where might you look to find the answers?

---FOLD---

▶ Reading Nonfiction   COMPREHENSION CARD 30

Before Reading

1. What is the topic of this selection?

2. What do you already know about this topic? Make a list.

During Reading

3. What do you want to learn about this topic? Write your questions. As you read, try to find the answers to your questions.

Harcourt

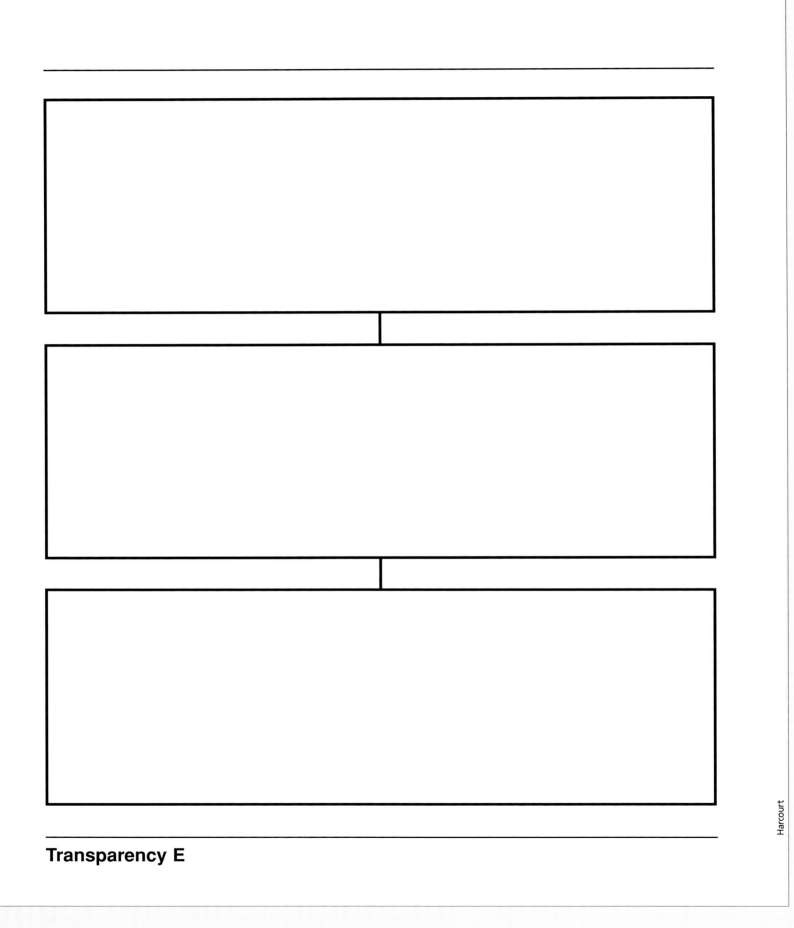

Harcourt

Transparency F

Transparency G

Harcourt

Using Student Rubrics

A rubric is a tool a teacher can use to score a student's work. A rubric lists the criteria for evaluating the work, and it describes different levels of success in meeting those criteria. Rubrics are useful assessment tools for teachers, but they can be just as useful for students. In fact, rubrics can be powerful teaching tools.

Before Writing

- When you **introduce** students to **a new kind of writing** through a writing model, discuss the criteria listed on the rubric, and ask students to decide how well the model meets each criterion. Have students add to the rubric other criteria they think are important.

- Before students attempt a new kind of writing, have them focus on the **criteria for excellence** listed on the rubric so that they have specific goals to aim for.

During Writing and Editing

- As students are **prewriting** and **drafting**, have them refer to the rubric for important aspects of organization and elaboration that they need to include in their writing.

- When students are ready to **revise**, have them check their writing against the rubric to determine if there are any aspects of organization and elaboration that they can improve.

- As students **proofread**, the rubric will remind them to pay attention to grammar, usage, punctuation, and sentence variety. You may wish to have individual students add to their rubrics, depending on particular language problems they have demonstrated.

After Writing

- The rubric can be used by individuals to **score their own writing** or by pairs or small groups for peer assessment. Students can highlight the parts of the rubric that they believe apply to a piece of writing.

- Students can keep the marked rubric in their portfolios with the piece of writing it refers to. The marked rubrics will help students **see their progress** through the school year. In conferences with students and family members, you can refer to the rubrics to point out both strengths and weaknesses.

	Score of 4	Score of 3	Score of 2	Score of 1
FOCUS/IDEAS	The paper is completely focused on the task and has a clear purpose.	The paper is generally focused on the task and the purpose.	The paper is somewhat focused on the task and purpose.	The paper does not have a clear focus or a purpose.
ORGANIZATION/PARAGRAPHS	The narrative has a clear beginning, middle, and ending. The ideas and details are presented in logical order. The writer groups related ideas in paragraphs. The paper seems complete.	The ideas and details are mostly presented in logical order. The writer usually groups related ideas in paragraphs.	The organization is not clear in some places.	The paper has little or no organization.
DEVELOPMENT	The sequence of events in the narrative is fully developed.	The sequence of events is developed.	The sequence of events is somewhat developed.	The paper does not have a sequence of events.
VOICE	The writer's viewpoint is clear. The writer uses creative and original phrases and expressions where appropriate.	The writer's viewpoint is somewhat clear. The writer uses some original phrases and expressions.	The writer's viewpoint is unclear.	The writer seems uninterested in what he or she is writing about.
WORD CHOICE	The writer uses colorful words and phrases. The writing is very descriptive and detailed.	The writer uses some colorful words and phrases.	The writer does not use many colorful words or phrases.	There are very few details and very little description.
SENTENCES	The writer uses a variety of sentences. The writing flows smoothly.	The writer uses some variety in sentences.	The writer does not use much variety in his or her sentences.	There is little or no variety in sentences. Some of the sentences are unclear.
CONVENTIONS	There are few or no errors in grammar, punctuation, capitalization, and spelling.	There are a few errors in grammar, punctuation, capitalization, and spelling.	There are some errors in grammar, punctuation, capitalization, and spelling.	There are many errors in grammar, punctuation, capitalization, and spelling.

Harcourt

SCORING RUBRIC FOR WRITING

	Score of 6	Score of 5	Score of 4	Score of 3	Score of 2	Score of 1
	☆☆☆☆☆☆	☆☆☆☆☆	☆☆☆☆	☆☆☆	☆☆	☆
FOCUS	The writing is completely focused on the topic and has a clear purpose.	The writing is focused on the topic and purpose.	The writing is generally focused on the topic and purpose.	The writing is somewhat focused on the topic and purpose.	The writing is related to the topic but does not have a clear focus.	The writing is not focused on the topic and purpose.
ORGANIZATION	The ideas in the paper are well-organized and presented in logical order. The paper seems complete to the reader.	The organization of the paper is mostly clear. The paper seems complete.	The organization is mostly clear, but the paper may seem unfinished.	The paper is somewhat organized, but seems unfinished.	There is little organization to the paper.	There is no organization to the paper.
SUPPORT	The writing has strong, specific details. The word choices are clear and fresh.	The writing has strong, specific details and clear word choices.	The writing has supporting details and some variety in word choice.	The writing has few supporting details. It needs more variety in word choice.	The writing uses few supporting details and word choices are unclear.	The writing uses few supporting details. The word choices are unclear.
CONVENTIONS	The writer uses a variety of sentences. There are few or no errors in grammar, spelling, punctuation, and capitalization.	The writer uses a variety of sentences. There are few errors in grammar, spelling, punctuation, and capitalization.	The writer uses some variety in sentences. There are a few errors in grammar, spelling, punctuation, and capitalization.	The writer uses simple sentences. There are some errors in grammar, spelling, punctuation, and capitalization.	The writer uses simple sentences. There are many errors in grammar, spelling, punctuation, and capitalization.	The writer uses unclear sentences. There are many errors in grammar, spelling, punctuation, and capitalization.

Harcourt

	Score of 6	Score of 5	Score of 4	Score of 3	Score of 2	Score of 1
	☆☆☆☆☆☆	☆☆☆☆☆	☆☆☆☆	☆☆☆	☆☆	☆
HANDWRITING	The slant of the letters is the same throughout the whole paper. The letters are clearly formed and the spacing between words is equal, which makes the text very easy to read.	The slant of the letters is almost the same through most of the paper. The letters are clearly formed. The spacing between words is usually equal.	The slant of the letters is usually the same. The letters are clearly formed most of the time. The spacing between words is usually equal.	The handwriting is readable. There are some differences in letter shape and form, slant, and spacing that make some words easier to read than others.	The handwriting is somewhat readable. There are many differences in letter shape and form, slant, and spacing that make some words hard to read.	The letters are not formed correctly. The slant and spacing are not the same throughout the paper, or there is no regular space between words. The paper is very difficult to read.
WORD PROCESSING	Fonts and sizes are used very well, which helps the reader enjoy reading the text.	Fonts and sizes are used well.	Fonts and sizes are used fairly well, but could be improved upon.	Fonts and sizes are used well in some places, but make the paper look cluttered in others.	Fonts and sizes are not used well. The paper looks cluttered.	The writer has used too many different fonts and sizes. It is very distracting to the reader.
MARKERS	The title, side heads, page numbers, and bullets are used very well. They make it easy for the reader to find information in the text. These markers clearly show how the writer organized the information.	The title, side heads, page numbers and bullets are used well. They help the reader find information.	The title, side heads, page numbers and bullets are used fairly well. They usually help the reader find information.	The writer uses some markers such as a title, page numbers, or bullets. However, the use of markers could be improved upon to help the reader get more meaning from the text.	The writer uses very few markers. This makes it hard for the reader to find and understand the information in the text.	There are no markers such as a title, page numbers, bullets, or side heads.
VISUALS	The writer uses visuals such as illustrations, charts, graphs, maps, and tables very well. The text and visuals clearly relate to each other.	The writer uses visuals well. The text and visuals relate to each other.	The writer uses visuals fairly well.	The writer uses visuals with the text, but the reader may not understand how they are related.	The writer tries to use visuals with the text, but the reader is confused by them.	The visuals do not make sense with the text.
SPEAKING	The speaker uses very effective pacing, volume, intonation, and expression.	The speaker uses effective pacing, volume, intonation, and expression.	The speaker uses mostly effective pacing, volume, intonation, and expression.	The speaker uses somewhat effective pacing, volume, intonation, and expression.	The speaker needs to work on pacing, volume, intonation, and expression.	The speaker's techniques are unclear or distracting to the listener.

Harcourt

I'm in Charge of Celebrations	Alejandro's Gift
signal	windmill
celebrations	cherished
choosy	furrows
average	ample
tracks	shunned
admiring	growth

Harcourt

Rocking and Rolling	Armadillo from Amarillo
magma	eventually
edges	converse
range	continent
epicenter	sphere
coast (n.)	universe
peak (n.)	homeward

Harcourt

Visitors from Space	
force	
nucleus	
loops	
solar wind	
particles	
fluorescent	

Harcourt

 # School–Home Connection

Your child is reading "I'm in Charge of Celebrations" by Byrd Baylor. In this narrative poem, a young girl creates holidays to celebrate the many special, wondrous natural events she witnesses in the American Southwest desert. You may enjoy discussing this poem and doing these activities with your child. Together you can develop and explore your child's language skills.

Nature Tales

Ask your child to tell you about some of the natural events the young girl celebrates in the poem. Look for these additional nature books in your local library:

- *Deserts* by Neil Morris. Raintree Steck-Vaughn, 1997.
- *By the Blazing Blue Sea* by S.T. Garne. Harcourt Brace, 1999.
- *Desert Voices* by Byrd Baylor. Scribner's, 1981.

AT THE LIBRARY

Vocabulary Lookout

The following words are new vocabulary your child has learned while reading "I'm in Charge of Celebrations":

signal	choosy
celebrations	average
tracks	admiring

To reinforce meanings, ask your child to choose one word each day of the week and use it as many times as possible throughout that day. Record the number of times your child uses each word correctly.

Let's Celebrate

Talk with your child about some of the special days that are celebrated in your home and in your community. If possible, take your child to a community celebration and talk about what is being celebrated and why. Then invite your child to ask family members and friends about the ways they like to celebrate their special days and to note the ways the celebrations are similar and different. Encourage your child to write what she or he has learned in a notebook.

Harcourt

 TIME TO READ Encourage your child to read for at least 30 minutes outside of class each day.

Visit *The Learning Site!* www.harcourtschool.com

 # School-Home Connection

Your child is reading "Alejandro's Gift," a story about a lonely man named Alejandro, who digs a water hole for the desert animals that live near his home. The animals stay away because the hole is too near Alejandro's house, so he digs a second hole that is more sheltered. In the end, he is no longer lonely. You may wish to work with your child to complete these activities as a way to develop your child's language skills.

Discuss Desert Details

Invite your child to describe what Alejandro's life was like. Prompt your child with questions such as these: What kind of home did Alejandro live in? Where was it? What kinds of plants were around his house? How did Alejandro get water? You and your child might also enjoy reading other fiction and nonfiction books about the desert.

VOCABULARY

Concentration

Have your child write each of these words on a separate index card:

windmill   cherished
furrows   ample
shunned   growth

Then work with your child to create sentences about the story for each word. Write the sentences on another set of cards, but leave a blank where the word should go. Then play Concentration with both sets of cards, placing the word cards face down in a row on one side of a table and the sentences face down on the other side. Ask your child to turn over a word card and a sentence card, read aloud both cards, and tell if the word belongs in the blank. If it does, remove both cards; if not, turn the cards face down again. Play until all cards are matched.

Harcourt

TIME TO READ   Encourage your child to read for at least 30 minutes outside of class each day.

Retell the Story

Invite your child to retell "Alejandro's Gift" in his or her own words. Then ask your child what he or she thinks are the three most important parts of the story. Ask your child to draw three pictures to show the order of these events. Then help your child write a sentence telling about each picture. Suggest that he or she begin each sentence with a word that shows the order in which the events happened, such as *first, next,* and *finally.*

Visit *The Learning Site!*
www.harcourtschool.com

School–Home Connection

Your child is reading "Rocking and Rolling" by Philip Steele. This nonfiction article tells what lies under the Earth's surface and how the forces of nature have shaped the Earth's features. As you and your child talk about these processes and try these activities together, you will be developing and exploring your child's language skills.

Read All About It

Help your child read and discuss other books about the Earth's land. Look for books like these in your local library:

- *A Walk Up the Mountain* by Caroline Arnold. Silver, 1990.
- *Volcanoes* by Keith Lye. Raintree Steck-Vaughn, 1993.
- *Our Earth* by Anne Rockwell. Harcourt Brace, 1998.

VOCABULARY

Word of the Day

While reading "Rocking and Rolling," your child has learned the following new words:

magma	epicenter
edges	coast
range	peak

You and your child might enjoy this game. Each day, choose one word as the Word of the Day, and discuss its meaning. Every time a family member uses the word correctly, he or she earns a point. The person with the most points at the end of the week is the champion.

Being Prepared

Help your child create a poster that lists what family members should do if a natural disaster strikes your area. Your child may want to take the poster to school to exchange ideas with other students after reading "Rocking and Rolling."

Harcourt

 TIME TO READ Encourage your child to read for at least 30 minutes outside of class each day.

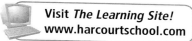
Visit *The Learning Site!*
www.harcourtschool.com

School–Home Connection

Your child is reading "The Armadillo from Amarillo" by Lynne Cherry. This fantasy is about an armadillo named Sasparillo, who wonders how big the world is and where his place is in it. The story teaches children about geography. You may enjoy discussing the story and doing these activities with your child. Together you and your child can enrich his or her language skills.

Reading Together

Your child may enjoy reading with you other award-winning books written and illustrated by Lynne Cherry. You may be able to find the following books and several others in your local library:

- *A River Ran Wild.* Harcourt Brace, 1992.
- *The Great Kapok Tree.* Harcourt Brace, 1990.
- *Flute's Journey.* Harcourt Brace, 1997.

VOCABULARY

Vocabulary Practice

The following words are new vocabulary your child has learned while reading "The Armadillo from Amarillo":

eventually	converse
continent	sphere
universe	homeward

Discuss when you might use or hear these words. During the week, to encourage your child to use the words, ask questions such as these: Where in the *universe* would you travel if you were an astronaut? When do you *converse* with your classmates?

TIME TO READ Encourage your child to read for at least 30 minutes outside of class each day.

Let's Take a Trip

Talk with your child about a trip you have taken or would like to take. Tell him or her what you learned about the place, why you wanted to go there, how you got there, and what happened on your journey. If you have mementos or photographs of your trip, share them with your child. Encourage your child to ask you questions and to share his or her ideas for a trip.

Visit *The Learning Site!* www.harcourtschool.com

Harcourt

 # School–Home Connection

Your child is reading "Visitors from Space" by Jeanne Bendick. This nonfiction selection explains why comets have tails, how comets orbit the sun, and much more. You may enjoy discussing the selection and doing these activities with your child. Together you can develop and explore your child's language skills.

Explore the Solar System

Talk about the solar system with your child. To find more information that you can explore together, look for these books in your local library:

- *The Magic School Bus Lost in the Solar System* by Joanna Cole. Scholastic, 1990.
- *Moons and Rings: Companions to the Planets* by Jeanne Bendick. Millbrook, 1991.
- *Comets and Shooting Stars* by Patrick Moore. Copper Beech, 1994.

VOCABULARY

Space Words

The following words are new vocabulary your child has learned while reading "Visitors from Space":

force	loops
nucleus	particles
solar wind	fluorescent

Discuss with your child how these words relate to comets and our solar system. Together you might think of other ways these words are used; for example, the *force* of the wind, *loops* around a track, *fluorescent* paint.

View the Night Sky

If possible, visit a planetarium with your child or view the sky on a clear night. You might also check out books on astronomy from a library. Have your child draw a picture of what he or she observes, such as the Moon or the Big Dipper. Help him or her label the picture with the date, the place, the time, and a brief caption. Your child can later share the night sky picture with classmates.

Harcourt

 TIME TO READ Encourage your child to read for at least 30 minutes outside of class each day.

 Visit *The Learning Site!* www.harcourtschool.com

SCHOOL-HOME CONNECTION

Additional Reading
On Your Mark

This list is a compilation of the additional theme- and topic-related books cited in the lesson plans. You may wish to use this list to provide students with opportunities to read at least thirty minutes a day outside of class.

THEME 3: CELEBRATE OUR WORLD

Ata, Te. *Baby Rattlesnake.* Children's Press, 1989. Willful Baby Rattlesnake throws tantrums to get his rattle before he's ready. When he misuses it, he learns a lesson. EASY

Baylor, Byrd. *Desert Voices.* Scribner's, 1981. Desert inhabitants describe the beauty of their home. ☃ *ALA Notable Book; Outstanding Science Trade Book.* CHALLENGING

Baylor, Byrd. *The Desert Is Theirs.* Aladdin, 1987. Simple text and illustrations describe the characteristics of the desert and its plant, animal, and human life. ☃ *Caldecott Honor; ALA Notable Book; Children's Choice.* AVERAGE

Bendick, Jeanne, et al. *Moons and Rings: Companions to the Planets.* Millbrook, 1991. Provides answers to children's questions about the moon. What is it made of? What does it do? What keeps it up in the sky? Do other planets have a moon? What are rings? AVERAGE

Bendick, Jeanne. *The Planets: Neighbors in Space.* Millbrook, 1991. An introduction to each of the planets, including how they compare to Earth. AVERAGE

Brett, Jan. *Armadillo Rodeo.* Putnam, 1995. Bo, an adventurous armadillo, scares himself up some trouble when his poor vision causes him to mistake a pair of cowboy boots for another armadillo. AVERAGE

Butler, Daphne. *What Happens When Volcanoes Erupt?* Raintree Steck-Vaughn, 1996. Questions about volcanoes are answered through illustrations, definitions, and explanations. EASY

Cherry, Lynne. *A River Ran Wild.* Harcourt Brace, 1997. An environmental history of the Nashua River, from its discovery by Indians through the polluting years of the Industrial Revolution to the ambitious clean-up that revitalized it. ☃ *Children's Choice; Notable Social Studies Trade Book; Outstanding Science Trade Book.* CHALLENGING

Chesworth, Michael. *Archibald Frisby.* Farrar, Straus & Giroux, 1994. Archibald Frisby, mad about science and wise beyond his years, is sent to camp to have fun and ends up broadening the horizons of his fellow campers. AVERAGE

Cole, Joanna. *The Magic School Bus: Inside the Earth.* Scholastic, 1989. On a special field trip in the magic school bus, Ms. Frizzle's class learns first hand about different kinds of rocks and the formation of the earth. AVERAGE

Fowler, Allan. *So That's How the Moon Changes Shape.* Children's Press, 1991. A simple explanation of the moon and why it changes shape throughout the month. EASY

Garne, S.T. *By a Blazing Blue Sea.* Harcourt, 1999. A rhyming description of the simple and colorful life of a Caribbean fisherman. EASY

George, Jean Craighead. *One Day in the Desert.* HarperCollins, 1996. Explains how the animal and human inhabitants of the Sonoran Desert of Arizona, including a mountain lion, a roadrunner, a coyote, a tortoise, and members of the Papago Indian tribe, adapt and survive the desert's merciless heat. CHALLENGING

Guiberson, Brenda Z. *Cactus Hotel.* Henry Holt, 1991. Describes the life cycle of the giant saguaro cactus, with an emphasis on its role as a home for other desert dwellers. ☃ *Teachers' Choice; Outstanding Science Trade Book; Parents' Choice.* EASY

King-Smith, Dick. *Dick King-Smith's Animal Friends: Thirty-One True Life Stories.* Candlewick, 1996. A collection of anecdotes about the author's encounters with animals beginning with his first elephant ride at the zoo and continuing through his years as a dairy farmer. AVERAGE

Locker, Thomas. *Water Dance.* Harcourt Brace, 1997. Water speaks of its existence in such forms as storm clouds, mist, rainbows, and rivers. Includes factual information on the water cycle. ☃ *Teachers' Choice; Outstanding Science Trade Book; Notable Children's Book in the Language Arts.* CHALLENGING

Morris, Neil. *Deserts.* Steck-Vaughn, 1997. Presents information about the location, features, and human and animal inhabitants of the ten largest deserts in the world, including the Sahara, Taklamakan, Sonoran, and Thar. CHALLENGING

Noble, Trinka Hakes. *Jimmy's Boa Bounces Back.* Dutton, 1992. A pet boa constrictor wreaks havoc on a posh garden party. ☃ *Children's Choice.* EASY

Pfister, Marcus. *Sun and Moon.* North-South, 1990. The Sun and Moon are sad and lonely until an eclipse lets them spend some time together. EASY

Phinney, Margaret Yatsevitch. *Exploring Land Habitats.* Mondo, 1994. Describes several different animal habitats such as the Amazon rainforest, Sonoran desert, and Canadian tundra. CHALLENGING

Rockwell, Anne. *Our Earth.* Harcourt Brace, 1998. A simple introduction to geography which explains such things as how the earth was shaped, how islands are born from volcanoes, and how gushing springs affect rivers. ☃ *Notable Social Studies Trade Book.* EASY

Ryan, Pam Muñoz. *Armadillos Sleep in Dugouts & Other Places Animals Live.* Disney, 1997. Examines the different types of homes animals make, including those of river otters, peregrine falcons, and two-toed sloths. AVERAGE

Simon, Seymour. *Comets, Meteors, and Asteroids.* Mulberry, 1994. Explores how comets, meteors, and asteroids move through our solar system. ☃ *Outstanding Science Trade Book.* CHALLENGING

Simon, Seymour. *Earthquakes.* Mulberry, 1995. Examines the phenomenon of earthquakes describing how and where they occur, how they can be predicted, and how much damage they can inflict. CHALLENGING

Steele, Philip. *The Egyptians and the Valley of the Kings.* Dillon, 1994. A glimpse at Howard Carter's remarkable find of Tutankhamen's tomb in Egypt's Valley of the Kings. CHALLENGING

Welsbacher, Anne. *The Earth.* Abdo & Daughters, 1997. Discusses our planet's atmosphere, land forms, seasons, weather, life forms, and constantly changing nature. AVERAGE

Teacher Notes

Celebrate Our World
Additional Resources

Writer's Handbook

Contents

419

Writer's Handbook

Introducing the Handbook

Teach/Model

Preview the handbook by focusing on the Table of Contents on page 419 of the *Pupil Edition.* Model as follows:

Model   Begin by saying: **Good writing is not just luck. There are steps to learning how to be a better writer. The Table of Contents shows you the main ideas about writing that are found in this handbook. The ideas are about ways to find information, organize it, and turn it into writing that is clear and interesting to read. I use these ideas to improve my own writing, and you can, too.**

Practice/Apply

Have students first read aloud the five major subheads, then go back and read the section topics under each subhead. Ask students to identify the page(s) on which each topic can be found.

Planning your Writing

Purposes for Writing

There are many different purposes for writing. You might be asked to write **to inform, to respond to something you read, to entertain or express feelings,** or **to persuade.** Sometimes you may write for more than one purpose. For example, when writing a friendly letter, you may write to inform the reader about an event and to express your feelings about the event. Before you write, it is important that you think about the task, the audience, and the purpose for writing. Ask yourself these questions:

Task
What am I going
to write?

Audience
Who will read this?

Purpose
Why am I writing?

Remember as you are writing to be creative and have fun with your topic. Place yourself in the place of your audience and ask yourself, "What can I write about this topic that will excite my audience?"

Expository Writing

The purpose for expository writing is to inform. This kind of writing explains something. Examples of expository writing are how-to essays, descriptive paragraphs, and research reports.

Sample prompt: *Explain how to get to your house from your school.*

> **Tips for Expository Writing**
> - Write a topic sentence that tells the main idea or what you are explaining.
> - Organize the information into paragraphs that tell about one idea.
> - Use vivid, descriptive language and specific details to convey your interest in the topic to your readers.

Literary Response

When you write to respond to something you have read, your purpose is to show that you understand the passage or selection.

420

> **Tips for Literary Response**
> - Write a topic sentence that answers the question.
> - Use your own experience and details from the selection to support your topic sentence.
> - Restate your main idea in the conclusion.

Expressive Writing

The purpose for expressive writing is to share your feelings or to entertain. Sometimes expressive writing describes something. Examples of expressive writing are personal narratives, stories, and poems.

Sample prompt: *There are many things to do on a rainy day. Think about what you would do on a rainy day. Now write a story about what you did on a rainy day.*

> **Tips for Expressive Writing**
> - Introduce yourself or your characters.
> - Use your personal voice to describe what you are writing about.
> - Include as many details about what you or your characters see, hear, touch, taste, and smell to draw your reader into the story.
> - Have an ending that makes sense.

Persuasive Writing

The purpose of persuasive writing is to persuade readers to agree with your opinions or to take action.

Sample prompt: *Imagine that you want to convince your parents to let you have a sleep over. Write a persuasive paragraph that gives reasons why having a sleep over is a good idea.*

> **Tips for Persuasive Writing**
> - Have an interesting beginning that explains your opinion.
> - Give at least three reasons why you feel the way you do.
> - In your conclusion, restate your opinion or ask your reader to take action.

> **Try This**
> What would be the purpose for each of these kinds of writing: a telephone message, a joke, a recipe, and an advertisement?

421

Purposes for Writing

Teach/Model

Remind students of the three basic prewriting questions that they should always keep in mind: *Who will read this? What am I going to write? Why am I writing?* Read *Pupil Edition* pages 420–421 with students to review and discuss those questions. Then model as follows:

Model Begin by saying: **Before I write something, I figure out my answers to the three questions about task, audience, and purpose. That way, I know which type of writing to use: expository, expressive, or persuasive.**

Practice/Apply

Have each student choose a fun topic to write about. Then have him or her write answers to the three prewriting questions, and decide which type of writing would be best suited for the topic.

The Writing Process

The writing process has five steps. You will go back and forth through these steps as you write.

Prewriting: In this step, you plan what you will write. Identify your purpose and who your audience is. Then choose a topic and organize your information.

Drafting: Write out your ideas in sentences and paragraphs. Follow your prewriting plan.

Revising: Make changes to make your writing easier to understand or more interesting to read.

Proofreading: In this step, check for errors in grammar, spelling, capitalization, and punctuation. Then make a final copy of your work.

Publishing: Choose a way to share your work. You may add pictures or read your writing aloud.

Here is an example, showing how Keesha used the writing process to write a personal narrative.

Prewriting

Keesha was asked to write a personal narrative. Her audience would be her classmates. She remembered the time she broke her leg. Her next step was to write down everything she could remember.

> Fell off bicycle.
> Broke leg.
> Got crutches.
> Couldn't get out of a chain
> Couldn't go up and down stairs.
> Then learned how to go really
>   fast on them.

Drafting

Keesha wrote about the events in the order that they took place. She also thought about details that would describe what happened.

Revising

Keesha made changes to improve her writing. She checked to see whether her ideas were in the right order. She added details and took out unnecessary information. She made a run-on sentence into two separate sentences. Here is her first draft with some changes she made in blue.

422

Proofreading

Keesha looked for mistakes in grammar, spelling, punctuation, and capitalization. The corrections in red show the changes she made while proofreading.

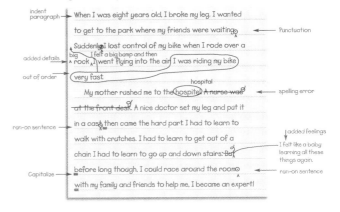

Publishing

Keesha decided to read her story aloud to the class. She brought her crutches to school. She showed how hard it was to get out of a chair. Then she answered questions.

Try This

Imagine you are writing a story about a time you tried something new. Decide what your purpose and audience will be. Then think of interesting ways to publish your story.

423

The Writing Process

Teach/Model

With the students, preview the five steps in the writing process explained on pages 422–423 of the *Pupil Edition*. Then model as follows:

Model Begin by saying: **When I think of a process, I think of something happening in order, step-by-step, like a recipe or a set of directions. Writing, directions, and recipes are all processes that are done step-by-step.**

Practice/Apply

Have students draw a large square on a piece of paper. Tell them to title it "The Writing Process Recipe." Have them number the five steps in order and copy the explanations for each of them from the text. They can add illustrations, if they like.

How to Get Ideas

Once you know your purpose and audience, here are ways to get ideas:

Keep **lists** in a Reading log or idea bank.

- **Think about things you like to do.**

Things I Like
arts and crafts
sports
board games
reading

- **Think about subjects you like in school.**

Interesting Lessons in School
air pressure experiment
estimation games
mock trial in social studies

- **Research people, places, and things you want to know more about.**

Things I want to learn more about
weather forecasting
Paris, France
Video games
art programs on the computer

Keep a **timeline** of interesting things that happen in your life.

- Record feelings and experiences in a personal journal.
- Draw pictures to remind you of memorable events.
- Describe yourself at different times in your life.

Use **freewriting** when you get stuck.

- Start with a topic word or a feeling word.
- Write freely for several minutes. Do not pick your pencil up off the paper.
- Write every thought that comes to your mind. You never know when a good idea will come to you.

424

When you find an idea you want to write about, you can explore it some more, using an idea web. Janna made a web like this one to describe an elephant that she saw at the zoo.

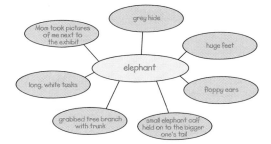

Guidelines for Making an Idea Web:

- Write a word as your starting point. Circle it.
- Around it, write ideas that pop into your head.
- Circle each idea.

Try This

Select an object that is important to you. Imagine that you will write a paragraph about it. Make a web like the web Janna made, but write your object in the center circle. In the outside circles, write all your ideas about the object.

425

How to Get Ideas

Teach/Model

First, direct students' attention to pages 424–425 of the *Pupil Edition* and the illustrations that show three ways to generate writing ideas: a list, a timeline, and an idea web. With students, read the explanations of each way. Then model as follows:
Model   Begin by saying: **Sometimes when I'm thinking about what to write, I simply doodle with ideas. That is, I just write down what pops into my head about a topic. A list, a timeline, and an idea web are all ways to doodle with ideas in this way.**

Practice/Apply

Have students think of three interesting or unusual events that have happened to them. Tell them to explore one as a list, one as a timeline, and one as an idea web.

Using References and Resources:
Reading Functional Texts

Library Resources

You can find books, magazines, videos, audiocassettes, and even games in a library. The library lends all of these items free to the people who live in the area. All you need to do is ask for a library card.

The books in a library are arranged so that you can find what you need easily. **Fiction books** are arranged in alphabetical order by the last names of the authors. **Nonfiction books** are grouped according to subject. **Reference books** such as dictionaries, atlases, almanacs, and encyclopedias, can be found in a special section of the library.

Libraries have card catalogs to help you find books. A card catalog has a card for every book in the library. These cards are put in alphabetical order in drawers. An **electronic card catalog** has the same information, but it is on a computer.

At the computer, you can type **keywords,** such as the name of an author, the title of a book, or the subject of a book. Then the computer will provide a list of titles. Each **entry,** or listing, includes a short summary of the book.

J974.45.C
Chandler, Timothy.
Pioneer Life in America.
Nonfic.
Children's Room
©1990
A close look at the everyday life of pioneers in this country

J971.04F
Fellers, Frances.
Life in the West. Nonfic.
Children's Room
©1994
Struggles of the early settlers in America's Western states

426

Using a Dictionary

A **dictionary** is a book that gives the meanings of words. It also shows how to say them.

Words in a dictionary are listed in alphabetical order. At the top of each dictionary page are **guide words.** The first guide word is the first word on the page. The next guide word is the last word on the page. Use the guide words to help you find the page that lists the word you need.

A **pronunciation key** can be found on every other page. The key shows the letters and symbols used in the pronunciation of each entry. Then it gives sample words to show how to pronounce each sound.

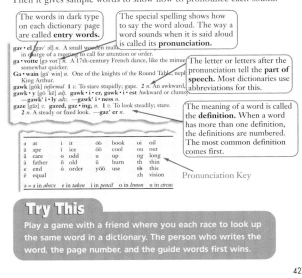

The words in dark type on each dictionary page are called **entry words.**

The special spelling shows how to say the word aloud. The way a word sounds when it is said aloud is called its **pronunciation.**

The letter or letters after the pronunciation tell the **part of speech.** Most dictionaries use abbreviations for this.

The meaning of a word is called the **definition.** When a word has more than one definition, the definitions are numbered. The most common definition comes first.

Pronunciation Key

Try This

Play a game with a friend where you each race to look up the same word in a dictionary. The person who writes the word, the page number, and the guide words first wins.

427

Library Resources

Teach/Model

Use page 426 of the *Pupil Edition* to discuss how information is arranged in a library. Model as follows:
Model   Begin by saying: **When I go into a library that is unfamiliar to me, I try to learn how the resources are arranged.**

Practice/Apply

Have each student make a map of the school library showing where resources can be found.

Using a Dictionary

Teach/Model

Use *Pupil Edition* page 427 to present guide words.
Model   Begin by saying: **I use guide words to narrow my dictionary search for a word.**

Practice/Apply

Have pairs of students write five words that would come, in alphabetical order, between their two last names.

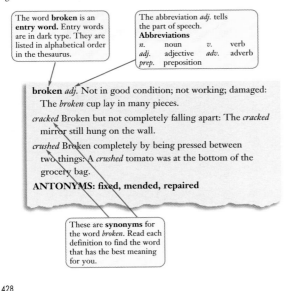

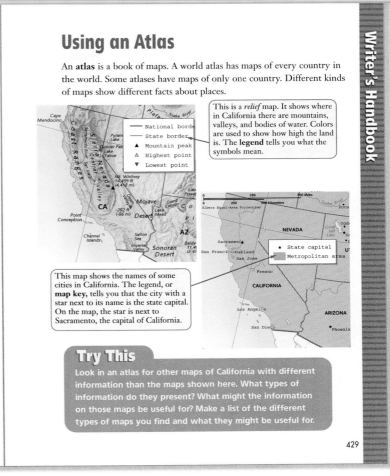

Using a Thesaurus

Teach/Model

Use *Pupil Edition* page 428 to discuss how a thesaurus *is* and *is not* like a dictionary. Then model as follows:

Model   Begin by saying: **I find that a thesaurus is useful when I am describing something and I need more colorful words.**

Practice/Apply

Have students fold a piece of paper in half. Suggest describing words, such as "sad," and have students write, on one side, what a dictionary would say about that word, and, on the other, what a thesaurus would say.

Using an Atlas

Teach/Model

Use page 429 in the *Pupil Edition* to present the topic. Model as follows:

Model   Begin by saying: **If I travel far, I sometimes use an atlas to learn more about where I'm going.**

Practice/Apply

Have students use atlases to find an interesting map fact about the state in which they were born.

Book Parts

Books are organized to help you find information.

Front of the Book

- The **title page** shows the name of the book, the author, and the name of the company that made, or published, the book. It also says where the book was published.

- The **copyright page** tells you in what year the book was made.

- The **table of contents** lists the names of the chapters or units. It tells on which page each chapter or unit begins.

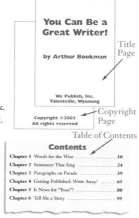

You Can Be a Great Writer!

by Arthur Bookman

We Publish, Inc.
Talentville, Wyoming

Copyright ©2003
All rights reserved

Title Page

Copyright Page

Table of Contents

Contents

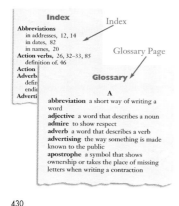

Index

Index

Abbreviations
    in addresses, 12, 14
    in dates, 82
    in names, 20
Action verbs, 26, 32–33, 85
    definition of, 46
Action
Adverb
    defini
    endi
Adverti

Glossary Page

Glossary

A

abbreviation a short way of writing a word

adjective a word that describes a noun

admire to show respect

adverb a word that describes a verb

advertising the way something is made known to the public

apostrophe a symbol that shows ownership or takes the place of missing letters when writing a contraction

Back of the Book

- The **glossary** gives the meanings of important words in the book. The glossary is arranged in alphabetical order.

- The **index** is a list of topics in the book. Page numbers next to each word tell where in the book you can find that information.

430

Using an Encyclopedia

An **encyclopedia** is a book or a set of books that gives information about many different subjects. In a printed set of encyclopedias, each **volume**, or book, has one or more letters on its spine (or side). The letters go from A to Z. Sometimes each book has a number as well. A CD-ROM version of a printed encyclopedia will sometimes have all the information from all the volumes on one disc!

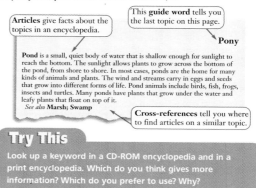

All the subjects in any kind of encyclopedia are arranged in alphabetical order. If you wanted to look up ponds in a printed encyclopedia, you would look in volume 8, *P.*

Articles give facts about the topics in an encyclopedia.

This **guide word** tells you the last topic on this page.

Pony

Pond is a small, quiet body of water that is shallow enough for sunlight to reach the bottom. The sunlight allows plants to grow across the bottom of the pond, from shore to shore. In most cases, ponds are the home for many kinds of animals and plants. The wind and streams carry in eggs and seeds that grow into different forms of life. Pond animals include birds, fish, frogs, insects and turtles. Many ponds have plants that grow under the water and leafy plants that float on top of it.
See also **Marsh; Swamp**

Cross-references tell you where to find articles on a similar topic.

Try This

Look up a keyword in a CD-ROM encyclopedia and in a print encyclopedia. Which do you think gives more information? Which do you prefer to use? Why?

431

Book Parts

Teach/Model

After reading page 430 of the *Pupil Edition*, discuss why the front of a book contains what it does.
Model Begin by saying: **I can find out quickly whether a book will be useful to me by looking at the front and back parts.**

Practice/Apply

Have students use any nonfiction book in the room to identify its front and back parts.

Using an Encyclopedia

Teach/Model

Use page 431 of the *Pupil Edition* to present the topic. Then model as follows:
Model Begin by saying: **The cross-reference in a printed encyclopedia can be like a keyword in a CD-ROM search.**

Practice/Apply

Have students see whether cross-references in a printed encyclopedia lead them back to the original topic.

Organizing Information

Note Taking

A good way to remember information you read is to **take notes.** You can look at your notes when you write a report or study for a test.

Putting your notes on cards can help you organize ideas and details. Make a separate card for each main idea. Then you will be able to put the cards in order in different ways if you need to. This can be useful if you are writing a report.

> On the card, write the **title** and **name of the author** of the book where you found the information you will use. If possible, include the **page numbers.**

Lorrie Lindstrom, All About Ants, pages 54–64

What kinds of ants are there?

1. army ants—travel, hunt
2. Amazon ants—slave makers
3. honey ants—juices
4. leaf-cutter ants—leaves above heads

> Write the **main idea** as a heading on the card. It may help to write the main idea as a question.

> Under the main idea write **details.** Use only enough words to help you remember the important facts.

Note Taking with Graphic Organizers

Sometimes it helps to use a graphic organizer when you take notes. A **K-W-L** chart is a good chart for note taking. The chart has three columns.

- Write what you **know** about the subject in the **K** column. Do this before you read.
- Write questions about what you **want** to find out in the **W** column.
- Write what you **learn** in the **L** column. Do this as you are reading.

432

Ants		
K	W	L
small black or red insects	What kinds of ants are there?	army ants: travel most of the time
live in large groups	What is special about each kind?	Amazon ants: kidnap other ants
very strong		honey ants: collect juice

A **web** is another helpful graphic organizer to use when you are taking notes. A web shows how facts or ideas are connected.

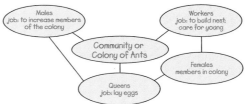

A **Venn diagram** helps you compare two things. This Venn diagram shows how ants and termites are alike and how they are different.

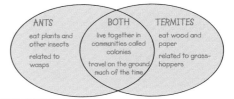

Try This

Think about two of your favorite things to do during your free time. On a sheet of paper, make a Venn diagram and use it to compare and contrast these two activities.

433

Writer's Handbook

Note Taking

Teach/Model

Reemphasize that note taking has two purposes: to remember information, and to organize ideas and details. Then read pages 432–433 of the *Pupil Edition* with students. Model as follows:

Model   Begin by saying: **When I'm reading new information that I need to remember, or when I'm trying to organize information so I can make sense of it, I take notes. This helps me learn because I'm not only reading, but I'm also working with the information by writing it down.**

Practice/Apply

Have students draw three large squares on a sheet of paper to represent note cards, one for each of the three types of graphic organizers for note taking: a **K-W-L** chart, a web organizer, and a Venn diagram. Have students describe in a sentence how each one works on its own note card.

Outlining

Outlining is a good way to organize information. When you read, an outline can help you keep track of the main ideas and the details in an article or book. When you write, an outline can help you plan your ideas into paragraphs.

Tips for Outlining

- Make an outline before you write.
- Write the topic of your outline at the top as its title.
- List the most important ideas, or the main ideas. Leave space between them for the details.
- Put a Roman numeral followed by a period in front of each main idea.
- List supporting details below each main idea.
- Put a capital letter followed by a period in front of each supporting detail.

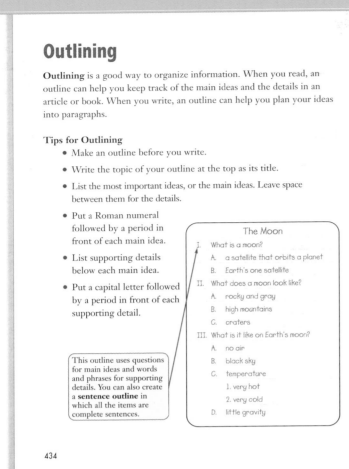

The Moon

I. What is a moon?
   A. a satellite that orbits a planet
   B. Earth's one satellite
II. What does a moon look like?
   A. rocky and gray
   B. high mountains
   C. craters
III. What is it like on Earth's moon?
   A. no air
   B. black sky
   C. temperature
      1. very hot
      2. very cold
   D. little gravity

This outline uses questions for main ideas and words and phrases for supporting details. You can also create a **sentence outline** in which all the items are complete sentences.

434

Here is a report about the moon that was written using the outline. Compare the outline and the report.

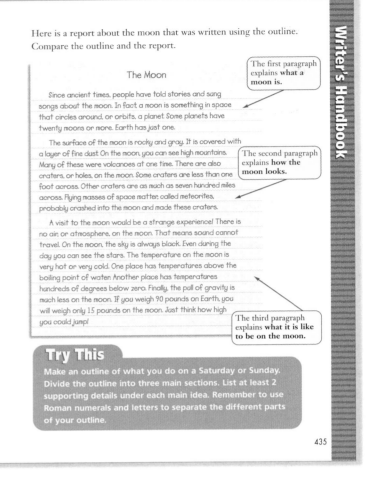

The Moon

Since ancient times, people have told stories and sung songs about the moon. In fact a moon is something in space that circles around, or orbits, a planet. Some planets have twenty moons or more. Earth has just one.

The surface of the moon is rocky and gray. It is covered with a layer of fine dust. On the moon, you can see high mountains. Many of these were volcanoes at one time. There are also craters, or holes, on the moon. Some craters are less than one foot across. Other craters are as much as seven hundred miles across. Flying masses of space matter, called meteorites, probably crashed into the moon and made these craters.

A visit to the moon would be a strange experience! There is no air, or atmosphere, on the moon. That means sound cannot travel. On the moon, the sky is always black. Even during the day you can see the stars. The temperature on the moon is very hot or very cold. One place has temperatures above the boiling point of water. Another place has temperatures hundreds of degrees below zero. Finally, the pull of gravity is much less on the moon. If you weigh 90 pounds on Earth, you will weigh only 15 pounds on the moon. Just think how high you could jump!

The first paragraph explains **what a moon is.**

The second paragraph explains **how the moon looks.**

The third paragraph explains **what it is like to be on the moon.**

Try This

Make an outline of what you do on a Saturday or Sunday. Divide the outline into three main sections. List at least 2 supporting details under each main idea. Remember to use Roman numerals and letters to separate the different parts of your outline.

435

Outlining

Teach/Model

Direct students to pages 434–435 of the *Pupil Edition*. Have students identify where the information in "The Moon" outline appears in the report called "The Moon." Then read the explanatory text on *Pupil Edition* pages 434–435 together. Model as follows:

Model   Begin by saying: **I find that I can write longer, more complete reports or descriptions by outlining first. That way, I can add information in places, and make sure all of the information is in the right order.**

Practice/Apply

Have students write an outline titled "My Home." Roman numeral I should be about the kind of home in which they live. Each numeral that follows the numeral I should be devoted to an important part of that home. Details about each part appear in order of importance.

Polishing Your Writing

Traits of Good Writing

Writing is like any other skill or activity. It takes time, practice, and effort. There are rules you have to learn and **traits,** or features, of good writing that you will learn to recognize. But once you understand those rules and traits, writing can be a lot of fun. Think about another activity you enjoy. When you did it for the first few times, learning the rules was important. Once you knew the rules, though, you could focus on having fun.

Think about drawing, for example. To draw well, an artist needs to be able to imagine what he wants to draw, sketch it out on whatever he's drawing on, and then add details and maybe colors to make the drawing look real. Very few people can do this well from the beginning. Most artists have to train their imaginations to see things in detail, and train their hands to make the marks and shapes that look like what they're imagining. Creating mental images, sketching, and detail drawing are **traits of good drawing.** They are skills that good artists practice and improve in order to draw well.

Good writing takes practice at these skills, too. This web shows the **traits of good writing.**

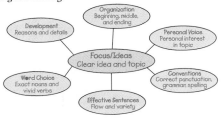

436

Quick Checklist for Good Writers

Good writers practice, practice, practice! As you practice, ask yourself these questions. If you can say "yes" to most of them, you are doing quite well indeed! If you need work in some areas, use the lessons in this handbook. Keep practicing!

✔ **FOCUS/IDEAS** Are my ideas clear? Do I stay on the topic?

✔ **ORGANIZATION** Do I have a clear beginning, middle, and ending? Are similar ideas grouped together in paragraphs?

✔ **DEVELOPMENT** Do I use details and reasons to support my ideas?

✔ **VOICE** Do I seem to care about my topic?

✔ **EFFECTIVE SENTENCES** Do I use a variety of sentence types?

✔ **WORD CHOICE** Do I use exact nouns and vivid verbs?

✔ **CONVENTIONS** Are my spelling, grammar, and punctuation correct?

Try This

Choose a piece of writing from your portfolio. Use the Quick Checklist. What are your strengths? What can you improve? Jot down your ideas in your Writer's Journal.

437

Traits of Good Writing

Teach/Model

Preview the section by asking students how they judge a good drawing, a good dance, or a good piece of music. Summarize by saying that certain traits separate "good" work from "not very good" work. Then, with students, read pages 436–437 of the *Pupil Edition.* Model as follows:

Model   Begin by saying: **While I read a piece of writing, I'm deciding whether I like its traits. Even when I'm reading over my own writing, I look to make sure that the traits of good writing are present.**

Practice/Apply

Have students rank, from 1 to 7, with 1 being the highest, the "Traits of Good Writing" shown in the web on page 436. Although most will probably agree that "Focus/Ideas" is the most important trait, encourage discussion about why students ranked the other traits as they did.

Using a Rubric

A rubric is a list you can use to check your writing. It spells out the main points of good writing.

Before writing   Use the list to remind you of the traits of good writing.

During writing   Use the list to see how you can improve your drafts.

After writing   Use the list to see if your essay or story has all the points of good writing.

Here is a checklist you can use to self-evaluate your writing.

My Best Score

✓ Do I make the topic and my ideas clear to the reader?

✓ Does my essay move from beginning to the middle to the end smoothly? Is it easy to follow?

✓ Do I support my ideas with specific reasons and details?

✓ Do my words show my interest and knowledge in the topic?

✓ Do I use different kinds of sentences in my essay?

✓ Are my choices of nouns and verbs specific and vivid?

✓ Do I use correct grammar, spelling, and punctuation?

438

Peer Conferences

You can make your writing better by reading your work to a classmate. **Peer conferences** are a good way to get helpful comments and suggestions.

Here are some questions to ask a friend when you want help with your writing:

1. Is my topic interesting to you? Can you figure out my point of view?
2. Do you understand the order of events? Is there anything I left out?
3. Is this detail important? Should I include it?
4. Can you suggest a better word for_____?
5. Do I have any choppy sentences? Can any sentences be combined?
6. Do I have any run-on sentences?
7. Are there mistakes in spelling, grammar, or punctuation?

Tips for peer conferences:
- Listen carefully to someone else's writing.
- Make suggestions, but don't tell the writer what to do.
- Remember to tell what you like about the writing.
- Be polite and encouraging. Agree or disagree in a pleasant way.

Try This

Write a paragraph about a time you went somewhere new and had a good time. Share your paragraph with a partner, and conduct a peer conference.

439

Using a Rubric

Teach/Model

Introduce the concept of a rubric by revisiting the "Practice/Apply" exercise about ranking the traits of good writing. Then read page 438 in the *Pupil Edition* with students. Model as follows:

Model   Begin by saying: **Sometimes when I visit a store or eat at a restaurant, I'm given a "customer satisfaction" card that asks me to fill out a rubric evaluating my experience. Was it good, or was it bad? Writing is an experience that must be evaluated, too.**

Practice/Apply

Have students discuss why each question in the sample rubric is important.

Peer Conferences

Teach/Model

Use page 439 in the *Pupil Edition* to present the topic. Then model as follows:

Model   Begin by saying: **When I show my writing to others for their opinion, I am doing what is called a *peer conference*.**

Practice/Apply

Have students create a list of ways in which peer conferences can help someone become a better writer.

Presenting Your Writing

Giving an Oral Presentation

One way to share your writing with classmates is to give an oral presentation.

Tips for giving an oral presentation:

1. Write the report on note cards in big print.
2. Practice reading your report aloud in front of a mirror or to a friend.
3. When you speak, look at your audience some of the time. Make motions with your hands, too. This will keep your listeners interested in your presentation.
4. Speak clearly and loudly enough for everyone to hear you. Speak slowly enough for everyone to understand you. Change your tone of voice every now and then to stress important parts of what you read.
5. Make your presentation more interesting by using props. You might use things that describe your topic, such as posters, pictures or charts.
6. When you finish, ask for questions from the audience.

Tips for listeners:

1. Listen politely to the speaker's presentation. Don't talk with your neighbors.
2. Look at the speaker to show your interest.
3. Save your questions for the end. You may also want to add information you have on the topic that might be interesting.

440

Giving a Multimedia Presentation

You can use different means of communication, such as pictures, videos, music, or drama, when you share a report with your class. This is called a **multimedia presentation.** Here are the steps to follow:

1. Decide which multimedia aids fit your report best. For example, if you are doing a report on state songs, you might bring a CD or cassette tape of music. If you are doing a report on tropical fish, you might bring photos, drawings, videotapes, or maps.
2. Get permission to use equipment that you need, such as a tape recorder or a videotape player. Learn how to operate the equipment ahead of time. If you are presenting your report as a play or skit, ask classmates to assist you by acting out parts.
3. Decide at what time during your presentation you will use the multimedia aids.
4. Organize the spoken part of your presentation. Write notes of what you will say. Practice reading your notes.
5. Invite your classmates to ask questions about your report.

Try This

Imagine that you have been asked to give an oral report about a hobby that you have or a club in which you are involved. Make a list of aids you could use in your presentation.

441

Giving an Oral Presentation

Teach/Model

Prepare the students for the lesson by asking, "What makes a good oral presentation?" Then read page 440 in the *Pupil Edition*. Model as follows:
Model Begin by saying: **Everyone gets nervous before making an oral presentation, even me. But I've found that being prepared helps get rid of nervousness.**

Practice/Apply

Have students create a rubric in the form of questions for evaluating oral presentations.

Giving a Multimedia Presentation

Teach/Model

Preview page 441 in the *Pupil Edition* by asking students to list all the visual aids they could show to people who had never heard of baseball. Model as follows:
Model Begin by saying: **I try to use multimedia aids in my presentations here in class. Which ones can you name?**

Practice/Apply

Have students choose a useful product to sell on TV. Then have them list the aids they would use if the TV had no sound.

Introducing the Glossary

Explain to students that a glossary often is included in a book so that readers can find the meanings of words used in the book. Read aloud the introductory pages. Then model looking up one or more words, pointing out how you rely on alphabetical order and the guide words at the top of the Glossary pages to help you locate the entry word. You may also want to demonstrate how to use the pronunciation key to confirm the correct pronunciation.

- As students look over the Glossary, point out that illustrations accompany some definitions. Have students read a Word Origins note and a Fact File note, and discuss the type of information in each.

- Encourage students to look up several words in the Glossary, identifying the correct page and the guide words. Then have them explain how using alphabetical order and the guide words at the top of each page helps them locate the words.

- Tell students to use the Glossary to confirm the pronunciations of vocabulary words during reading and to help them better understand the meanings of unfamiliar words.

Using the Glossary

Like a dictionary, this glossary lists words in alphabetical order. To find a word, look it up by its first letter or letters.

To save time, use the **guide words** at the top of each page. These show you the first and last words on the page. Look at the guide words to see if your word falls between them alphabetically.

Here is an example of a glossary entry:

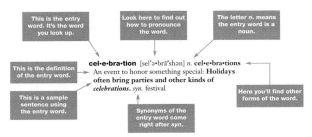

This is the entry word. It's the word you look up.

Look here to find out how to pronounce the word.

The letter *n.* means the entry word is a noun.

This is the definition of the entry word.

This is a sample sentence using the entry word.

Synonyms of the entry word come right after *syn.*

Here you'll find other forms of the word.

cel·e·bra·tion [sel′ə·brā′shən] *n.* **cel·e·bra·tions**
An event to honor something special: **Holidays often bring parties and other kinds of** *celebrations.* *syn.* festival

Word Origins

Throughout the glossary, you will find notes about word origins, or how words get started and change. Words often have interesting backgrounds that can help you remember what they mean.

Here is an example of a word origin note:

harvest Until the 1700s, *harvest* named the season we now know as *autumn.* That was the time when many crops were picked.

442

Pronunciation

The pronunciation in brackets is a respelling that shows how the word is pronounced.

The **pronunciation key** explains what the symbols in a respelling mean. A shortened pronunciation key appears on every other page of the glossary.

PRONUNCIATION KEY*

a	add, map	m	move, seem	u	up, done
ā	ace, rate	n	nice, tin	û(r)	burn, term
â(r)	care, air	ng	ring, song	yŏŏ	fuse, few
ä	palm, father	o	odd, hot	v	vain, eve
b	bat, rub	ō	open, so	w	win, away
ch	check, catch	ô	order, jaw	y	yet, yearn
d	dog, rod	oi	oil, boy	z	zest, muse
e	end, pet	ou	pout, now	zh	vision, pleasure
ē	equal, tree	ŏŏ	took, full	ə	the schwa, an
f	fit, half	ōō	pool, food		unstressed vowel
g	go, log	p	pit, stop		representing the
h	hope, hate	r	run, poor		sound spelled
i	it, give	s	see, pass		*a* in *above*
ī	ice, write	sh	sure, rush		*e* in *sicken*
j	joy, ledge	t	talk, sit		*i* in *possible*
k	cool, take	th	thin, both		*o* in *melon*
l	look, rule	ŧ	this, bathe		*u* in *circus*

Other symbols:
• separates words into syllables
′ indicates heavier stress on a syllable
′ indicates light stress on a syllable

Abbreviations: *adj.* adjective, *adv.* adverb, *conj.* conjunction, *interj.* interjection, *n.* noun, *prep.* preposition, *pron.* pronoun, *syn.* synonym, *v.* verb

* The Pronunciation Key, adapted entries, and the Short Key that appear on the following pages are reprinted from *HBJ School Dictionary* Copyright © 1990 by Harcourt Brace & Company. Reprinted by permission of Harcourt Brace & Company.

443

A

ad·mire [ad·mīr′] *v.* **ad·mir·ing** To look upon with pleasure and approval: **Bonnie strolled through the park,** *admiring* the rose garden.

ad·vice [ad·vīs′] *n.* Suggestions or directions on what to do: **Tom asked for** *advice* **on how to set up his computer.**

a·mount [ə·mount′] *n.* A certain number of: **We saved our money in the bank until we had the** *amount* **we needed for our trip.** *syn.* quantity

Word Origins

amount *Amount* comes from the Latin *ad montem,* which means "to the mountain," and so "going in an upward direction." As you add up numbers to find the amount, or sum, you are "climbing a mountain" of numbers!

am·ple [am′pəl] *adj.* Enough or more than enough: **We had** *ample* **food for everyone, so no one went hungry.**

ar·range [ə·rānj′] *v.* **ar·ranged** To place things in a certain order: **Lian** *arranged* **the books on the shelf from tallest to shortest.** *syn.* organize

auc·tion·eer [ôk′shən·ir′] *n.* A person who sells things at a public sale to people offering the highest prices: **The** *auctioneer* **spoke very fast as he called out the prices being offered.**

av·er·age [av′rij] *adj.* Usual or ordinary: **Juan is an** *average* **runner, not unusually fast or slow.**

B

bar·gain [bär′gən] *v.* To work out an agreement about selling or trading something: **Mother had to** *bargain* **with our neighbor to trade some of our corn for some of his eggs.**

bid [bid] *n.* An offer to pay a certain price for something: **Sally wanted to buy the lamp, so she made a** *bid* **of five dollars for it.**

boom town [bŏŏm′ toun] *n.* A town that grows quickly and has successful businesses: **This is becoming a** *boom town* **as more people move in and open new stores.**

bram·ble [bram′bəl] *n.* **bram·bles** A rough and prickly plant, smaller than a tree: **Be careful not to get scratched if you step into the** *brambles* **growing along the road.**

bramble

brit·tle [brit′əl] *adj.* Easily broken: **This old clay pot is very** *brittle,* **so handle it carefully.**

444

C

can·yon [kan′yən] *n.* A deep valley with high cliffs on both sides: **When you look down into a** *canyon,* **you may see a river running through it.**

canyon

cel·e·bra·tion [sel′ə·brā′shən] *n.* **cel·e·bra·tions** An event to honor something special: **Holidays often bring parties and other kinds of** *celebrations.* *syn.* festival

cher·ish [cher′ish] *v.* **cher·ished** To care about or hold dear: **Helga** *cherished* **the doll her grandmother had given her.**

choice [chois] *n.* **choic·es** What you decide to have or to do: **When you decide what you want to eat and to wear, you are making** *choices.* *syn.* selection

choos·y [chōō′zē] *adj.* Very careful about deciding; paying close attention to: **Joan is** *choosy* **about what she wears, so it takes her a long time to dress.** *syn.* fussy

clutch [kluch] *v.* **clutched** To hold onto something tightly: **Larisa** *clutched* **her purse in both hands on the crowded bus.** *syn.* grasp

coast [kōst] *n.* Land that is along the sea: **Cities along the** *coast* **can be reached by ship as well as by train.** *syn.* seashore

Word Origins

coast What does a rib have to do with a coast? In Latin, *costa* means "rib," and people in the past used *coast* to mean "side." People now use *coast* to mean "seashore" or "seaside" because we think of the coast as being the land at the "side" or "edge" of the ocean.

colo·nel [kûr′nəl] *n.* A senior officer in the military: **The** *colonel* **commanded his troops to carry supplies across the river.**

com·bi·na·tion [kom′bə·nā′shən] *n.* **com·bi·na·tions** Something made by putting other things together: **Salads usually are** *combinations* **of different kinds of vegetables or fruits.**

con·grat·u·la·tions [kən·grach′ə·lā′shənz] *n.* Good wishes to someone who has done well: **When our team won the game, the coach gave us his** *congratulations.*

con·ti·nent [kon′tə·nənt] *n.* One of the main areas of land that make up the earth: **The United States is part of the** *continent* **of North America.**

continent

a add	e end	o odd	ōō pool	oi oil	ŧh this	*a* in *above*
ā ace	ē equal	ō open	u up	ou pout	zh vision	*e* in *sicken*
â care	i it	ô order	û burn	ng ring		ə = *i* in *possible*
ä palm	ī ice	ŏŏ took	yŏŏ fuse	th thin		*o* in *melon*
						u in *circus*

445

---

con·verse [kən·vûrs′] *v.* To talk: **If you would like to *converse* with me, call me on the telephone.**

cor·ral [kə·ral′] *n.* A fenced-in space for farm animals: **The cattle were put in a *corral* to keep them from wandering away.** *syn.* pen

coun·cil [koun′səl] *n.* A group of people who meet to talk about something or to make plans: **The *council* met, and its members decided to clean up the park.**

Fact File
council A city *council* is a group of men and women who are chosen by the people of the city. They make laws that help the city run smoothly. The American colonies modeled their first city councils after those in England.

coun·ty [koun′tē] *n.* One of the parts into which a state is divided: **My uncle lives in the same state as I do, but in a different *county*.**

county

cun·ning [kun′ing] *adj.* Crafty or sly: **The *cunning* squirrel took a nut from my plate when I wasn't looking.**

D

de·light·ed [di·līt′ed] *adj.* Highly pleased: **Maya was *delighted* to get so many wonderful gifts.**

dread·ful [dred′fəl] *adj.* Awful; very bad: **The *dreadful* tornado struck the town with a roar.** *syns.* terrible, fearful

dusk [dusk] *n.* The time just between sunset and nightfall: **It is hard to see where you are going at *dusk* before the streetlights come on.**

du·ty [d(y)oō′tē] *n.* Something that should be done because it is right or important: **Police officers have a *duty* to keep people safe.**

E

edge [ej] *n.* **edg·es** The line where a thing begins or ends: **Tomeka put the dishes near the *edges* of the table to make room for the turkey.**

edges

em·brace [im·brās′] *v.* **em·braced** To hug: **Their arms went around each other as they *embraced*.**

ep·i·cen·ter [ep′i·sen′tər] *n.* The place on the earth's surface that is right above the point where an earthquake begins: **Scientists said that the *epicenter* of the earthquake was five miles south of the city.**

e·ven·tu·al·ly [i·ven′choō·əl·ē] *adv.* Over time; in the end: **At first the kitten was afraid, but *eventually* it learned to trust us.** *syn.* finally

446

F

fare [fâr] **far·ing** *v.* To get along; to manage: **We were *faring* just fine on our nature walk until a skunk crossed our path.**

fare·well [fâr·wel′] *n.* Words spoken when leaving; a good-bye: **As Teresa was leaving, she told her friends *farewell*.**

feast [fēst] *n.* A special meal with a large amount of food: **The king gave a great *feast* to celebrate his daughter's wedding.** *syn.* banquet

fluo·res·cent [floō·res′ənt] *adj.* Describes something that gives off cool light: **Some *fluorescent* lightbulbs are in the shape of long, white tubes.**

force [fôrs] *n.* Power or energy to cause something to move or to stop moving: **A sailboat uses the *force* of the wind to move across the water.** *syn.* strength

fur·row [fûr′ō] *n.* **fur·rows** A long groove or cut made in the ground by a plow or another tool: **The farmer plowed neat *furrows* in the soil and planted seeds in them.**

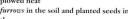
furrows

G

gal·lop [gal′əp] *v.* **gal·loped** To ride a horse that is running fast: **Henry was in a hurry to get home, so he got on his horse and *galloped* across the field.**

gaze [gāz] *v.* **gaz·ing** To look at something in away that shows great interest or wonder: **Jamal spent hours *gazing* at the clouds as they moved and changed.** *syn.* stare

glis·ten [glis′ən] *v.* **glis·tened** To shine or sparkle: **The lake *glistened* in the sunshine.**

growth [grōth] *n.* Plants or things that become greater in size and number in a certain place: **There was a *growth* of weeds around the empty house.**

H

har·vest [här′vist] *v.* To pick or gather a crop, such as grain, fruits, or vegetables: **When the apples are ripe, it's time to *harvest* them.**

Word Origins
harvest Until the 1700s, *harvest* named the season we now know as *autumn*. That was the time when many crops were picked.

home·ward [hōm′wərd] *adv.* Toward home: **After we walked to the pond and fed the ducks, we turned *homeward*.**

a add	e end	o odd	oō pool	oi oil	th this		a in *above*
ā ace	ē equal	ō open	u up	ou pout	zh vision		e in *sicken*
â care	i it	ô order	û burn	ng ring		ə =	i in *possible*
ä palm	ī ice	oō took	yoō fuse	th thin			o in *melon*
							u in *circus*

447

L

land·mark [land′märk′] *n.* An outstanding object in a landscape, such as a building or a mountain: **The oak tree on the corner serves as a *landmark* for finding our street.**

latch [lach] *v.* To close and fasten shut: **Be sure to *latch* the door with a strong lock.**

loop [loōp] *v.* **loops** To move in a circle or an oval: **The plane leaves a white trail as it *loops* across the sky.**

loop

M

ma·chet·e [mə·shet′ē *or* mə·shet′] *n.* A large knife with a heavy blade, often used as a tool, especially in Latin American countries: **Manuel uses a *machete* to cut sugarcane in the fields.**

mag·ma [mag′mə] *n.* Very hot, partly melted rock inside the earth: **Can you imagine how hot it must be inside the earth to melt rocks into *magma*?**

mar·ket [mär′kit] *n.* A place where goods are sold: **After the peaches are picked, trucks take them to the *market* to be sold.**

min·er [mīn′ər] *n.* **min·ers** A person who digs minerals from the earth: **Gold *miners* dig large holes in search of gold.**

mis·chief [mis′chif] *n.* Action that is naughty or that may cause harm: **My mother has to watch my younger brother all the time to keep him out of *mischief*.**

N

non·sense [non′sens′] *n.* Something that is silly or that does not make sense: **The story about pigs flying is *nonsense*.** *syn.* foolishness

nu·cle·us [n(y)oō′klē·əs] *n.* The center of something: **The pit is the *nucleus* of a peach.**

nug·get [nug′it] *n.* **nug·gets** A lump, especially of gold: **These *nuggets* are valuable pieces.**

O

out·stretched [out′strecht′] *adj.* Extended out: **His *outstretched* arms reached for the flying ball.**

P

par·ti·cle [pär′ti·kəl] *n.* **par·ti·cles** A very tiny bit of something: **Did you know that grains of sand are really *particles* of broken rock?**

448

---

peak [pēk] *n.* The pointed top of a hill or mountain: **This mountain *peak* is so high that there is always snow on it, even in summer.**

peak

pride [prīd] *n.* A feeling of being proud or having respect for; a feeling of worth: **We keep our streets clean and safe because we have *pride* in our city.**

prof·it [prof′it] *n.* Money gained by selling something: **After Carlos and Isabel paid for the lemons and sugar, they found that they hadn't made much *profit* from selling lemonade.**

pulp [pulp] *n.* The soft, juicy inside of some fruits and vegetables: **Eat the *pulp* of the melon, not the skin.**

R

ranch·er [ran′chər] *n.* **ranch·ers** A person who owns a large farm for raising animals, such as cattle, sheep, or horses: **Ranchers need a lot of land so that their animals will have enough grass to eat.**

range [rānj] *n.* A row or line of mountains: **The mountain *range* looks small on the map, but it is long in real life.**

range

re·ceive [ri·sēv′] *v.* To get something: **I like to give gifts, and I like to *receive* them, too.**

S

sat·is·fy [sat′is·fī] *v.* **sat·is·fied** To meet someone's needs or wishes: **Dawn kept changing her picture until she was *satisfied* with the way it looked.** *syn.* please

schoon·er [skoō′nər] *n.* A sailing ship that has two or more masts, or poles, that hold up the sails: **We saw a model of an old-fashioned *schooner* at the ship museum.**

schooner

a add	e end	o odd	oō pool	oi oil	th this		a in *above*
ā ace	ē equal	ō open	u up	ou pout	zh vision		e in *sicken*
â care	i it	ô order	û burn	ng ring	ə =	i in *possible*
ä palm	ī ice	oō took	yoō fuse	th thin			o in *melon*
							u in *circus*

449

GLOSSARY

set·tle [set′əl] *v.* To make a home: **The families will *settle* in the country.**

shun [shun] *v.* **shunned** To stay away from: **The duckling was *shunned* by the mother hen and her chicks.** *syn.* avoid

sig·nal [sig′nəl] *v.* To use an action, a symbol, or an object to send a message or to make something known: **We tied balloons to our mailbox to *signal* my sister's birthday.**

skil·let [skil′it] *n.* A shallow metal pan with a handle: **Mother likes to fry food in her *skillet*.**

skill·ful [skil′fəl] *adj.* Having the ability to do something very well: **Mr. Green is a *skillful* carpenter who knows how to build fine houses.**

so·lar wind [sō′lər wind] *n.* A flow of gases or particles given off by the sun: **The *solar wind* is different from the kind of wind we have on Earth.**

Fact File

solar wind On Earth, hurricane winds can have speeds of 100 miles per hour. In space, the speed of *solar wind* is about 310 miles per *second!* However, the earth's magnetic forces stop particles in the solar wind from reaching the earth.

---

sol·dier [sōl′jər] *n.* A person who serves in the army: **My grandfather was a *soldier* and was wounded in battle.**

sphere [sfir] *n.* An object that has a shape like a ball: **A baseball is a small *sphere*, and a beach ball is a larger one.** *syn.* globe

stage·coach [stāj′kōch′] *n.* A carriage pulled by horses and having a regular route for picking up passengers or packages: **The *stagecoach* delivered mail to settlers who lived out West.**

stray [strā] *adj.* Wandering or lost: **We helped the *stray* dog find its way home.**

stum·ble [stum′bəl] *v.* **stum·bling** To move along in an unsteady way: **We knew that George was sleepy when we saw him *stumbling* out of his bedroom.**

sup·port [sə·pôrt′] *v.* To hold the weight of something or someone: **The old wooden bridge isn't strong enough to *support* a car.**

swift·ly [swift′lē] *adv.* In a very fast way: **The jet moved *swiftly* across the sky.** *syns.* quickly, rapidly

T

tend [tend] *v.* **tend·ing** To take care of: **The mother bird was busy *tending* her babies.**

ten·der [ten′dər] *adj.* Soft and easily injured: **The *tender* fruit was bruised from being touched.**

tid·bit [tid′bit′] *n.* A small, very good bit of food: **Jay selected the tastiest *tidbit* from the tray of snacks.**

track [trak] *n.* **tracks** Footprints or other marks left by a person, an animal, or a thing: **We could see from the *tracks* in the snow that a deer had walked there.**

trad·ing [trā′ding] *adj.* Having to do with exchanging goods: **A *trading* post was a place where hunters exchanged animal skins for things they needed.**

U

u·ni·verse [yoo′nə·vûrs′] *n.* Everything that is, including the Earth, the sun, planets, stars, and all of space: **Earth is like a tiny dot compared to the size of the *universe*.**

Word Origins

Universe comes from *universus*, the Latin word for "whole" or "entire."

---

ur·gent [ûr′jənt] *adj.* Needing prompt attention: **Kim's *urgent* letter demanded a quick reply.**

V

val·ue [val′yoo] *n.* How much something is worth: **Even though a dime is smaller in size than a nickel, the dime has a greater *value*.** *syn.* worth

W

wail [wāl] *v.* **wail·ing** To cry: **The baby was *wailing* to be fed.**

wea·ry [wir′ē] *adj.* Tired: **After a long day, Joan felt *weary* and went straight to bed.**

wind·mill [wind′mil′] *n.* A machine that uses the power of the wind to grind grain, pump water, or do other work: **As the wind blew, the long blades of the *windmill* turned around and around.**

windmill

wits [wits] *n. (pl.)* The ability to think; good sense: **I needed my *wits* about me to find my way home in the snowstorm.**

a add	e end	o odd	oo pool	oi oil	th this		a in *above*
ā ace	ē equal	ō open	u up	ou pout	zh vision	ə =	e in *sicken*
â care	i it	ô order	û burn	ng ring			i in *possible*
ä palm	ī ice	oo took	yoo fuse	th thin			o in *melon*
							u in *circus*

450   451

Index *of* Titles *and* Authors

Page numbers in color refer to biographical information.

Managing the Classroom

Setting the Stage

Designing a Space

One of the keys to productive learning is the physical arrangement of your classroom. Each classroom has unique characteristics, but the following areas should be considered in your floor plan.

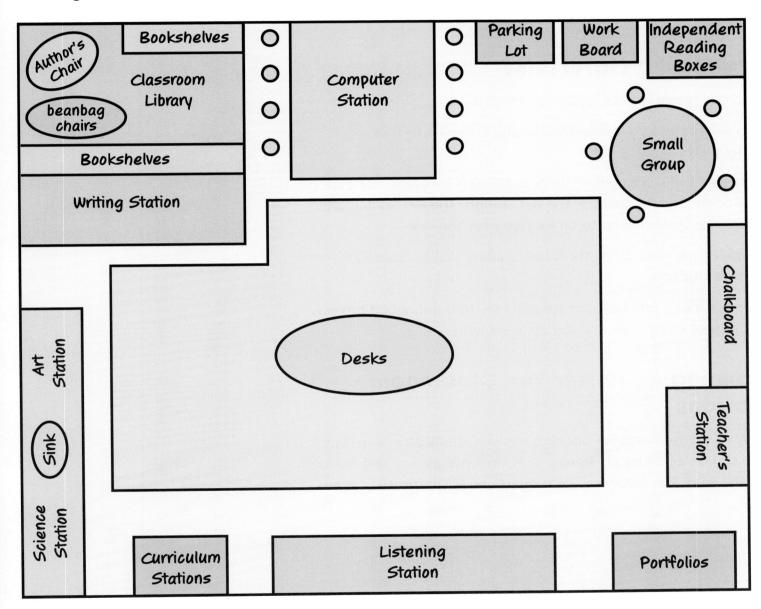

When arranging your classroom, consider traffic patterns and usage of areas. Place quiet stations near small group and independent work areas. Provide some private spaces for students to work.

A three-sided cardboard divider can instantly become a "private office" or a portable learning station.

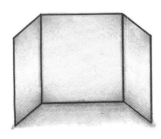

MANAGING THE CLASSROOM

Introducing the Stations

Before beginning a routine, acquaint students with procedures for and use of each area. All station activities should involve literacy with a balance of reading and writing tasks.

Help students understand how much time they will spend in a station. For example, they can read several chapters in a book from the Classroom Library, listen to one tape recording in the Listening Station, and play one game in the Technology Station.

Show students how to use the computer, tape recorder, and headphones. Demonstrate proper usage of art supplies.

Organizing Materials

Clean and resupply each station as needed.

Get students into the habit of returning materials to their proper places.

Determine the placement of items in stations by usage. For example, you'll need a wastebasket in the Art Station. The Art Station and the Science Station need to be located near the sink.

Set aside time once a day for room cleaning. Assign specific tasks for each student.

Have a "parking lot" table for students to store unfinished projects that require more than one day for completion.

Planning Activities for Classroom Stations

Many of the materials for ongoing stations are at your fingertips. Base station activities on literacy skills students are learning throughout the year. The following are suggestions for particular stations.

Classroom Library

One corner of your room can house books students can freely choose and enjoy reading on their own. Include books of all kinds: reference books, chapter books, and books students have made themselves.

Independent Reading Boxes

Provide boxes of books for each small guided reading group. Use color-coded boxes or bins to hold fifteen or more books. Provide multiple copies if possible. Books can include those that have been shared during group sessions and books that are appropriate for independent reading.

Listening Station

Include tape recorder and headsets. Provide audiotexts and a variety of commercial tapes and tapes recorded by volunteers and students. If you are providing text with a tape, make multiple copies and store the tape and books in a plastic bag. Suggest an extension activity following listening.

Technology Station

Students can write on the computer using word processing software, such as ClarisWorks for Kids, or interact with literature software, such as Instant Readers and Living Books™. See technology references throughout the lessons.

Writing Station

This should be a clearly defined space where writing materials are stored. Possible materials include:

blank books	a variety of paper	stationery and envelopes
stickers	poster board	stapler and staple remover
pencils	markers	hole punch and yarn

Curriculum Stations

Ideas for cross-curricular activities are provided before each lesson in the Teacher's Edition. Supply materials as needed for students to:

- create graphs in a math activity

- perform an experiment and keep a log in a science activity

- make a map in a social studies activity

- create new verses to perform a song in a music activity

- create artwork in response to stories

Establishing Flexible Work Groups

In order for the teacher to work with small groups without interruption, the other class members must clearly understand what they are to do. To plan a series of tasks these students can do independently, establish small work groups. These are heterogeneous groups of students who are scheduled for the same station activities on a daily basis. You can change these groups as often as you like.

The Value of Flexible Grouping

Flexible grouping is a way to insure that all students will achieve instructional standards. Grouping should be a fluid process—changing on a daily, weekly, or monthly basis—based upon your assessment of individual students' progress.

Whole-Class Instruction   Students can be grouped all together for activities, such as reading literature and discussing literature, writing compositions, and creating art.

Small-Group Instruction   You may wish to use small-group instruction for:

■ a group of students who do not understand a skill and need another approach to learning it

■ a group of students who have already mastered a skill and need an additional challenge

The Teacher's Role   With some groups, the teacher may establish the group's goal and then step aside, letting the group decide how to achieve that goal. With other groups, the teacher may remain close by, monitoring the group as needed to achieve the goal. With still others, the teacher may provide direct instruction and assistance to help group members achieve the goal.

Introducing a Work Board

One way to schedule classroom activity is with a Work Board. A typical Work Board includes the names of small-group members and icons that represent independent tasks. For example, you may wish to use an atom to represent the Science Station or headphones to represent the Listening Station. The Work Board can be a cork board, a peg board with hooks, or a magnetic board. Its design should be flexible, enabling you to move cards on a daily basis.

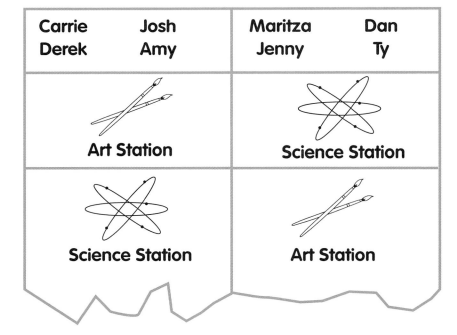

Carrie Josh Derek Amy	Maritza Dan Jenny Ty
Art Station	Science Station
Science Station	Art Station

Vowel

A vowel is *a*, *e*, *i*, *o*, or *u*—and sometimes *y*.

Syllable

A syllable usually has one vowel or vowel pattern in it.

Example: re̱do̱ (2 syllables)

Consonant

A consonant is any letter that is not a vowel.

One-Syllable Words

Never divide a one-syllable word.

Examples: seat   chair   rug

Harcourt

Compound Words

Divide a compound word between the two smaller words in it.

Examples: hot/dog   sail/boat

Closed Syllables

When a vowel is between two consonants in a syllable, the vowel is usually short.

Example: fin/ish

Open Syllables

When a syllable ends in a single vowel, the vowel is usually long.

Example: be/gin

Vowel Patterns

Use vowel patterns you know to help you read a long word.

Example: farmer

Harcourt

Suffixes

Divide a word between the base word and the suffix.

Examples: glad<u>ly</u>   fear<u>less</u>   fast<u>er</u>

Prefixes

Divide a word between the prefix and the base word.

Examples: <u>re</u>read   <u>un</u>kind

V/CV Pattern

When a single consonant is between two vowels, divide before the consonant. Try the first syllable long. If the word makes sense, keep it!

Example: ti/ger   pa/per

VC/V Pattern

If a consonant is between two vowels, always try the V/CV pattern. Try the first syllable long. If the word doesn't make sense, divide after the consonant and try it short.

Examples: drag/on   vis/it

Harcourt

Consonant -le Words

When a word ends in a consonant and le, divide the word before the consonant.

Examples: cir/cle peo/ple gen/tle

VC/CV Words

When two consonants come between two vowels in a word, divide after the first consonant.

Examples: num/ber pen/cil bot/tle

VC/CCV Words

When more than two consonants come between two vowels, divide after the first consonant.

Examples: hun/gry chil/dren

Harcourt

Handwriting

Individual students come to third grade with various levels of handwriting skills, but they all have the desire to communicate effectively. To write correctly, they must be familiar with concepts of

- size (tall, short).
- open and closed.
- capital and lowercase letters.
- manuscript vs. cursive letters.
- letter and word spacing.
- punctuation.

To assess students' handwriting skills, review samples of their written work. Note whether they use correct letter formation and appropriate size and spacing. Note whether students follow the conventions of print such as correct capitalization and punctuation. Encourage students to edit and proofread their work and to use editing marks. When writing messages, notes, and letters, or when publishing their writing, students should leave adequate margins and indent new paragraphs to help make their work more readable for their audience.

Stroke and Letter Formation

Most manuscript letters are formed with a continuous stroke, so students do not often pick up their pencils when writing a single letter. When students begin to use cursive handwriting, they will have to lift their pencils from the paper less frequently and will be able to write more fluently. Models for Harcourt and D'Nealian handwriting are provided on pages R29–R32.

Position for Writing

Establishing the correct posture, pen or pencil grip, and paper position for writing will help prevent handwriting problems.

Posture   Students should sit with both feet on the floor and with hips to the back of the chair. They can lean forward slightly but should not slouch. The writing surface should be smooth and flat and at a height that allows the upper arms to be perpendicular to the surface and the elbows to be under the shoulders.

Writing Instrument   An adult-sized number-two lead pencil is a satisfactory writing tool for most students. As students become proficient in the use of cursive handwriting, have them use pens for writing final drafts. Use your judgment in determining what type of instrument is most suitable.

Paper Position And Pencil Grip   The paper is slanted along the line of the student's writing arm, and the student uses his or her nonwriting hand to hold the paper in place. The student holds the pencil or pen slightly above the paint line—about one inch from the lead tip.

Reaching All Learners

The best instruction builds on what students already know and can do. Given the wide range in students' handwriting abilities, a variety of approaches may be needed.

Extra Support   For students who need more practice keeping their handwriting legible, one of the most important understandings is that legible writing is important for clear communication. Provide many opportunities for writing that communicates among students. For example, students can

- make a class directory listing names and phone numbers of their classmates.
- record observations in science.
- draw and label maps, pictures, graphs, and picture dictionaries.
- write and post messages about class assignments or group activities.

ELL   English-Language Learners can participate in meaningful print experiences. They can

- write signs, labels for centers, and messages.
- label drawings.
- contribute in group writing activities.
- write independently in journals.

You may also want to have students practice handwriting skills in their first language.

Challenge   To ensure continued rapid advancement of students who come to third grade writing fluently, provide

- a wide range of writing assignments.
- opportunities for independent writing on self-selected and assigned topics.

Handwriting
Manuscript Alphabet

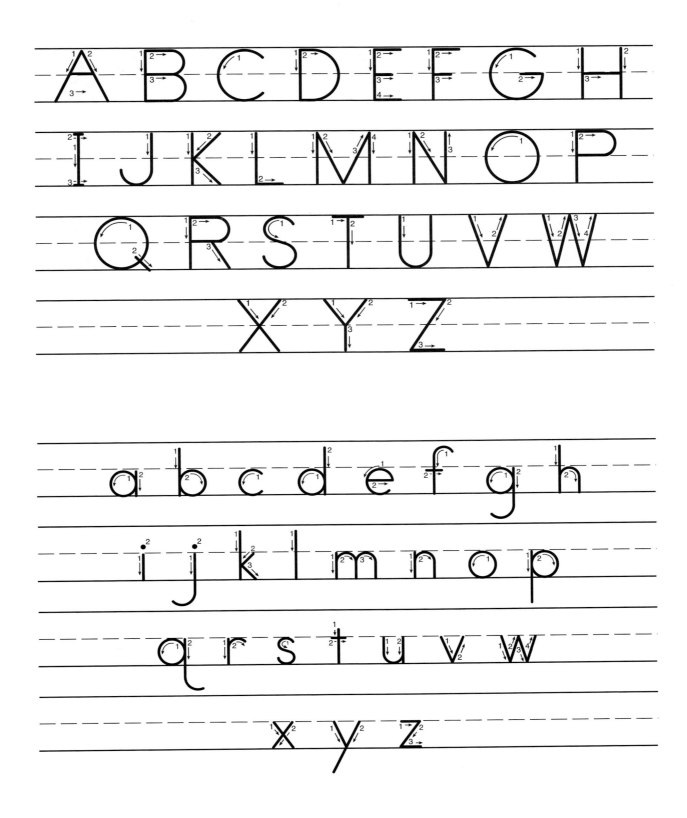

Handwriting
Cursive Alphabet

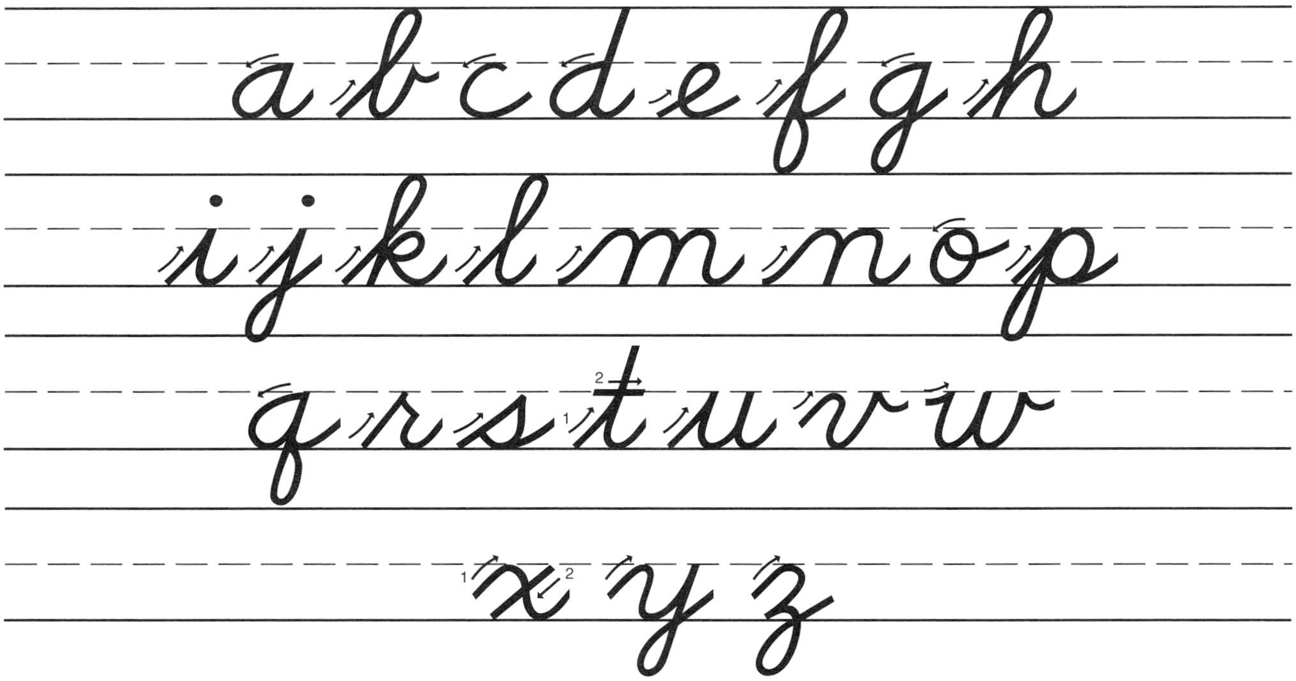

A B C D E F G H
I J K L M N O P
Q R S T U V W
X Y Z

a b c d e f g h
i j k l m n o p
q r s t u v w
x y z

D'Nealian
Handwriting
Manuscript Alphabet

A B C D E F G H

I J K L M N O P

Q R S T U V W

X Y Z

a b c d e f g h

i j k l m n o p

q r s t u v w

x y z

D'Nealian
Handwriting
Cursive Alphabet

A B C D E F G H
I J K L M N O P
Q R S T U V W
X Y Z

a b c d e f g h
i j k l m n o p
q r s t u v w
x y z

HANDWRITING MODEL

Hands-on Grammar Activities

Photocopy the page, cut apart the strips, and distribute them to students. One or more sentences can be distributed at a time. You may also need to distribute blanks and punctuation marks. Students can cut the strips apart into cards and can write replacement words on the backs of cards for some activities. Depending on the needs of your students, have them use the cards to practice and reinforce word order and other grammatical concepts with activities such as the following:

Sentences

- rearrange words to change a statement to a question
- change the sentence type by adding, replacing, or rearranging words
- identify the correct end mark
- combine sentences by using conjunctions

Subjects/Nouns

- replace common nouns with proper nouns, and vice versa
- identify simple and complete subjects
- combine sentences by using compound subjects
- replace general nouns with specific nouns

Predicates/Verbs

- identify complete and simple predicates
- combine sentences by using compound predicates
- replace common verbs with more interesting verbs
- change the subject and then change the verb to agree
- change present-tense verbs to past-tense verbs

Pronouns

- replace nouns with pronouns
- replace possessive nouns with possessive pronouns
- change the pronoun and then change the verb to agree

Adjectives and Adverbs

- add or remove adjectives or adverbs
- replace common adjectives or adverbs with more vivid ones
- experiment with changing the order of two adjectives

School   is   closed   every   Sunday   .

Is   her   dog   '   s   name   Pogo   ?

Jody   plays   the   piano   ,   sings   ,   and

dances   .

One   kitten   '   s   face   is   white   .

There   are   many   different   apples   .

First   ,   you   must   read   the   directions   .

Popcorn   is   a   good   snack   .

Ranchers   help   sick   cows   get   better   .

.   ?   !   ,   "   "   ,   .

Monica washes the dishes , and I dry them .

Did the mayor read your letter ?

My watch is broken again .

The family prepares to celebrate .

A train engine puffs smoke and steam .

We have eaten ripe berries .

George took my ball .

What lovely eyes she has !

| . | ? | ! | , | " | " | , | . |

Harcourt

A   soft   breeze   was   blowing   .

She   is   a   talented   artist   .

The   magazine   printed   an   interesting   article   .

Juan   runs   faster   than   Pete   .

A   marathon   is   the   longest   race   of   all   .

A   few   people   watched   silently   .

There   was   no   school   that   day   .

.   ?   !   ,   "   "   ,   .

HANDS-ON GRAMMAR ACTIVITIES

Harcourt

Mr . Hart will mow the lawn .

My parents bought theater tickets .

Some mammals have very sharp teeth .

They chase butterflies outdoors .

The girls ' masks are colorful .

Uncle Ryan is an astronomer .

Sue and Lakeesha rode the bus .

They watch my mother water the flowers .

| . | ? | ! | , | " | " | ' | . |

Harcourt

Betty   forgot   her   lunch   money   .

It   is   a   small   ,   furry   ,   gentle   animal   .

Kari ' s   address   is   2832   W   .   Fairbanks   St   .

Which   was   the   better   speech   ?

This   rain   is   never   going   to   stop   .

The   tall   ,   gray   stalk   looks   like   a   bird ' s

neck   .

Lisa   is   a   good   pitcher   .

Houston   ,   Texas   ,   is   a   busy   city   .

.   ?   !   ,   "   "   ,   .

Using the Student Record Form

Using the Student Record Form

The record form on the following pages is a tool for tracking each student's progress toward grade-level standards. In addition to formal records on assessment results and instructional plans, you may also wish to complete this form several times yearly for each student. Make one copy of the form for each student. Record the date at the top of the column, and use the codes provided to record student progress. You may wish to add comments at the bottom or on the back of the form.

Sharing Student Progress with Family Members

The record form can be one vehicle for communicating with families about how students are making progress toward grade-level standards. Explain that students are expected to master the standards toward the end of the school year. Therefore, a code of B, or Beginning, at the start of the year is expected for most students. After that time, most students should be receiving a P for Making Progress, and by the end of the year they should meet or exceed each standard.

Students who are not making progress, of course, require intervention and frequent assessment to monitor progress and adapt instruction. Explain to family members the levels of support offered by *Trophies* and how you are using these tools to help their students succeed. On the other hand, some students may begin to meet or exceed the standards early in the year. For these families, you can explain how you are using *Trophies* to extend and accelerate progress. (For more information about levels of support in *Trophies*, see Theme Assessment to Plan Instruction at the beginning of each theme.)

Encouraging Family Involvement

Besides explaining student progress, there are several things you can do to encourage parents and guardians to support their students' achievement:

- Use the School-Home Connection pages in the Theme Resources section to suggest activities and reading materials on a weekly basis.
- Copy the Additional Homework Ideas pages at the beginning of each theme, and send them home with students. Encourage family members to use at least one activity per day.
- Have students use My Reading Log (provided on page R42 in this tabbed section) daily, to record their reading outside of class. Stress repeatedly that sustained daily reading is essential to student growth. Request that parents or guardians sign off on the My Reading Log form, to encourage them to monitor students' reading.
- Above all, offer praise and recognition for all efforts that family members make to support students' literacy.

Student Record Form

Student _____ Teacher _____ Grade _____

	Date____	Date____	Date____	Date____	Date____	Date____
WORD ANALYSIS, FLUENCY, AND SYSTEMATIC VOCABULARY DEVELOPMENT						
Know and use complex word families when reading to decode unfamiliar words.						
Decode regular multisyllabic words.						
Read aloud narrative and expository text fluently and accurately and with appropriate pacing, intonation, and expression.						
Use knowledge of antonyms, synonyms, homophones, and homographs to determine the meanings of words.						
Demonstrate knowledge of levels of specificity among grade-appropriate words and explain the importance of these relations.						
Use sentence and word context to find the meaning of unknown words.						
Use a dictionary to learn the meaning and other features of unknown words.						
Use knowledge of prefixes and suffixes to determine the meaning of words.						
READING COMPREHENSION						
Use titles, tables of contents, chapter headings, glossaries, and indexes to locate information in text.						
Ask questions and support answers by connecting prior knowledge with literal information found in, and inferred from, the text.						
Demonstrate comprehension by identifying answers in the text.						
Recall major points in the text and make and modify predictions about forthcoming information.						
Distinguish the main idea and supporting details in expository text.						
Extract appropriate and significant information from the text, including problems and solutions.						
Follow simple multiple-step written instructions.						
LITERARY RESPONSE AND ANALYSIS						
Distinguish common forms of literature.						
Comprehend basic plots of classic fairy tales, myths, folktales, legends, and fables from around the world.						
Determine what characters are like by what they say or do and by how the author or illustrator portrays them.						
Determine the underlying theme or author's message in fiction and nonfiction text.						
Recognize the similarities of sounds in words and rhythmic patterns in a selection.						
Identify the speaker or narrator in a selection.						
WRITING STRATEGIES						
Create a single paragraph:						
a. Develop a topic sentence.						
b. Include simple supporting facts and details.						
Write legibly in cursive or joined italic, allowing margins and correct spacing between letters in a word and words in a sentence.						
Understand the structure and organization of various reference materials.						
Revise drafts to improve the coherence and logical progression of ideas by using an established rubric.						
WRITING APPLICATIONS (Genres and Their Characteristics)						
Write narratives:						
a. Provide a context within which an action takes place.						
b. Include well-chosen details to develop the plot.						
c. Provide insight into why the selected incident is memorable.						

Harcourt

Write descriptions that use concrete sensory details to present and support unified impressions of people, places, things, or experiences.						
Write personal and formal letters, thank-you notes, and invitations:						
a. Show awareness of the knowledge and interests of the audience and establish a purpose and context.						
b. Include the date, proper salutation, body, closing, and signature.						

WRITTEN AND ORAL ENGLISH LANGUAGE CONVENTIONS

Understand and be able to use complete and correct declarative, interrogative, imperative, and exclamatory sentences in writing and speaking.						
Identify subjects and verbs that are in agreement and identify and use pronouns, adjectives, compound words, and articles correctly in writing and speaking.						
Identify and use past, present, and future verb tenses properly in writing and speaking.						
Identify and use subjects and verbs correctly in speaking and writing simple sentences.						
Punctuate dates, city and state, and titles of books correctly.						
Use commas in dates, locations, and addresses, and for items in a series.						
Capitalize geographical names, holidays, historical periods, and special events correctly.						
Spell correctly one-syllable words that have blends, contractions, compounds, orthographic patterns, and common homophones.						
Arrange words in alphabetic order.						

LISTENING AND SPEAKING STRATEGIES

Retell, paraphrase, and explain what has been said by a speaker.						
Connect and relate prior experiences, insights, and ideas to those of a speaker.						
Respond to questions with appropriate elaboration.						
Identify the musical elements of literary language.						
Organize ideas chronologically or around major points of information.						
Provide a beginning, a middle, and an end, including concrete details that develop a central idea.						
Use clear and specific vocabulary to communicate ideas and establish the tone.						
Clarify and enhance oral presentations through the use of appropriate props.						
Read prose and poetry aloud with fluency, rhythm, and pace, using appropriate intonation and vocal patterns to emphasize important passages of the text being read.						
Compare ideas and points of view expressed in broadcast and print media.						
Distinguish between the speaker's opinions and verifiable facts.						

SPEAKING APPLICATIONS
(Genres and Their Characteristics)

Make brief narrative presentations:						
a. Provide a context for an incident that is the subject of the presentation.						
b. Provide insight into why the selected incident is memorable.						
c. Include well-chosen details to develop character, setting, and plot.						
Plan and present dramatic interpretations of experiences, stories, poems, or plays with clear diction, pitch, tempo, and tone.						
Make descriptive presentations that use concrete sensory details to set forth and support unified impressions of people, places, things, or experiences.						

Comments:

Harcourt

Key:

B = Beginning

P = Making Progress

M = Meets Standard

E = Exceeds Standard

My Reading Log

Student: _____ Date: _____ Grade: _____

Teacher: _____ School: _____

Book Title: _____ Book Author: _____

Total number of pages: _____

Date I started the book: _____ Date I finished the book: _____

I read:

(date/time) _____ (pages) _____ (date/time) _____ (pages) _____

(date/time) _____ (pages) _____ (date/time) _____ (pages) _____

(date/time) _____ (pages) _____ (date/time) _____ (pages) _____

I am spending   more time/less time   reading because _____

_____.

I chose this book to read because _____

_____.

My favorite part of the book was _____

_____.

This book was   easy/difficult   to read because:

❑ I could figure out _____ of the words.   (all, most, some, a few)

❑ I   understood/didn't understand   the topic.

❑ I   liked/disliked   the author.

Other: _____

I   would/would not   choose another book like this because _____

_____.

Harcourt

SELF-ASSESSMENT FORMS

Thinking About My Reading and Writing

Student: _____ Date: _____ Grade: _____

Teacher: _____ School: _____

When I read,

I think about why I am reading something.	**Always**	**Sometimes**	**Need to work on this**
I think about what I already know about the topic.	**Always**	**Sometimes**	**Need to work on this**
I think about what might happen in the story.	**Always**	**Sometimes**	**Need to work on this**
I picture in my mind what I am reading.	**Always**	**Sometimes**	**Need to work on this**
I ask myself if what I'm reading makes sense.	**Always**	**Sometimes**	**Need to work on this**
I think about what kind of story it might be.	**Always**	**Sometimes**	**Need to work on this**

When I write,

I think about my purpose and my reader.	**Always**	**Sometimes**	**Need to work on this**
I list or draw my main ideas.	**Always**	**Sometimes**	**Need to work on this**
I use an organization that makes sense.	**Always**	**Sometimes**	**Need to work on this**
I use my own words and ideas.	**Always**	**Sometimes**	**Need to work on this**
I choose exact, vivid words.	**Always**	**Sometimes**	**Need to work on this**
I use a variety of sentences.	**Always**	**Sometimes**	**Need to work on this**
My writing sounds smooth when I read it aloud.	**Always**	**Sometimes**	**Need to work on this**
I add facts and details when they are needed.	**Always**	**Sometimes**	**Need to work on this**
I group my ideas in paragraphs.	**Always**	**Sometimes**	**Need to work on this**
I proofread to check for errors.	**Always**	**Sometimes**	**Need to work on this**

Harcourt

Listening and Speaking Checklist

Student _____ Teacher _____ Grade _____

	Date____	Date____	Date____	Date____	Date____	Date____
LISTENING AND SPEAKING STRATEGIES						
Retell, paraphrase, and explain what has been said by a speaker.						
Connect and relate prior experiences, insights, and ideas to those of a speaker.						
Respond to questions with appropriate elaboration.						
Identify the musical elements of literary language (e.g., rhymes, repeated sounds, instances of onomatopoeia).						
Organize ideas chronologically or around major points of information.						
Provide a beginning, a middle, and an end, including concrete details that develop a central idea.						
Use clear and specific vocabulary to communicate ideas and establish the tone.						
Clarify and enhance oral presentations through the use of appropriate props (e.g., objects, pictures, charts).						
Read prose and poetry aloud with fluency, rhythm, and pace, using appropriate intonation and vocal patterns to emphasize important passages of the text being read.						
Compare ideas and points of view expressed in broadcast and print media.						
Distinguish between the speaker's opinions and verifiable facts.						
SPEAKING APPLICATIONS						
Make brief narrative presentations: Provide a context for an incident that is the subject of the presentation.						
Provide insight into why the selected incident is memorable.						
Include well-chosen details to develop character, setting, and plot.						
Plan and present dramatic interpretations of experiences, stories, poems, or plays with clear diction, pitch, tempo, and tone.						
Make descriptive presentations that use concrete sensory details to set forth and support unified impressions of people, places, things, or experiences.						

Comments:

Key:

N = Not Observed

O = Observed Occasionally

R = Observed Regularly

Harcourt

Traveling on the Internet

There are so many things to see and do on the Internet that new users may wish they had a "tour guide" to help them see the most interesting sites and make sure they don't miss anything. There are many ways to become a savvy Web traveler—one is by learning the language. Here are some common terms.

bookmark A function that lets you return to your favorite Web sites quickly.

browser Application software that allows you to navigate the Internet and view a Web site.

bulletin board/newsgroup Places to leave an electronic message or to share news that anyone can read and respond to.

chat room A place for people to converse online by typing messages to each other. Once you're in a chat room, others can contact you by e-mail. Some online services monitor their chat rooms and encourage participants to report offensive chatter. Some allow teachers and parents to deny children access to chat rooms altogether.

cookie When you visit a site, a notation known as a "cookie" may be fed to a file in your computer. If you revisit the site, the cookie file allows the Web site to identify you as a return guest—and offer you products tailored to your interests or tastes. You can set your online preferences to limit or let you know about cookies that a Web site places on your computer.

cyberspace Another name for the Internet.

download To move files or software from a remote computer to your computer.

e-mail Messages sent to one or more individuals via the Internet.

filter Software that lets you block access to Web sites and content that you may find unsuitable.

ISP (Internet Service Provider) A service that allows you to connect to the Internet.

junk e-mail Unsolicited commercial e-mail; also known as "spam."

keyword A word you enter into a search engine to begin the search for specific information or Web sites.

links Highlighted words on a Web site that allow you to connect to other parts of the same Web site or to other Web sites.

listserv An online mailing list that allows individuals or organizations to send e-mail to groups of people at one time.

modem An internal or external device that connects your computer to a phone line that can link you to the Internet.

password A personal code that you use to access your Internet account with your ISP.

privacy policy A statement on a Web site describing what information about you is collected by the site and how this information is used.

search engine A function that helps you find information and Web sites. Accessing a search engine is like using the catalog in a library.

URL (Uniform Resource Locator) The address that lets you locate a particular site. For example, **http://www.ed.gov** is the URL for the U.S. Department of Education. All government URLs end in **.gov**. Nonprofit organizations and trade associations end in **.org**. Commercial companies now end in **.com**, and non-commercial educational sites end in **.edu**. Countries other than the United States use different endings.

virus A file maliciously planted in your computer that can damage files and disrupt your system. Antivirus software is available.

Web site An Internet destination where you can look at and retrieve data. All the Web sites in the world, linked together, make up the World Wide Web or the "Web."

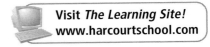

Visit *The Learning Site!*
www.harcourtschool.com

My Rules for Internet Safety

I agree that

- **I will never give out private information,** such as my last name, my address, my telephone number, or my parents' work addresses or telephone numbers on the Internet.

- **I will never give out the address or telephone number** of my school on the Internet without first asking an adult's permission.

- **I understand which sites I can visit** and which ones are off-limits.

- **I will tell an adult right away** if something comes up on the screen that makes me feel uncomfortable.

- **I will never agree to meet in person** with anyone I meet online.

- **I will never e-mail a person any pictures** of myself or my classmates without an adult's permission.

- **I will tell an adult** if I get an inappropriate e-mail message from anyone.

- **I will remember that going online** on the Internet is like going out in public, so all the safety rules I already know apply here as well.

- **I know the Internet is a useful tool,** and I will always use it responsibly.

- **I will follow these same rules when I am at home,** in school, at the library, or at a friend's.

X

_____   _____
(Student signs here)   (Parent/Guardian signs here)

Visit *The Learning Site!*
www.harcourtschool.com

Harcourt

Professional Bibliography

Adams, M. J. 1990. *Beginning to Read: Thinking and Learning About Print.* Cambridge: Massachusetts Institute of Technology Press.

Adams, M. J., et al. 1998. "The Elusive Phoneme: Why Phonemic Awareness Is So Important and How to Help Children Develop It," *American Educator: The Unique Power of Reading and How to Unleash It,* Vol. 22, Nos. 1 and 2, 18–29.

Adams, M. J.; R. Treiman; and M. Pressley. 1998. "Reading, Writing, and Literacy," in *Handbook of Child Psychology: Child Psychology in Practice* (Fifth edition). Vol. 4. Edited by I. E. Sigel and K. A. Renninger. New York: Wiley.

Allen, L. 1998. "An Integrated Strategies Approach: Making Word Identification Instruction Work for Beginning Readers," *The Reading Teacher,* Vol. 52, No. 3, 254–68.

American Association of School Librarians and the Association of Educational Communications and Technology. 1998. *Information Power: Building Partnerships for Learning.* Chicago: American Library Association.

Anderson, R. C., et al. 1985. *Becoming a Nation of Readers: The Report of the Commission on Reading.* Washington, D.C.: National Academy of Education, Commission on Education and Public Policy.

Anderson, R. C.; P. T. Wilson; and L. G. Fielding. 1988. "Growth in Reading and How Children Spend Their Time Outside of School," *Reading Research Quarterly,* Vol. 23, No. 3, 285–303.

Anderson, R. C., and W. E. Nagy. 1991. "Word Meanings," in *Handbook of Reading Research.* Vol. 2. Edited by R. Barr, et al. New York: Longman.

Ball, E. W., and B. A. Blachman. 1991. "Does Phoneme Awareness Training in Kindergarten Make a Difference in Early Word Recognition and Developmental Spelling?" *Reading Research Quarterly,* Vol. 26, No. 1, 49–66.

Barinaga, M. 1996. "Giving Language Skills a Boost," *Science,* Vol. 271, 27–28.

Baumann, J. F., and E. J. Kame'enui. 1991. "Research on Vocabulary Instruction: Ode to Voltaire," in *Handbook of Research on Teaching the English Language Arts.* Edited by J. Flood, J. J. D. Lapp, and J. R. Squire. New York: Macmillan.

Beck, I., et al. 1996. "Questioning the Author: A Year-Long Classroom Implementation to Engage Students with Text," *The Elementary School Journal,* Vol. 96, 385–414.

Beck, I., et al. 1998. "Getting at the Meaning: How to Help Students Unpack Difficult Text," *American Educator: The Unique Power of Reading and How to Unleash It,* Vol. 22, Nos. 1 and 2, 66–71, 85.

Beck, I., et al. 1997. *Questioning the Author: An Approach for Enhancing Student Engagement with Text.* Newark, Del.: International Reading Association.

Berninger, V. W., et al. 1994. "Developmental Skills Related to Writing and Reading Acquisition in the Intermediate Grades," *Reading and Writing: An Interdisciplinary Journal,* Vol. 6, 161–96.

Berthoff, A. E. 1984. "Recognition, Representation, and Revision," in *Rhetoric and Composition: A Sourcebook for Teachers and Writers.* Edited by R. Graves. Portsmouth, N.H.: Boynton Cook.

Blachman, B. A., et al. 1994. "Kindergarten Teachers Develop Phoneme Awareness in Low-Income, Inner-City Classrooms," *Reading and Writing: An Interdisciplinary Journal,* Vol. 6, 1–18.

Blachowicz, C. L. Z., and P. Fisher. 1996. *Teaching Vocabulary in All Classrooms.* Englewood Cliffs, N.J.: Merrill/Prentice Hall.

Bloom, B. S., ed. 1985. *Developing Talent in Young People.* New York: Ballantine Books.

Bus, A. G.; M. H. vanIJzendoorn; and A. D. Pellegrini. 1995. "Joint Book Reading Makes for Success in Learning to Read: A Meta-Analysis on Inter-generational Transmission of Literacy," *Review of Educational Research,* Vol. 65, 1–21.

Byrne, B., and R. Fielding-Barnsley. 1995. "Evaluation of a Program to Teach Phonemic Awareness to Young Children: A One- and Three-Year Follow-Up and a New Preschool Trial," *Journal of Educational Psychology,* Vol. 87, No. 3, 488–503.

California Department of Education. 1996. *Connect, Compute, and Compete: The Report of the California Education Technology Task Force.* Sacramento: California Department of Education.

California Department of Education. 1994. *Differentiating the Core Curriculum and Instruction to Provide Advanced Learning Opportunities.* Sacramento: California Department of Education.

California Department of Education. 1998. *English-Language Arts Content Standards for California Public Schools, Kindergarten Through Grade Twelve.* Sacramento: California Department of Education.

California Department of Education. 1995. *Every Child a Reader: The Report of the California Reading Task Force.* Sacramento: California Department of Education.

California Department of Education. 1998. *Fostering the Development of a First and a Second Language in Early Childhood.* Sacramento: California Department of Education.

California Department of Education. 1999. *Reading/Language Arts Framework for California Public Schools: Kindergarten Through Grade Twelve.* Sacramento: California Department of Education.

California Department of Education. 1996. *Recommended Readings in Literature, Kindergarten Through Grade Eight* (Revised annotated edition). Sacramento: California Department of Education.

Calkins, L. 1996. "Motivating Readers," ERIC Clearinghouse on Assessment and Evaluation (No. SP525606), *Instructor,* Vol. 106, No. 1, 32–33.

Campbell, F. A., and C. T. Ramsey. 1995. "Cognitive and Social Outcomes for High-Risk African American Students at Middle Adolescence: Positive Effects of Early Intervention," *American Educational Research Journal,* Vol. 32, 743–72.

Carlisle, J. F., and D. M. Nomanbhoy. 1993. "Phonological and Morphological Awareness in First-Graders," *Applied Psycholinguistics,* Vol. 14, 177–95.

Carnine, D.; J. Silbert; and E. J. Kame'enui. 1990. *Direct Instruction Reading.* Columbus, Ohio: Merrill Publishing Company.

Chall, J.; V. Jacobs; and L. Baldwin. 1990. *The Reading Crisis: Why Poor Children Fall Behind.* Cambridge: Harvard University Press.

Cornwall, A., and H. Bawden. 1992. "Reading Disabilities and Aggression: A Critical Review," *Journal of Learning Disabilities,* Vol. 25, 281–88.

Corson, D. 1995. *Using English Words.* Dordrecht, Netherlands: Kluwer.

Cunningham, A. E., and K. E. Stanovich. 1993. "Children's Literacy Environments and Early Word Recognition Subskills," *Reading and Writing: An Interdisciplinary Journal,* Vol. 5, 193–204.

Cunningham, A. E., and K. E. Stanovich. 1998. "What Reading Does for the Mind," *American Educator: The Unique Power of Reading and How to Unleash It,* Vol. 22, Nos. 1 and 2, 8–15.

Cunningham, P. M. 1998. "The Multisyllabic Word Dilemma: Helping Students Build Meaning, Spell, and Read 'Big' Words," *Reading and Writing Quarterly,* Vol. 14, 189–218.

Daneman, M. 1991. "Individual Differences in Reading Skills," in *Handbook of Reading Research* (Vol. 2). Edited by R. Barr, M. L. Kamil, P. B. Mosenthal, and P. D. Pearson. New York: Longman.

Defior, S., and P. Tudela. 1994. "Effect of Phonological Training on Reading and Writing Acquisition," *Reading and Writing,* Vol. 6, 299–320.

Delpit, L. D. 1986. "Skills and Other Dilemmas of a Progressive Black Educator," *Harvard Educational Review,* Vol. 56, 379–85.

Dickinson, D. K., and M. W. Smith. 1994. "Long-Term Effects of Preschool Teachers' Book Readings on Low-Income Children's Vocabulary and Story Comprehension," *Reading Research Quarterly,* Vol. 29, No. 2, 104–22.

Dillard, A. 1998. "What Reading Does for the Soul: A Girl and Her Books," *American Educator: The Unique Power of Reading and How to Unleash It,* Vol. 22, Nos. 1 and 2, 88–93.

Ediger, M. 1988. "Motivation in the Reading Curriculum," ERIC Clearinghouse on Assessment and Evaluation (No. CS009424).

Ehri, L. 1994. "Development of the Ability to Read Words: Update," in *Theoretical Models and Processes of Reading.* Edited by R. Ruddell, M. Ruddell, and H. Singer. Newark, Del.: International Reading Association.

Ehri, L. C., and S. McCormick. 1998. "Phases of Word Learning: Implications for Instruction with Delayed and Disabled Readers," *Reading and Writing Quarterly,* Vol. 14, 135–63.

Ehri, L. C. 1991. "Development of the Ability to Read Words," in *Handbook of Reading Research* (Vol. 2). Edited by R. Barr, et al. New York: Longman.

Ehrlich, M. F.; B. Kurtz-Costess; and C. Loridant. 1993. "Cognitive and Motivational Determinants of Reading Comprehension in Good and Poor Readers," *Journal of Reading Behavior,* Vol. 25, No. 4, 365–81.

Eisenberg, M., and R. Berkowitz. 1990. *Information Problem Solving: The Big Six Skills Approach to Library and Information Skills Instruction.* Norwood, N.J.: Ablex.

Englert, C. S., et al. 1995. "The Early Literacy Project: Connecting Across the Literacy Curriculum," *Learning Disability Quarterly,* Vol. 18, 253–75.

Epstein, J. L. 1995. "School-Family-Community Partnerships: Caring for Children We Share," *Phi Delta Kappan,* Vol. 76, No. 9, 701–2.

Felton, R. H., and P. P. Pepper. 1995. "Early Identification and Intervention of Phonological Deficits in Kindergarten and Early Elementary Children at Risk for Reading Disability," *School Psychology Review,* Vol. 24, 405–14.

Fielding, L. G., and Pearson, P. D. 1994. "Synthesis of Research—Reading Comprehension: What Works," *Educational Leadership,* Vol. 51, No. 5, 62–7.

Fielding-Barnsley, R. 1997. "Explicit Instruction in Decoding Benefits Children High in Phonemic Awareness and Alphabet Knowledge," *Scientific Studies of Reading,* Vol. 1, No. 1, 85–98.

Fitzgerald, J. 1995. "English-as-a-Second-Language Learners' Cognitive Reading Processes: A Review of Research in the U.S.," *Review of Educational Research,* Vol. 65, 145–90.

Flower, L. 1985. *Problem-Solving Strategies for Writing.* New York: Harcourt Brace Jovanovich.

Foorman, B., et al. 1998. "The Role of Instruction in Learning to Read: Preventing Reading Failure in At-Risk Children," *Journal of Educational Psychology,* Vol. 90, 37–55.

Foster, K. C., et al. 1994. "Computer-Assisted Instruction in Phonological Awareness: Evaluation of the DaisyQuest Program," *Journal of Research and Development in Education,* Vol. 27, 126–37.

Fuchs, L. S., et al. 1993. "Formative Evaluation of Academic Progress: How Much Growth Can We Expect?" *School Psychology Review,* Vol. 22, No. 1, 27–48.

Gambrell, L. B., et al. 1996. *Elementary Students' Motivation to Read.* Reading Research Report No. 52. Athens, Ga.: National Reading Research Center.

Gardner, H. 1983. *Frames of Mind: The Theory of Multiple Intelligences.* New York: Basic Books.

Gersten, R., and J. Woodward. 1995. "A Longitudinal Study of Transitional and Immersion Bilingual Education Programs in One District," *Elementary School Journal,* Vol. 95, 223–39.

Giles, H. C. 1997. "Parent Engagement as a School Reform Strategy," ERIC Clearinghouse on Urban Education (Digest 135).

Goldenberg, C. N., and R. Gallimore. 1991. "Local Knowledge, Research Knowledge, and Educational Change: A Case Study of Early [First-Grade] Spanish Reading Improvement," *Educational Researcher,* Vol. 20, No. 8, 2–14.

Goldenberg, C. 1992–93. "Instructional Conversations: Promoting Comprehension Through Discussion," *The Reading Teacher,* Vol. 46, 316–26.

Good, R. III; D. C. Simmons; and S. Smith. 1998. "Effective Academic Interventions in the United States: Evaluating and Enhancing the Acquisition of Early Reading Skills," *School Psychology Review,* Vol. 27, No. 1, 45–56.

Greene, J. F. 1998. "Another Chance: Help for Older Students with Limited Literacy," *American Educator: The Unique Power of Reading and How to Unleash It,* Vol. 22, Nos. 1 and 2, 74–79.

Guthrie, J. T., et al. 1996. "Growth of Literacy Engagement: Changes in Motivations and Strategies During Concept-Oriented Reading Instruction," *Reading Research Quarterly,* Vol. 31, 306–25.

Hanson, R. A., and D. Farrell. 1995. "The Long-Term Effects on High School Seniors of Learning to Read in Kindergarten," *Reading Research Quarterly,* Vol. 30, No. 4, 908–33.

Hart, B., and T. R. Risley. 1995. *Meaningful Differences in the Everyday Experience of Young American Children.* Baltimore: Paul H. Brookes Publishing Co.

Hasbrouck, J. E., and G. Tindal. 1992. "Curriculum-Based Oral Reading Fluency Norms for Students in Grades 2 Through 5," *Teaching Exceptional Children,* Vol. 24, 41–44.

Hiebert, E. H., et al. 1992. "Reading and Writing of First-Grade Students in a Restructured Chapter I Program," *American Educational Research Journal,* Vol. 29, 545–72.

Hillocks, G., Jr. 1986. *Research on Written Composition: New Directions for Teaching.* Urbana, Ill.: National Council for Teachers of English.

Honig, B.; L. Diamond; and L. Gutlohn. 2000. *Teaching Reading Sourcebook for Kindergarten Through Eighth Grade.* Emeryville, CA: CORE, Consortium on Reading Excellence.

Honig, B.; L. Diamond; and R. Nathan. 1999. *Assessing Reading: Multiple Measures for Kindergarten Through Eighth Grade.* Emeryville, CA: CORE, Consortium on Reading Excellence.

Hoover-Dempsey, K. V., and H. M. Sandler. 1997. "Why Do Parents Become Involved in Their Children's Education?" *Review of Educational Research,* Vol. 67, No. 1, 3–42.

Hunter, M., and G. Barker. 1987. "If at First . . . : Attribution Theory in the Classroom," *Educational Leadership,* Vol. 45, No. 2, 50–53.

Jimenez, R. T.; G. E. Garcia; and P. D. Pearson. 1996. "The Reading Strategies of Latina/o Students Who Are Successful Readers: Opportunities and Obstacles," *Reading Research Quarterly,* Vol. 31, 90–112.

Juel, C. 1991. "Beginning Reading," in *Handbook of Reading Research* (Vol. 2). Edited by R. Barr, M. L. Kamil, P. B. Mosenthal, and P. D. Pearson. New York: Longman.

Juel, C. 1988. "Learning to Read and Write: A Longitudinal Study of 54 Children from First Through Fourth Grades," *Journal of Educational Psychology,* Vol. 80, 437–447.

Kame'enui, E. J. 1996. "Shakespeare and Beginning Reading: 'The Readiness Is All,'" *Teaching Exceptional Children,* Vol. 28, No. 2, 77–81.

Kuhn, M. R., and S. A. Stahl. 1998. "Teaching Children to Learn Word Meanings from Context: A Synthesis and Some Questions," *Journal of Literacy Research,* Vol. 30, No. 1, 119–38.

Lance, K. C.; L. Welborn; and C. Hamilton-Pennell. 1993. *The Impact of School Library Media Centers on Academic Achievement.* San Jose, Calif.: Hi Willow Research and Publishing.

Leather, C. V., and L. A. Henry. 1994. "Working Memory Span and Phonological Awareness Tasks as Predictors of Early Reading Ability," *Journal of Experimental Child Psychology,* Vol. 58, 88–111.

Levy, B. A.; A. Nicholls; and D. Kohen. 1993. "Repeated Readings: Process Benefits for Good and Poor Readers," *Journal of Experimental Child Psychology,* Vol. 56, 303–27.

Liberman, I. Y.; D. Shankweiler; and A. M. Liberman. 1991. "The Alphabetic Principle and Learning to Read," in *Phonology and Reading Disability: Solving the Reading Puzzle.* Edited by D. Shankweiler and I. Y. Liberman. Ann Arbor: University of Michigan Press.

Lie, A. 1991. "Effects of a Training Program for Stimulating Skills in Word Analysis in First-Grade Children," *Reading Research Quarterly,* Vol. 26, No. 3, 234–50.

Lipson, M. Y., and K. K. Wixson. 1986. "Reading Disability Research: An Interactionist Perspective," *Review of Educational Research,* Vol. 56, 111–36.

Louis, K. S.; H. M. Marks; and S. Kruse. 1996. "Teachers' Professional Community in Restructuring Schools," *American Educational Research Journal* (Vol. 33).

Lundberg, I.; J. Frost; and O. P. Petersen. 1988. "Effects of an Extensive Program for Stimulating Phonological Awareness in Preschool Children," *Reading Research Quarterly,* Vol. 23, 263–284.

Lyon, G. R. 1995. "Toward a Definition of Dyslexia," *Annals of Dyslexia,* Vol. 45, 3–27.

Lyon, G. R., and V. Chhabra. 1996. "The Current State of Science and the Future of Specific Reading Disability," *Mental Retardation and Developmental Disabilities Research Reviews,* Vol. 2, 2–9.

Markell, M. A., and S. L. Deno. 1997. "Effects of Increasing Oral Reading: Generalization Across Reading Tasks," *The Journal of Special Education,* Vol. 31, No. 2, 233–50.

McCollum, H., and A. Russo. 1993. *Model Strategies in Bilingual Education: Family Literacy and Parent Involvement.* Washington, D.C.: United States Department of Education.

McGuinness, D.; C. McGuinness; and J. Donahue. 1996. "Phonological Training and the Alphabetic Principle: Evidence for Reciprocal Causality," *Reading Research Quarterly,* Vol. 30, 830–52.

McWhorter, J. 1998. *The Word on the Street: Fact and Fable about American English.* New York: Plenum.

Moats, L. C. 1995. *Spelling: Development, Disability, and Instruction.* Baltimore: York Press.

Moats, L. C. 1998. "Teaching Decoding," *American Educator: The Unique Power of Reading and How to Unleash It,* Vol. 22, Nos. 1 and 2, 42–49, 95–96.

Moffett, J., and B. J. Wagner. 1991. *Student-Centered Language Arts, K-12.* Portsmouth, N.H.: Boynton Cook.

Morrow, L. M. 1992. "The Impact of a Literature-Based Program on Literacy, Achievement, Use of Literature, and Attitudes of Children from Minority Backgrounds," *Reading Research Quarterly,* Vol. 27, 250–75.

Mosenthal, P. 1984. "The Problem of Partial Specification in Translating Reading Research into Practice," *The Elementary School Journal,* Vol. 85, No. 2, 199–227.

Mosenthal, P. 1985. "Defining Progress in Educational Research," *Educational Researcher,* Vol. 14, No. 9, 3–9.

Mosteller, F.; R. Light; and J. Sachs. 1996. "Sustained Inquiry in Education: Lessons from Skill Grouping and Class Size," *Harvard Educational Review,* Vol. 66, No. 4, 797–842.

National Center to Improve the Tools of Educators. 1997. *Learning to Read, Reading to Learn—Helping Children to Succeed: A Resource Guide.* Washington, D.C.: American Federation of Teachers.

National Research Council. 1998. *Preventing Reading Difficulties in Young Children.* Edited by M. S. Burns, P. Griffin, and C. E. Snow. Washington, D.C.: National Academy Press.

National Research Council. 1999. *Starting Out Right: A Guide to Promoting Children's Reading Success.* Edited by M. S. Burns, P. Griffin, and C. E. Snow. Washington, D.C.: National Academy Press.

Neuman, S. B. 1996. "Children Engaging in Storybook Reading: The Influence of Access to Print Resources, Opportunity, and Parental Interaction," *Early Childhood Research Quarterly,* Vol. 11, 495–513.

O'Connor, R. E.; J. R. Jenkins; and T. A. Slocum. 1995. "Transfer Among Phonological Tasks in Kindergarten: Essential Instructional Content," *Journal of Educational Psychology,* Vol. 87, 202–17.

Pearson, P. D., et al. 1992. "Developing Expertise in Reading Comprehension," in *What Research Says to the Teacher.* Edited by S. J. Samuels and A. E. Farstrup. Newark, Del.: International Reading Association.

Pearson, P. D., and K. Camperell. 1985. "Comprehension in Text Structures," in *Theoretical Models and Processes of Reading.* Edited by H. Singer and R. B. Ruddell. Newark, Del.: International Reading Association.

Perfetti, C. A., and S. Zhang. 1995. "The Universal Word Identification Reflex," in *The Psychology of Learning and Motivation* (Vol. 33). Edited by D. L. Medlin. San Diego: Academic Press.

Phillips, L. M.; S. P. Norris; and J. M. Mason. 1996. "Longitudinal Effects of Early Literacy Concepts on Reading Achievement: A Kindergarten Intervention and Five-Year Follow-Up," *Journal of Literacy Research,* Vol. 28, 173–95.

Pinnell, G. S., and L C. Fountas. 1997. *Help America Read: A Handbook for Volunteers.* Portsmouth, N.H.: Heinemann.

Pressley, M.; J. Rankin; and L. Yokoi. 1996. "A Survey of Instructional Practices of Primary Teachers Nominated as Effective in Promoting Literacy," *The Elementary School Journal,* Vol. 96, 363–84.

Purcell-Gates, V.; E. McIntyre; and P. Freppon. 1995. "Learning Written Storybook Language in School: A Comparison of Low-SES Children in Skills-Based and Whole-Language Classrooms," *American Educational Research Journal,* Vol. 32, 659–85.

Robbins, C., and L. C. Ehri. 1994. "Reading Storybooks to Kindergartners Helps Them Learn New Vocabulary Words," *Journal of Educational Psychology,* Vol. 86, No. 1, 54–64.

Rosenshine, B., and C. Meister. 1994. "Reciprocal Teaching: A Review of the Research," *Review of Educational Research,* Vol. 64, No. 4, 479–530.

Ross, S. M., et al. 1995. "Increasing the Academic Success of Disadvantaged Children: An Examination of Alternative Early Intervention Programs," *American Educational Research Journal,* Vol. 32, 773–800.

Ruddell, R.; M. Rapp Ruddell; and H. Singer, eds. 1994. *Theoretical Models and Processes of Reading* (Fourth edition). Newark, Del.: International Reading Association.

Ryder, R. J., and M. F. Graves. 1994. "Vocabulary Instruction Presented Prior to Reading in Two Basal Readers," *Elementary School Journal*, Vol. 95, No. 2, 139–53.

Sacks, C. H., and J. R. Mergendoller. 1997. "The Relationship Between Teachers' Theoretical Orientation Toward Reading and Student Outcomes in Kindergarten Children with Different Initial Reading Abilities," *American Educational Research Journal*, Vol. 34, 721–39.

Samuels, S. J. 1979. "The Method of Repeated Reading," *The Reading Teacher*, Vol. 32, 403–08.

Sanacore, J. 1988. "Linking Vocabulary and Comprehension Through Independent Reading," ERIC Clearinghouse on Assessment and Evaluation (No. CS009409).

Shefelbine, J. 1991. *Encouraging Your Junior High Student to Read.* Bloomington, Ind.: ERIC Clearinghouse on Reading, English, and Communication.

Shefelbine, J. L. 1990. "Student Factors Related to Variability in Learning Word Meanings from Context," *Journal of Reading Behavior*, Vol. 22, No. 1, 71–97.

Shore, B. M., et al. 1991. *Recommended Practices in Gifted Education: A Critical Analysis.* New York: Teachers College Press.

Shore, W. J., and F. T. Durso. 1990. "Partial Knowledge in Vocabulary Acquisition: General Constraints and Specific Detail," *Journal of Educational Psychology*, Vol. 82, 315–18.

Simmons, D. C., and E. J. Kame'enui. 1996. "A Focus on Curriculum Design: When Children Fail," in *Strategies for Teaching Children in Inclusive Settings.* Edited by E. Meyen, G. Vergason, and R. Whelan. Denver: Love Publishing.

Simmons, D. C., and E. J. Kame'enui, eds. 1998. *What Reading Research Tells Us About Children with Diverse Learning Needs: Bases and Basics.* Mahwah, N.J.: Lawrence Erlbaum Associates.

Sindelar, P. T.; L. Monda; and L. O'Shea. 1990. "Effects of Repeated Readings on Instructional- and Mastery-Level Readers," *Journal of Educational Research*, Vol. 83, 220–26.

Slavin, R. E.; N. L. Karweit; and B. A. Wasik, eds. 1993. *Preventing Early School Failure: Research, Policy, and Practice.* 1993. Boston: Allyn and Bacon.

Snider, V. E. 1995. "A Primer on Phonological Awareness: What It Is, Why It's Important, and How to Teach It," *School Psychology Review*, Vol. 24, 443–55.

Spear-Swerling, L., and R. J. Sternberg. 1998. "Curing Our 'Epidemic' of Learning Disabilities," *Phi Delta Kappan*, Vol. 79, No. 5, 397–401.

Spear-Swerling, L., and R. J. Sternberg. 1996. *Off Track: When Poor Readers Become Learning Disabled.* Boulder, Colo.: Westview Press.

Stanovich, K. E. 1986. "Matthew Effects in Reading: Some Consequences of Individual Differences in the Acquisition of Literacy," *Reading Research Quarterly*, Vol. 21, 360–407.

Stanovich, K. E. 1994. "Constructivism in Reading Education," *The Journal of Special Education*, Vol. 28, 259–74.

Stanovich, K. E. 1993–94. "Romance and Reality," *The Reading Teacher*, Vol. 47, 280–90.

Sulzby, E., and W. Teale. 1991. "Emergent Literacy," in *Handbook of Reading Research* (Vol. 2). Edited by R. Barr, M. L. Kamil, P. B. Mosenthal, and P. D. Pearson. New York: Longman.

Topping, K. 1998. "Effective Tutoring in America Reads: A Reply to Wasik," *The Reading Teacher*, Vol. 52, No. 1, 42–50.

Torgesen, J. K. 1998. "Catch Them Before They Fall: Identification and Assessment to Prevent Reading Failure in Young Children," *American Educator: The Unique Power of Reading and How to Unleash It*, Vol. 22, Nos. 1 and 2, 32–39.

Treiman, R. 1985. "Onsets and Rimes as Units of Spoken Syllables: Evidence from Children," *Journal of Experimental Child Psychology*, Vol. 39, 161–81.

Treiman, R.; S. Weatherston; and D. Berch. 1994. "The Role of Letter Names in Children's Learning of Phoneme-Grapheme Relations," *Applied Psycholinguistics*, Vol. 15, 97–122.

Vandervelden, M. C., and L. S. Siegel. 1995. "Phonological Recoding and Phoneme Awareness in Early Literacy: A Developmental Approach," *Reading Research Quarterly*, Vol. 30, 854–73.

Vellutino, F. R., et al. 1996. "Cognitive Profiles of Difficult-to-Remediate and Readily Remediated Poor Readers: Early Intervention as a Vehicle for Distinguishing Between Cognitive and Experiential Deficits as Basic Causes of Specific Reading Disability," *Journal of Educational Psychology*, Vol. 88, 601–38.

Wagner, R. K., et al. 1993. "Development of Young Readers' Phonological Processing Abilities," *Journal of Educational Psychology*, Vol. 85, 83–103.

Walberg, H. J. 1984. "Families as Partners in Educational Productivity," *Phi Delta Kappan*, Vol. 65, No. 6, 397–400.

Wasik, B. A., and R. E. Slavin. 1993. "Preventing Early Reading Failure with One-to-One Tutoring: A Review of Five Programs," *Reading Research Quarterly*, Vol. 28, 178–200.

Wells, G. 1986. *The Meaning Makers: Children Learning Language and Using Language to Learn.* Portsmouth, N.H.: Heinemann.

White, T. G.; M. F. Graves; and W. H. Slater. 1990. "Growth of Reading Vocabulary in Diverse Elementary Schools: Decoding and Word Meaning," *Journal of Educational Psychology*, Vol. 82, 281–90.

Whitehurst, G. J., et al. 1994. "Outcomes of an Emergent Literacy Intervention in Head Start," *Journal of Educational Psychology*, Vol. 86, 542–55.

Yopp, H. K. 1988. "The Validity and Reliability of Phonemic Awareness Tests," *Reading Research Quarterly*, Vol. 23, No. 2, 159–77.

PROFESSIONAL BIBLIOGRAPHY

Program Reviewers

Dr. Judylynn Baily-Mitchell
Principal
West Salisbury
Elementary School
Salisbury, Maryland

Dr. Judith F. Barry
Coordinator of Reading/
Language Arts
Taunton Public Schools
Taunton, Massachusetts

Carol Berman
Lead Teacher
Crestview Elementary School
Miami, Florida

Angela Berner
Language Arts Staff Developer
Huntington Unified
School District
Administration Offices
Huntington Station, New York

Susan Birch
Teacher
Dunns Corners
Elementary School
Westerly, Rhode Island

Candace Bouchard
Teacher
Sandburg Elementary School
San Diego, California

Sandra Carron
Teacher
Moreno Valley Unified
School District
Moreno Valley, California

Loretta Cudney
Teacher
Riverside Unified School District
Riverside, California

Justyne Davis
Teacher
Wallbridge Community
Education Center
St. Louis, Missouri

Dr. Ann Dugger
Reading Teacher/Title I
Will Rogers Elementary School
Stillwater, Oklahoma

Rosemary Forsythe
Reading Specialist
West Pottsgrove
Elementary School
Pottstown, Pennsylvania

Stanley Foster
Teacher
Magnolia Avenue School
Los Angeles, California

Kimberly Griffeth
Teacher
Fulton Elementary
Aurora, Colorado

Jeffrey Guerra
Teacher
Westchase Elementary School
Tampa, Florida

Anne Henry
Teacher
Northern Hills
Elementary School
Edmond, Oklahoma

Carol Hookway
Teacher
Memorial Elementary School
Natick, Massachusetts

Arlene Horkey
Curriculum/Technology
Specialist
Belleair Elementary School
Clearwater, Florida

Carolyn M. Horton
District Reading Facilitator
Cedar Rapids Community
School District,
Educational Service Center
Cedar Rapids, Iowa

Patty Jacox
Teacher
Lansing Elementary School
Aurora, Colorado

Beverly Keeley
Teacher
Grant Foreman
Elementary School
Muskogee, Oklahoma

Rebecca L. Kelly
Teacher
Wekiva Elementary School
Longwood, Florida

Lisa Leslie
Teacher
Costello Elementary School,
Troy Public Schools
Troy, Michigan

Arlene D. Loughlin
Student Achievement Specialist
Curlew Creek
Elementary School
Palm Harbor, Florida

Christin Machado
Teacher
Jefferson Elementary School
Burbank, California

Alicia L. Marsh
Teacher
Pearl Sample
Elementary School
Culpeper, Virginia

K. Gale Martin
Teacher
JEB Stuart Elementary School
Richmond, Virginia

Anne M. Merritt
Teacher
Citrus Glen Elementary School
Ventura, California

Joan Miller
Teacher
Carlton Hills Elementary School
Santee, California

Bobbie A. Overbey
Teacher
Carillon Elementary School
Oviedo, Florida

Katherin Pagakis
English Teacher
Washington Elementary School
Waukegan, Illinois

Barbara Pitts
Administrator
Joy Middle School
Detroit, Michigan

Sundee Preedy
Teacher
Aloma Elementary School
Winter Park, Florida

Dr. Carolyn Reedom
Principal
Vanderberg Elementary School
Henderson, Nevada

Dorina Rocas
Teacher
Corono-Norco Unified
School District
Corona, California

Josephine Scott
Language Arts
Curriculum Director
Columbus City School District,
Northgate Center
Columbus, Ohio

Renee Seifert
Teacher
Serrano Elementary School
Moreno Valley, California

Gayle E. Sitter
Mathematics Resource
Teacher
Educational Leadership Center
Orlando, Florida

Linda Smolen
Director of Reading
Buffalo City School District
Buffalo, New York

Gail Soft
Teacher
Vermillion Primary School
Maize, Kansas

Alejandro Soria
Teacher
Leo Politi Elementary
Los Angeles, California

Jan Strege
Vice-Principal
Schlegel Road
Elementary School
Webster, New York

Dahna Taylor
Teacher
Chavez Elementary School
San Diego, California

Dr. Sandra Telfort
Teacher
Palmetto Elementary School
Miami, Florida

Dana Thurm
Teacher
Olivenhain Pioneer
Elementary School
Carlsbad, California

Geralyn Wilson
Literacy Coordinator
James McCosh Intermediate
Chicago, Illinois

John L. York
Teacher
Cedar Heights
Elementary School
Cedar Falls, Iowa

Maureen A. Zoda
Reading Specialist Coordinator
Meadow Brook
Elementary School
East Longmeadow,
Massachusetts

KINDERGARTEN REVIEWERS

Janice Allocco
Teacher
Klem Road South
Elementary School
Webster, New York

Irma A. Barr
Teacher
Embassy Creek
Elementary School
Cooper City, Florida

Dikki Cie Chanski
Teacher
Martell Elementary School
Troy, Michigan

Rosemary Gaskin
Reading Specialist
Broad Rock Elementary School
Richmond, Virginia

Carol Grenfell
District Language
Arts Specialist
Ventura Unified School District
Ventura, California

Cathleen Hunter
Teacher
Peterson Elementary
Huntington Beach, California

Karen A. Kuritar
Teacher
Allen Elementary School
Dayton, Ohio

Charlotte Otterbacher
Teacher
Hamilton Elementary
Troy, Michigan

Gwendolyn Perkins
Teacher
Ginter Park Elementary School
Richmond, Virginia

Kelly Schmitt
Teacher
Public School #225 Seaside
Rockaway Parkway, New York

Corene Selman
Teacher
Westwood Early
Childhood Center
Woodward, Oklahoma

Laureen B. Stephens
Teacher
Mountainview
Elementary School
Saycus, California

Pam Styles
Teacher
World of Wonder
Community School
Dayton, Ohio

Scope and Sequence

Reading	GR K	GR 1	GR 2	GR 3	GR 4	GR 5	GR 6
Concepts about Print							
Understand that print provides information	▨						
Understand how print is organized and read	▨						
Know left-to-right and top-to-bottom directionality	▨						
Distinguish letters from words	▨						
Recognize name	▨						
Name and match all uppercase and lowercase letter forms	▨						
Understand the concept of word and construct meaning from shared text, illustrations, graphics, and charts	▨	▨					
Identify letters, words, and sentences	▨	▨					
Recognize that sentences in print are made up of words	▨						
Identify the front cover, back cover, title page, title, and author of a book	▨						
Match oral words to printed words	▨						
Phonemic Awareness							
Understand that spoken words and syllables are made up of sequences of sounds	▨						
Count and track sounds in a syllable, syllables in words, and words in sentences	▨	▨	▨				
Know the sounds of letters	▨	▨					
Track and represent the number, sameness, difference, and order of two or more isolated phonemes	▨	▨					
Match, identify, distinguish, and segment sounds in initial, final, and medial position in single-syllable spoken words	▨						
Blend sounds (phonemes) to make words or syllables	▨						
Track and represent changes in syllables and words as target sound is added, substituted, omitted, shifted, or repeated	▨						
Distinguish long- and short-vowel sounds in orally stated words	▨						
Identify and produce rhyming words	▨	▨					
Decoding: Phonic Analysis							
Understand and apply the alphabetic principle	▨						
Consonants: single, blends, digraphs in initial, final, medial positions	•	•	•				
Vowels: short, long, digraphs, r-controlled, variant, schwa		•	•				
Match all consonant and short-vowel sounds to appropriate letters	•	•					
Understand that as letters in words change, so do the sounds	•	•					
Blend vowel-consonant sounds orally to make words or syllables	•	•					
Blend sounds from letters and letter patterns into recognizable words	▨	▨					
Decoding: Structural Analysis							
Inflectional endings, with and without spelling changes: plurals, verb tenses, possessives, comparatives-superlatives		•	•				
Contractions, abbreviations, and compound words		•	•				
Prefixes, suffixes, derivations, and root words			•	•	•	•	•
Greek and Latin roots					•	•	•
Letter, spelling, and syllable patterns			▨	▨	▨	▨	▨
Phonograms/word families/onset-rimes		▨	▨				
Syllable rules and patterns				•			

Key

Shaded area Explicit Instruction / Modeling / Practice and Application

• Tested

Assessment resources include: Kindergarten Assessment Handbook; Placement and Diagnostic Assessments, Grades 1, 2, and 3–6; Reading and Language Skills Assessments, Grades 1–6; Holistic Assessments, Grades 1–6; End-of-Selection Tests, Grades 1–6; and Oral Reading Fluency Assessment, Grades 1–6

	GR K	GR 1	GR 2	GR 3	GR 4	GR 5	GR 6
Decoding: Strategies							
Visual cues: sound/symbol relationships, letter patterns, and spelling patterns		▒	▒	▒	▒	▒	▒
Structural cues: compound words, contractions, inflectional endings, prefixes, suffixes, Greek and Latin roots, root words, spelling patterns, and word families		▒	▒	▒	▒	▒	▒
Cross check visual and structural cues to confirm meaning			▒	▒	▒	▒	▒
Syllabication rules and patterns			▒	▒	▒	▒	▒
Word Recognition							
One-syllable and high-frequency words	•	•	•				
Common, irregular sight words	•	•	•				
Common abbreviations			•				
Lesson vocabulary		•	•	•	•	•	•
Fluency							
Read aloud in a manner that sounds like natural speech		•	•				
Read aloud accurately and with appropriate intonation and expression			•	•			
Read aloud narrative and expository text with appropriate pacing, intonation, and expression				•	•	•	•
Read aloud prose and poetry with rhythm and pace, appropriate intonation, and vocal patterns				▒	▒	▒	▒
Vocabulary and Concept Development							
Academic language	▒	▒	▒	▒	▒	▒	▒
Classify-categorize		•		•		•	
Antonyms			•	•	•		
Synonyms			•	•	•		
Homographs				•	•		
Homophones			•	•	•	•	
Multiple-meaning words			•	•		•	
Figurative and idiomatic language							•
Context/context clues			•	•	•	•	•
Content-area words							
Dictionary, glossary, thesaurus				•	•		
Foreign words							
Connotation-denotation						•	•
Word origins (acronyms, clipped and coined words, regional variations, etymologies, jargon, slang)							
Analogies							
Word structure clues to determine meaning			•	•	•	•	•
Inflected nouns and verbs, comparatives-superlatives, possessives, compound words, prefixes, suffixes, root words			•	•	•	•	•
Greek and Latin roots, prefixes, suffixes, derivations, and root words					•	•	•
Develop vocabulary							
Listen to and discuss text read aloud	▒	▒	▒	▒	▒	▒	▒
Read independently	▒	▒	▒	▒	▒	▒	▒
Use reference books	▒	▒	▒	▒	▒	▒	▒
Comprehension and Analysis of Text							
Ask/answer questions	▒	▒	▒	▒	▒	▒	▒
Author's purpose				•	•	•	•
Author's perspective						•	•
Propaganda/bias							•

Key

Shaded area Explicit Instruction / Modeling / Practice and Application

• Tested

Assessment resources include: Kindergarten Assessment Handbook; Placement and Diagnostic Assessments, Grades 1, 2, and 3–6; Reading and Language Skills Assessments, Grades 1–6; Holistic Assessments, Grades 1–6; End-of-Selection Tests, Grades 1–6; and Oral Reading Fluency Assessment, Grades 1–6

	GR K	GR 1	GR 2	GR 3	GR 4	GR 5	GR 6
Background knowledge: prior knowledge and experiences							
Cause-effect			•	•	•	•	•
Compare-contrast			•	•	•	•	•
Details		•	•	•	•	•	•
Directions: one-, two-, multi-step	•	•	•	•	•		
Draw conclusions				•	•	•	•
Fact-fiction							
Fact-opinion				•	•	•	•
Higher order thinking							
Analyze, critique and evaluate, synthesize, and visualize text and information							
Interpret information from graphic aids			•	•	•	•	•
Locate information		•	•	•	•	•	•
Book parts				•			•
Text features				•		•	
Alphabetical order		•					
Main idea: stated/unstated		•	•	•	•	•	•
Main idea and supporting details				•	•	•	•
Make generalizations							
Make inferences			•	•	•	•	•
Make judgments							
Make predictions/predict outcomes							
Monitor comprehension							
Adjust reading rate, create mental images, reread, read ahead, set/adjust purpose, self-question, summarize/paraphrase, use graphic aids, text features, and text adjuncts							
Paraphrase/restate facts and details			•	•	•	•	•
Preview							
Purpose for reading							
Organize information							
Alphabetical order							
Numerical systems/outlines							
Graphic organizers							
Referents							
Retell stories and ideas							
Sequence		•	•	•	•	•	•
Summarize			•	•	•	•	•
Text structure							
Narrative text			•	•	•	•	•
Informational text (compare and contrast, cause and effect, sequence/chronological order, proposition and support, problem and solution)					•	•	•
Study Skills							
Follow and give directions			•	•	•		
Apply plans and strategies: KWL, question-answer-relationships, skim and scan, note taking, outline, questioning the author, reciprocal teaching							
Practice test-taking strategies							

Key

Shaded area Explicit Instruction / Modeling / Practice and Application

• Tested

Assessment resources include: Kindergarten Assessment Handbook; Placement and Diagnostic Assessments, Grades 1, 2, and 3–6; Reading and Language Skills Assessments, Grades 1–6; Holistic Assessments, Grades 1–6; End-of-Selection Tests, Grades 1–6; and Oral Reading Fluency Assessment, Grades 1–6

	GR K	GR 1	GR 2	GR 3	GR 4	GR 5	GR 6
Research and Information							
Use resources and references							
Understand the purpose, structure, and organization of various reference materials							
Title page, table of contents, chapter titles, chapter headings, index, glossary, guide words, citations, end notes, bibliography				•			•
Picture dictionary, software, dictionary, thesaurus, atlas, globe, encyclopedia, telephone directory, on-line information, card catalog, electronic search engines and data bases, almanac, newspaper, journals, periodicals			•	•	•	•	•
Charts, maps, diagrams, timelines, schedules, calendar, graphs, photos			•	•			•
Choose reference materials appropriate to research purpose							•
Viewing/Media							
Interpret information from visuals (graphics, media, including illustrations, tables, maps, charts, graphs, diagrams, timelines)			•	•	•	•	•
Analyze the ways visuals, graphics, and media represent, contribute to, and support meaning of text							
Select, organize, and produce visuals to complement and extend meaning							
Use technology or appropriate media to communicate information and ideas							
Use technology or appropriate media to compare ideas, information, and viewpoints							
Compare, contrast, and evaluate print and broadcast media							
Distinguish between fact and opinion							
Evaluate the role of media							
Analyze media as sources for information, entertainment, persuasion, interpretation of events, and transmission of culture							
Identify persuasive and propaganda techniques used in television and identify false and misleading information							
Summarize main concept and list supporting details and identify biases, stereotypes, and persuasive techniques in a nonprint message							
Support opinions with detailed evidence and with visual or media displays that use appropriate technology							
Literary Response and Analysis							
Genre Characteristics							
Know a variety of literary genres and their basic characteristics			•	•	•	•	•
Distinguish between fantasy and realistic text							
Distinguish between informational and persuasive texts							
Understand the distinguishing features of literary and nonfiction texts: everyday print materials, poetry, drama, fantasies, fables, myths, legends, and fairy tales			•	•	•	•	•
Explain the appropriateness of the literary forms chosen by an author for a specific purpose							
Literary Elements							
Plot/Plot Development							
Important events		•	•	•	•	•	•
Beginning, middle, end of story		•	•				
Problem/solution			•				
Conflict				•			
Conflict and resolution/causes and effects					•	•	•
Compare and contrast							
Character							
Identify		•					
Identify, describe, compare and contrast			•	•	•	•	•
Relate characters and events					•	•	•

Key

Shaded area Explicit Instruction/Modeling/Practice and Application

•   Tested

     Assessment resources include: Kindergarten Assessment Handbook; Placement and Diagnostic Assessments, Grades 1, 2, and 3–6; Reading and Language Skills Assessments, Grades 1–6; Holistic Assessments, Grades 1–6; End-of-Selection Tests, Grades 1–6; and Oral Reading Fluency Assessment, Grades 1–6

SCOPE AND SEQUENCE

	GR K	GR 1	GR 2	GR 3	GR 4	GR 5	GR 6
Traits, actions, motives				•	•	•	•
Cause for character's actions					•		
Character's qualities and effect on plot							•
Setting							
Identify and describe		•	•	•	•	•	•
Compare and contrast			•	•	•	•	•
Relate to problem/resolution							
Theme							
Theme/essential message				•	•	•	•
Universal themes							
Mood/Tone							
Identify							•
Compare and contrast							•

Literary Devices/Author's Craft

	GR K	GR 1	GR 2	GR 3	GR 4	GR 5	GR 6
Rhythm, rhyme, pattern, and repetition							
Alliteration, onomatopoeia, assonance, imagery							
Figurative language (similes, metaphors, idioms, personification, hyperbole)				•	•	•	•
Characterization/character development				•		•	
Dialogue				•	•	•	•
Narrator/narration					•	•	•
Point of view (first-person, third-person, omniscient)					•	•	•
Informal language (idioms, slang, jargon, dialect)							

Response to Text

	GR K	GR 1	GR 2	GR 3	GR 4	GR 5	GR 6
Relate characters and events to own life							
Read to perform a task or learn a new task							
Recollect, talk, and write about books read							
Describe the roles and contributions of authors and illustrators							
Generate alternative endings and identify the reason and impact of the alternatives							
Compare and contrast versions of the same stories that reflect different cultures							
Make connections between information in texts and stories and historical events							
Form ideas about what had been read and use specific information from the text to support these ideas							
Know that the attitudes and values that exist in a time period or culture affect stories and informational articles written during that time period							
Explore origin and historical development of words and changes in sentence patterns over the years							

Self-Selected Reading

	GR K	GR 1	GR 2	GR 3	GR 4	GR 5	GR 6
Select material to read for pleasure							
Read a variety of self-selected and assigned literary and informational texts							
Use knowledge of authors' styles, themes, and genres to choose own reading							
Read literature by authors from various cultural and historical backgrounds							

Cultural Awareness

	GR K	GR 1	GR 2	GR 3	GR 4	GR 5	GR 6
Connect information and events in texts to life and life to text experiences							
Compare language, oral traditions, and literature that reflect customs, regions, and cultures							
Identify how language reflects regions and cultures							
View concepts and issues from diverse perspectives							
Recognize the universality of literary themes across cultures and language							

Key

Shaded area Explicit Instruction / Modeling / Practice and Application

• Tested

Assessment resources include: Kindergarten Assessment Handbook; Placement and Diagnostic Assessments, Grades 1, 2, and 3–6; Reading and Language Skills Assessments, Grades 1–6; Holistic Assessments, Grades 1–6; End-of-Selection Tests, Grades 1–6; and Oral Reading Fluency Assessment, Grades 1–6

Writing

Writing Strategies

	GR K	GR 1	GR 2	GR 3	GR 4	GR 5	GR 6
Writing process: prewriting, drafting, revising, proofreading, publishing							
Collaborative, shared, timed writing, writing to prompts		•	•	•	•	•	•
Evaluate own and others' writing							
Proofread writing to correct convention errors in mechanics, usage, punctuation, using handbooks and references as appropriate				•	•	•	•

Organization and Focus

	GR K	GR 1	GR 2	GR 3	GR 4	GR 5	GR 6
Use models and traditional structures for writing							
Select a focus, structure, and viewpoint							
Address purpose, audience, length, and format requirements							
Write single- and multiple-paragraph compositions			•	•	•	•	•

Revision Skills

	GR K	GR 1	GR 2	GR 3	GR 4	GR 5	GR 6
Correct sentence fragments and run-ons					•	•	•
Vary sentence structure, word order, and sentence length							
Combine sentences					•	•	•
Improve coherence, unity, consistency, and progression of ideas							
Add, delete, consolidate, clarify, rearrange text							
Choose appropriate and effective words: exact/precise words, vivid words, trite/overused words						•	•
Elaborate: details, examples, dialogue, quotations							
Revise using a rubric							

Penmanship/Handwriting

	GR K	GR 1	GR 2	GR 3	GR 4	GR 5	GR 6
Write uppercase and lowercase letters							
Write legibly, using appropriate word and letter spacing							
Write legibly, using spacing, margins, and indention							

Writing Applications

	GR K	GR 1	GR 2	GR 3	GR 4	GR 5	GR 6
Narrative writing (stories, paragraphs, personal narratives, journal, plays, poetry)		•	•	•	•	•	•
Descriptive writing (titles, captions, ads, posters, paragraphs, stories, poems)		•	•	•	•	•	•
Expository writing (comparison-contrast, explanation, directions, speech, how-to article, friendly/business letter, news story, essay, report, invitation)			•	•	•	•	•
Persuasive writing (paragraph, essay, letter, ad, poster)						•	•
Cross-curricular writing (paragraph, report, poster, list, chart)							
Everyday writing (journal, message, forms, notes, summary, label, caption)							

Written and Oral English Language Conventions

Sentence Structure

	GR K	GR 1	GR 2	GR 3	GR 4	GR 5	GR 6
Types (declarative, interrogative, exclamatory, imperative, interjection)		•	•	•	•	•	•
Structure (simple, compound, complex, compound-complex)		•	•	•	•	•	•
Parts (subjects/predicates: complete, simple, compound; clauses: independent, dependent, subordinate; phrase)		•	•	•	•	•	•
Direct/indirect object							
Word order		•					

Grammar

	GR K	GR 1	GR 2	GR 3	GR 4	GR 5	GR 6
Nouns (singular, plural, common, proper, possessive, collective, abstract, concrete, abbreviations, appositives)		•	•	•	•	•	•
Verbs (action, helping, linking, transitive, intransitive, regular, irregular; subject-verb agreement)		•	•	•	•	•	•
Verb tenses (present, past, future; present, past, and future perfect)		•	•	•	•	•	•
Participles; infinitives							

Key

Shaded area Explicit Instruction/Modeling/Practice and Application

•   Tested

Assessment resources include: Kindergarten Assessment Handbook; Placement and Diagnostic Assessments, Grades 1, 2, and 3–6; Reading and Language Skills Assessments, Grades 1–6; Holistic Assessments, Grades 1–6; End-of-Selection Tests, Grades 1–6; and Oral Reading Fluency Assessment, Grades 1–6

	GR K	GR 1	GR 2	GR 3	GR 4	GR 5	GR 6
Adjectives (common, proper; articles; comparative, superlative)		•	•	•	•	•	•
Adverbs (place, time, manner, degree)				•	•	•	•
Pronouns (subject, object, possessive, reflexive, demonstrative, antecedents)		•	•	•	•	•	•
Prepositions; prepositional phrases					•	•	•
Conjunctions							
Abbreviations, contractions				•	•	•	•
Punctuation							
Period, exclamation point, or question mark at end of sentences		•	•	•	•	•	•
Comma			•	•	•	•	•
Greeting and closure of a letter				•	•	•	•
Dates, locations, and addresses				•	•	•	•
For items in a series				•	•	•	•
Direct quotations							
Link two clauses with a conjunction in compound sentences					•	•	•
Quotation marks			•	•	•	•	•
Dialogue, exact words of a speaker				•	•	•	•
Titles of books, stories, poems, magazines						•	•
Parentheses/dash/hyphen						•	•
Apostrophes in possessive case of nouns and in contractions				•	•	•	•
Underlining or italics to identify title of documents					•	•	•
Colon					•	•	•
Separate hours and minutes					•	•	•
Introduce a list					•	•	•
After the salutation in business letters						•	•
Semicolons to connect independent clauses							
Capitalization							
First word of a sentence, names of people, and the pronoun *I*	•	•	•	•	•	•	•
Proper nouns, words at the beginning of sentences and greetings, months and days of the week, and titles and initials of people		•	•	•	•	•	•
Geographical names, holidays, historical periods, and special events							•
Names of magazines, newspapers, works of art, musical compositions, organizations, and the first word in quotations when appropriate							•
Use conventions of punctuation and capitalization							
Spelling							
Spell independently by using pre-phonetic knowledge, sounds of the alphabet, and knowledge of letter names							
Use spelling approximations and some conventional spelling							
Common, phonetically regular words			•	•	•	•	•
Frequently used, irregular words		•	•	•	•	•	•
One-syllable words with consonant blends			•	•	•	•	•
Contractions, compounds, orthographic patterns, and common homophones				•	•	•	•
Greek and Latin roots, inflections, suffixes, prefixes, and syllable constructions					•	•	•
Use a variety of strategies and resources to spell words							
Listening and Speaking							
Listening Skills and Strategies							
Listen to a variety of oral presentations such as stories, poems, skits, songs, personal accounts, or informational speeches							
Listen attentively to the speaker (make eye contact and demonstrate appropriate body language)							

Key

Shaded area   Explicit Instruction / Modeling / Practice and Application

•   Tested

Assessment resources include: Kindergarten Assessment Handbook; Placement and Diagnostic Assessments, Grades 1, 2, and 3–6; Reading and Language Skills Assessments, Grades 1–6; Holistic Assessments, Grades 1–6; End-of-Selection Tests, Grades 1–6; and Oral Reading Fluency Assessment, Grades 1–6

	GR K	GR 1	GR 2	GR 3	GR 4	GR 5	GR 6
Listen for a purpose							
Follow oral directions (one-, two-, three-, and multi-step)	▓	▓	▓	▓			
For specific information	▓	▓	▓	▓			
For enjoyment	▓	▓	▓	▓			
To distinguish between the speaker's opinions and verifiable facts				▓	▓	▓	
To actively participate in class discussions				▓	▓	▓	
To expand and enhance personal interest and personal preferences							▓
To identify, analyze, and critique persuasive techniques							▓
To identify logical fallacies used in oral presentations and media messages						▓	
To make inferences or draw conclusions							
To interpret a speaker's verbal and nonverbal messages, purposes, and perspectives							
To identify the tone, mood, and emotion							
To analyze the use of rhetorical devices for intent and effect							
To evaluate classroom presentations							
To respond to a variety of media and speakers		▓	▓	▓			
To paraphrase/summarize directions and information				▓	▓		
For language reflecting regions and cultures				▓	▓		
To recognize emotional and logical arguments						▓	
To identify the musical elements of language				▓			
Listen critically to relate the speaker's verbal communication to the nonverbal message							
Speaking Skills and Strategies							
Speak clearly and audibly and use appropriate volume and pace in different settings	▓	▓	▓	▓	▓	▓	▓
Use formal and informal English appropriately	▓	▓	▓	▓	▓	▓	▓
Follow rules of conversation	▓	▓	▓	▓	▓	▓	▓
Stay on the topic when speaking	▓						
Use descriptive words							
Recount experiences in a logical sequence							
Clarify and support spoken ideas with evidence and examples							
Use eye contact, appropriate gestures, and props to enhance oral presentations and engage the audience				▓	▓	▓	▓
Give and follow two-, three-, and four-step directions		▓	▓	▓			
Recite poems, rhymes, songs, stories, soliloquies, or dramatic dialogues	▓	▓	▓	▓	▓	▓	▓
Plan and present dramatic interpretations with clear diction, pitch, tempo, and tone				▓	▓	▓	▓
Organize presentations to maintain a clear focus							
Use language appropriate to situation, purpose, and audience				▓	▓	▓	▓
Make/deliver							
Oral narrative, descriptive, informational, and persuasive presentations							
Oral summaries of articles and books						▓	
Oral responses to literature						▓	
Presentations on problems and solutions						▓	
Presentation or speech for specific occasions, audiences, and purposes						▓	▓
Vary language according to situation, audience, and purpose							
Select a focus, organizational structure, and point of view for an oral presentation							
Participate in classroom activities and discussions	▓	▓	▓	▓	▓	▓	▓

Key

Shaded area   Explicit Instruction/Modeling/Practice and Application

•   Tested
    Assessment resources include: Kindergarten Assessment Handbook; Placement and Diagnostic Assessments, Grades 1, 2, and 3–6;
    Reading and Language Skills Assessments, Grades 1–6; Holistic Assessments, Grades 1–6; End-of-Selection Tests, Grades 1–6; and
    Oral Reading Fluency Assessment, Grades 1–6

Index

A

Abbreviations.
See **Grammar, Word Study.**
Academic Language: 3-1: 16, 44, 70, 102, 132, 148, 158, 163, 172, 184, 187, 193, 208, 211, 226, 258, 263, 284, 293, 306, 332, 358, 390; **3-2:** 16, 23, 38, 41, 62, 77, 87, 96, 120, 148, 170, 196, 224, 264, 302, 326, 350, 372, 402
Access Prior Knowledge.
See **Building Background and Concepts; Comprehension, prior knowledge; Prereading Strategies.**
Acknowledgements: 3-1: R91–R93; **3-2:** R91–R93
Acronyms.
See **Word Study.**
Active Reading Strategies.
See **Strategies Good Readers Use.**
Additional Reading.
See **Independent Reading; Independent Reading Books; Library Books Collection; Trade Books.**
Additional Support Activities: 3-1: S1–S31, S33–S63, S65–S95; **3-2:** S1–S31, S33–S63, S65–S95
Adjectives.
See **Grammar.**
Adjust Reading Rate.
See **Strategies Good Readers Use.**
Advanced Students, Activities for.
See **Reaching All Learners.**
Adverbs.
See **Author's Craft; Grammar.**
Advertisement
"Stupendous Sticker Store," **3-2:** 292–293
See also **Genre.**
Affixes.
See **Decoding/Phonics; Prefixes and Suffixes; Vocabulary and Concepts, prefixes, suffixes, and roots.**
Alliteration.
See **Author's Craft.**
Almanac.
See **Reference Sources.**
Alphabetic Knowledge.
See **Decoding/Phonics; Spelling.**
Alphabetical Order.
See **Research and Information Skills.**
Alternative Teaching Strategies: 3-1: T2–T9, T36–T43, T68–T76; **3-2:** T2–T9, T38–T45, T70–T77
American Sign Language: 3-1: 269
Analogies.
See **Vocabulary and Concepts, synonyms and antonyms; Word Study.**

Antonyms.
See **Word Study; Vocabulary and Concepts, synonyms and antonyms.**
Apostrophe.
See **Mechanics.**
Appreciating the Literature.
See **Literary Response and Analysis.**
Art Activities.
See **Content Areas; Cross-Curricular Connections; Viewing.**
Articles:
3-1: "Dogs and People Today," 256G
3-1: "A Guide to Basketball," 122–125
3-1: "The Hitting Machine of San Diego," 330G
3-1: "Sue, the Tyrannosaurus Rex," 246–251
3-2: "Mapping the World," 394–395
3-2: "Our Nation's Oldest City: St. Augustine, Florida," 216–217
3-2: "Seeds Can Sleep," 342–343
Articles: (a, an, the).
See **Grammar.**
Assessment
diagnostic check
grammar: **3-1:** 41E, 67G, 99G, 129E, 153G, 181G, 205G, 223G, 255E, 279E, 303G, 329G, 355G, 387G, 407E; **3-2:** 35G, 59G, 93G, 117E, 143E, 167E, 193G, 221G, 261G, 297G, 323E, 347E, 369G, 399G, 417E
skills: **3-1:** 40, 66, 98, 128, 152, 180, 204, 222, 254, 294, 328, 354, 386, 406; **3-2:** 34, 58, 92, 116, 142, 166, 192, 220, 260, 296, 322, 346, 368, 398, 416
vocabulary: **3-1:** 14K, 42K, 68K, 100K, 130K, 156K, 182K, 206K, 224K, 256K, 282K, 304K, 330K, 356K, 388K; **3-2:** 14K, 36K, 60K, 94K, 118K, 146K, 168K, 194K, 222K, 262K, 300K, 324K, 348K, 370K, 400K
formal
End-of-Selection Tests: **3-1:** 12F, 34, 62, 94, 118, 146, 154F, 174, 198, 216, 244, 274, 280F, 296, 320, 348, 380, 402; **3-2:** 12F, 28, 82, 112, 134, 144F, 160, 186, 214, 252, 288, 297S, 298F, 316, 340, 364, 390, 410
End-of-Year Reading and Language Skills Assessment: **3-2:** 298G
Holistic Assessment: **3-1:** 12G, 154F, 280F; **3-2:** 12F, 143Q, 144F, 297S, 298F, 417Q
Mid-Year Reading and Language Skills Assessment: **3-1:** 280G

Oral Reading Accuracy and Fluency Assessment: **3-1:** 12F, 33, 41A, 61, 67C, 93, 99C, 117, 129A, 145, 153C, 154F, 173, 181C, 197, 205C, 223A, 243, 255A, 273, 279A, 280F, 295, 303C, 319, 329C, 347, 355A, 379, 387A, 401, 407A, T10–T12, T44–T46, T77–T79; **3-2:** 12F, 25, 35C, 49, 59A, 81, 93A, 111, 117A, 133, 143A, 143Q, 144F, 159, 167A, 183, 193C, 213, 221A, 251, 261C, 287, 297C, 297S, 298F, 315, 323A, 339, 347A, 363, 369C, 389, 399A, 409, 417A, T10–T12, T46–T48, T78–T80
Placement and Diagnostic Assessments: **3-1:** 12F, 154F, 280F; **3-2:** 12F, 144F, 298F
Reading and Language Skills Assessment: **3-1:** 12F, 14B, 42B, 68B, 100B, 130B, 153S, 154F, 156B, 182B, 206B, 224B, 256B, 280F, 282B, 304B, 330B, 356B, 388B; **3-2:** 12F, 14B, 36B, 60B, 94B, 118B, 144F, 146B, 168B, 194B, 222B, 262B, 297S, 298F, 300B, 324B, 348B, 370B, 400B
informal
anecdotal records: **3-1:** 153W, 279U, 407U; **3-2:** 143U, 297W, 417U
benchmarks: **3-1:** R39–R41; **3-2:** R39–R41
comprehension skills.
See **diagnostic check, skills.**
conferences: **3-1:** 41D, 99F, 129D, 181F, 205F, 223F, 255D, 303F, 329F, 355F, 387F; **3-2:** 35F, 59F, 93F, 117D, 193F, 261F, 297F, 323D, 347D, 369F, 399F, 417D
literary response and analysis.
See **diagnostic check, skills.**
ongoing oral reading fluency: **3-1:** 41A, 67C, 99C, 129A, 153C, 181C, 205C, 223A, 255A, 279A, 303C, 329C, 355A, 387A, 407A; **3-2:** 35C, 59A, 93A, 117A, 143A, 167A, 193C, 221A, 261C, 297C, 323A, 347A, 369C, 399A, 417A
peer assessment.
See **student self- and peer assessment.**
portfolio assessment: **3-1:** 99F, 129D, 153F, 223F, 255D, 279D, 355F, 387F, 407D; **3-2:** 93F, 117D, 143D, 261F, 297F, 347D, 369F, 417D
See also **portfolio opportunities.**
record forms, student: **3-1:** R39–R41; **3-2:** R39–R41

Books on Tape.
See **Audiotexts.**
Building Background and Concepts: 3-1: 12, 14K, 42K, 68K, 100K, 130K, 154, 156K, 182K, 206K, 224K, 256K, 280, 282K, 304K, 330K, 356K, 388K, S3; **3-2:** 12, 14K, 36K, 60K, 94K, 118K, 144, 146K, 168K, 194K, 222K, 262K, 298, 300K, 324K, 348K, 370K, 400K
See also **Prereading Strategies.**
Brainstorming.
See **Writing Process, prewriting.**

Capitalization and Punctuation.
See **Mechanics.**
Captions.
See **Research and Information Skills; Text Structure, expository text.**
Card Catalog.
See **Library/Media Center; Research and Information Skills, library/media center.**
Categorizing/Classifying.
See **Classify and Categorize; Vocabulary and Concepts, classify and categorize.**
Cause and Effect: 3-1: 28, 32, 48, 52, 54, 60, 62, 88, 100H, 108, 122, 124, 136, 194, 200, 218, 224H, 234, 244, 266, 274, 310, 322, 362, 364, 366, 370, 372, 374, 376, 378; **3-2:** 18, 28, 44, 64, 66, 80, 88, 98, 102, 106, 108, 124, 152, 164, 178, 182, 198, 200, 206, 210, 238, 244, 272, 282, 312, 324I, 328, 330, 336, 338, 342, 346–347, 358, 360, 362, 364, 369D, 370I, 376, 382, 384, 386, 388, 390, 398–399, 406, 408, 417P, S74, S75, S86, S87, T71
See also **Comprehension.**
Centers.
See **Cross-Curricular Stations.**

Challenge.
See **Additional Support Activities; Books for All Learners; Reaching All Learners, advanced.**
Character Map.
See **Research and Information Skills, organizing information graphically.**
Characterization.
See **Literary Response and Analysis.**
Characters' Feelings and Actions.
See **Literary Response and Analysis, narrative elements.**
Charts, Use and Interpret.
See **Research and Information Skills, graphic aids, organizing information graphically.**
Classify and Categorize: 3-1: 181A–181B, 223C, 279B, T37; **3-2:** 21, 47, 79, 125, 168E, 193K, 205, 209, 210, 233, 239, 324E, 333, 370E
See also **Vocabulary and Concepts.**
Classroom Library.
See **Classroom Management, stations, library center; Library Books Collection; Trade Books.**
Classroom Management: 3-1: R19–R22; **3-2:** R19–R22
managing small groups: **3-1:** 41L, 41N, 67N, 67P, 99N, 99P, 129L, 129N, 153N, 153P, 181N, 181P, 205N, 205P, 223N, 223P, 255L, 255N, 279L, 279N, 303N, 303P, 329N, 329P, 355N, 355P, 387N, 387P, 407L, 407N; **3-2:** 35N, 35P, 59N, 59P, 93N, 93P, 117L, 117N, 143L, 143N, 167L, 167N, 193N, 193P, 221N, 221P, 261N, 261P, 297N, 297P, 323L, 323N, 347L, 347N, 369N, 369P, 399N, 399P, 417L, 417N
planning charts: **3-1:** 14C–14D, 42C–42D, 68C–68D, 100C–100D, 130C–130D, 156C–156D, 182C–182D, 206C–206D, 224C–224D, 256C–256D, 282C–282D, 304C–304D, 330C–330D, 356C–356D, 388C–388D; **3-2:** 14C–14D, 36C–36D, 60C–60D, 94C–94D, 118C–118D, 146C–146D, 168C–168D, 194C–194D, 222C–222D, 262C–262D, 300C–300D, 324C–324D, 348C–348D, 370C–370D, 400C–400D
stations
art: **3-1:** 156E; **3-2:** 36E
health/physical education: **3-1:** 130E, 282E
inquiry projects: **3-1:** 14F, 42F, 68F, 100F, 130F, 156F, 182F, 206F, 224F, 256F, 282F, 304F, 330F, 356F, 388F; **3-2:** 14F, 36F, 60F, 94F, 118F, 146F, 168F, 194F, 222F, 262F, 300F, 324F, 348F, 370F, 400F
library center: **3-1:** 14F, 42F, 68F, 100F, 130F, 156F, 182F, 206F,

D

Daily Language Practice: 3-1: 14C–14D, 41E–41F, 42C–42D, 67G–67H, 68C–68D, 99G–99H, 100C–100D, 129E–129F, 130C–130D, 153G–153H, 154C–154D, 181G–181H, 182C–182D, 205G–205H, 206C–206D, 223G–223H, 224C–224D, 255E–255F, 256C–256D, 279E–279F, 282C–282D, 303G–303H, 304C–304D, 329E–329H, 330C–330D, 355G–355H, 356C–356D, 387E–387H, 388C–388D, 407E–407F; **3-2:** 14C–14D, 35E–35H, 36C–36D, 59G–59H, 60C–60D, 93G–93H, 94C–94D, 117E–117F, 118C–118D, 143E–143F, 146C–146D, 167E–167F, 168C–168D, 193G–193H, 194C–194D, 221G–221H, 222C–222D, 261G–261H, 262C–262D, 297G–297H, 300C–300D, 323E–323F, 324C–324D, 347E–347F, 348C–348D, 369G–369H, 370C–370D, 399G–399H, 400C–400D, 417E–417F

Daily Routines.
See **Question of the Day, Daily Language Practice, Writing Prompts, Daily Writing Prompts.**

Daily Writing Prompts.
See **Writing Prompts.**

Debate.
See **Listening and Speaking, speaking.**

Declarative Sentences.
See **Grammar, statements and questions.**

Decodable Text.
See **Decoding/Phonics.**

Decode Long Words: 3-1: 22, 24, 30, 41K, 41L, 41M, 72, 84, 88, 99M, 99N, 99O, 143, 260, 266, 268, 279K, 279L, 279M, 279P, 303C, S5; **3-2:** 323A, 347A
  introduce: **3-1:** 14I
  reteach: **3-1:** S5, T2
  review: **3-1:** 40–41, 67D, 68I, 98–99, 256I
  maintain: **3-1:** 278–279
  See also **Decoding/Phonics, Decoding Multisyllabic Words, Vocabulary Strategies.**

Decoding.
See **Decoding/Phonics.**

Decoding Multisyllabic Words: 3-1: 388L, 388
  syllables
    C*le* syllable pattern: **3-2:** 417A
    closed syllables: **3-1:** 153C
    CVC spelling pattern: **3-1:** 41A
    CVC*e* spelling pattern: **3-1:** 99C
    CVVC spelling pattern: **3-1:** 99C
    open syllables: **3-1:** 255A
    schwa: **3-2:** 369C
    unaccented syllables: **3-2:** 399A
    VCCV syllable pattern: **3-1:** 293; **3-2:** 193C, 231
    VCV syllable pattern: **3-2:** 221A
  word structure

compound words: **3-1:** 355A; **3-2:** 153, 167A, 181, 315, 417I
prefix + root word: **3-1:** 303C; **3-2:** 35C, 117A, 230
prefix + root word + suffix: **3-2:** 323A
root word + inflection: **3-1:** 67C, 205C; **3-2:** 261C, 347A
root word + root word: **3-1:** 143, 407A
root word + suffix: **3-1:** 143, 387A; **3-2:** 143A, 297C, 323I
See also **Decoding/Phonics, compound words, decode long words, prefixes and suffixes.**

Decoding/Phonics
  blending: **3-1:** 182J, 191, 374; **3-2:** 107, 117A
  compound words: **3-1:** 104, 181K, 279I, 303K, 355A, 355K, 366; **3-2:** 153, 167A, 181, 315, 417I
  context clues: **3-1:** 14J, 21, 23, 31, 34, 41L, 41M, 41N, 81, 87, 91, 107, 109, 139, 169, 200, 231, 256J, 261, 263, 267, 274, 279K, 279L, 313, 347, 356J, 359, 365, 369, 377, 380, 381; **3-2:** 104, 168J, 171, 175, 177, 183, 209, 331
  decode long words: **3-1:** 22, 24, 30, 41K, 41L, 41M, 72, 84, 88, 99M, 99N, 99O, 260, 266, 268, 279K, 279L, 279M, 279P, 303C, S5; **3-2:** 323A, 347A
    introduce: **3-1:** 14I
    reteach: **3-1:** S5, T2
    review: **3-1:** 40–41, 67D, 68I, 98–99
    maintain: **3-1:** 256I, 278–279
  See also **Decoding Multisyllabic Words.**
  letter patterns
    "soft" *c* and *g*: **3-1:** 223A
    words with *igh* and e*igh*: **3-2:** 59A
    words with *kn, wr,* and *gn*: **3-1:** 181C
    words with /ô/: **3-1:** 329C
    words with *ough*: **3-1:** 279A
    long vowel /(y) o͞o/ (u, u_e, ew, ue): **3-2:** 203
  morphemes: **3-1:** 14I, 67C, 68I, 117, 205C, 256I, 260, 266, 268, 303C, 304I, 308, 314, 328, 347, 356I, 362, 364, 365, 369, 372, 386, 387A; **3-2:** 35C, 35D, 75, 107, 153, 167A, 168L, 181, 194L, 297C, 315, 323I, 399K, 417I
  phonemic awareness: **3-1:** 14I, 22, 24, 27, 40, 41A, 53, 67D, 68I, 72, 79, 84, 88, 98, 99C, 117, 129A, 153C, 173, 181C, 181I, 191, 193, 205C, 205I, 211, 223A, 223I, 255A, 255G, 256I, 260, 266, 268, 271, 278, 279A, 279G, 293, 303C, 304I, 313, 329C, 329I, 347, 355A, 355I, 356J, 365, 369, 374, 377, 387A, 387I, 407A, 407G; **3-2:** 45, 107, 133, 153, 181, 203, 231, 271, 315, 339, 407
  phonetic respellings: **3-2:** 93A, 143I, 221K, 399K, 417H, 417I

phonograms: **3-2:** 35I, 59I, 93I, 117G, 143G, 167G, 193I, 221I, 261I, 297I
prefixes and suffixes: **3-1:** 303C, 304I, 308, 314, 328–329, 355B, 356I, 356L, 356, 362, 364, 365, 369, 372, 376, 386–387, 407P, S74–S75, S86, T71; **3-2:** 35C, 35D, 75, 107, 168L, 168, 194L, 230, 297C, 323I, 399K, 417I
strategic reading: **3-1:** 14J, 42J, 68J, 100J, 130J, 156J, 182J, 206J, 224J, 256J, 282J, 304J, 330J, 356J, 388J; **3-2:** 14J, 36J, 60J, 94J, 118J, 146J, 168J, 194J, 222J, 262J, 300J, 324J, 348J, 370J, 400J
structural analysis
  base root words: **3-1:** 387A, 407A
  compound words: **3-1:** 355A
  inflected endings: **3-1:** S5; **3-2:** 261C
  prefixes and suffixes: **3-1:** 303C, 304I, 308, 314, 328–329, 355B, 356I, 356L, 356, 364, 365, 369, 372, 374, 387A; **3-2:** 35C, 35D, 75, 107, 168L, 168, 194L, 230, 297C, 323I, 399K, 417I
syllabication: **3-1:** 173, 374, R23–R26; **3-2:** R23–R26
syllables
  accent marks: **3-2:** 93A
  closed syllables: **3-1:** 153C
  consonant-*le* syllable pattern: **3-2:** 417A
  CVC spelling pattern: **3-1:** 41A
  CVC*e* spelling pattern: **3-1:** 99C, 129A
  CVVC spelling pattern: **3-1:** 99C, 129A, 193
  open syllables: **3-1:** 255A
  schwa: **3-2:** 369C
  unaccented syllables: **3-2:** 399A
  VCCV syllable pattern: **3-1:** 293, 347; **3-2:** 193C, 231
  VCV syllable pattern: **3-2:** 221A
vowel variant *oo*: /o͞o/, /o͝o/: **3-2:** 203
word identification strategies.
  See **Vocabulary Strategies.**
word structure
  compound words: **3-1:** 355A; **3-2:** 153, 167A, 181, 315, 417I
  prefix + root word: **3-1:** 303C; **3-2:** 35C, 117A, 230
  prefix + root word + suffix: **3-2:** 323A
  root word + inflection: **3-1:** 67C, 205C; **3-2:** 261C, 347A
  root word + root word: **3-1:** 143, 407A
  root word + suffix: **3-1:** 143, 387A; **3-2:** 143A, 297C, 323I
  See also **Decoding Multisyllabic Words; Spelling.**

Decoding Strategies.
See **Decoding Multisyllabic Words; Decoding/Phonics; Strategies Good Readers Use; Vocabulary Strategies.**

Denotation.
> *See* **Word Study, connotation/denotation.**

Description.
> *See* **Author's Craft, descriptive images; Writing, student writing models, analyze; paragraphs that describe; writing activities; Writing Forms, expressive.**

Details, Noting Important.
> *See* **Comprehension, important details; Thinking.**

Diagnostic Check.
> *See* **Assessment.**

Diagrams, Use and Interpret.
> *See* **Research and Information Skills, graphic aids, organizing information graphically.**

Dialogue.
> *See* **Author's Craft; Writing, writing activities.**

Dictionary, Use a: 3-1: 41I, 67A–67B, 122, 129B, 153D, S75, S87, T5; **3-2:** 93A, 143I, 221K, 399K, 417H, 417I
> *See also* **Reference Sources; Research and Information Skills, references and resources.**

Differentiated Instruction.
> *See* **Reaching All Learners.**

Digraphs.
> *See* **Decoding/Phonics, letter patterns.**

Directed Reading.
> *See* **Reading, Options for.**

Directions, Following.
> *See* **Research and Information Skills, follow written directions; Writing, writing activities, directions/how-to.**

Domains of Writing.
> *See* **Writing, purposes.**

Drama.
> *See* **Genre, play; Literary Response and Analysis, literary forms; Writing, writing activities.**

Drama Activities.
> *See* **Listening and Speaking, speaking, dramatic interpretations.**

Draw Conclusions: 3-1: 18, 22, 24, 26, 28, 52, 74, 80, 84, 94, 104, 110, 134, 162, 164, 168, 170, 186, 212, 246, 264, 272, 286, 310, 329A–329B, 336, 344, 348, 355C, 362, 364, 366, 376, 387C, T72; **3-2:** 20, 24, 26, 28, 64, 74, 78, 98, 114, 122, 138, 154, 174, 176, 190, 198, 204, 210, 214, 221D, 226, 236, 238, 266, 268, 270, 278, 282, 314, 354, 362, 374, 386, 394
> *See also* **Comprehension, Thinking.**

Editing.
> *See* **Writing, editing skills.**

Elaboration.
> *See* **Writing, editing skills, revision focus: adding.**

Elements of Nonfiction: 3-1: 130I, 136, 138, 140, 142, 146, 152–153, 153M, 153N, 153O, 153R; **3-2:** 297D
> *See also* **Expository Nonfiction, Literary Response and Analysis.**

Encyclopedia: 3-1: 156E, 160, 182E, 206E, 213, 224E, 282E, 282F, 304E, 388E; **3-2:** 14F, 21, 36F, 60F, 103, 105, 115, 168E, 191, 193A–193B, 221C, 222E, 262F, 324E, 348E, 370E, 370F, 383, 400E, 400F, 415
> *See also* **Reference Sources; Research and Information Skills, multiple resources, references and resources.**

Encyclopedia Articles
> **3-1:** "Turtles," 156G

End Marks.
> *See* **Grammar, sentences; Mechanics, punctuation, sentence.**

End-of-Selection Tests.
> *See* **Assessment.**

English as a Second Language (ESL).
> *See* **Reaching All Learners, English-language learners, English-Language Learners Resource Kit.**

English for Speakers of Other Languages.
> *See* **Reaching All Learners, English-language learners.**

English-Language Learners, Activities for.
> *See* **Reaching All Learners, English-language learners.**

English-Language Learners Resource Kit.
> *See* **Reaching All Learners.**

Environmental Print.
> *See* **Real-Life Reading.**

Etymologies.
> *See* **Vocabulary and Concepts, word origins.**

Evaluation.
> *See* **Assessment.**

Exclamations.
> *See* **Grammar, commands and exclamations.**

Expository Nonfiction
> **3-1:** "The Olympic Games: Where Heroes Are Made," 132–147
> **3-2:** "If You Made a Million": 264–291
> **3-2:** "Rocking and Rolling": 350–365
> **3-2:** "Visitors from Space": 402–413
> **3-2:** "Yippee-Yay!": 170–187
> *See also* **Genre; Literary Response and Analysis, elements of nonfiction.**

Expository Text.
> *See* **Genre, Expository Nonfiction, Text Structure.**

Expository Writing.
> *See* **Writing Forms, expository, informative, nonfiction, research report.**

Expressive Writing.
> *See* **Writing Forms.**

Extend.
> *See* **Additional Support Activities, Reaching All Learners, advanced.**

Extra Support.
> *See* **Additional Support Activities, Books for All Learners; Intervention Resource Kit; Reaching All Learners; Reteach Lessons.**

Fable
> **3-1:** "The Camel Dances," 304G
> **3-1:** "Sayings We Share: Proverbs and Fables," 390–403
> **3-1:** "The Thirsty Crow," 68G
> *See also* **Genre.**

Fact and Opinion: 3-2: 146I, 150, 152, 156, 166–167, 193D, 194I, 198, 202, 204, 206, 210, 220–221, 297R, 323B, S36, S37, S48, S49, T38
> *See also* **Comprehension, fact and opinion.**

Family Involvement.
> *See* **School-Home Connection.**

Fantasy
> **3-1:** "Little Grunt and the Big Egg," 226–245
> **3-2:** "The Armadillo from Amarillo": 372–395
> *See also* **Genre.**

Fiction
> **3-1:** "Dinosaur Dreams," 224G
> **3-1:** "Officer Buckle and Gloria," 16–35
> **3-1:** "Pepita Talks Twice," 44–63
> **3-2:** "How Many Stars in the Sky?": 36G
> *See also* **Genre.**

Fiction from Nonfiction, Distinguish.
> *See* **Comprehension.**

Figurative Language: 3-1: 46, 47, 48, 49, 52, 76, 86, 109, 112, 148, 187, 193, 294, 335, 338, 363, 392, 394; **3-2:** 35A–35B, 59C, 93D, 167I, 200, 203, 208, 247, 256, 323C, 387

characters: **3-1:** 45, 285, T14, T80
comparing texts: **3-2:** 97, T16
plot: **3-1:** T15; **3-2:** 39, T14
QTA: **3-1:** 17, 359, T13, T51, T83; **3-2:** 121, 225, 351, T17, T52, T83
reading nonfiction: **3-2:** 171, 403, T50, T85
setting: **3-1:** 159, T47
theme: **3-1:** 307, T81; **3-2:** 327, T82
think along: **3-1:** 133, 185, 391, T17, T48, T84; **3-2:** 17, 149, 303
contrast actions, motives, characters: **3-1:** 88, 96, 100H, 150, 160, 236, 260; **3-2:** 123, 132, T13, T49
elements of nonfiction: **3-1:** 136, 138, 140, 142, 146, 153M, 153N, 153O, 153R
 introduce: **3-1:** 130I
 review: **3-1:** 152–153; **3-2:** 297D
fantasy-realism.
 See **Comprehension, reality and fantasy.**
figurative language: **3-1:** 46, 47, 48, 49, 52, 76, 86, 109, 112, 148, 187, 193, 294, 335, 338, 363, 392, 394; **3-2:** 40, 124, 167I, 200, 203, 208, 247, 256, 323C, 387
 introduce: **3-2:** 35A–35B
 reteach: **3-2:** T3
 review: **3-2:** 59C
 maintain: **3-2:** 93D
 See also **Author's Craft; Figurative Language; Word Study.**
humor: **3-1:** 21, 42H, 79
identify with characters: **3-1:** 106, 166, 268, 310, 368; **3-2:** 310, 388
illustrations as context: **3-1:** 23
illustrator's craft/purpose: **3-1:** 300; **3-2:** 288, 377
interpreting text ideas through discussion.
 See **Listening and Speaking, purposes for listening and speaking, oral activities, participate in discussion; Oral Communication.**
literary devices: **3-1:** 187, 336
literary forms: **3-1:** 293, 341; **3-2:** 41, 82
 introduce: **3-1:** 99A–99B
 review: **3-1:** 223D, 387D
main problem.
 See **Comprehension, main idea and details.**
mood: **3-2:** 150, 331
narrative analysis: **3-1:** 163, 174; **3-2:** 109, 390
narrative elements (setting, character, and plot): **3-1:** 44, 47, 48, 50, 58, 59, 60, 62, 67M, 67N, 67O, 80, 94, 110, 114, 116, 118, 129K, 129L, 129M, 153Q, 163, 244, 312, 318, 320, 324, 390, 396, 398, 400, 407P; **3-2:** 16, 18, 20, 24, 26, 28, 38, 40, 42, 46, 48, 50, 66, 68, 70, 72, 74, 77, 78, 80, 82, 96, 98, 100, 102, 104, 106, 108, 109, 110,

112, 114, 122, 123, 126, 130, 132, 134, 150, 152, 154, 156, 158, 160, 167B, 198, 202, 204, 208, 212, 214, 222I, 224, 226, 228, 234, 236, 240, 242, 252, 328, 331, 332, 338, 340, 374, 376, 378, 380, 382, 386, 388, 390, 417C–417D
 introduce: **3-1:** 42I
 reteach: **3-1:** T4
 review: **3-1:** 66, 99D, 100I, 128; **3-2:** 167B
 maintain: **3-1:** 388I, 406
poetic devices (rhyme, rhythm, assonance, alliteration).
 See **Author's Craft.**
point of view: **3-1:** 211, 287, 326
responding to selections
 personal response: **3-1:** 34, 62, 64, 94, 118, 130H, 142, 146, 174, 198, 202, 216, 220, 244, 248, 256H, 274, 296, 320, 348, 380, 402; **3-2:** 28, 50, 82, 112, 134, 138, 160, 186, 214, 216, 252, 288, 316, 340, 364, 390, 410
 Response Journal: **3-1:** 14H, 42H, 68H, 100H, 130H, 156H, 182H, 206H, 224H, 256H, 282H, 304H, 330H, 356H, 388H; **3-2:** 14H, 36H, 60H, 94H, 118H, 146H, 168H, 194H, 222H, 262H, 300H, 324H, 348H, 370H, 400H
 Think and Respond Questions: **3-1:** 34, 62, 94, 118, 146, 174, 198, 216, 244, 274, 296, 320, 348, 380, 402; **3-2:** 28, 50, 82, 112, 134, 138, 160, 186, 214, 216, 252, 288, 316, 340, 364, 390, 394, 410
 story map: **3-1:** 99D, 358, 381; **3-2:** 14I, 16, 29, 60E
 See also **Research and Information Skills, organizing information graphically, selection chart.**
suspense.
 See **Author's Craft.**
theme: **3-1:** 126, 178, 220, 272, 290, 300, 316, 324, 346, 352, 404; **3-2:** 80, 88, 90, 114, 218, 256, 294, 344, 366, 396, 414
theme connections: **3-1:** 178, 220; **3-2:** 80, 88, 90, 114, 218, 256, 294, 344, 366, 396, 414
through enactments.
 See **Listening and Speaking, speaking, dramatic interpretations.**
through journal writing.
 See **responding to selections, Response Journal.**
Literary Terms.
 See **Author's Craft, Literary Response and Analysis.**
Locate Information: **3-1:** 150, 178, 282E, 282F, 304E, 330E, 356F, 388E, 388F; **3-2:** 194E, 219, 261D, 354, 360, 362, 404, 406, 417P, S83, S93
 introduce: **3-2:** 348I
 reteach: **3-2:** S80, S81, S92, T73
 review: **3-2:** 368, 399B, 400I, 416–417

See also **Reference Sources, Research and Information Skills.**

Magazine Article:
 3-1: "A Place of Their Own": 218–219
 3-1: "Wild Shots, They're My Life": 208–217
 3-2: "Mission to Mars": 400G
 See also **Genre.**
Main Idea and Details: 3-1: 42H, 46, 60, 64, 100H, 136, 138, 246, 256H, 264, 344, 348, 374, 396; **3-2:** 66, 114, 132, 134, 168I, 172, 176, 180, 182, 188, 192–193, 206, 216, 221B, 250, 262I, 266, 272, 276, 296–297, 297R, 356, 394, S42, S43, S60, S61, T40
 See also **Comprehension, main idea and details, important details; Text Structure.**
Make and Confirm Predictions.
 See **Comprehension, predict outcomes; Strategies Good Readers Use.**
Make Inferences: 3-1: 153A–153B, 188; **3-2:** 93C, 399D
 See also **Comprehension, make inferences; Thinking, inferential thinking.**
Make Judgments: 3-1: 160, 190, 294, 334, 392, 396, 404; **3-2:** 22, 70, 72, 80, 82, 86, 102, 244, 276, 286, 292, 314, 344
 See also **Comprehension, Thinking.**
Managing the Classroom.
 See **Classroom Management.**
Maps.
 See **Reference Sources.**
Math Activities.
 See **Content Areas, Cross-Curricular Connections; Cross-Curricular Stations.**
Mechanics
 apostrophe: **3-1:** 387F; **3-2:** 167F, 369F, 369H, 399H, 417D
 capitalization: **3-1:** 41F, 67H, 181G, 181H, 223F, 223H, 255D, 329H, 355F, 387F; **3-2:** 93F, 117D, 261F, 369F, 399F, 417D
 comma: **3-1:** 181G, 181H
 proofreading: **3-1:** 41H, 65, 99F, 99J, 129D, 223F, 223H, 255D, 355F, 387F; **3-2:** 93F, 117D, 143D, 193F, 261F, 369F, 369H, 399F, 417D, 417F
 punctuation, sentence: **3-1:** 41F, 65, 67H, 181G, 181H, 223F, 223H, 255D, 329H, 355F, 387F, S7; **3-2:** 93F, 117D, 167F, 221H, 321, 399F, 417D, 417F
 See also **Daily Language Practice; Writing Process, proofread.**
Media.
 See **Research and Information Skills, library/media center; Technology;**

Reference Sources, CD–ROM/ on-line encyclopedias, magazine, newspaper.

Meeting Individual Needs.
 See **Reaching All Learners.**

Metacognitive Thinking.
 See **Thinking.**

Metaphors.
 See **Author's Craft.**

Modalities of Learning.
 See **Reteach Lessons.**

Modeling: 3-1: 14I, 14J, 14L, 21, 23, 25, 27, 31, 40, 41B, 42J, 42L, 45, 49, 53, 57, 59, 66, 67A, 67D, 68I, 68J, 68L, 73, 75, 77, 79, 81, 83, 85, 87, 89, 91, 98, 99A, 99D, 100J, 103, 104, 105, 107, 109, 111, 115, 117, 128, 129B, 130J, 130L, 133, 137, 139, 141, 143, 145, 152, 153A, 153D, 156J, 156L, 159, 161, 163, 165, 167, 169, 171, 173, 180, 181A, 181D, 182J, 185, 187, 189, 193, 195, 204, 205A, 205D, 206J, 206L, 209, 211, 213, 215, 223B, 223D, 224J, 224L, 229, 231, 233, 237, 239, 241, 249, 254, 255B, 256J, 256L, 261, 263, 265, 267, 269, 271, 278, 279B, 282J, 282L, 285, 287, 289, 291, 293, 295, 303D, 304J, 304L, 307, 309, 311, 313, 315, 317, 319, 328, 329A, 330J, 330L, 333, 335, 337, 339, 340, 341, 345, 347, 354, 355B, 355C, 355D, 356J, 361, 363, 365, 367, 369, 371, 373, 377, 379, 386, 388J, 391, 393, 395, 397, 399, 406, 407B; **3-2:** 14J, 14L, 17, 19, 21, 23, 25, 27, 35A, 36J, 36L, 38, 41, 43, 45, 49, 53, 59B, 59C, 59D, 60J, 60L, 63, 65, 67, 69, 71, 73, 75, 77, 79, 81, 87, 92, 93B, 93C, 93D, 94J, 94L, 99, 101, 103, 105, 107, 109, 111, 116, 118J, 118L, 121, 123, 125, 127, 129, 131, 133, 142, 146J, 146L, 149, 151, 153, 155, 157, 159, 166, 167B, 168J, 168L, 171, 173, 175, 177, 179, 181–183, 192, 193A, 193D, 194J, 194L, 197, 199, 201, 203, 205, 207, 209, 211, 219, 220, 221B, 221C, 221D, 222J, 222L, 225, 227, 229, 231, 233, 235, 241, 245, 249, 251, 260, 261A, 261D, 262J, 262L, 265, 269, 271, 273, 277, 279, 281, 283, 285, 296, 297A, 300J, 300L, 303, 305, 307, 309, 311, 313, 315, 322, 323B, 324J, 324L, 327, 329, 331, 333, 335, 337, 339, 346, 347B, 348J, 348L, 351, 353, 355, 357, 359, 361, 368, 369A, 369D, 370J, 370L, 373, 375, 377, 379, 383, 385, 398, 399B, 399C, 399D, 400J, 400L, 403, 405, 407, 409, 416, 417B
 See also **Guided Comprehension.**

Models of Writing Purposes.
 See **Writing, purposes, student writing models.**

Modified Instruction.
 See **Reaching All Learners.**

Monitor Comprehension.
 See **Guided Comprehension.**

Monitor Progress.
 See **Assessment.**

Mood.
 See **Author's Craft, Literary Response and Analysis.**

Morphemes.
 See **Decoding/Phonics.**

Morphological Analysis.
 See **Decoding/Phonics.**

Multi-Age Classrooms: 3-1: 12I, 154I, 280I; **3-2:** 12I, 144I, 298I
 See also **Reaching All Learners.**

Multimedia.
 See **Technology.**

Multiple-Meaning Words.
 See **Vocabulary and Concepts, Word Study.**

Music Activities.
 See **Content Areas, Cross-Curricular Connections.**

Mystery
 3-1: "Nate the Great, San Francisco Detective": 70–95
 3-1: "The Last Case of the I. C. Detective Agency": 322–325
 See also **Genre.**

Narration.
 See **Listening and Speaking, speaking, oral activities.**

Narrative Elements (setting, character, plot): 3-1: 42I, 44, 47, 48, 50, 58, 59, 60, 62, 66, 67M, 67N, 67O, 80, 94, 100I, 110, 114, 116, 118, 129K, 129L, 129M, 153R, 163, 244, 312, 318, 320, 324, 388I, 390, 396, 398, 400, 406, 407, 407P, T4; **3-2:** 16, 18, 20, 24, 26, 28, 38, 40, 42, 46, 48, 50, 66, 68, 70, 72, 74, 77, 78, 80, 82, 96, 98, 100, 102, 104, 106, 108, 109, 110, 112, 114, 122, 123, 126, 130, 132, 134, 150, 152, 154, 156, 158, 160, 167B, 198, 202, 204, 208, 212, 214, 224, 226, 228, 234, 236, 240, 242, 252, 328, 331, 332, 338, 340, 374, 376, 378, 380, 382, 386, 388, 390
 See also **Genre, Literary Response and Analysis.**

Narrative Nonfiction
 3-1: "Balto, the Dog Who Saved Nome": 184–199
 3-1: "My Dolphin Encounter": 206G
 3-1: "Rosie, a Visiting Dog's Story": 258–275
 See also **Genre.**

Narrative Poem
 3-1: "Nine Gold Medals": 130G
 See also **Genre.**

Narrative Text, Reading.
 See **Genre Study, Literary Response and Analysis.**

Narrative Text, Writing.
 See **Writing, writing activities, personal narrative, story; Writing Forms, expressive.**

Native American Legend
 3-2: "Coyote Places the Stars": 38–55
 See also **Genre.**

Negatives.
 See **Grammar, contractions.**

Nonfiction
 3-1: "Dogs and People Today": 256G
 3-1: "The Hitting Machine of San Diego": 330G
 3-1: "My Dolphin Encounter": 206G
 3-2: "Home Ranges": 324G
 3-2: "Moving West": 168G
 3-2: "Seeds Can Sleep": 342–343
 3-2: "Sourdough": 194G
 3-2: "Starry, Starry Night": 52–55
 See also **Genre, expository nonfiction, narrative nonfiction; Text Structure.**

Note-Taking Strategies.
 See **Research and Information Skills; Research Report; Writing Forms, research report.**

Nouns.
 See **Grammar, common and proper nouns, more plural nouns, singular and plural nouns, singular possessive nouns, plural possessive nouns.**

Ongoing Assessment.
 See **Guided Comprehension, Assessment.**

Onomatopoeia.
 See **Author's Craft; Listening and Speaking, purposes for listening/speaking, musical elements of literary language; Word Study.**

Oral and Media Communications.
 See **Listening and Speaking, speaking; Technology.**

Oral Communication
 Read Alouds: **3-1:** 14G–14H, 42G–42H, 68G–68H, 100G–100H, 130G–130H, 156G–156H, 182G–182H, 206G–206H, 224G–224H, 282G–282H, 304G–304H, 330G–330H, 356G–356H, 388G–388H; **3-2:** 14G–14H, 36G–36H, 60G–60H, 94G–94H, 118G–118H, 146G–146H, 168G–168H, 194G–194H, 222G–222H, 262G–262H, 300G–300H, 324G–324H, 348G–348H, 370G–370H, 400G–400H

Oral English Language Conventions
 grammar: **3-1:** 205G–205H, 223G–223H, 279E–279F, 303G–303H, 329G–329H, 355G–355H, 387G–387H, 407E–407F; **3-2:** 35G–35H, 59G–59H, 93G–93H, 117E–117F, 143E–143F, 167E–167F, 193G–193H, 221G–221H, 261G–261H,

Reaching All Learners

revision focus: clarifying sentences: **3-2:** 35F, 59F

revision focus: clarifying words: **3-2:** 323D, 347D

revision focus: consolidating: **3-2:** 261E

revision focus: deleting: **3-1:** 181F, 205F; **3-2:** 261E

revision focus: rearranging: **3-1:** 303F, 329F; **3-2:** 261E

elaboration.

  See **editing skills, revision focus: adding.**

evaluation

  effective features of a piece of writing, identify: **3-1:** 41C, 67E, 181E, 205E, 303E, 329E; **3-2:** 35F, 59F, 297F, 323D, 347D, 369F, 399F, 417D

  others' writing, respond effectively to: **3-1:** 41D, 99F, 129D, 181F, 205F, 223F, 255D, 303F, 329F, 355F, 387F; **3-2:** 35F, 60E, 93F, 193F, 261F, 297F, 323D, 347D, 369F, 399F, 417D

  writing, assess own: **3-1:** 153F, 279D, 407F; **3-2:** 143D, 261F, 297F

  writing models, use published pieces as: **3-1:** 41C, 67F, 129C, 181E, 205F; **3-2:** 323C–323D, 417C

  writing revisions: **3-1:** 303F, 329F, 355F, 387F; **3-2:** 35F, 59F, 93F, 117D, 143D, 193F, 261E–261F, 323D, 347D, 369F, 399F, 417D

inquiry/research.

  See **Inquiry and Research.**

interactive.

  See **Writing Approaches, Interactive.**

organization: **3-1:** 41D, 99F, 129C, 129D, 153E, 153F, 181E, 181F, 205E, 205F, 223F, 255C, 255D, 279C, 303E, 303F, 329F, 355E, 355F, 387F, 407C; **3-2:** 93F, 117D, 167C–167D, 193E, 323C, 347C, 369E, 399F, 417D, S6

penmanship, gain more proficient control of.

  See **Handwriting Tips.**

process writing.

  See **Writing Process.**

publish: **3-1:** 99F, 129D, 223F, 255D, 355F, 387F; **3-2:** 93F, 117D, 297E–297F, 369F, 399F, 417D

purposes

  audiences, communicate with a variety of: **3-1:** 41D, 153E, 181E, 181F, 205F, 255C, 255D, 279C, 279D, 303F, 329E, 329F, 355E, 387E, 387F, 407C, 407D; **3-2:** 35F, 59F, 117C, 143C, 167D, 297E–297F, 323C, 347C, 369E, 417C

  selecting form based on purpose/task to compare and contrast: **3-2:** 35E–35F, 59E–59F, 117C–117D

to describe: **3-1:** 41C–41D, 67E–67F, 99E–99F, 129C–129D, 153E–153F; **3-2:** 323C–323D

to entertain: **3-2:** 369E–369F, 417C–417D

to explain/inform: **3-1:** 181E–181F, 205E–205F, 223E–223F, 255C–255D, 279C–279D; **3-2:** 93E–93F, 143C–143D, 167C–167D, 193E–193F, 221E–221F, 261E–261F, 297E–297F

to invite someone: **3-2:** 399E–399F

to persuade: **3-1:** 303E–303F, 329E–329F, 355E–355F, 387E–387F, 407C–407D; **3-2:** 82

to thank someone: **3-2:** 347C–347D

research.

  See **Research and Information Skills.**

revision.

  See **editing skills.**

student writing models, analyze

  essay: **3-1:** 255C

  invitation: **3-2:** 399E

  journal entry: **3-1:** 67E

  letter: **3-2:** 347C

  paragraphs

    that compare: **3-2:** 35E

    that contrast: **3-2:** 59E

    that describe: **3-1:** 41C

    that explain/inform: **3-1:** 181E, 205E; **3-2:** 93E

    that persuade: **3-1:** 303E, 387E

  persuasive letter: **3-1:** 355E

  play: **3-2:** 369E

  poem: **3-2:** 323C

  research report: **3-2:** 221E–221F, 261E–261F, 297E–297F

  review: **3-1:** 387E

  speech: **3-1:** 329E

  stories

    imaginative: **3-1:** 129C; **3-2:** 417C

    personal: **3-1:** 99E

    summary: **3-1:** 223E

technology: **3-1:** 41C, 67E, 99E, 99F, 129C, 129D, 153E, 181E, 205E, 223E, 223F, 255C, 279C, 303E, 329E, 355E, 335F, 387E, 387F, 407E; **3-2:** 35F, 59F, 93E, 117C, 143C, 167C, 193E, 221E–221F, 261E, 297E, 323C, 347C, 369E, 399E, 417C

  See also **Technology, software, *Writing Express*; word processor.**

test prep: **3-1:** 153E–153F, 279C–279D, 407C–407D; **3-2:** 143C–143D

traits of good writing: **3-1:** 279C

  conventions: **3-1:** 99E, 129C, 223E, 255C, 303E, 355E, 387E; **3-2:** 93E, 117C, 167C, 347C

development: **3-1:** 41C, 67E, 153E, 329E; **3-2:** 35E, 59E, 93E, 167C, 323C, 347C, 369E, 399E

effective paragraphs: **3-1:** 67E, 99E; **3-2:** 93E, 117C, 297E, 399E

effective sentences: **3-2:** 59E, 59F, 369E, 399E, 417C

focus: **3-1:** 41C, 67E, 99E, 153E, 329E; **3-2:** 35E, 59E, 93E, 167C, 297E, 323C, 369E, 399E

ideas: **3-1:** 129C, 153E, 223E, 255C, 303E, 355E, 387E; **3-2:** 93E, 117C, 323C, 369E, 399E, 417C

organization: **3-1:** 41C, 67E, 99E, 129C, 153E, 223E, 255C, 303E, 329E, 355E, 387E; **3-2:** 35E, 59E, 93E, 117C, 167C, 297E, 323C, 347C, 369E, 399E, 417C

sentence fluency: **3-1:** 99E, 129C, 223E, 255C, 355E, 387E; **3-2:** 93E, 117C, 297E, 323C

voice: **3-1:** 67E, 99E, 129C, 153E, 223E, 255C, 355E, 387E; **3-2:** 93E, 117C, 297E, 323C, 369E, 399E, 417C

word choice: **3-1:** 67E, 99E, 129C, 223E, 255C, 303E, 355E, 387E; **3-2:** 93E, 117C, 297E, 323C, 347C, 369E, 399E, 417C

writing activities

  advertisement: **3-2:** 115, 323H

  bibliography: **3-2:** 221F

  captions: **3-2:** 175, 348E

  character sketch: **3-1:** 34; **3-2:** S39

  conversation: **3-1:** 255H

  description: **3-1:** 41C–41D, 198, 225, S6, S7; **3-2:** 59H, 112, 297H, 364, 417H, S13

  dialogue: **3-2:** 221K, 321, S94, S95

  diary/journal: **3-1:** 67E–67F, 127, 327; **3-2:** 261J, 297B, 345

  directions: **3-1:** 181E–181F

    See also **how-to.**

  email: **3-2:** 222F

  explanation: **3-1:** 97, 131, 146, 296, 320, 348, 380, 402, S70; **3-2:** 214, 252, 262E, 288, 410, S19, S31

  fable: **3-1:** 405

  friendly letter: **3-1:** 65, 99H; **3-2:** 141, 340

    See also **persuasive letter.**

  handbook: **3-1:** 181F, 205F

  how-to: **3-1:** 179, 255C–255D, 279C–279D, 301; **3-2:** 259

  informative composition: **3-1:** 301

  instruction sequence: **3-1:** 179; **3-2:** 416

  invitation: **3-2:** 399E–399F, S88, S89

  journal entry: **3-1:** 67E–67F

  letter: **3-2:** 82

  magazine article: **3-2:** 219

news story: **3-1:** 256E; **3-2:** 165, 367

outline: **3-2:** 193F, 216

paragraph of information: **3-1:** 99K, 205E–205F; **3-2:** 168E

paragraph of opinion: **3-1:** 43, 69, 216, 221; **3-2:** 28, 134, 191, 316, S51

paragraph that compares or contrasts: **3-2:** 35E–35F, 59E–59F, 117C–117D, 160, 219, S6, S7, S24, S25

paragraph that explains: **3-2:** 93E–93F

personal narrative: **3-1:** 99E–99F, 153E–153F

persuasive letter: **3-1:** 355E–355F, S71, S82–S83; **3-2:** 82

persuasive paragraph: **3-1:** 174, 303E–303F, S71

play: **3-2:** 369E–369F

poem: **3-1:** 99J, 129H; **3-2:** 323C–323D, 397, S71

postcard: **3-1:** 203

poster: **3-1:** 256E

pourquoi tale: **3-2:** 60E

proposal: **3-1:** 179

questions: **3-2:** 297J

quickwrite: **3-1:** 13, 15, 43, 69, 101, 131, 155, 157, 183, 207, 225, 257, 281, 283, 305, 331, 357, 389; **3-2:** 13, 15, 37, 61, 95, 119, 145, 147, 169, 195, 223, 263, 299, 301, 325, 349, 371, 401

research report: **3-1:** 304E; **3-2:** 167C–167D, 193E–193F, 221E–221F, 261E–261F, 297E–297F, 367

response to literature: **3-1:** 34, 62, 94, 118, 146, 153Q, 174, 198, 216, 244, 274, 279O, 296, 320, 348, 380, 402, 407O; **3-2:** 28, 50, 82, 112, 134, 143O, 160, 186, 214, 252, 288, 297Q, 316, 340, 364, 390, 410, 417O

review: **3-1:** 387E–387F, S88–S89; **3-2:** 94E, S37

rules: **3-1:** 39

sequel: **3-2:** S89

song: **3-2:** 415

speech: **3-1:** 151, 329E–329F, S76–S77

sportscast: **3-1:** 353

story: **3-1:** 41F, 129C–129D; **3-2:** 194E, 417C–417D

summary: **3-1:** 35, 63, 95, 119, 147, 175, 199, 217, 223E–223F, 245, 275, 297, 321, 349, 381, 403; **3-2:** 29, 51, 83, 113, 135, 161, 187, 193J, 215, 253, 289, 317, 341, 365, 391, 411, S5, S17

summons: **3-2:** 91

thank-you letter: **3-2:** 347C–347D, 390, S76, S77

timed writing: **3-1:** 146, 153E–153F, 274, 279C–279D, 402,

407C–407D; **3-2:** 134, 143C–143D, 288, 410

travel guide: **3-2:** 295, S63

See also **Writing Process.**

Writing Approaches, Interactive: 3-1: S6, S12, S18, S24, S30, S38, S44, S50, S56, S62, S70, S76, S82, S88, S94; **3-2:** 297H, S6, S7, S12, S18, S24, S30, S38, S44, S50, S56, S62, S70, S76, S82, S88, S94

Writing Express™ **CD–ROM.**

See **Technology, software.**

Writing Forms:

everyday

email: **3-2:** 222F

friendly letter: **3-1:** 65, 99H, 355E–355F; **3-2:** 141, 340

invitation: **3-2:** 399E–399F, S88, S89

thank-you letter: **3-2:** 347C–347D, 390, S76, S77

expository

comparison and contrast: **3-2:** 117C–117D

how-to paragraph: **3-1:** 179, 255C–255D, 279C–279D; **3-2:** 259

paragraph that compares: **3-2:** 35E–35F, S6

paragraph that contrasts: **3-2:** 59E–59F, S12

summary: **3-1:** 223E–223F

expressive

character sketch: **3-1:** 34; **3-2:** S39

description: **3-1:** 41C–41D, 101, 198, 225, S6, S7; **3-2:** 59H, 112, 297H, 364, 417H, S13

journal entry: **3-1:** 67E–67F, 127, 327; **3-2:** 261J, 297B, 345

personal narrative: **3-1:** 99E–99F, 153E–153F

play: **3-2:** 369E–369F, S82, S83

story: **3-1:** 41F, 129C–129D; **3-2:** 60E, 417C–417D, S94, S95

unrhymed poem: **3-2:** 323C–323D, S70

informative

directions/how-to: **3-1:** 179, 181E–181F, 255C–255D, 279C–279D, 301; **3-2:** 259

paragraph of information: **3-1:** 99K, 205E–205F, 301

paragraph that explains: **3-2:** 93E–93F

persuasive

paragraph: **3-1:** 174, 303E–303F

letter: **3-1:** 355E–355F, S71, S82–S83; **3-2:** 82

review: **3-1:** 387E–387F, S88–S89; **3-2:** 94E, S37

speech: **3-1:** 151, 329E–329F

nonfiction: **3-1:** 97, 99K, 131, 146, 205E–205F, 296, 320, 348, 380, 402; **3-2:** 93E–93F, 168E, 219

research report

draft: **3-2:** 221E–221F, 261E–261F, S50

edit: **3-2:** 261E–261F, S56

outline: **3-2:** 193E–193F, S44

prewrite: **3-2:** 167C–167D, S38

share and publish: **3-2:** 297E–297F, S62

Writing Growth, Monitor Own.

See **Writing, evaluation, writing, assess own.**

Writing Process

audience, identifying: **3-1:** 355E, 387E; **3-2:** 369E, 399E, 417C

edit: **3-1:** 99F, 129D, 223F, 255D, 355F, 387F; **3-2:** 93F, 117D, 261E–261F, 369F, 399F, 417D

prewriting/draft: **3-1:** 99E–99F, 129C–129D, 223E–223F, 255C–255D, 355E–355F, 387E–387F; **3-2:** 93E, 93F, 117C–117D, 143C, 221E–221F, 369E–369F, 399E–399F, 417D

proofread: **3-1:** 99F, 129D, 223F, 255D, 355F, 387F; **3-2:** 93F, 117D, 143C, 369F, 399F, 417D

publish: **3-1:** 99F, 129D, 223F, 255D, 355F, 387F; **3-2:** 93F, 117D, 297E–297F, 369F, 399F, 417D

purpose/task, writer's: **3-1:** 99E, 129C, 223E, 255C, 355E, 387E; **3-2:** 93E, 117C, 143C, 167C–167D, 369E, 399E, 417C

revise: **3-1:** 99F, 129D, 223F, 255D, 355F, 387F; **3-2:** 93F, 117D, 143C, 193F, 261E–261F, 369F, 399F, 417F

spelling, check: **3-1:** 99F, 129D, 223F, 255D, 355F, 387F; **3-2:** 117D, 143D, 369F, 399F

see also **Technology, spell-checker.**

technology, use available: **3-1:** 129D, 223F, 255D, 355F, 387F; **3-2:** 117C, 146F

word processing: **3-1:** 129D, 223F, 255D, 355F, 387F; **3-2:** 146F, 369F

Writing Prompts: 3-1: 41D, 67F, 99E, 129C, 153F, 181F, 205F, 223E, 255C 279D, 303F, 329F, 355E, 387E, 407D; **3-2:** 35F, 59F, 93E, 117C, 143D, 167C, 323D, 347D, 369E, 399E, 417C

Daily Writing Prompts: **3-1:** 14C–14D, 42C–42D, 68C–68D, 100C–100D, 130C–130D, 156C–156D, 182C–182D, 206–206D, 224C–224D, 256C–256D, 282C–282D, 304C–304D, 330C–330D, 356C–356D, 388C–388D; **3-2:** 14C–14D, 36C–36D, 60C–60D, 94C–94D, 118C–118D, 146C–146D, 168C–168D, 194C–194D, 222C–222D, 262C–262D, 300C–300D, 324C–324D, 348C–348D, 370C–370D, 400C–400D

Written English Language Conventions.

See **Grammar, Mechanics, Usage**

Teacher Notes

Acknowledgments

For permission to reprint copyrighted material, grateful acknowledgment is made to the following sources:

Atheneum Books for Young Readers, an imprint of Simon & Schuster Children's Publishing Division: "Trot Along, Pony" from *Open the Door* by Marion Edey and Dorothy Grider. Published by Charles Scribner's Sons, 1949.

Brandt & Brandt Literary Agents, Inc.: "The Old Dog's Song" from *Merlin & The Snake's Egg* by Leslie Norris. Text copyright © 1978 by Leslie Norris. Published by The Viking Press.

Curtis Brown, Ltd.: "What Is Science?" by Rebecca Kai Dotlich from *Spectacular Science*, edited by Lee Bennett Hopkins. Text copyright © 1999 by Rebecca Kai Dotlich. Published by Simon & Schuster Books for Young Readers.

Children's Better Health Institute, Indianapolis, IN: "Dinosaur Dreams" by Susan Costantino from *Jack and Jill* Magazine, September 1990. Text copyright © 1990 by Children's Better Health Institute, Benjamin Franklin Literary & Medical Society, Inc. "Mission to Mars" from *U.S. Kids*, A *Weekly Reader* Magazine, January/February 1993. Text copyright © 1993 by Children's Better Health Institute, Benjamin Franklin Literary & Medical Society, Inc.

Cobblestone Publishing Company, 30 Grove St., Suite C, Peterborough, NH 03458: "The Hitting Machine of San Diego" by Stephen Currie from *Appleseeds: American Places, San Diego*, May 2000. Text copyright © 2000 by Cobblestone Publishing Company. "Sourdough" by Jane Scherer from *Cobblestone: The California Gold Rush*, December 1997. Text © 1997 by Cobblestone Publishing Company.

The Cousteau Society, Inc.: From "My Dolphin Encounter" by Joan Bourque in *Dolphin Log* Magazine, January 2000. Text copyright © 2000 by the Cousteau Society, Inc.

Doubleday, a division of Random House, Inc.: "Celebration" by Alonzo Lopez from *Whispering Wind* by Terry Allen. Text copyright © 1972 by the Institute of American Indian Arts.

Hampton-Brown Books: "The Outside/Inside Poem" by Sarah Yim Hong Chan from *A Chorus of Cultures: Developing Literacy Through Multicultural Poetry* by Alma Flor Ada, Violet J. Harris, and Lee Bennett Hopkins. Text copyright © 1993 by Hampton-Brown Books.

Harcourt, Inc.: "Brother" from *The Llama Who Had No Pajama* by Mary Ann Hoberman. Text copyright © 1959, renewed 1987 by Mary Ann Hoberman.

HarperCollins Publishers: From "Friend Dog" by Arnold Adoff. Text copyright © 1980 by Arnold Adoff. From *Secrets of a Wildlife Watcher: A Beginner's Field Guide* by Jim Arnosky. Text copyright © 1983, 1991 by Jim Arnosky. "Rudolph Is Tired of the City" from *Bronzeville Boys and Girls* by Gwendolyn Brooks. Text copyright © 1956 by Gwendolyn Brooks Blakely. *How Many Stars in the Sky?* by Lenny Hort. Text copyright © 1991 by Lenny Hort. "Here and There" from *Silly Times with Two Silly Trolls* by Nancy Jewell. Text copyright © 1992 by Nancy Jewell. "The Camel Dances" from *Fables* by Arnold Lobel. Text copyright © 1980 by Arnold Lobel. "I Am Flying!" from *The New Kid on the Block* by Jack Prelutsky. Text copyright © 1984 by Jack Prelutsky. "I Met a Rat of Culture" from *Something Big Has Been Here* by Jack Prelutsky. Text copyright © 1990 by Jack Prelutsky. "A Lesson Well Learned" from *Still More Stories to Solve: Fourteen Folktales From Around the World,* told by George Shannon. Text copyright © 1994 by George W. B. Shannon.

NBA Properties Inc.: "Rebecca Lobo" (Retitled: "Rebecca Lobo, WNBA Superstar") from *WNBA Superstars* by Molly Jackel and Joe Layden. Text copyright © 2001 by WNBA Enterprises.

North-South Books Inc., New York: The Friendship Trip by Wolfgang Slawski, translated by Rosemary Lanning. Text copyright © 1996 by Nord-Süd Verlag AG, Gossau, Zürich, Switzerland; English translation copyright © 1996 by North—South Books Inc. Originally published in Switzerland under the title, *Die Besucher-Sucher.*

Oxford University Press: "Turtles" from *Oxford Children's Encyclopedia: Sea to Zulus,* Volume 5. Text copyright © 1991 by Oxford University Press.

Pearson Education Inc.: "Ears Hear" by Lucia and James Hymes, Jr. from *Oodles of Noodles.* Text © 1964 by Lucia and James Hymes Jr.

Marian Reiner, on behalf of August House, Inc. Publishers: "The Theft of a Smell: A Peruvian Tale" from *Twenty-Two Splendid Tales to Tell from Around the World* by Pleasant DeSpain. Text copyright © 1979, 1990, 1994 by Pleasant DeSpain. Published by August House, Inc. Publishers.

Marian Reiner, on behalf of Aileen Fisher: "If I Had a Pony" from *Out in the Dark and Daylight* by Aileen Fisher. Text copyright © 1980 by Aileen Fisher.

Marian Reiner: "A Cliché" from *It Doesn't Always Have to Rhyme* by Eve Merriam. Text copyright © 1964 by Eve Merriam; text © renewed 1992 by Eve Merriam.

Elizabeth Ring: "Dogs and People Today" from *Companion Dogs: More Than Best Friends* by Elizabeth Ring. Text copyright © 1994 by Elizabeth Ring.

David Roth: "Nine Gold Medals" by David Roth. Text © 1988 by David Roth.

Anne Rockwell: "The Thirsty Crow" from *The Acorn Tree and Other Folktales* by Anne Rockwell. Text copyright © 1995 by Anne Rockwell.

Myra Stilborn: "A mosquito in the cabin" from *Round Slice of Moon* by Myra Stilborn. Text copyright © 1980 by Myra Stilborn.

Gloria Vando: "Childhood Country" by Gloria Vando. Text © by Gloria Vando.

John Wiley & Sons, Inc.: From *Wild West Days: Discover the Past with Fun Projects, Games, Activities, and Recipes* by David C. King. Text copyright © 1998 by David C. King.

Acknowledgments
For permission to reprint copyrighted material, grateful acknowledgment is made to the following sources:
George Ancona: Photographs of money by George Ancona from *If You Made a Million* by David M. Schwartz. Photographs copyright © 1989 by George Ancona.
Atheneum Books for Young Readers, Simon & Schuster Children's Publishing Division: *I'm in Charge of Celebrations* by Byrd Baylor, illustrated by Peter Parnall. Text copyright © 1986 by Byrd Baylor; illustrations copyright © 1986 by Peter Parnall.
Jeanne Bendick: From *Comets and Meteors: Visitors from Space* by Jeanne Bendick. Text copyright © 1991 by Jeanne Bendick.
Boyds Mills Press, Inc.: *Leah's Pony* by Elizabeth Friedrich, illustrated by Michael Garland. Text copyright © 1996 by Elizabeth Friedrich; illustrations copyright © 1996 by Michael Garland.
Candlewick Press, Inc., Cambridge, MA, on behalf of Walker Books Ltd., London: "Starry, Starry Night" from *Seeing Stars* by James Muirden. From *Rocking and Rolling* by Phillip Steele. Text © 1997 by Phillip Steele; illustrations © 1997 by Walker Books Ltd.
Chronicle Books: *Alejandro's Gift* by Richard E. Albert, illustrated by Sylvia Long. Text copyright © 1994 by Richard E. Albert; illustrations copyright © 1994 by Sylvia Long.
Dial Books for Young Readers, a division of Penguin Putnam Inc.: *Why Mosquitoes Buzz in People's Ears: A West African Tale,* retold by Verna Aardema, illustrated by Leo and Diane Dillon. Text copyright © 1975 by Verna Aardema; illustrations copyright © 1975 by Leo and Diane Dillon.
Harcourt, Inc.: *The Armadillo from Amarillo* by Lynne Cherry. Copyright © 1994 by Lynne Cherry. Stamp designs copyright © by United States Postal Service. Reproduction of images courtesy of Gilbert Palmer, the National Aeronautics and Space Administration, the Austin News Agency, Festive Enterprises, Jack Lewis/Texas Department of Transportation, the Baxter Lane Company, Wyco Colour Productions, Frank Burd, and City Sights. *Worksong* by Gary Paulsen, illustrated by Ruth Wright Paulsen. Text copyright © 1997 by Gary Paulsen; illustrations copyright © 1997 by Ruth Wright Paulsen.
HarperCollins Publishers: *If You Made a Million* by David M. Schwartz, illustrated by Steven Kellogg. Text copyright © 1989 by David M. Schwartz; illustrations copyright © 1989 by Steven Kellogg.
Holiday House, Inc.: *The Ant and the Grasshopper* by Amy Lowry Poole. Copyright © 2000 by Amy Lowry Poole.
Kalmbach Publishing Co.: *The Crowded House* by Eva Jacob from PLAYS: *The Drama Magazine for Young People.* Text copyright © 1959, 1970 by Plays, Inc. This play is for reading purposes only; for permission to produce, write to Kalmbach Publishing Co., 21027 Crossroads Circle, P.O. Box 1612, Waukesha, WI 53187-1612.
Kingfisher Publications plc: From "Mapping the World" in *Young Discoverers: Maps and Mapping* by Barbara Taylor, cover illustration by Kevin Maddison. Text and cover illustration copyright © 1992 by Grisewood and Dempsey Ltd.
Little, Brown and Company (Inc.): *Yippee-Yay! A Book About Cowboys and Cowgirls* by Gail Gibbons. Copyright © 1998 by Gail Gibbons.
Ludlow Music, Inc., New York, NY: "This Land Is Your Land," words and music by Woody Guthrie. TRO—©—copyright 1956 (Renewed) 1958 (Renewed) and 1970 (Renewed) by Ludlow Music, Inc.
Philomel Books, an imprint of Penguin Putnam Books for Young Readers, a division of Penguin Putnam Inc.: *Lon Po Po: A Red Riding Hood Story from China,* translated and illustrated by Ed Young. Copyright © 1989 by Ed Young.

Scholastic Inc.: *Cocoa Ice* by Diana Appelbaum, illustrated by Holly Meade. Text copyright © 1997 by Diana Appelbaum; illustrations copyright © 1997 by Holly Meade. Published by Orchard Books, an imprint of Scholastic Inc. *Boom Town* by Sonia Levitin, illustrated by Cat Bowman Smith. Text copyright © 1998 by Sonia Levitin; illustrations copyright © 1998 by Cat Bowman Smith. Published by Orchard Books, an imprint of Scholastic Inc.
Simon & Schuster Books for Young Readers, Simon & Schuster Children's Publishing Division: *Papa Tells Chita a Story* by Elizabeth Fitzgerald Howard, illustrated by Floyd Cooper. Text copyright © 1994 by Elizabeth Fitzgerald Howard; illustrations copyright © 1994 by Floyd Cooper. *Coyote Places the Stars* by Harriet Peck Taylor. Copyright © 1993 by Harriet Peck Taylor.

Photo Credits
Key: (t)=top; (b)=bottom; (c)=center; (l)=left; (r)=right.
Page 51, Black Star; 52, The Granger Collection, New York; 53(t), Harcourt Photo Library; 53(b), Zefa / H. Armstrong Roberts; 60, Lawrence Migdale / Photo Researchers, Inc.; 113, Tom Sobolik / Black Star; 162, Rick Friedman / Black Star; 163, Black Star; 168, Barry Levy / Index Stock Photography; 169, Superstock; 187, courtesy, Gail Gibbons; 188, National Gallery of Art, Washington, DC; 215(t), Rose Eichenbaum; 215(b), courtesy, Scholastic; 216(t), Nik Wheeler / Corbis; 216(c), C.J. Collins / Photo Researchers, Inc.; 217(t), Walter Coker / Silver Image; 217(b), George E. Jones III / Photo Researchers, Inc.; 222, Superstock; 223(t), Tim Page / Corbis; 223(c), (cb), Harcourt Photo Library; 223(b), Jeff Schultz / AlaskaStock; 254, 255, Rick Friedman / Black Star; 290, Dale Higgins; 291, Tom Sobolik / Black Star; 292, 293, Ken Kinzie / Harcourt; 318, Black Star; 319, Rick Friedman / Black Star; 324, Simon Jauncey / Stone; 325, Mickey Gibson / Earth Scenes; 342, Patti Murray / Earth Scenes; 343, Harry Rogers / Photo Researchers, Inc.; 365, courtesy, Philip Steele; 392, Black Star; 394-395, Corbis Stock Market; 395(t), The Granger Collection, New York; 395(cl), (cr), Harcourt Photo Library; 400, 402(l), 402-403, Aaron Horowitz / Corbis; 410, Corbis; 412, Black Star; 415, Bettmann / Corbis; 445(t), Jim Steinberg / Photo Researchers, Inc.; 445(b), Harcourt Photo Library; 446(l), Gail Shumway / FPG; 446(r), Harcourt Photo Library; 447, Inga Spence / Tom Stack & Associates; 449(tl), Richard Johnston / Stone; 449(br), Joyce Photographics / Photo Researchers, Inc.; 451, Bob Krist / Corbis Stock Market.

Illustration Credits
Dan Craig, Cover Art; Jennie Oppenheimer, 4-5, 12-13; Paul Cox, 6-7, 144-145; Dave LeFleur, 8-9, 298-299; Ethan Long 10-11, 33, 165, 259, 345, 416; Art Valero, 14-15; Floyd Cooper, 16-31; Nancy Davis, 34, 92, 116, 141, 260, 370-371; Lizi Boyd, 36-37; Harriet Peck Taylor, 38-51; Terry Widener, 52-55; Tom Leonard, 55; Cathy Bennett, 57, 58, 191, 321, 367; Leo and Diane Dillon, 62-85; Tracy Sabin, 94-95; Ed Young, 96-113; Jackie Snider, 115; Paul Meisel, 118-119; Holly Cooper, 120-135; Diane Paterson, 136-139; Tuko Fujisaki, 142, 219, 448; Lisa Carlson, 146-147; Michael Garland, 148-163; Chris Van Dusen, 166, 415; Gail Gibbons, 170-187; Thomas Hart Benton, 188; Stephen Snider, 194-195; Laura Ovresat, 220-221; Holly Meade, 224-255; Ruth Wright Paulsen, 256-257; Tracy McGuinness, 262-263; Steven Kellogg, 264-291; Nancy Coffelt, 295, 296, 346, 397; Hideko Takahashi, 300-301; Peter Parnall, 302-319; Sylvia Long, 326-341; Sharron O'Neil, 342-343; Rick Allen, 348-349; Philip Steele, 350-365; Lynne Cherry, 372-393; Richard Hull, 400-401; David Schleinkofer, 402-413.

Pupil Edition Acknowledgments

Teacher Notes